God's Hope on the Glory Road

Other Books about Bill's Journey

Yes, God! Volume 1

Daily Devotionals
Our Walk of Faith: The Journey to Bill's Healing
God's Grace on the Winding Road: The Journey to Bill's Healing
God's Peace on the Glory Road: Our Journey to Healing

Miracle Man Trilogy
#1 Musings of the Miracle Man: Words of Wisdom Words of Hope
#2 Adventures of the Miracle Man: Dreams, Visions & Miracles
#3 Lessons of the Miracle Man: Wit, Wisdom & Wonder (Coming February 2023)

God's Hope on the Glory Road:

Our Journey to Healing

Barbara Hollace

Published by Hollace House Publishing Spokane Valley, Washington

For more information or to contact the author: barbara@barbarahollace.com
Website: www.barbarahollace.com

Book layout/Cover design: Ann Mathews
Book editing: Barbara Hollace, www.barbarahollace.com
Book Cover photograph: Valle del Lago, Somiedo Nature Park, Asturias, Spain, iStock.com
Line Drawings: Freedom Girl, iStock.com
Photo inside book: Freedom Girl, by guvendemir at iStock.com
ISBN: 978-1-7345159-4-7

Printed in the United States of America

Dedication

This book is dedicated to those who have chosen faith over fear.
You have found joy in your journey with Jesus
no matter your circumstances.

Acknowledgments

This book wouldn't be in your hands without the amazing grace of God.

My heavenly Father has been so faithful. On this book journey, I have known Him as Jehovah Rapha, my healer; Jehovah Jireh, my provider; Jehovah Gibbor, the Lord mighty in battle, and Jehovah Shalom, my peace.

Many thanks to my family, church family, and friends who have walked alongside me during 2022. You have been with me over the mountains and through the valleys. Your prayers and love have sustained me.

My dear friend, Ann Mathews, has patiently walked with me through the creation of this book. She is an incredibly talented woman who loves the Lord. Ann, I'm so grateful for your expertise and our partnership on this journey. God is so good to me.

I have been blessed with amazing prayer partners who hold up my arms, whether they are near, or hundreds, or thousands of miles away. There is no distance in the spirit. God has heard your prayers on my behalf and answered them… again and again. I'm forever grateful.

And last, but not least, thank you to Mr. Bill, my forever love. God took you home to heaven in 2020 but your spirit hovers close by, and your wit and wisdom are my constant companions. I love you.

Introduction

They that wait on the Lord… (Isaiah 40:31)

Waiting – it's one of our least favorite activities. Why? Because it requires patience, another one of those character qualities we don't rush to the front of the line to receive.

This is the fourth book in my devotional series about our journey to healing. My husband, Bill, and I both have been blessed with the opportunity to put our hand in God's hand and go to a place we did not know.

Let me give you a quick recap if you are new to our life and our story.

We are Bill and Barb Hollace, ordinary people God called to walk an extraordinary path.

My husband, Bill, walked through an intense storm of health issues that began on January 10, 2018. From the moment the curtain opened, Bill was diagnosed with pneumonia and his heart was in afib (atrial fibrillation.) Three days later, he was diagnosed with Influenza A, and the next morning had a brain bleed.

From there, we went to the second hospital where Bill had surgery to remove the pool of blood in his brain. There are too many details to explain here, but our initial journey covered five and a half months, in five hospitals and a skilled care facility in two states. Several surgeries including brain surgery, a pacemaker, heart stents, and an aortic valve replacement. And more than one life and death moment where God intervened with a miracle, which earned Bill the title, "Miracle Man." Our journey was so much more than the health issues Bill overcame through God's miraculous healing.

The morning Bill entered the hospital God started me on another path that would give even greater meaning to this adventure. Every morning God knew I needed heavenly manna to sustain me. He would direct me to a specific Bible passage and then "feed" me with new revelation and how it pertained to our journey. Daily, I posted them on Facebook, because my blessings were for others too.

Our friend, Evelyne Ello-Hart, months into our journey shared I should bring these devotions together into a book. I was surprised by her suggestion, but later understood it was exactly what God had in mind.

In the early days of 2020, two years after we started this journey, the first daily devotional was born, "Our Walk of Faith." December 2020, the second book, "God's Grace on the Winding Road" was released. December 2021, the third book, "God's Peace on the Glory Road" became reality. And now you hold my fourth "book baby" in this series in your hands, "God's Hope on the Glory Road."

"God's Hope on the Glory Road" covers the calendar year of 2021. God closed some open doors as I waited for my healing to be completed. He was at work beneath the surface where no one else could see.

Maybe you are waiting for God to answer your prayers, or complete your healing. Or you could be the one with a broken heart that needs mending.

As I put this book together, once again, I was met by my heavenly Father who loves me so much and comforts us in our sorrow, and rejoices with us in our victories.

My prayer is you will find whatever you are looking for as you read about our journey. Whether you decide to read this one day at a time, digest it one bite at a time, or devour larger pieces of it, the choice is yours.

God has prepared a banqueting table for you where you can taste of His goodness and His grace.

Blessings,

Barb

This pose is very symbolic of my journey. For those of you who don't know, in July 2020, I was diagnosed with breast cancer just two months after my husband died, and four months after my mom died. It was a tough year.

The tumor had attached itself to my left pectoral muscle and it restricted my arm movement. It was an aggressive enemy and I was its target.

To give you a visual, take your left arm and move it into a 90-degree angle across your body at waist level (as if your arm were in a sling). Then raise your whole arm in the same position about an inch away from your body and hold it there. Stop for a moment. What you see is how much I could move my left arm in July 2020.

But God wasn't done yet. (More of this story in another book.)

Fast forward to May, 2022, I had surgery to remove the remains of the tumor. However, in April, 2022, about three weeks prior to my surgery, God restored my left arm movement so I could raise my left arm above my head. Praise the Lord!

Today, as I write this in December 2022, as I am recovering from surgery and going through physical therapy, in partnership with God, this drawing represents me. It is not only my physical posture, but God has given me unspeakable joy on this journey. Not only do I lift my hands in praise, but as long as I have breath, I will declare His faithfulness to all generations.

Let everything that has breath praise the Lord!
(Psalm 150:6)

January 2021

Be joyful in hope, Patient in affliction,
Faithful in prayer.

~ Romans 12:2 ~

Day#257 January 1

 Anchor Verse: Genesis 1:31
Then God looked over all that he had made, and it was excellent in every way.
(TLB)

Welcome to a brand-new year. Take a deep breath and experience this fresh new start.

In many ways, a new year is reminiscent of the initial creation of the world. God created a brand-new world for Adam and Eve to occupy and where they were called to be fruitful and multiply.

For six days, layer after layer, God created all that we see today – day and night, sky and seas, vegetation on the earth, creatures in the sky, land, and sea, and God's crowning achievement, man and woman. Not only was it orderly, but it was "excellent." God always does His best work and expects us to do the same. "Good enough" or "better" are just steps toward the "best" – the excellence that God has planned for us.

On our journey to Bill's healing, we learned a lot about how God created us, especially the intricate design of our bodies. Truly we are fearfully and wonderfully made. We were created to live and bring honor and glory to our heavenly Father.

The Glory Road this morning has a new signpost, "2021" – it's a marker to remind me that I have stepped into a new place and God is here. Every year is filled with "surprises" and this year will be no different. But what I do know, the lessons I have learned in the last three years, is that God is faithful. What I need, God will provide.

His plans and purposes are greater than I can imagine or even understand. But one thing I know without reservation is that I trust my heavenly Father to do what is best for me. It may be the winding road I follow, a short flight, a leap of faith, going through a mountain or over it, but I never walk alone.

Join me as we begin this journey into a new year. The Lord is asking us to bring our "best" to Him, an excellent offering of our lives, time, and talent. Come with joy and thanksgiving. The Lord has done great things for us, the Lord has done great things.

Thank you for taking this leap of faith.#Godisfaithful#TheGloryRoad

Day#258 January 2

 Anchor Verse: Genesis 6:8
But Noah found favor and grace in the eyes of the LORD. (AMP)

In Genesis 6, it says wickedness had overcome the world. EVERY inclination of the thoughts of the human heart was only evil ALL the time.

Our world is pretty messed up right now but in Noah's time, it was even worse. The Lord regretted that He made human beings and His heart was deeply troubled.

However, one man stood out to God, Noah. The Lord found a way to save a remnant on the face of the earth. "Noah found favor and grace in the eyes of the Lord."

It would start with Noah building an ark. We don't even know that Noah had any carpentry skills. In Genesis 6:9 it says, "Noah was a righteous man, blameless among the people of his time, and he walked faithfully with God."

Obedience and faithfulness marked Noah's life. Does it describe your life today?

On our journey to Bill's healing, our ears were tuned to the voice of the Lord and our eyes to watch what He was doing. Just like Noah, we learned that obedience and faithfulness were what God desired from us.

The Glory Road is a path through a world in chaos. The battle is intense; the solution is still the same as it was in Noah's day. We must faithfully follow the Lord. We must choose righteousness above popularity.

Lord, we praise and thank you for Your grace and mercy this morning. We thank you that You alone are worthy of our praise. May we walk humbly before You today always choosing to do what is right in Your sight. We love you, Lord, in Jesus' name, amen.

Thank you for your persistent prayers.#Godisfaithful#TheGloryRoad

Day#259 January 3

 Anchor Verse: Genesis 9:16
For I will see the rainbow in the cloud and remember My eternal promise to every living being on the earth. (TLB)

After the earth and all that was in it were destroyed by a worldwide flood (except Noah and his family and the creatures in the ark), God established a covenant with Noah and all his descendants.

God promised there would never again be a flood that would destroy the whole earth and its inhabitants. He didn't promise that there wouldn't be "local" floods. But that the whole world wouldn't be destroyed as it was in Noah's time.

In Genesis 9:16, it is brought to our attention that the "rainbow" in the cloud is a reminder to God, about His covenant with us. God made an eternal promise to every living being on the earth and for generations yet to come.

Isn't it interesting that the rainbow is God's reminder to Himself about His promise?

God knew that man would not live a perfect life after the flood. In fact, within a few verses, we see evidence of that from Noah's own son. Maybe God knew He would need to be reminded of His covenant because mankind was still going to have some "bad days."

On our journey to Bill's healing, we were blessed daily by God's grace through His promises. Jesus was the ultimate gift from God for our redemption but the rainbow in the sky reminds us of God's grace and love for the whole world.

The Glory Road is a place to see God's signs and wonders. Every day my eyes are open to see God's handiwork – in my life, in my world, in my own body. My ears are open to hear the sounds of creation – the sounds of life, the sounds of love – they are the sounds of God's pleasure.

Lord, we praise and thank you for the gift of Your love. Thank you for Your mercy and grace for without them we would surely perish. We ask for forgiveness of our shortcomings and for Your help to get back on the narrow road. We love you, Lord. In Jesus' name we pray, amen.

Thank you for your faithfulness in prayer.#Godisfaithful#TheGloryRoad

Day#260 January 4

 Anchor Verse: Matthew 4:24
News about him spread all over Syria, and people brought to him all who were ill with various diseases, those suffering severe pain, the demon-possessed, those having seizures, and the paralyzed; and he healed them. (NIV)

Shortly after Jesus called His first disciples to join His ministry, Jesus moved throughout Galilee, "teaching in their synagogues, proclaiming the good news of the kingdom, and healing every disease and sickness among the people."

Healing *every* disease and sickness is difficult for us to grasp. Even with all the medical breakthroughs over the years, there are many people who still need to be healed.

The word spread from Galilee over all Syria. In Matthew 4:24 it states the medical conditions Jesus healed. "People brought to him all who were ill with various diseases, those suffering severe pain, the demon-possessed, those having seizures, and the paralyzed; and he healed them."

Lord, hear the cries of our heart and send Your healing power to our world.

On our journey to Bill's healing, daily we prayed for Bill's body to be healed. We saw miracle after miracle happen. When a new problem would arise, we took it to God in prayer. And God touched and healed Bill.

The Glory Road is filled with many who need healing, many who are suffering, those who cannot sleep because of the pain, and God sees their need. Who gets healed and how they get healed and when they get healed is above my pay grade.

Jesus is so much more than our physical healer. He comes to share the "good news of the kingdom" that we might have a new life forever, beginning today. Our earthly bodies are just our temporary home.

Jehovah Rapha, our healer, come in Your power today. Touch and heal those who need to be healed. Lord, I pray for those suffering severe pain. Bring relief, and realign their bodies to perfect harmony. By His authority, we declare them healed and whole in Jesus' name. Amen.

Thank you for believing in miracles.#Godisfaithful#TheGloryRoad

Day#261 January 5

 Anchor Verse: Genesis 5:1
After these things the word of the LORD came to Abram in a vision, saying, "Do not be afraid, Abram, I am your shield; Your reward [for obedience] shall be very great." (AMP)

Often in the Bible, the Lord tells people to "not be afraid." Have you noticed? Put your name in the blank, personalize His promise.

"Do not be afraid, _____, I am your shield. Your reward for obedience shall be very great."

Your reward is still coming. It was for Abram, later called Abraham. In Genesis chapter 12:2, God tells Abram that "I will make you into a great nation, and I will bless you." This is God's promise to a man who has no children.

But that didn't stop God. God knew the end result even as Abram's wife Sarai remained childless. He was counting us as Abraham's descendants even before Isaac was born. God was rejoicing over you and the story He had written about your life.

God is our shield today as we face the blank pages of this year, even with some of the uncertainties that follow us. His promises are true. There IS and always will be a REWARD for our obedience, and it will be very great.

On our journey to Bill's healing, we learned about the power of God as our shield and defender. When the enemy was shooting his arrows left and right and full-on, the Lord protected us. Not only was our shield of faith in place, but God sent many of you to stand with us and tip your shields our way.

The Glory Road is a place where I hear the Lord say, "Do not be afraid, Barb, I am your shield." That is God's promise to me this morning. As every cancer cell is flipped into a healthy cell, God is fighting for me. I am filled with hope. I am filled with praise. I rejoice in the God of my salvation.

Lord, as we stand in victory, we look toward heaven, and thank you for the great things You have done for us and the greater things that are yet to come. We sing praises to Your name today, and every day. We live for Your honor and glory. In Jesus' name we pray, amen.

Thank you for your perseverance in prayer. #Godisfaithful#TheGloryRoad

Day#262 January 6

 Anchor Verse: Joshua 23:8
But you are to cling to the LORD your God, just as you have done to this day. (AMP)

To be successful on the path ahead, we must remember the victories that have brought us to this place.

Joshua in his final days on earth is sharing with God's people words of wisdom about how to carry on along the path that lies ahead of them. It won't be easy but they need to remember God's faithfulness.

When Moses sent 12 men on a recon mission into the "Promised Land" – 10 of them returned with reports of fear about the people who inhabited the land. The blessings of this new place were great but they believed the challenges were greater.

Joshua and Caleb saw things differently. They saw not only the blessings but a mighty God that would help them occupy the land just as He had promised. God rewarded their faithfulness. Joshua was a man of faith, a man who saw God do the miraculous.

Joshua 23:8 tells us, "But you are to cling to the LORD your God, just as you have done to this day." We are to "cling" to God, hold fast, remain faithful and follow Him whatever the future holds, wherever He may lead us.

On our journey to Bill's healing, we quickly learned that our best course of action was to hold fast to God and His promises. Just like an anchor in a stormy sea that cannot be moved, the Lord was our anchor through the storms in our life.

The Glory Road may be a new path but I must cling to the Lord my God. Jesus is the same yesterday, today and forever. He doesn't change. The same God who created the world is still on His throne. His love is unconditional. His truth is uncompromising.

Heavenly Father, we praise and thank you for Your faithfulness. You open Your arms wide to draw us near. You are a God who stays close, attentive to our every move, to our every cry. Lord, may You find us faithful. We love you and praise you in Jesus' name, amen.

Thank you for standing with me in every season.
#Godisfaithful#TheGloryRoad

Day#263 January 7

 Anchor Verse: Matthew 6:17-18
When you fast, don't let it be obvious, but instead, wash your face and groom yourself and realize that your Father in the secret place is the one who is watching all that you do in secret and will continue to reward you openly. (TPT)

Fasting and praying are often used in combination to accelerate the effectiveness of our prayers.

Since the early days of 2020, and for many of you, long before that, praying became a regular discipline, not just a "foxhole" prayer. As our friends and families were touched by the covid virus, our prayers took on a new urgency. They became our lifeline of hope to our heavenly Father who loves us beyond what our minds can conceive.

Jesus speaks of fasting in His Sermon on the Mount in Matthew 6. There was a "twist" that Jesus added. In the earlier verse, Jesus addresses those who when they fasted "looked somber as the hypocrites do." Jesus tells His disciples that they don't need to "look" the part on the outside, it's the inner man that gets God's attention. Fasting is a tool to bring us closer to God not to look "more holy" to others.

"When you practice some appetite-denying discipline to better concentrate on God, don't make a production out of it. It might turn you into a small-time celebrity but it won't make you a saint. If you 'go into training' inwardly, act normal outwardly. Shampoo and comb your hair, brush your teeth, wash your face. God doesn't require attention-getting devices. He won't overlook what you are doing; he'll reward you well." (Matthew 6:17-18 MSG)

On our journey to Bill's healing, there were times in critical places where I called for a day of prayer and fasting. I wanted God to know how serious I was about what was happening and that God's grace and power alone would turn the tide.

The Glory Road has become a place where praying without ceasing has taken on a new urgency. Fasting added to this can accelerate our prayer effectiveness. Lord, we need Your multiplied blessing and grace.

Lord, we praise and thank you for the gift of prayer. We thank you for better strategies of how to increase our effectiveness. Give us the self-discipline to add fasting to our prayer life. Lord, hear the cry of our hearts as we speak peace over our nation. In Jesus' name we pray, amen.

Thank you for standing with me.#Godisfaithful#TheGloryRoad

Day#264 January 8

 Anchor Verse: Proverbs 11:24
The world of the generous gets larger and larger; the world of the stingy gets smaller and smaller. (MSG)

Daily, Jesus asks us to follow Him. This doesn't mean walking along focused just on ourselves and our needs. Our hearts are to beat with His heart, and our minds be filled with His thoughts and His compassion for others.

Out of that love and compassion Jesus placed in us, we are to have a generous heart.

You may not understand the gifts and blessings in your own home. It's not just about our possessions, but rather the gifts that God has placed in us.

Coming from a "frugal" heritage, we strive to get the most value out of our time and our money. My heavenly Father calls me to live with a generous heart that obeys quickly at His command. Often I hear Him say, just as Jesus said to His disciples, "Freely you have received, freely give."

Do you understand what a powerful gift your time is to those who love you and need you?

On our journey to Bill's healing, I was blessed with the opportunity to spend every day with Bill while he was in the hospital, and in some places, the nights too. This is one of the greatest treasures I carry in my heart from our adventure.

The Glory Road has been a place of shifting. My life took a big shift when God took Bill home to be with Him. Our apartment only echoes with our conversations and our laughter, but in its place, I am learning a new cadence, a new path, as I listen for the Lord's heartbeat and His still small voice.

Lord, we praise and thank you for the gift of Jesus. Thank you for the greatest gift of all Your love. May we be good stewards of all You have entrusted to us. Open our eyes to see the needs that we can fill. And then in obedience, may we freely give. In Jesus' name we pray, amen.

Thank you for your generosity in my life.#Godisfaithful#TheGloryRoad

Day#265 January 9

 Anchor Verse: Matthew 7:7
Ask and keep on asking and it will be given to you; seek and keep on seeking and you will find; knock and keep on knocking and the door will be opened to you. (AMP)

Matthew 7 is part of Jesus' Sermon on the Mount and it is packed full of much wisdom and many lessons. It's like a good meal that needs to savored.

More than just nuggets of wisdom, Jesus described for us a "way of life." Not just moments of faithfulness of following God, but a lifelong pursuit of God's highest and best for us.

From the beginning of Jesus' ministry, His focus was not only about how to change and improve our own lives but how we should treat others. The lesson remains the same today.

This verse in Matthew 7 is often quoted – you may have heard it many times. So many times that it just rolls off your tongue and you move on to the next subject.

It's not a "magic pill" that we swallow and all our problems are cured, or a solution appears. Jesus is reminding us that the kingdom of God is worth pursuing. But more than that, it will take our entire lifetime to learn more and more about God's plans for us, and we will enjoy Him for all eternity.

On our journey to Bill's healing, we learned the necessity of "asking" and "seeking" and "knocking" in every area of our lives. It was only through persistence that we received all that God had for us as we experienced the fullness of His joy even in hard places.

The Glory Road continues to teach me that God is worth pursuing with all I have, every part of me. As I continue to seek His face and know His will for me, I ask and keep on asking, and God gives His best to me. I seek more wisdom, more revelation, and even as I receive a little at a time, I continue to press on and ask God for the "more" He has for me.

Thank you, Lord, that Your best is worth pursuing. May we not "settle" for "good enough" or even "better" but may we press on to receive Your "best" for us in this new year. We praise and thank you, Lord, that You are a good, good Father. In Jesus' name, amen.

Thank you for your faithful prayers.#Godisfaithful#TheGloryRoad

Day#266 January 10

 Anchor Verse: Matthew 8:8
Lord, I don't deserve to have You in my house. And, in truth, I know You don't need to be with my servant to heal him. Just say the word, and he will be healed. (VOICE)

As Jesus' reputation spread far and wide, people from many places, many walks of life came to Jesus with their problems looking for solutions.

In Matthew 8, we read that Jesus has just entered Capernaum, and a Roman centurion approaches Him because his servant is sick.

This is a man of stature and authority, yet he recognized that Jesus' power and authority was greater than his.

"Just say the word and he will be healed." (Matthew 8:8)

That is our truth today. "Just say the word" and we will be healed. "Just say the word" and our nation will be healed. "Just say the word" and our churches will be healed.

On our journey to Bill's healing, we knew Jesus as Bill's healer. There is power and authority in the name of Jesus. We watched the miracles unfold.

The Glory Road is a path of hope. As I approach the throne room of grace, I ask not only for my healing but for yours. He is Jehovah Rapha, the Lord our Healer. Jesus has the power to heal, deliver, and set people free.

Lord, we praise and thank you for Your healing power. Your love makes healing possible. All praise and honor are due Your name. You are the Lord, our healer. In Jesus' mighty and matchless name we pray, amen.

Thank you for believing with me.#Godisfaithful#TheGloryRoad

Day#267 January 11

 Anchor Verse: Matthew 6:12
Forgive us the wrongs we have done as we ourselves release forgiveness to those who have wronged us. (TPT)

In Matthew 6, Jesus' disciples came to Him and said, "Lord, teach us how to pray." His disciples didn't ask Jesus how to preach or how to do mighty miracles, but they knew the "key" was that Jesus would teach them how to pray.

Prayer connects us to our heavenly Father's heart.

Forgiveness – just the word probably stirs up some emotions in you. It might bring people to mind or situations or viewpoints that you either agree or disagree with in your heart and mind.

In Matthew 6:12 it says, "Forgive us the wrongs we have done as we ourselves release forgiveness to those who have wronged us."

God will forgive us as we forgive those who have wronged us. The Amplified verse adds this phrase, "letting go of both the wrong and the resentment." It's not just lip service, we must "let go" of the darkness that has crept into our hearts.

On our journey to Bill's healing, we learned how powerful the act of forgiveness is. When God begins a healing work in you, it's not just about your "physical" issues but He wants to heal you in every area of your life.

The Glory Road in this interesting season of our lives, as we experience things we have never experienced before, we may find ourselves at a loss for words when we pray. It is in those moments I go back to the "solid rock" of the prayer Jesus shared with His disciples.

Lord, we come this morning grateful that You are a God who forgives our sins. We ask for Your help to forgive those who have wronged us. We don't want to carry this burden any more. Take this load from my heart, my mind, and my soul. Restore my relationships with others and especially my relationship with You, O Lord. In Jesus' name, I pray, amen.

Thank you for loving God and loving me.#Godisfaithful#TheGloryRoad

Day#268 January 12

 Anchor Verse: Matthew 9:10
Later, Jesus went to Matthew's home to share a meal with him. Many other tax collectors and outcasts of society were invited to eat with Jesus and his disciples. (TPT)

When Jesus began His ministry, He chose those who would become His disciples, His inner circle. Jesus approached some fishermen and asked them if they wanted to become "fishers of men." In Matthew 4:20, 22 it says, "Immediately" they left their nets and followed Jesus.

Jesus saw a man named Matthew sitting at the tax collector's booth and said "Follow me" and Matthew got up and followed Jesus.

When these men began following Jesus, it didn't change who they were professionally… they were still men who had been fishermen and a tax collector. Jesus saw their potential. He was bringing together men who were unconventional, just like Jesus was.

In Matthew 9:10, during the meal at Matthew's home, "many other tax collectors and outcasts of society were invited to eat with Jesus and His disciples." The "saved" and the "lost" ate at the same table side by side. Jesus, the Son of God, rubbed shoulders and ate food with those who didn't really even know what "love" meant.

Darkness and light were not separated that day, they dined at the same table. Their conversation was mingled yet the light of the love of Jesus was the most powerful, it respected each person at that table.

On our journey to Bill's healing, we learned about walking through places where darkness and light were in the same room. Keeping our eyes on Jesus, we continued to walk in the light and not be overcome by the darkness.

The Glory Road is like that dining table in Matthew's house. Wherever I walk or stand, wherever I am online, Jesus is there as so are those who are "the tax collectors and outcasts of society" of our day. I am called to be an image bearer of Jesus in that place.

Lord, we praise and thank you for Your love. We are called to be love in action. Give us eyes to see beyond the surface to the heart of the problem. Jesus' love always pierces the darkness. We love you and worship you, in Jesus' name we pray, amen.

Thank you for loving like Jesus loves.#Godisfaithful#TheGloryRoad

Day#269 January 13

 Anchor Verse: Revelation 4:11
"Worthy are You, our Lord and God, to receive the glory and the honor and the power; for You created all things, and because of Your will they exist, and were created and brought into being." (AMP)

Sometimes we need to turn our eyes away from the "train wreck" in front of us and turn our eyes toward heaven to God, our Maker, and Jesus, our Savior.

One thing we know without exception is that God is still on His throne. God's plans do not change based on our failures or shortcomings. His plans for us are good. (Jeremiah 29:11)

In the last week, some of you have become discouraged, angry, frustrated, and frightened; some have even lost their hope. For just a moment, let's take a peek into heaven as we see it in Revelation 4:11.

"Worthy are You, our Lord and God, to receive the glory and the honor and the power; for You created all things, and because of Your will they exist, and were created and brought into being."

Bask in His presence. Be restored by the Light of His love. Be empowered by Jesus' resurrection power that overcame death, hell, and the grave.

On our journey to Bill's healing, we learned the power of praising the Lord and resting in His Presence. It was in heaven's throne room where we were equipped to fight our battles here on earth because Jesus had already won the victory for us.

The Glory Road is a place of praise and adoration. Every day I choose to trust that my heavenly Father knows the path ahead. As a widowed woman diagnosed with cancer, Jesus is my husband, my healer, and provider. Because of the resurrection power of Jesus that lives in me, I have victory every day in every way.

Lord, this morning we come to lay your burdens down at Your feet. We see You high and lifted up. We join with all the saints and angels and sing praises to Your name. We declare Your glory and honor and majesty. Blessed is He who comes in the name of the Lord. We praise you and thank you the work has already been done. In Jesus' mighty name we pray, amen.

Thank you for your faithful prayers.#Godisfaithful#TheGloryRoad

Day#270 January 14

 Anchor Verse: 2 Corinthians 4:8-9
We are pressed on every side by troubles, but not crushed and broken. We are perplexed because we don't know why things happen as they do, but we don't give up and quit. We are hunted down, but God never abandons us. We get knocked down, but we get up again and keep going. (TLB)

Hard times, trials, tribulations, natural disasters, health issues, heart issues, and political turmoil are not new to this world.

What feels different is that instead of reading it as a "historical" account – something that happened to somebody else, it's happening to us. There are days that tears are more prevalent than words, and the groaning of our soul reaches heaven's gates.

The apostle Paul helps us "reframe" our reaction to what is happening around us

"We are pressed on every side by troubles, but not crushed and broken. We are perplexed because we don't know why things happen as they do, but we don't give up and quit. We are hunted down, but God never abandons us. We get knocked down, but we get up again and keep going." (2 Corinthians 4:8-9)

Like a breath of fresh air, we are empowered by the Spirit of God through the resurrection power of the risen Savior, Jesus Christ, to stand and believe in FAITH even when we can't see the outcome.

On our journey to Bill's healing, every day we had a choice – to walk in despair or walk in hope. We chose to walk in the way of the Lord – the path of hope, love, and faith.

The Glory Road has been filled with the same choices. The circumstances we see rising up around us seem like great mountains and the winds blowing for our destruction.

Lord, give us eyes to see life from Your perspective. Please give us the courage to stand on Your truth and speak blessings even on the darkest nights. Our hope is in You, Lord. Our hope is in You alone. We praise you and thank you, in Jesus' name, Amen.

Thank you for sharing God's love.#Godisfaithful#TheGloryRoad

Day#271 January 15

 Anchor Verse: Matthew 9:29
Then He touched their eyes, saying, "According to your faith [your trust and confidence in My power and My ability to heal] it will be done to you." (AMP)

"According to your faith it will be done to you." Does that statement make you "swallow hard" or fill you with great joy?

These are the words that Jesus spoke to the two blind men that had followed Him.

Jesus' first question to them was, "Do you believe I am able to do this?" And they replied, "Yes, Lord."

"Then He touched their eyes, saying, "According to your faith [your trust and confidence in My power and My ability to heal] it will be done to you." (Matthew 9:29)

It was because of their faith that the blind men were healed. The Amplified version breaks it down into two pieces: Your trust and confidence in 1. My power and 2. My ability to heal.

Do I have trust and confidence in Jesus' power and His ability to heal?

On our journey to Bill's healing, we had a team of medical doctors in five hospitals in two states and an amazing follow-up team. But we knew Bill's healing would not come through the hands of men (and women) but through God's hands. We were not disappointed.

The Glory Road is a place of great faith. My hope and faith are in the Lord. I am grateful for those the Lord has chosen to be on "my team." But my confidence rests at the foot at the cross, where Jesus overcame death, hell, and the grave.

Lord, we thank you that You are the Lord our Healer. You lead us beside still waters and You restore not only our souls, but our body and mind as well. Thank you that at "Your word" and by "Your touch" we are healed. In Jesus' name, we pray, amen.

Thank you for your persistent prayers. Three years ago today, Bill had a brain bleed that put us on an amazing course of faith and miracles. Thank you, Lord, for Your faithfulness.#Godisfaithful#TheGloryRoad

Day#272 January 16

 Anchor Verse: Psalm 143:11
Lord, saving me will bring glory to your name. Bring me out of all this trouble because you are true to your promises. (TLB)

King David knew what it was like to be in the middle of trouble – lots of trouble. Often David found himself being pursued by his enemies who were trying to kill him.

Psalm 143 is one of the psalms written when David was facing trouble and he was tired, weary, and even feeling hopeless. His spirit is growing "faint" within him. Some translations say, "Answer me quickly, Lord, for my depression deepens."

In the midst of all his troubles, David reaches out to God. David is "real" with God. He tells God the "score" – "my enemy crushes me to the ground."

David does not "remain" in the pit… he remembers what God did for him in the past. In verse 11, David says, "Lord, saving me will bring glory to your name. Bring me out of all this trouble because you are true to your promises."

On our journey to Bill's healing, we cried out to the Lord immediately. In January 2018, even as I called 911 because Bill's breathing was so labored, I laid my hands on Bill and cried out to the Lord to breathe the breath of life into him and save his life.

The Glory Road is a place of contrasts as well. We live in a world that is in conflict, still fighting a virus, and desperately needs healing on every level. There are days that I sit with the Lord and remember times gone by and rejoice in His faithfulness.

Sometimes through the tears, tears of grief and gratitude, I recall the journey I have walked these last few years. The hand of God is everywhere. I hear His still small voice, during the day while I am taking care of "life stuff" and even in the nighttime hours.

Thank you, Lord, that You fight for us and the battle belongs to You. Set our feet on higher ground. May we see the deliverance of the Lord as You fight for us. You will receive all the honor and glory in Jesus' name. Amen.

Thank you for your faithful prayers.#Godisfaithful#TheGloryRoad

Day#273 January 17

 Anchor Verse: Exodus 4:2
Eternal One: *What do you have in your hand?* **Moses**: *My shepherd's staff.*
(VOICE)

In times of turmoil, conflict, and discontent, we "forget" the resources God
has already given us. We see our shortcomings; God sees our strengths.

If you know the story of Moses, it's a story of both tragedy and triumph.
Looking at Moses' life in graphic form, the lines would be zigzagging all over
the page.

God's plan for our lives is rarely a "straight line" from birth to death – there
are many starts and stops, and twists and turns from our first breath to our
last breath.

We often see chaos and confusion, but God sees the way through the storm.

In Exodus 4:2, when God is speaking to Moses about his new "assignment",
Moses has one excuse after another about why he isn't qualified for the task.
God sees it differently and asks Moses, "What do you have in your hand?"
God is asking us the same question today.

On our journey to Bill's healing, God showed us daily the ways we were
equipped to handle the assignment God had for us. With God on our side,
our well of resources was deep. Truly the resources in our hands were greater
than we imagined.

The Glory Road is a place of sowing and reaping, a place of discovering the
resources God has placed in my hand and my heart. We so greatly
underestimate what we can do with God on our side. Lord, give me eyes to
see.

Lord, we praise and thank you that You can make a way when there seems to
be no way. We surrender what we have and put it in Your hands. It's by
Your power that we can overcome every obstacle. In every victory, You will
receive all the praise and honor and glory. In Jesus' mighty name, amen.

Thank you for your faithfulness in prayer.#Godisfaithful#TheGloryRoad

Day#274 January 18

 Anchor Verse: Psalm 143:6
I lift my hands to you in prayer. I thirst for you as parched land thirsts for rain.
(NLT)

Prayer is a direct communication link to the heart of God. There isn't an operator you must go through to get in contact with your heavenly Father. It doesn't involve an elaborate "phone tree" – press#1 or#2 or#3 – where often the option you're looking for doesn't even exist.

In the Old Testament days, before Jesus came into the world, God's people had to go through the priest, and the priest entered the Holy of Holies to meet the Lord there.

Hallelujah that we can raise our hands in prayer, wherever, whenever, however, and even "whyever" (a new word) we have a need that only Lord God Almighty, Maker of heaven and earth can handle.

We don't have to wait until we are "desperate" before we reach out in God in prayer. The best advice is to run to God "first."

Notice the second part of this verse, "I thirst for you as parched land thirsts for rain." Do you "thirst" for God in that way? Is your soul parched this morning? You may be feeling like those "dry bones" that Ezekiel talks about in the Old Testament.

On our journey to Bill's healing, prayer was our lifeline. Prayer – communication with God – was woven into the tapestry of each day. Not only our prayers, but your prayers were brought to the throne room of grace as we sought help in our time of need.

The Glory Road is really a prayer walk, my steps and my prayers are mingled together. In these last few years, especially on our healing journey, I thirst for God like the parched land thirsts for rain. There's a hunger for God's Word. I long to hear His voice, because I want to walk in rhythm with Him, and not run ahead or lag behind.

Lord, we come this morning, so grateful for the gift of prayer. We lift our hands to You in praise for what You have done for us. We thank you that You are always available to listen to our heart cry. Fill our hearts and souls anew with Your refreshing springs of living water. We love you, Lord. In Jesus' name we pray, amen.

Thank you for the many prayers.#Godisfaithful#TheGloryRoad

Day#275 January 19

 Anchor Verse: Matthew 6:13
And don't let us yield to temptation, but rescue us from the evil one. (NLT)

The Lord's Prayer – the prayer that Jesus shared with His disciples the day they asked Him, "Lord, teach us to pray."

Today, it is still our heart's cry, "Lord, teach us to pray." As believers, we know prayer is a gift from God. Maybe even more importantly, it's a direct communication link to the heart of God. His ears are always attentive to the cries of His children, just as a mother to her child.

Whether it is a one-word prayer, "Jesus" or your prayers prayed through the night when you can't sleep. God has called you to be a watchman on the wall for others, for our nation. God inhabits our praise; God hears our prayers.

In the chaos of our land and our world, we are crying out to God to deliver us, to rescue us from "the evil one." Other versions say, "Deliver us from evil."

One thing we need to remember is that our "target" in this prayer is NOT "people." But we are praying against the powers and principalities of darkness. In Ephesians 6:12 it says, "For our struggle is not against flesh and blood [contending only with physical opponents], but against the rulers, against the powers, against the world forces of this [present] darkness, against the spiritual *forces* of wickedness in the heavenly (supernatural) *places*."

On our journey to Bill's healing, we were so grateful for God's hand of protection over us – not only in the flesh but in the spirit, our mind, and our emotions. The "evil one" daily would "take a run" at us – you know exactly what I mean.

The Glory Road often resembles a battlefield, not only on the outside but on the inside. My heart is full as I pray through the day. It's so important to have the full armor of God in place as we go into battle daily. (Ephesians 6)

Lord, we praise and thank you for the gift of prayer. It is a weapon against the darkness in our world, and in our own hearts. We pray for our nation. May the Prince of Peace rule in our land as we stand in the gap and pray for God's love to engulf our nation's capital. May His peace be yours as well. Our victory is assured in You, O Lord. In Jesus' mighty name we pray, amen.

Thank you for standing with me.#Godisfaithful#TheGloryRoad

Day#276 January 20

 Anchor Verse: Psalm 33:11
His destiny-plan for the earth stands sure. His forever-plan remains in place and will never fail. (TPT)

We have good news. God's Word never changes. His Jeremiah 29:11 plans and purposes for us are the same today as they were yesterday.

Our eyes are focused on our nation's capital today (11.20.21), Washington DC. Today the 46th President will be sworn into office. This will be a very unique inauguration based on these unparalleled times in which we are living. None of this has taken God by surprise. God is unshakeable, unstoppable, and unchangeable.

I recently heard this expression, "Administrations will come and go, but the Word of God remains forever." God is still on His throne. His plans and purposes for the United States have not changed.

On our journey to Bill's healing, we quickly learned that God's promises stand strong for generations. (Psalm 33:11) Bill and I were so grateful to God that "the thoughts of His heart" awakened and stirred us and our faith through our greatest trials.

The Glory Road is a place to praise Him and to cling to His promises. I have found this to be true so many times, not only on Bill's journey, but my health journey too. During chemo there were steroids in some of medications, so there were some nights when sleep was a little elusive. His Presence gave me strength but also helped me to finally go to sleep with a song in my heart and praise on my lips.

Lord, we lift our hands in praise. You are Jehovah Jireh, our provider, Jehovah Rapha, our healer, and Jehovah Shalom, our peace. Humbly we ask for a blessing over this nation and its people. Give our leaders heavenly wisdom. We commit to uphold them in prayer. All glory and honor belong to You, King of kings and Lord of lords. In Jesus' name we pray, amen.

Thank you for standing in the gap with me for our nation and for all of us who need healing. God's arm is not too short. We give Him all the praise and honor and glory. #Godisfaithful#TheGloryRoad

Day#277 January 21

 Anchor Verse: Mathew 14:18
Jesus: Bring the bread and the fish to Me. So the disciples brought Him the five rounds of flatbread and the two fish. (VOICE)

"Bring what you have to Me." These are the words of Jesus that echo down through time to us today. Jesus knows what we can "bring to the table."

In Matthew 14, Jesus went to a solitary place after He hears the news of the death of John the Baptist. People followed Him. Not just a few people, thousands of people.

Jesus has compassion on them and "healed their sick." He met their need. The disciples being practical men tell Jesus to send the crowd away so they can find something to eat – it's dinner time. Jesus says, "Don't send them away, you feed them."

Five loaves and two fish feed a crowd of 5000 men PLUS women and children. Jesus doesn't do math like we do. Just the thought of feeding 5000 people is pretty daunting.

What is the need that Jesus is asking us to meet today?

On our journey to Bill's healing, there were often places where the need seemed greater than our resources. God was faithful, we brought what we had – financially, physically, emotionally and mentally, and our "five loaves and two fish" were multiplied.

The Glory Road has been a place of such great testimony to God's faithfulness. At so many junctures in the road, especially in the early days, I was wounded and weary, yet God took all my brokenness and my perceived "lack" and He met every need.

On this path to rebuilding, my body, mind, and spirit, I am grateful this portion of the path is "quieter" and less "noisy" as the Great Physician continues my healing daily.

Lord, thank you for asking us to partner with You to meet the needs of those around us who are hungry and weary. You could do it on Your own, but You invite us to experience the joy of giving and watch our resources multiply. Thank you, Lord, for Your provision. In Jesus' name, amen.

Thank you for your persevering prayers.#Godisfaithful#TheGloryRoad

Day#278 January 22

 Anchor Verse: Exodus 6:2-3
Then God spoke further to Moses and said to him, "I am the Lord. I appeared to Abraham, to Isaac, and to Jacob (Israel) as God Almighty [El Shaddai], but by My name, Lord, I did not make Myself known to them [in acts and great miracles]. (AMP)

When God chose Moses, a shepherd on the backside of the desert to be God's mouthpiece, Moses had lots of excuses why he wasn't "the man."

Now that Moses is in Egypt, Pharaoh isn't willing to let God's people go.

Moses goes back to God and in our language today would say, "What's the deal? You said You were going to get them out of Egypt but I've only made it worse."

"Then God spoke further to Moses and said to him, "I am the LORD. I appeared to Abraham, to Isaac, and to Jacob (Israel) as God Almighty [El Shaddai], but by My name, LORD, I did not make Myself known to them [in acts and great miracles]."

God says to Moses, "Your ancestors knew "about" Me, as God Almighty [El Shaddai] but today and in the days ahead, you will "see" Me "act" on your behalf as Yahweh, it's going to get really personal."

What was once a "long-distance" relationship, knowing God from afar would forever be changed in those moments – the Israelites would have "experiential" knowledge of God.

On our journey to Bill's healing, our understanding of who God is changed forever. We had seen His mighty miracles in the lives of others – read about them, believed it was possible for "them." God showed us it was possible for us too.

On the Glory Road, I am learning another facet of God's love and mighty power. Daily, He reveals more of Himself as I draw closer to Him. Spending time in His Presence is like food and drink to me – to my soul. He gives us abundant life.

Thank you, Lord, for the intimate relationship You desire to have with us. Our relationship with You is "personal." You are not a distant God but are with us wherever we go. Thank you, Lord. In Jesus' name we pray, amen.

Thank you for your faithful prayers.#Godisfaithful#TheGloryRoad

Day#279 January 23

 Anchor Verse: Matthew 15:18
But what comes out of your mouth reveals the core of your heart. Words can pollute, not food. (TPT)

Words spoken to ourselves, or others, can leave scars that last a lifetime or provide "good fuel" on the days you are feeling down.

The Pharisees and teachers of the law often pursued Jesus to find fault with Him or His teachings. This particular day when they approached Jesus, they asked why His disciples didn't wash their hands before they ate.

Jesus used the opportunity to teach the crowd a lesson. What you eat isn't the problem, but it's what comes out of your mouth that is a reflection of your heart.

The food we eat passes through our bodies and into the sewer. But what comes out of our mouth is a reflection of our heart. What's in our heart is not only reflected in the words we speak but in our actions. (Example: murder, adultery, slander, theft, etc.)

On our journey to Bill's healing, we learned about the power of words spoken and the actions that stem from them. As God was rebuilding Bill from the inside out, it was important to be aware of the words spoken by those who surrounded him. The seeds planted in our lives always bear fruit.

The Glory Road, on this new journey, God is teaching me new things about my body, mind, and spirit. Keeping my vessel "clean" is not just about what I eat, but what I watch, what I read, what I listen to, who I listen to, and where I invest my time.

God breathed life into me at the moment of my creation. Every moment of every day, my heavenly Father breathes "new" life into me, but I must do my part. God continues to teach me how to tend to the "garden" in my heart. Time spent with the Lord in quietness is the best medicine for our souls.

Lord, our hearts are easily polluted by the things of this world. Clean our hearts. Pull out the weeds, trim the underbrush, and prune the trees, so our lives may reflect Jesus' love at work in us. Give us clean hands and a pure heart so we can enter Your presence, in Jesus' name we pray, amen.

Thank you for your encouraging words.#Godisfaithful#TheGloryRoad

Day#280 January 24

 Anchor Verse: Psalm 23:6
So why would I fear the future? For your goodness and love pursue me all the days of my life. Then afterward, when my life is through, I'll return to your glorious presence to be forever with you! (TPT)

Psalm 23 is a place of refuge and strength. It is a place where believer and unbeliever have found comfort. It is often quoted, but it's also a strong statement of our faith.

In Psalm 23:1, we begin with the present, "I lack nothing" but what about what lies ahead? Do we have the same reassurance for our future?

Verse 6 reminds us, as believers, we are in a win-win situation. "So why would I fear the future? For your goodness and love pursue me all the days of my life. Then afterward, when my life is through, I'll return to your glorious presence to be forever with you!"

Goodness and love (mercy) pursue me all the days of my life here on earth and then I will live in God's glorious presence forever. Thank you, Lord.

On our journey to Bill's healing, we learned about God's goodness and love pursuing us every day. Not only your prayers and encouragement, but God's favor everywhere. So many miracles as God touched and healed Bill so many times. Now Bill is experiencing life forever in God's glorious presence.

The Glory Road has definitely been a place of God's goodness and love. I couldn't walk another step without His presence and His power, and most of all His tender loving care. I do not fear the future; I choose to live for His honor and glory every day.

Lord, we thank you that You are the Good Shepherd. We lack nothing. Hope and joy are our constant companions. Praise the Lord that even though we walk through the darkest valleys the light of Your love lights the way. We love you and praise you. In Jesus' name we pray, amen.

Thank you for your companionship.#Godisfaithful#TheGloryRoad

Day#281 January 25

 Anchor Verse: Psalm 94:19
Lord, when doubts fill my mind, when my heart is in turmoil, quiet me and give me renewed hope and cheer. (TLB)

There are moments in our lives when we feel things are coming at us faster than we can handle. It reminds me of those old pitching machines where baseballs would be lobbed at the batter in the batter's box as he tried to tune up his batting skills. But when the baseballs start coming too fast, it overwhelms you – a few bruises might be the result.

You might be feeling "bruised" this morning – not necessarily in the flesh, but in your mind and spirit. Your circumstances and troubles have multiplied, or concerning someone you love, and your heart is in turmoil.

The Message translation says it this way, in verses 16-19, "Who stood up for me against the wicked? Who took my side against evil workers? If GOD hadn't been there for me, I never would have made it. The minute I said, "I'm slipping, I'm falling," your love, GOD, took hold and held me fast. When I was upset and beside myself, you calmed me down and cheered me up."

"If God hadn't been there for me, I never would have made it." Amen and amen.

On our journey to Bill's healing, we wouldn't have made it, without God's help. God wrapped us up in His arms of love and held us close to His heart. Some days we let the rest of the world pass by as God kept us protected through the storms of our lives. He calmed us down, cheered us up, and prepared us for the next step ahead.

The Glory Road has its own "issues" shall we say. I am so grateful that God created us to be able to learn from the past, so we can use those lessons to change our present and future. There is peace in God's presence. There is power in God's promises. There is hope because Jesus lives.

Lord, we come into Your presence this morning grateful You are always there. We praise you and thank you for who You are and who You call us to be. Lord, we surrender our doubts and fears and leave them at Your feet. In exchange, we will walk forward filled with new hope, new joy, and new peace, in Jesus' name we pray, amen.

Thank you for your faithfulness in prayer.#Godisfaithful#TheGloryRoad

Day#282 January 26

 Anchor Verse: Psalm 57:8

Awake, O my soul, with the music of his splendor-song! Arise, my soul, and sing his praises! My worship will awaken the dawn, greeting the daybreak with my songs of praise! (TPT)

Good morning. Are you one of those "cheerful" morning people or more of an evening person?

As you can probably guess, I am at my best in the morning and yes, I love to meet with the Lord before dawn – when it's still pitch-black outside. Inside, the glory of the Lord is here and it is as bright as noonday.

In Psalm 57, our call is to "awaken the dawn" because we are worshiping the King of kings and the Lord of lords that our praises fill not only our homes but the heavens.

Verse 8 says, "Awake, O my soul, with the music of his splendor-song! Arise, my soul, and sing his praises! My worship will awaken the dawn, greeting the daybreak with my songs of praise!"

If you look closely, David is talking about his "soul" waking up… not speaking to your flesh, but to your inner spirit, your inner man. Isn't that really where we need to awakened?

How much of your day do you do on auto-pilot? Probably too much.

On our journey to Bill's healing, we learned about shifting our perspective, about lifting our voices in praise to the Lord. Bill once said about his own singing, "The Bible says to make a joyful noise but my singing is pure agony." Then we both laughed.

The Glory Road is a place of praise and worship – day and night. As I lift my hands and heart in praise, the things of this world grow dim. Praise more, worry less. Sing more, grumble less. Believe what God says, not what the enemy whispers into our ear.

Lord, we praise Your holy name for You are great and greatly to be praised. Forgive us when we are so burdened with life all we see are the troubles and not the blessings. We trust you and love you. In Jesus' name we pray, amen.

Thank you for speaking life over me.#Godisfaithful#TheGloryRoad

Day#283 January 27

 Anchor Verse: Exodus 18:23
If you do what I advise and God directs you, then you will be able to handle the pressure. Not only that, but all these people standing around needing help, they will be able to return to their tents at peace. (VOICE)

Where are you feeling pressured? Is there a load that's not yours to carry?

The American independent spirit has taught us to pursue our dreams and push through every obstacle in front of us. Many of tried to "go it alone" when in truth, our heavenly Father had in mind that "others" would be walking alongside us to our destination.

If we were to speak the truth of the matter, all of us have had seasons of our lives when we pushed through even when the fallout from the pressure almost "took us out."

In Exodus 18, Jethro, Moses' father-in-law sees all these people lined up waiting to talk to Moses. He inquires of Moses what's happening. Moses tells Jethro that the people come to him to settle disputes, "the people come to seek God's will."

Jethro replies, "What you are doing is good but…" You might be in that same place.

On our journey to Bill's healing, we too learned we couldn't do it all. Bill and I were the ones always helping others, but God turned the tables and taught us how to receive with great grace and humility.

The Glory Road may follow a new path but God's truth is still the same. There are places I need to ask for help. Tasks that are "easy" when you are in full health are sometimes not as easy when you aren't. It blesses others as they bless you.

In this new season, God is teaching me new prayer strategies and to invite others to join me. There is power in unity. There is even greater joy and pleasure as we pursue God and use our unique gifts and talents.

Thank you, Lord, for the gift of others. You do not call us to carry our burdens alone. Thank you for the grace and humility You give us as we surrender our lives to You and graciously receive the gift in Your hands.

Thank you for helping me carry this load.#Godisfaithful#TheGloryRoad

Day#284 January 28

 Anchor Verse: Matthew 18:21
Then Peter came to Him and asked, "Lord, how many times will my brother sin against me and I forgive him and let it go? Up to seven times?" (AMP)

The only dumb (stupid) question is the question you don't ask. "I have a dumb question to ask" has been my entry into a question I didn't feel confident about asking – because of the content of the question or I was skittish about asking the person.

Peter, Jesus' disciple didn't have that problem. Peter asked a lot of questions and made some bold declarations as well. ("Even if I have to die with You, I will never deny You (Jesus).")

In Matthew 18:21, Peter asks Jesus this question, "Lord, how many times will my brother sin against me and I forgive him and let it go? Up to seven times?"

Does it make you wonder who Peter had in mind when he asked the question? Was it one of the other disciples he was thinking of or a family member?

I was really struck by this phrase in the Amplified translation, "and I forgive him AND let it go." Forgive and forget... once our sins are forgiven, they are covered by the blood of Jesus and God sees them no more... and neither should we. Choosing to forgive and to forget, an offense no longer has a hold on you.

On our journey to Bill's healing, we learned a lot about life and not being offended by others' words or deeds, even sins of omission (what wasn't done.) Making it a daily pattern now in the calm places prepares you for "life" in the storm. Lord, give us clean hands and a pure heart.

The Glory Road in 2020/2021 is lived out on a landscape where there's a lot of conflict. Many opportunities arise to forgive others and ask for forgiveness. It may not even be your battle to fight but you are invited into the fray. Innocent bystanders often have become casualties. Forgive as Jesus forgave. Love like Jesus loves.

Lord, may we walk in forgiveness – forgiving others even as we need to be forgiven. Thank you for forgiving us, O Lord. Help us to pass that gift along to those who cross our path in Jesus' name. Amen.

Thank you for your love and support.#Godisfaithful#TheGloryRoad

Day#285 January 29

 Anchor Verse: Psalm 63:6
If I'm sleepless at midnight, I spend the hours in grateful reflection. (MSG)

Psalm 63 offers a different perspective on sleepless nights. The psalmist turns to the Lord and finds refuge, solace there. The MESSAGE translation says, "If I'm sleepless at midnight, I spend the hours in grateful reflection."

The VOICE translation, "Often at night I lie in bed and remember You, meditating on Your greatness till morning smiles through my window."

This perspective may be a lot different than how you have viewed those nights of insomnia where your troubles pursued like a spotlight in the darkness.

On our journey to Bill's healing, our sleep was often interrupted. Often after the interruption, God would put both of us right back to sleep. If that wasn't the case, then I would lay there and pray or "sing praises to His name." We survived the storm because we kept our eyes on Jesus, the captain of the ship, the only one who could speak peace to the waves.

The Glory Road has had its own learning curve. In the early days, just learning how to sleep without Bill at my side was difficult. My heart and mind had been so tuned to Bill's heart it was like half of me was missing.

Some nights my heavenly Father turned the darkness into a classroom. Other nights I could feel the power of His presence, even the rush of angel's wings as God reminded me He was near. New songs of praise from the depths of my spirit were born in those early morning hours. At times my tears were my prayers to the only one who could heal my heart.

God is merciful and mighty. He is gentle and full of grace. With hope, our spirits are infused with new life as we rest in the shadow of His wings.

Lord, I pray for those who had a sleepless night, or a sleep interrupted night. Lord, bless them with Your strength and Your song throughout this day. We lift our hands in praise, thanking you that You are the God who sees, knows, and loves us all the days of our lives, and the nights too. We love you, Lord, in Jesus' name, we pray, amen.

Thank you for praying for me in the night.#Godisfaithful#TheGloryRoad

Day#286 January 30

 Anchor Verse: Psalm 24:1
The earth is the Lord's, and everything in it. The world and all its people belong to him. (NLT)

"In the beginning God created the heavens and the earth." (Genesis 1:1) And on the sixth day, God created man in His own image.

From the very beginning, God has been the creator of all things and creation continues in motion every day. New babies are born. New crops, new life burst forth from the earth. In Christ, we are new creations when we say "yes" to the new life He offers.

God has written a story about our lives – it's a great story because our heavenly Father only writes best sellers. It's a story of hope with a great ending when we are reunited with God in glory at the end of our lives. We just need to choose to live out that story.

This morning I hear the Lord proclaiming to us this truth. You might even hear the Lion of the tribe of Judah roaring – "The earth is the Lord's, and everything in it. The world and all its people belong to Him."

It's like the Lord saying, "No matter what you think, it all belongs to Me. And I take care of what belongs to Me – all of it, all of you."

On our journey to Bill's healing, we were so blessed that in the stripping away of so many things, God alone remained. He was faithful every day. What we needed God's hand provided. Great is His faithfulness.

The Glory Road and its wonders often cause me to stop and praise the Lord. My perspective has changed. Daily, God opens my eyes to see the wonders of the day. His glory shines in all of us who know Him and love Him. His majesty brings beauty to all things, this is who God is.

Lord, open our eyes to see that there is more that unites us than divides us. Open our mouths to speak life to each other and to ourselves. Open our hearts to receive Your love and freely pass it along, in Jesus' name, amen.

Thank you for your love.#Godisfaithful#TheGloryRoad

Day#287 January 31

 Anchor Verse: Matthew 20:33
They answered Him, "Lord, we want our eyes to be opened." (AMP)

The two blind men couldn't "see" Jesus but they could hear Him. I believe they could feel the power of His presence. Today was the day they would encounter their healer, who could restore their sight.

As Jesus asks, "What do want me to do for you?" there was no hesitation. In the Amplified version, verse 33 says, "Lord, we want our eyes to be opened." Other translations say, "We want to see." Or "We want our sight." And Jesus healed them.

This morning in my spirit, I am sensing that as individuals, families, a nation, a world, this is the cry of our heart, "Lord, we want our eyes to be opened." We want to see things as You see them. We want to wake up from what has felt like a nightmare for the last few years. We want to be healed. The only way that's going to happen is to have an encounter with Jesus, our healer.

On our journey to Bill's healing, there was a time in the early days after Bill's brain surgery, when he couldn't see. It was during the time he was sedated and unable to communicate with us. Bill knew and yet his faith was so strong. Later he said, "I reasoned that even though I was blind, I had Barb. Not sure the quality of life we would have but I had life. Thank you, God."

The Glory Road has offered a new perspective, a new line of vision, to see as God sees. That my heart would be touched with compassion as I stand on Christ the solid rock, and I would not be moved. That my faith in what Jesus can do is greater than the circumstances my eyes can see. Or even more so, the things I can't see.

This morning as I chose to abide in His Presence before I launched myself into the day, I believe I felt what those blind men felt, the power of Jesus' presence. There is peace and strength intertwined. There we are equipped to face the battles of our days.

Lord, we thank you that Your heart's desire is to heal our "blindness." Heavenly Father, You want us to see with Your eyes of love so Your heart of compassion will move us to do Your will, Your way. Lord, touch and heal the broken today. Thank you, Lord. In Jesus' name, amen.

Thank you for your faithful prayers.#Godisfaithful#TheGloryRoad

February 2021

But the eyes of the Lord are on those who fear him, on those whose hope is in his unfailing love.

~ Psalm 33:18 ~

Day#288 February 1

 Anchor Verse: 1 Corinthians 16:14
Let everything you do be done in love [motivated and inspired by God's love for us]. (AMP)

Do everything in love. Sounds simple, doesn't it? Then why is it so difficult for billions of people to do this daily? Why is difficult for you and for me to do it consistently?

The key is found in the Amplified translation of 1 Corinthians 16:14, "Let everything you do be done in love [motivated and inspired by God's love for us]." As we are motivated and inspired by God's love for us, we can then love each other.

Not everyone understands how much God loves them. Life might have thrown them some curve balls. Loved ones – friends and family, or even strangers have not acted in love and many people have become disillusioned with life and with love.

When we get hurt, we are quick to generalize. The actions of one person have caused a ripple effect that have altered the course of many people, even generations.

Toward the end of Paul's letter to the church in Corinth, as he is about to say goodbye, there are two verses, filled with powerful instruction and encouragement. "Be on your guard; stand firm in the faith; be courageous; be strong. Do everything in love."

On our journey to Bill's healing, the power of God's love was multiplied in our lives, our relationship with God, and with each other. I loved God and Bill for many years before our "trials and tribulations" began in 2018, but the depth of my love for both of them catapulted to a new level.

The Glory Road is a place to love without counting the cost. Daily, there are divine appointments God has for me. I ask for spiritual eyes to see them and many days I entertain angels unaware.

Lord Jesus, thank you for Your example of what it looks like to love others in all that we say and do, even as You taught us to love ourselves. Be honored and glorified in our lives, O Lord. In Jesus' name, we pray, amen.

Thank you for your love for us.#Godisfaithful#TheGloryRoad

Day#289 February 2

 Anchor Verse: Joel 1:3
Tell your children about it in the years to come, and let your children tell their children. Pass the story down from generation to generation. (NLT)

What a blessing it is to share family stories from generation to generation.

As powerful as our own family history, even greater is the record of what God has done in the Bible. Their revelation can be our revelation. The Lord's promises in the past pave the way for our hope today and tomorrow.

"Tell your children about it in the years to come, and let your children tell their children. Pass the story down from generation to generation." (Joel 1:3)

On our journey to Bill's healing, from the very beginning, God instructed me to share our story. Facebook is a place where once it is in writing, it doesn't go away. God reassured me, "I want to do a work there (Facebook)." I obeyed and now more than three years (2018-2021) down the road, many lives have been touched by the account of God's faithfulness in our lives.

The Glory Road was birthed out of God's continued "command" to share my story, to let you see how I walk out this path of grieving, and an unexpected "bonus" of my journey to healing. God knew all about this – Bill's journey and my journey, and the greater good would come from it.

Will we "hoard" the blessing, the miracle or will we hold it with open hands and let the world see what a mighty God we serve?

Lord, we praise and thank you for the gift of miracles. Thank you for Your hand at work in our lives. May we share what You have done with this generation and generations yet to come. Help us to encourage others to share their story for God's glory. May we be good stewards of God's gift of love. In Jesus' name we pray, amen.

Thank you for holding up my arms.#Godisfaithful#TheGloryRoad

Day#290 February 3

 Anchor Verse: Matthew 22:16
"Teacher," they said, "we know that you are a man of integrity and that you teach the way of God in accordance with the truth. You aren't swayed by others, because you pay no attention to who they are." (NIV)

When you set a trap, you may be the one who gets caught in it.

The religious leaders are trying to "trap" Jesus because of what He is teaching, or not teaching. They send their disciples to ask Jesus a question. Ultimately the question is about paying taxes, but the heart of the story lies in verse 16.

"Teacher," they said, "we know that you are a man of integrity and that you teach the way of God in accordance with the truth. You aren't swayed by others, because you pay no attention to who they are." (Matthew 22:16)

The words spoken intended to "trap" Jesus, instead revealed the truth of who Jesus was and what Jesus taught.

Jesus was just as comfortable being in the midst of the sick and those who needed to know the way to life or being in the synagogue. Jesus spoke to the Samaritan woman, the woman at the well with a checkered past. His own disciples included a wide representation of all men from fisherman to tax collectors (a hated profession.)

We are to love without counting the cost, to see with eyes of compassion those whose outward appearance might communicate their challenges.

On our journey to Bill's healing, it was always a blessing to be salt and light wherever we went, sharing Jesus' love. In our years together, we walked with those who were knocked down by the world and those on top of the world. Jesus taught us how to love like He loved – without judgment.

The Glory Road may have new scenery but it's also a place to walk as Jesus walked. May I walk in integrity and love unconditionally. We are called not to be swayed by the opinions of others but to speak the truth in love.

Lord, today may our words and our actions bring honor and glory to Your holy name. Open our eyes to see those who need Your love and kindness today and may we be Your hands and feet in Jesus' name. Amen.

Thank you for your love and kindness.#Godisfaithful#TheGloryRoad

Day#291 February 4

 Anchor Verse: Galatians 5:1
Let me be clear, the Anointed One has set us free—not partially, but completely and wonderfully free! We must always cherish this truth and stubbornly refuse to go back into the bondage of our past. (TPT)

Freedom ~ what is it?

Is it freedom from bondage? Maybe freedom to do what you want to do when you want to do it. Or is it the freedom we have in Christ to become ALL that God wants us to be?

When Jesus entered the scene, He came to make a "new" way to God. It would no longer be the sacrifices that the law demanded because Jesus came to be the ultimate sacrifice for us.

Freedom in Christ means we have a new relationship. The same God who walked in the garden with Adam and Eve wants to spend time with you and me.

"Let me be clear, the Anointed One has set us free—not partially, but completely and wonderfully free! We must always cherish this truth and stubbornly refuse to go back into the bondage of our past." (Galatians 5:1)

We are completely free. It was the gift that Jesus paid such a high price for at Calvary. With this freedom, comes this longing from the heart of God that we would cherish this truth of freedom in Christ and refuse to go back into the bondage of our past.

On our journey to Bill's healing, we had a greater revelation about what freedom in Christ meant. In the midst of ICU units, therapy sessions, caregivers to help at home, Bill knew that he had freedom in Christ. It wasn't his circumstances that determined his course, but his loving heavenly Father.

The Glory Road is a path of freedom in the midst of a world landscape that looks anything but free. As I was asking the Lord for my "word" for 2021, the word He gave me was "freedom." What an amazing gift.

Lord, set us free from the bondage of our past that we might live a life pleasing to You. May we show others this path to freedom. Jesus, thank you for the amazing gift of Your unconditional love. You died so that we could live with You for eternity. We love you, Lord. In Jesus' name we pray, Amen.

Thank you for your faithfulness.#Godisfaithful#TheGloryRoad

Day#292 February 5

 Anchor Verse: Exodus 36:2
Then Moses summoned Bezalel and Oholiab and every skilled person to whom the Lord had given ability and who was willing to come and do the work. (NIV)

When God has a task in mind, He equips and calls people to accomplish His purposes. In Exodus 36:2, God told Moses it was time to build a tabernacle.

Bezalel and Oholiab were given the ability to teach others – from engraving, designing, embroidering to weaving. God had equipped them perfectly for this task.

In Exodus 36:2, Moses calls these two men and every skilled person who the Lord had given ability AND who was <u>willing</u> to come and do the work. Having talent wasn't enough, you needed to be willing. This message is for us today too.

You may have the skills God needs to use you to do His work in the world, but if you are not willing, it's not going to happen… it's as simple as that.

Pastor Dave, our senior pastor, often imparts this nugget of wisdom, "Without God, man cannot. Without man, God will not." We need God and God needs us to live our lives to the fullest in this world and to share the good news of Jesus.

On our journey to Bill's healing, we learned that we were equipped for the path God had called us to walk. The question from the onset was: Are you willing? Bill and I both answered "yes" and in our surrender, we found abundant life.

The Glory Road is a path of obedience and surrender. It is a path mixed with tears of many kinds – joy, gratitude, grief, and surrender. All of them touch the heart of my heavenly Father. In that release, I am ready to take the next step, not only to exercise my gifts but to teach others, just like Bezalel and Oholiab. Thank you for Your ways which are higher than our ways. Thank you for the way You have gifted us. We give You our willing hearts. Please use them to reach others with Your love. In Jesus' name, amen.

Thank you for your 24-hour prayers.#Godisfaithful#TheGloryRoad

Day#293 February 6

 Anchor Verse: Matthew 23:37
How often I wanted to gather your children together, as a hen gathers her chicks under her wings, but you were not willing! (NKJV)

Jesus often used parables to explain truth to people, even His own disciples.

We do the same thing when we are trying to teach a lesson. Finding common ground, an image can be created in our own mind to help us understand the message our friend, teacher, or even God is trying to teach us.

In Matthew 23, we encounter the "woe" statements of Jesus to the teachers of the law and the Pharisees who were leading people astray through their teachings. As we near the end of the chapter, Jesus relays the message of His heart about Jerusalem, those who were refusing to accept His teachings and going their own way.

"How often I wanted to gather your children together, as a hen gathers her chicks under her wings, but you were not willing!" (Matthew 23:37)

Jesus was conveying how much He loved them. Other translations say, "You were too stubborn to let me" (TPT) or "you wouldn't let me" (NLT).

On our journey to Bill's healing, we quickly learned the best place to be was tucked under "the wings" of Jesus. Without divine intervention, wisdom, and understanding, we would have been in trouble. We chose to surrender to God's plans and His purposes and submit to His leadership.

The Glory Road is another place where "daily" Jesus asks if I am willing to follow Him. Am I willing to simply trust that He knows best? Jesus knows not only what I am facing today but He knows all about tomorrow.

Yes, life is a wild adventure to live this way, but isn't life a wild adventure anyway? When I trust Jesus to be the captain of my ship, I can "sleep" in the boat knowing that I am safe in the hollow of His hands.

Lord, we praise and thank you for the gift of Your lovingkindness. Nothing is too hard for You. In Your arms of love, we find safety from life's storms. We trust you even when our eyes can't see the outcome. Guide us through the hard places and protect us by Your mighty hand. In Jesus' name, amen.

Thank you for your persistent prayers.#Godisfaithful#TheGloryRoad

Day#294 February 7

 Anchor Verse: Psalm 119:45
I will walk with you in complete freedom, for I seek to follow your every command.
(TPT)

Freedom – it's the foundation of this nation, it's the foundation of our Christian faith.

Even in a nation that has freedom woven into the bedrock of its existence, there are so many who don't walk in that freedom. Whether those restrictions are self-imposed or from the hands of others, there is a longing to be free.

As believers, our calling from the Lord is to walk in "freedom" with Him. It's freedom in the Spirit. It's freedom to become all that God created you to be.

"I will walk with you in complete freedom, for I seek to follow your every command." It's not just about the letter of the law but the spirit of the law.

Freedom is my "word" for 2021. In a world turned upside down, our freedom has been restricted as we have attempted to stop the spread of sickness. Freedom is not about a "place" but rather about our "perspective."

On our journey to Bill's healing, there were many places where Bill's ability to move about freely was restricted by his physical health challenges. But that didn't stop Bill from imagining "better tomorrows." Those days Bill's spirit soared with the eagles.

The Glory Road is about perspective as well. I look to the hills where my help comes from. It comes in the name of the Lord, Maker of heaven and earth. (Psalm 121:1-2) Where I choose to focus my attention will determine the distance I can run that day.

Lord, we praise and thank you for the gift of strength, for in Christ we are free indeed. When our eyes remain focused on You, the sky is the limit. Obedience brings life. May You be honored and glorified in all that we say and do. And may we share the freedom that You have given us in Christ. In Jesus' mighty name we pray, amen.

Thank you for your companionship.#Godisfaithful#TheGloryRoad

Day#295 February 8

 Anchor Verse: Psalm 105:8
For though a thousand generations may pass away, he is still true to his word. He has kept every promise he made to Abraham and to Isaac. (TPT)

God's promises never fail. Though a thousand generations come and go, yet God's word remains true forever.

When our world becomes so focused on our own lives and this current generation, we are prone to forget generations past and generations yet to come. We are part of billions of people that have lived on this earth and impacted the world.

Sometimes we need to look at the "bigger" picture, especially if we are struggling with the right perspective.

Looking at a small piece of an elephant – tail, tusk, ear, foot – you have no clue about the magnitude of its presence until you see the whole animal.

That's why two things are so important. One is to read the Bible and the stories of generations past so we can see God's faithfulness. How people were in difficult situations, even life and death situations, and yet, God rescued them.

The second thing to remember is our part in passing along our testimony about what the Lord has done in our lives. It is the "oral" testimony – telling our stories that make an impact on our own friends and families. It's personal – and it's powerful.

On our journey to Bill's healing, we witnessed God's faithfulness so many times. What an honor and privilege to share those testimonies with you. Great is His faithfulness.

The Glory Road is a path filled with testimonies – both written and oral. Every opportunity I have I share of God's faithfulness and let His light shine through me. What a blessing to be the canvas on which God paints another chapter of His faithfulness to all generations – a thousand generations.

Lord, You are a promise keeper. Give us the strength, courage, and integrity to keep our promises. In Jesus' name, amen.

Thank you for your faithfulness in prayer.#Godisfaithful#TheGloryRoad

Day#296 February 9

 Anchor Verse: Leviticus 6:13
Remember, the fire must be kept burning on the altar at all times. It must never go out. (NLT)

The Israelites didn't have the internet, Google, or social media to get their information or to shape their opinions. It was through the leaders God appointed and His message through them that they lived their lives and walked in obedience.

This morning, Leviticus 6:13 "jumped" off the page. I heard my heavenly Father whisper this truth to me. "Your heart is your altar to Me. The fire of the Holy Spirit resides there. Never let that fire go out. Never let your love for Me grow dim. It is through the holy fire that you love others just as I love you – unconditionally and forever. Go and do the work I have called you to do. Love the Lord your God with all your heart, and soul, and mind, and strength and your neighbor as yourself. With My help, nothing is impossible –absolutely nothing."

In His Kingdom, "good enough" is not enough. God wants nothing less than His best for you. May our hearts be ablaze with His holy fire of love.

On our journey to Bill's healing, we were baptized in the fire of God's love. We were purified in the fire. As Bill's sickness was stripped away by God's loving hands, it was replaced with new joy and new strength. The fire of God's love was never quenched.

The Glory Road is a beautiful place for the fire of God's love in my heart, on my altar to shine brightly for Him. Whether that is in the chemo clinic, doctor's offices, my home, my church, on social media, I cannot contain the fire of the Holy Spirit the bright light of God's glory and grace within me.

Lord, we thank you for the fire of Your love that ignites our hearts. May we share that fire with others so everyone can hear the good news of Jesus. We yield our hearts, our lives, and our dreams to you and ask for Your best in exchange. In Jesus' mighty name we pray, amen.

Thank you for keeping His holy fire alive.#Godisfaithful#TheGloryRoad

Day#297 February 10

 Anchor Verse: Hebrews 4:12-13
God means what he says. What he says goes. His powerful Word is sharp as a
surgeon's scalpel, cutting through everything, whether doubt or defense, laying us
open to listen and obey. Nothing and no one can resist God's Word. We can't get
away from it—no matter what. (MSG)

There are very few "constants" in this world. Gravity is one of them. In the spiritual realm, God never changes. God's Word – the Bible doesn't change either.

"God means what he says. What he says goes. His powerful Word is sharp as a surgeon's scalpel, cutting through everything, whether doubt or defense, laying us open to listen and obey. Nothing and no one can resist God's Word. We can't get away from it—no matter what." (Hebrews 4:13 MSG)

What powerful imagery. No one likes to have a surgeon cut on your body, but sometimes it's necessary to remove what is hurtful, a hindrance to your life and your well-being. The Bible does the same thing. It is God's Word, that is so powerful it removes "anything" that is holding us back from giving "everything" we have to God.

On our journey to Bill's healing, Bill had several surgical procedures to fix and repair his body that was wounded from life's battles. At the same time that God was directing the surgeon's hands, the Great Physician's hands were "doing surgery" on the spirit man, and preparing Bill's "spiritual" heart for the next stage of his journey.

The Glory Road is a new adventure for me. As I walk out my own health journey, I have encountered the Great Physician, physically and spiritually. On one of my nighttime encounters with the Lord, He asked, "Would you rather trust a scalpel in the hands of your human surgeon or in My hands?" I answered, "In Your hands."

God has been "doing the work" to heal my physical body and fine-tuning my spirit so I am better fit for His service.

Lord, we praise for the work You are doing in our lives. May we be willing to submit to the sharp scalpel found in God's Word. God hands are hands that heal, not destroy. Embrace the path God has for you. Be at peace. He is the Lord your Healer. Touch and heal us, heavenly Father. In Jesus' name, amen.

Thank you for your faithful prayers.#Godisfaithful#TheGloryRoad

Day#298 February 11

 Anchor Verse: Deuteronomy 7:9
Understand, therefore, that the Lord your God is indeed God. He is the faithful God who keeps his covenant for a thousand generations and lavishes his unfailing love on those who love him and obey his commands. (NLT)

In a world where there are days when we feel like we are walking on shifting sand, it is so powerful to remember that our God never changes.

There is no one on earth that measures up to that standard. We are human, and there are times we will fail, even with our best intentions. Our God never fails.

And God keeps His covenant for "a thousand generations." Think of how many people exist just in "one" generation. A thousand generations are more people than we can count. God's faithfulness is infinite – it goes on forever.

God also "lavishes" His unfailing love on those who love Him and obey His commands. What does "lavish" mean? The dictionary says lavish means to "bestow something in generous or extravagant quantities."

That's what God does for you and for me – He gives us generous and extravagant quantities of unfailing love. In modern terms we might say, "Valentine's Day on steroids" … more than we could ever imagine.

It's not a free ride. In any good relationship, it's a two-way street. With God's unfailing love being poured into us, we "love" to love God back.

On our journey to Bill's healing, we learned that God is God. Nothing happens beyond His reach, beyond His control, and truly His love never fails. Loving God fueled the fire within us, not only to love each other but to love those who served us.

The Glory Road is a glorious road. As the Lord calls me to pray daily (and "nightly" too) my prayer list includes generations yet to come. May my legacy be filled with my faithfulness to God and God's faithfulness to me.

Lord, we praise you this morning for Your unfailing love. You are the rock on which we stand. You haven't change since the creation of the world, and You cannot, and will not, ever be shaken! May we lavishly share that love with others we meet. In Jesus' name, we pray, amen.

Thank you for your love and faithfulness.#Godisfaithful#TheGloryRoad

Day#299 February 12

 Anchor Verse: Proverbs 18:24
One who has unreliable friends soon comes to ruin, but there is a friend who sticks closer than a brother. (NIV)

The book of Proverbs is filled with much wisdom – small nuggets to be "chewed" and reflected on before they are "swallowed" and become part of our own "heart tapestry."

In this season of my life, I am more aware of the power of friendship and the blessing from God's hands that a true friend brings to us.

Bill and I were friends first before God fanned the flame for it to be "more." I am missing my best (human) friend.

Proverbs 18:24 reminds us that unreliable friends will cause our ruin. But the last half of this verse is where the "power" lies. "There is a friend who sticks closer than a brother."

The friend spoken of here is Jesus, a friend like no other. What a blessing to be able to talk with our friend, Jesus, day or night. You don't need any technology to connect with Jesus; He's as close as the breath you breathe.

On our journey to Bill's healing, we learned a lot about friendship – both new friends and old friends. A friendship can sprout up in unlikely places. Praise God for the gift of amazing friends.

The Glory Road is a place of new beginnings and new friendships. One of the blessings of this Covid season is the use of technology to connect us across time zones, and in some cases, thousands of miles. The Lord continues to bring "new" friends into my life to sharpen me and with whom I can share the encouragement and revelation God gives to me.

Thank you, Lord, for the gift of friends. Jesus is the greatest gift, the greatest friend of all. May we be that friend to others, in Jesus' name, amen.

"A true friend is one who walks in when the rest of the world walks out." ~ Walter Winchell. Thank you.#Godisfaithful#TheGloryRoad

Day#300 February 13

 Anchor Verse: Isaiah 35:8
And a great road will go through that once deserted land. It will be named the Highway of Holiness. Evil-minded people will never travel on it. It will be only for those who walk in God's ways; fools will never walk there. (NLT)

When you live in a country, in a location, where the infrastructure has been built – roads, electricity, water systems, etc. we take for granted what so many do not have.

It's not like everywhere. Where I live on the West Coast of America, it used to be called, the "Wild, Wild West." Definitely not that same picture today – it definitely looks more "civilized" (at least in some respects.)

Isaiah 35:8 says, "And a great road will go through that once deserted land."

God alone can bring joy out of our sorrow. God alone can bring peace out of our chaos. God alone rebuilds what the enemy has destroyed.

That new place is called the "Highway of Holiness." It is a place reserved for God's people that have chosen to follow Him to a place they do not know. It is the road of faith – just like Abraham, trusting God without seeing the end result, but trusting God's faithfulness.

On our journey to Bill's healing, our loving heavenly Father brought us from a desolate land to that Highway of Holiness, the Sacred Way. We walked hand in hand with Jesus as He spoke new life into us even while the rest of the world wandered in chaos.

The Glory Road is similar to that Highway of Holiness. "The Glory Road" is the Highway of Holiness where God has called me to walk. You have been invited as well to be my companions on this journey.

It is not an easy path, but Jesus' walk on this earth wasn't easy either. It was filled with God's glory. The easy path is not always the most blessed path.

Lord, we thank you and praise you for providing this place of blessing for us, Your children. May we share with others what You have taught us. We live for Your glory. We love you and praise you, in Jesus' name we pray, amen.

Thank you for walking this path with me.#Godisfaithful#TheGloryRoad

Day#301 February 14

 Anchor Verse: Isaiah 49:16
...I have written your name on the palms of my hands. (NLT)

Today is Valentine's Day, a day that we as a society set aside to recognize and celebrate "love."

Our focus today is on the power of love, especially God's love. The Bible tells us that "God is love." We were created because of God's love. With God's love as our genealogy and woven into our DNA, there is so much to celebrate.

Jesus was God's greatest "love" gift to us. When we accept the gift of Jesus, we have the guarantee of spending eternity with God in heaven.

God's love for us in a tangible way, "I have written your name on the palms of my hands." (Isaiah 49:16) It is a reminder of how much He loves us. The palms of His hands remind us of how God protects us, just as we want to protect those we love.

On our journey to Bill's healing, we experienced not only God's love, but an amazing gesture of love from a new friend. There were moments in Bill's travels where his life hung in the balance between life and death. Our friend took a marker and wrote Bill's name on her hand as a reminder to pray for him. What an amazing love gift.

The Glory Road is an opportunity for me to show God's love to others even as I know that my name is written on the palms of God's hands as He daily meets my needs. My heavenly Father fans the flames of the hopes and dreams for my future.

Daily, you and I have the opportunity to love and be loved, to encourage and be encouraged, to pray and to let others pray for us. There is nothing more beautiful to God than to see His children imitate their Father's love.

Lord, thank you for the gift of Your love. Thank you for Jesus, the greatest love gift of all. We pray for those who have lost loved ones this year, this day may be a difficult day for them. Lord, send them an extra measure of Your love to fill the empty places in their heart. You are love and we celebrate that love today. In Jesus' name, amen.

Thank you for your encouragement.#Godisfaithful#TheGloryRoad

Day#302 February 15

 Anchor Verse: Psalm 44:8
O God, we give glory to you all day long and constantly praise your name. (NLT)

We have often heard the expression about giving credit where credit is due. How often do you and I give credit to God for all that He has done? Are we like the psalmist here in Psalm 44:8?

"O God, we give glory to you all day long and constantly praise your name." Giving glory "all day long" and "constantly" praising God's name is our goal.

Why was the psalmist giving God all the glory and praise? In verse 6-7 it says, "I put no trust in my bow, my sword does not bring victory; but You give us victory over our enemies, You put our adversaries to shame."

The same is true today. It is not by our own strength and power that we prevail and have victory, but it's by God's grace, mercy, and love that we are victorious.

On our journey to Bill's healing, we learned the power of praise and boasting in what the Lord was doing in Bill's life. It wasn't our own willpower or strength that helped Bill move forward in his recovery. God gets all the credit for the mighty miracles we witnessed on the path to Bill's healing.

The Glory Road is filled with praising the Lord for the great things He has done and is still doing. Note the name of my path, the "Glory" Road. In those early days after Bill went to heaven, those were the words that my heavenly Father whispered into my spirit. My posture is to praise Him and obey Him and let God have His way in me.

What is your heart filled with today? Where are your eyes focused? What is the nature of the words that roll off your tongue?

A tree is known by its fruit. May the fruit of the Spirit be evidenced in our lives (love, joy, peace, patience, kindness, goodness, gentleness, faithfulness, and self-control).

Lord, we thank you for the gift of life, for the gift of Your love. Our heart's desire is to be more like You in all we say and do. May our lives, words, and actions be pleasing to You every day. In Jesus' name we pray, amen.

Thank you for your faithful prayers.#Godisfaithful#TheGloryRoad

Day#303 February 16

 Anchor Verse: Leviticus 19:32
Stand up in the presence of the aged, show respect for the elderly and revere your God. I am the Lord. (NLT)

There is great wisdom that comes with age and experience and much for us to learn from each other.

This verse from Leviticus 19:32 is a reminder of the respect and honor we should give to each other and to the Lord. "Stand up in the presence of the aged, show respect for the elderly and revere your God. I am the Lord."

In the long list of things the Lord shares with His people in the book of Leviticus about what to do and not to do that showing respect to the elderly and standing in the presence of the aged was among them.

I'm not sure at what age that you officially become "aged" or "elderly" – I don't think I'm there yet. Although based on the number of my times "around the sun," others might have another opinion.

It always amazed me that in the church I grew up in, the group of older adults (the Caleb group) didn't see themselves as "old" even though they were in their 70s, 80s, and 90s… they were still young at heart and full of life.

When you are blessed to have grandparents or great grandparents who have lived many years, soak in their wisdom and honor them.

On our journey to Bill's healing, we learned even more about honor and respect and honoring God. Bill was given respect and he gave it to others as well. It was beautiful.

The Glory Road is a place where God has opened the doors of opportunity to love well and live well. In that beautiful tapestry, there are people of all ages, races, cultural backgrounds, and geographical locations. The family of God is full of life, wisdom, knowledge, and understanding – oh that we would learn from each other.

Lord, we thank you that Your love never ends. It is for every generation and every age. Help us respect our elders and learn well from them. May the light of the love of Jesus light our way every day. We will give you all the praise and honor and glory. In Jesus' name we pray, amen.

Thank you for your love and prayers.#Godisfaithful#TheGloryRoad

Day#304 February 17

 Anchor Verse: Deuteronomy 28:2
And all these blessings shall come upon you and overtake you, because you obey the voice of the Lord your God. (NKJV)

Obedience brings life. It is a phrase that our pastor often repeats. It is a good word from the Lord that I have engraved on my heart.

Obedience isn't easy, and definitely not always the popular choice. Obedience to the Lord means that sometimes you will stand alone in the face of adversity, in the hour of trial or temptation. Yet, you are never alone because Jesus Christ is standing right next to you with His hand linked with yours.

Gently Jesus will "squeeze" your hand reminding you that you are not alone. His peace floods your heart when you take the action that brings God glory.

Deuteronomy 28 outlines the blessings that come to those who obey the voice of the Lord our God. The latter part of the chapter talks about the consequences of disobedience – you might want to read those as well.

"All these blessings shall come upon and overtake you." The NIV translation says they will "accompany" you.

On our journey to Bill's healing, we experienced the blessings as we obeyed the voice of the Lord. Sometimes our decisions were misunderstood by others. There were times we stood alone – but Jesus was always there.

The Glory Road is a pathway of blessings as I walk in obedience to the voice of God. First of all, our ears need to be tuned to God's voice, even a whisper, or a gentle nudge in our heart. Often Bill and I knew what the other one was thinking or feeling without words, this is the intimacy that your heavenly Father wants with you and me.

Obedience is the pathway to life. Every time I choose to obey, even in the hard places, a new rush of abundant life, floods my soul. I'm refreshed and more committed to walk the path of life with Jesus, my Lord and Savior.

Lord, we thank you for the blessings that flow from our acts of obedience. Remove anything that is blocking my path to a deeper intimacy with You. My life is Yours. Lead me on that path of truth in Jesus' name, amen.

Thanks for your faithful prayers.#Godisfaithful#TheGloryRoad

Day#305 February 18

 Anchor Verse: Mark 1:17
"Come, follow me," Jesus said. (NIV)

Are you a better leader or follower? Some people "always" want to be the one calling the shots, taking the lead, being the "boss." Following is a hard thing for them to do.

It might be a "control" issue – always being in control, having expectations about the outcome, knowing the outcome, and not giving that power to someone else.

When Jesus called His disciples to join Him on this incredible journey, the words Jesus used were simple, "Come, follow me."

The simplicity of those words, that invitation, that command is still the same for us. In the depths of your heart, Jesus is standing at the "door" and saying, "My child, come and follow Me." Jesus will show you glorious things you do not know.

This was not an invitation for an opportunity days, weeks, or months down the road, Jesus' invitation was for them to follow Him immediately.

Jesus is asking us to make that same decision today.

On our journey to Bill's healing, we left our "old life" behind the moment Bill left our apartment via ambulance on the way to the hospital on the morning of January 10, 2018. Jesus said, "Come, follow me and I will show you things you do not know." And He did. Jesus showed us new depths of His love for us and our love for each other.

The Glory Road is a place where daily I hear Jesus whisper, "Come, follow Me." Every day is an adventure, a word that Bill and I came to call the places we had never been before, but places where God was always there with us.

Lord, we thank you for the gift of Your invitation to follow you. There is no greater love than Your love and no greater blessing than what comes from Your hands and heart. We surrender control of our lives and place them in Your hands. Be honored and glorified in us. In Jesus' name we pray, amen.

Thank you for being willing to follow Jesus.#Godisfaithful#TheGloryRoad

Day#306 February 19

 Anchor Verse: Mark 1:38
Jesus replied, "Let us go somewhere else—to the nearby villages—so I can preach there also. That is why I have come." (NIV)

"What are you doing here?" I was asked this question in my late 20s. I thought I knew the answer. God had a deeper revelation. It changed the course of my life.

In Mark 1, we see the contrast in Jesus' life between time with God and time serving others. It was in the solitary place where Jesus was refreshed and renewed and filled with more strength and power, so He could effectively preach, teach, and heal.

Mark 1:38 says, "Jesus replied, "Let us go somewhere else—to the nearby villages—so I can preach there also. That is why I have come.""

Jesus' ministry wasn't confined to one small "dot" on the map. Jesus planted seeds of love and hope wherever He went.

What a great reminder that God has a plan and purpose for our lives. It is in that solitary place, time alone with our heavenly Father that we learn about His heart, His passion, His purpose for us.

On our journey to Bill's healing, we learned so much about how God uses some of the most difficult seasons in our lives to shine most for His glory. In the flesh, Bill had many trials, but in the spirit, God was birthing a mighty warrior fit for serving the King of kings and the Lord of lords.

The Glory Road is a new "dot" on my map. It is a place I've never been, yet there are familiar markers on the road. Signs of God's love and faithfulness dot the landscape. There are places to rest and places to run (in the spirit.) I am well acquainted with the solitary place where I spend time alone with my heavenly Father. Around the next bend, there are new places and new people that God has called me to reach and even messages to preach.

Lord, may Your light in us shine brightly today. Lord, may we discover why we are here so that You would be honored and glorified. Thank you that You are our strength and our song. In Jesus' name, amen.

Thank you for your perseverance.#Godisfaithful#TheGloryRoad

Day#307 February 20

 Anchor Verse: 2 Samuel 22:29
You, Lord, are my lamp; the Lord turns my darkness into light. (NIV)

Praise the Lord that He turns my darkness into light. Hallelujah!

The greatest darkness of all is the absence of God when we make poor choices and walk away from Him. The good news – His light is only a whisper away. Just speaking His name, "Jesus" turns the light on in our hearts and lives.

The MESSAGE translation paints a powerful picture of verse 29 and the verses following: "Suddenly, God, your light floods my path, God drives out the darkness…What a God! His road stretches straight and smooth. Every God-direction is road-tested. Everyone who runs toward him makes it."

A few years ago, when a windstorm in our area knocked out the power, Bill and I were without power and heat for five days. I remember how dark the darkness was, you could "feel" it in the air. Praise the Lord, God drives out the darkness.

On our journey to Bill's healing, we hit patches in the road that were pretty dark from our human standpoint. How beautiful the contrast when God's light flooded our path. Even in an ICU unit, where life and death are only a breath apart, God's light gave us hope. It made a way.

The Glory Road is a path of contrasts. In 2 Samuel 22:31 it says, "His road stretches straight and smooth. Every God-direction is road-tested. Everyone who runs toward Him makes it." That's God's promise to us this morning.

This path isn't a foreign place to God; it's already "road-tested." God's promise is that when we run to Him, we make it. If you are in the cold, the darkness, lonely, anxious, feeling abandoned, know that God is there with you. You're going to make it.

Lord, I pray for those in the darkness – in the flesh or their soul. Flood their path with light. May Your promises be a lamp to our feet and a light to our path. Do, Lord, what we cannot do ourselves. In Jesus' name, amen.

Thank you for being my companions.#Godisfaithful#TheGloryRoad

Day#308 February 21

 Anchor Verse: Mark 3:8
… [Jesus] deeply distressed at their stubborn hearts, said to the man, "Stretch out your hand." He stretched it out, and his hand was completely restored. (NIV)

The Gospels of Matthew, Mark, Luke, and John are filled with stories of Jesus' miracles, especially healing miracles. They are not "cookie cutter" miracles. Each miracle fit the person Jesus wanted to heal, with all the glory going to God.

Sometimes people were healed as the crowd pressed in, believing that if they could only touch Jesus they would be healed. Other times, it was done "quietly" – one on one. Some were instructed to go show themselves to the priests, while others were told to remain silent and not "broadcast" the news.

In Mark 3:8, Jesus asks the man with the shriveled hand to come and stand in front of everyone. Jesus wants them to see what was about to happen.

What struck me this morning was that Jesus was "deeply distressed at their stubborn hearts." (Yet He still healed the man.)

Is Jesus deeply distressed at our stubborn hearts? We see the miraculous. We have the Bible filled with His truth. Yet many do not believe. Even among believers, we fall short of receiving "all" that God has for us. We lack faith.

On our journey to Bill's healing, we saw God's healing hand at every turn. We heard our heavenly Father's invitation to press in and open our hands and hearts to receive ALL that God had for Bill, all that He had for me.

The Glory Road is filled with opportunities to see God's healing hand at work. It's more than just physical healing. It's the restoration of families, one neighbor helping another, the food that is lovingly made for a family with a new baby or a word of encouragement to a child or an elderly person.

Lord, we come before you asking for forgiveness. We lay our "stubborn" hearts down and ask that You would give us a new heart filled with faith and love. May we trust You, Lord, even when our eyes can't see the outcome. You alone are worthy of our praise. In Jesus' name we pray, amen.

Thank you for your faithful prayers.#Godisfaithful#TheGloryRoad

Day#309 February 22

 Anchor Verse: Proverbs 27:9
Sweet friendships refresh the soul and awaken our hearts with joy, for good friends are like the anointing oil that yields the fragrant incense of God's presence. (TPT)

Friends, good friends, are such a gift. They aren't wrapped up with bright wrapping paper with a beautiful bow on top instead they are wrapped in a blanket of love and ask you to join them there.

Proverbs 27:9 says, "Sweet friendships refresh the soul and awaken our hearts with joy, for good friends are like the anointing oil that yields the fragrant incense of God's presence."

What a blessing to have this kind of friendship that refreshes your soul and awakens your heart with joy. The "secret sauce" of a good friendship is that it's the "fragrant incense" of God's presence. Our ability to love others comes from the heart of God because God is love.

On our journey to Bill's healing, we were blessed by the kind deeds of long-time friends, and the prayers and encouraging words of new friends. Our friends and family helped carry us through the good times and challenges.

The Glory Road is a blessed road because of those who line my path. After Bill died, there was a hole in my life, in my heart, that no one else can fill. But I am so grateful for those who have walked with me especially during this health challenge, so I did not walk alone. Many of my friends chose to walk through uncomfortable places, places that stretched them too.

What about you? Have you been the recipient of such a friendship? Maybe the better question is, have you been that kind of friend?

The best friendships are not about what "I" get out of the deal but how I can best love my friend and be with them when they walk through deep valleys and also celebrate their mountaintop victories.

Ralph Waldo Emerson said, "The only way to have a friend is to be one."

Lord, we thank you for the gift of friendship. Jesus is a friend like no other. May we learn to love like Jesus loves. Thank you for trusting us to love others as You love them. In Jesus' mighty name we pray, amen.

Thank you for your friendship.#Godisfaithful#TheGloryRoad

Day#310 February 23

 Anchor Verse: Mark 4:18-19
The seed cast in the weeds represents the ones who hear the kingdom news but are overwhelmed with worries about all the things they have to do and all the things they want to get. The stress strangles what they heard, and nothing comes of it. (MSG)

Maybe your experience with planting is from your youth when in school you planted seeds in an "egg carton" and watched the wonder of nature unfold.

When God created the world, He put in place "laws of nature" that haven't changed since the beginning of time like the law of sowing and reaping.

The parable of the Sower appears in three gospels: Matthew, Mark, and Luke. It talks about the seed that is sown in various types of soil. Jesus explains the "seed" is the word of God – the good news of God's kingdom.

"The seed cast in the weeds represents the ones who hear the kingdom news but are overwhelmed with worries about all the things they have to do and all the things they want to get. The stress strangles what they heard, and nothing comes of it." (Mark 4:18-19)

This reads like a chapter out of 2020/2021 in this pandemic season. Many are overwhelmed by worry. What a powerful word, "The stress strangles what they heard, and nothing comes of it." Does this describe your life?

On our journey to Bill's healing, there were many stressful moments. We laid our stressful circumstances at the feet of Jesus, the Prince of Peace. He exchanged our cares for His compassion. Our worries were replaced with worship in the presence of the King of kings and the Lord of lords.

The Glory Road carves a path through a nation, a world that is overwhelmed by what they see, hear, and experience. Daily, I choose God's peace, God's presence. God's truth written in the Bible can withstand any storm in my life. It will not fail, it will not fall, and it will not bow to anything in this world. Jesus was victorious, and because He lives, my victory is certain too.

Lord, we worship you this morning. We choose to trust You when the hurricane-force winds surround us and threaten to blow us away. Lord Jesus, You are our shelter in the storm. You alone are worthy of our praise. May You be high and lifted up in our lives today. In Jesus' name we pray, amen.

Thank you for choosing faith, not fear.#Godisfaithful#TheGloryRoad

Day#311 February 24

 Anchor Verse: Mark 4:26-27
This is what the kingdom of God is like. A man scatters seed on the ground. Night and day, whether he sleeps or gets up, the seed sprouts and grows, though he does not know how. (NIV)

There are many mysteries in this world we do not understand. Maybe God designed it that way so we wouldn't try and take the credit. Otherwise, I can hear "Joe Blow" taking credit for "General Sherman" a sequoia tree that stands 275 feet tall. Thank you, Lord, for the mysteries of nature.

Jesus wants to expand their thinking beyond the natural phenomenon of sowing and reaping of crops, and turn our eyes to the kingdom of God.

"This is what the kingdom of God is like. A man scatters seed on the ground. Night and day, whether he sleeps or gets up, the seed sprouts and grows, though he does not know how." (Mark 4:26-27)

What a great reality check, said nicely of course, "Buddy, it's not about you." It's not because we are so smart or responsible or creative or gifted. It will grow no matter what we do. God who brings the increase.

There are two things that are our responsibility in this story about the kingdom of God. We are to sow the seed and reap the harvest. Daily, this should be our mindset. Surveying the landscape and seeing where we can sow, and in God's time, reap the harvest.

On our journey to Bill's healing, we were able to sow many seeds of faith as we let the light of Jesus shine through us. There is no place in this world where God tells us "not" to sow seed… every place is fertile ground for God's kingdom.

The Glory Road is a place of sowing and reaping. A portion of that reaping comes from the seeds Bill and I planted together. All of us are partners in this quest to sow and reap. You may be reaping a harvest from seeds planted by generations past and watered by the tears and prayers of many.

Lord, open our eyes, our ears, our hearts to be used by You. May we be vessels of honor, O Lord. May people see the hope that lives in us because You live in us. May we be Your hands and feet, in Jesus' name, amen.

Thank you for your faithful prayers.#Godisfaithful#TheGloryRoad

Day#312 February 25

 Anchor Verse: Mark 5:19
Jesus did not let him [come], but [instead] He said to him, "Go home to your family and tell them all the great things that the Lord has done for you, and how He has had mercy on you." (AMP)

In Mark 5, Jesus healed a man and the man wanted to go with Him. It is understandable he would want to follow this man who totally changed his life. Yet, that was not Jesus' plan for him.

"…He [Jesus] said to him, "Go home to your family and tell them all the great things that the Lord has done for you, and how He has had mercy on you." (Mark 5:19)

When something amazing happens in our lives, we want to share the good news with those we care about the most. In fact, often our families are those who have suffered the most with us during an illness or impairment. That's what Jesus asked of him.

From a heart of compassion, in His mercy, Jesus decided to heal him and rescue him from a life of agony. Thank you, Jesus.

On our journey to Bill's healing, Jesus met Bill many times. Every time, He reached out with a merciful heart, a heart of compassion, and saw Bill's need and met him there. God is a merciful God who loves us so much.

The Glory Road is a path where Jesus walks with me. He knows my past, my present, and my future. His presence goes with me daily. There are times when I am "stretched" in my faith or my physical strength and abilities – and mentally too. All this is done from a heart of compassion. My heavenly Father's heart hurts when I hurt, and rejoices when I rejoice.

Lord, we praise and thank you for the gift of Your love and mercy. Surely we would perish without Your grace. Lord, may we extend that grace and mercy to others. May our families be blessed because of Your love in and through us. We live for Your glory, O God. In Jesus' mighty name we pray, amen.

Thank you for your obedience. #Godisfaithful#TheGloryRoad

Day#313 February 26

 Anchor Verse: Numbers 12:13
So Moses cried out to the Lord, "Please, God, heal her!" (NIV)

The trouble all started with backtalk against their leader, their brother.

Numbers 12 starts out with Miriam and Aaron (Moses' sister and brother) talking against him because of his wife, a Cushite. "Has the Lord spoken only through Moses?" they asked. "Hasn't he also spoken through us?" And the Lord heard them. Yikes! Big trouble!

Moses was not misusing his authority or the power that God had given him. He wasn't bragging about meeting with God or how "wonderful" he was. Moses had his eyes on God, and God alone.

The anger of the Lord burned against Miriam and Aaron. When God left the tent of meeting, Miriam had leprosy. Aaron asked Moses for mercy.

In verse 13 we hear Moses, the one who had been "thrown under the bus" by his siblings, cry out to God on Miriam's behalf, "Please, God, heal her!"

You can feel Moses' gut-wrenching pain. Even though Moses had been wronged, his love for his sister was greater than being vindicated. God heard his cry. Miriam was placed outside the camp for 7 days and God healed her.

On our journey to Bill's healing, we encountered places in the road where Bill and I cried out to the Lord on behalf of others. God heard our cries and was merciful. Others may "wrong" you or speak against you, but it's an opportunity to ask for God's love and mercy on their behalf.

The Glory Road is a place of God's grace and mercy. In this season of our lives, many are flailing as they look at the storms that surround them. Many are so focused on themselves that they miss God's handiwork. It is there we have the opportunity to cry out for God's mercy and grace.

Lord, we praise and thank you for the gift of forgiveness. May we walk uprightly before You, our Creator. Help us to forgive others, so You can forgive us. You are a God of second chances. May You be honored and glorified in our lives. In Jesus' mighty name we pray, amen.

Thank you for your faithfulness in prayer.#Godisfaithful#TheGloryRoad

Day#314 February 27

 Anchor Verse: Isaiah 43:18-19
Forget about what's happened; don't keep going over old history. Be alert, be present. I'm about to do something brand-new. It's bursting out! Don't you see it? There it is! I'm making a road through the desert, rivers in the badlands. (MSG)

"The good old days" – we run to the past when the present is more than we can bear. In Isaiah 43:18-19, we are reminded that we are to "forget about what's happened; don't keep going over old history. Be alert, be present!"

Being present can be difficult when you are facing something that seems too hard. We all have our "comfort zone" – equilibrium, a little bubble in which we live – that sweet spot, you know what I'm talking about.

In this season of our lives, where we have experienced tumultuous times, many are caught up in the tangled web of the world. Their eyes are mesmerized by the chaos that surrounds them rather than looking for signs of what the Lord is doing.

God is making a road through the desert, rivers in the badlands. He is doing something brand new. Just as spring draws closer each day, so, too, are the wonders that God has planned for us.

I'm excited. I hope you are too.

On our journey to Bill's healing, there were moments, especially in the early days, looking back to once was "normal" had an attraction. The Lord showed us that better things were coming, and keeping our eyes on Him and His handiwork is where we would find great joy.

The Glory Road is a place where God is making things brand new. He is building a new hope and future. May our eyes not be looking behind us like Lot's wife, who bore the consequences of her disobedience. My eyes are fixed on You, Lord. I trust you. I love you. I praise you, my Lord.

Lord, we give thanks with a grateful heart that the old is gone and the new has come. Open our eyes to see our best days are before us, not behind us. We love and adore you, Lord God Almighty. In Jesus' name, we pray, amen.

Thank you for your persistent prayers.#Godisfaithful#TheGloryRoad

Day#315 February 28

 Anchor Verse: Mark 6:31
"...Come with me by yourselves to a quiet place and get some rest." (NIV)

Rest...it's a beautiful, necessary part of our lives. Most of us don't get enough rest. Rest is more than just sleep – it's also a state of mind.

Jesus in His wisdom tells the disciples they need to do three things: 1. Come with Jesus, 2. Go to a quiet place, and 3. Get some rest. This is a recipe for our crazy, busy lives as well.

We must follow Jesus as He leads us to the place where we can get some rest. At the end of a busy day, Jesus would go to a solitary place and spend time with His heavenly Father. This is where we will be refreshed too.

It needs to be a quiet place. Sometimes that is a challenge in a world that is so "connected" today, to find a quiet place. In the quietness, our senses are calmed. We can hear the voice of our heavenly Father there.

Get some rest. Sleep for the body and rest for the soul is so necessary for good physical and mental health. Without it, we get a little "cranky" and "overwhelmed." Praise the Lord for the gift of rest and its benefits.

On our journey to Bill's healing, we learned about the necessity of what is described here in Mark 6. What a beautiful place it is to enter into that rest. Even if it's your own home, there is new hope and energy that comes from choosing peace, quiet, and rest.

The Glory Road is a place where I am learning the value of this lifestyle. Without Bill at my side, it's easy to keep "pushing" through, and "doing" rather than just "being." There will always be things to do and people to see and places to go, but choosing quiet and rest needs to be a priority.

Lord, thank you for the pattern Jesus showed us about the importance of spending time with You in a quiet place, and getting rest. We give our days and nights to God. Make us more like You. In Jesus' name we pray, amen.

Thank you for your encouraging words.#Godisfaithful#TheGloryRoad

March 2021

But as for me, I waited in hope for the Lord. I wait for God my Savior, my God will hear me.

~ Micah 7:7 ~

Day#316 March 1

 Anchor Verse: Numbers 22:18
Balaam answered the servants of Balak, "Even if Balak were to give me his house full of silver and gold, I could not do anything, either small or great, contrary to the command of the Lord my God." (AMP)

Can your obedience be bought? Is there a price at which you are willing to walk away from what the Lord is commanding you to do?

The "world" and the things of this world can be attractive. We see the "wicked" flourish. It seems that the world is upside down, and what is evil is called good and what is good is called evil.

Balaam was a man of God and Balak came to him because Balak was having trouble with the Israelites. He wanted Balaam to put a curse on the Israelites. Balaam's response was that he would do "nothing" unless God told him. He refused to move without the Lord's permission.

"Balaam answered the servants of Balak, "Even if Balak were to give me his house full of silver and gold, I could not do anything, either small or great, contrary to the command of the Lord my God." (Numbers 22:18)

Are you that committed to the Lord that NOTHING the world has to offer could cause you to compromise your faith and walk away from God?

On our journey to Bill's healing, we found ourselves in a new place, but God was there too. Everything we said and did went through the "filter" of whether it was what God wanted. God knew our voices well because we always wanted to be in His presence, doing His will.

The Glory Road is a path through new territory, places I have never been before. There are principles that remain the same. My faith, trust, and hope are in my heavenly Father, Creator of heaven and earth. He is Lord God Almighty, and my first allegiance, now and forever, is to Him.

Lord, You love us with an everlasting love. Through Your strength, we meet the demands of this day. Please strengthen our resolve, as you grow our faith. May we not compromise our walk with You. Keep us faithful. Lord, we love and praise you in Jesus' name, amen.

Thank you for your faithfulness.#Godisfaithful#TheGloryRoad

Day#317 March 2

 Anchor Verse: Mark 7:37
They were thoroughly astounded and completely overwhelmed, saying, "He has done everything well! He even makes the deaf hear and the mute speak!" (AMP)

When heaven touches earth, miracles happen. In the Bible, we read how the hand of God moved on behalf of His people in the Old Testament and the miracles of Jesus throughout the gospels.

"They were thoroughly astounded and completely overwhelmed, saying, "He [Jesus] has done everything well! He even makes the deaf hear and the mute speak!" (Mark 7:37)

What is a miracle? In Hebrew, a miracle is a symbol of victory held high for all to see (also a banner or flag).

The scientific/medical community doesn't have a category for a healing miracle because a miracle defies explanation. That's why it's a miracle.

When we can't explain it, we put a tag or a name on it. When some of have been healed miraculously, the term used was "spontaneous remission." Can you hear God's laughter? I can. Shaking His head, and yet, loving us, because our finite minds can't comprehend God's love and how He moves.

On our journey to Bill's healing, we were blessed by so many miracles. All five of the hospitals where Bill was a patient, he was known as the "Miracle Man." Even those who aren't believers, recognize a miracle when it happens. Today, I still praise the Lord for the mighty miracles, the gift of life that God gave Bill time and again, so God's glory could be seen in him.

The Glory Road is also a place of miracles. I am a miracle. You are a miracle. Many parts of this journey have no logical explanation. Only God. That is my response. I sing His praises to His name for He is greatly to be praised.

Lord, open our eyes to see the miracles. May our hearts be healed as the love of Christ turns what the enemy meant for evil into good. May we receive God's healing miracle. His love will set you free. In Jesus' name, amen.

Thank you for rejoicing in our victories.#Godisfaithful#TheGloryRoad

Day#318 March 3

 **Anchor Verse: Mark 8:12**
He [Jesus] sighed deeply… (TLB)

When was the last time you let out a deep sigh? Maybe you just did…

Sometimes we sigh and we don't even know it. It's often our body's way of releasing overwhelm, sorrow, disappointment, even anxiety. It's a pressure release valve the Creator installed in us. God knew we would have days that our souls needed to release what was weighing us down.

It is an "audible" manifestation of the weight our spirit is carrying. The groaning of our soul expressed out loud.

In Mark 8:12, it says Jesus sighed deeply. How difficult it must have been to carry the answer to the world's problems, to be able to meet the needs of everyone He met, and yet encounter, the "blindness" of men's hearts.

On our journey to Bill's healing, there were moments when sighs escaped our lips. You don't make a decision to sigh; your spirit releases it on your behalf. Your heavenly Father comes alongside of you and says, "You can't carry all that by yourself, release it to Me. I will carry you. Just trust Me." It is there we encountered God's peace, and the load was lifted.

The Glory Road is a place where I encounter God daily. As I rush into His presence, it is there I find the fullness of His joy. My sorrow and sighing flee away. When the Glory of the Lord is released in me, I can shine more brightly for Him. The cares of this world have no hold on me when I dwell in the secret place of the Most High.

There are still times when a sigh escapes from my spirit, but not as often as it once did. Daily, I am enrolled in God's classroom where He teaches me how to walk this road called life. My heavenly Father teaches me how to keep my eyes on Him, and remain in His presence, there I lack nothing.

Lord, thank you for the gift of life, the gift of Your love. You exchange our sorrow and sighing for a greater measure of Your joy. Touch and heal our physical needs and also our soul wounds. In Jesus' name, we pray. Amen.

Thank you for your faithfulness in prayer. #Godisfaithful#TheGloryRoad

Day#319 March 4

 Anchor Verse: Psalm 34:4
Listen to my testimony: I cried to God in my distress and he answered me. He freed me from all my fears! (TPT)

We overcome by the blood of the Lamb and the word of our testimony. (Revelation 12:11)

The testimony about what God has done in our lives not only encourages us but it encourages those who are fighting their own battles. When we share a spark of hope with another, it rekindles the fire of hope in their hearts, when their hope is only a pile of embers.

Psalm 34:4 says, "Listen to my testimony: I cried to God in my distress and he answered me. He freed me from all my fears!"

Often in our distress, chaos, fear, we cry out to the Lord, and sometimes we just cry. He always answers and God FREES US from our fears.

When the enemy of our souls attempts to derail God's peace in our hearts, we have a choice. Will we choose to let fear guide our decisions and our path or will our faith in God keep us secure as we are anchored to Jesus?

On our journey to Bill's healing, from the moment I made that 9-1-1 call on January 10, 2018 until the day God took Bill home on April 19, 2020, the spirit of fear "tried" to sink our boat. Our trust and faith in God allowed us to choose FAITH over fear. Praise triumphs over our problems every day.

The Glory Road is a path I am exploring as a widow. It is paved with memorial stones of God's faithfulness. There are days when a strong crosswind crosses my path and the spirit of fear blows in from a foreign land. By God's strength, I am not blown away, literally or figuratively.

A couple of days ago, an enemy ambush had me crying out to God. God in His mercy delivered me, as I declared out loud so the enemy could hear it and so could I, "I will not fear. I will not fear. I will not fear."

My heavenly Father stepped in and said, "She's my girl, back off!" The spirit of fear left and so did the enemy. God's peace came rushing in like a flood.

Thank you for your faithfulness in prayer.#Godisfaithful#TheGloryRoad

Day#320 March 5

 Anchor Verse: Mark 9:32
But the disciples didn't have a clue what he meant and were too embarrassed to ask him to explain it. (TPT)

Some passages of the Bible are just "real" – they describe exactly how we feel or might have reacted.

When we think about Jesus' disciples, we might view them as "super spiritual" because they spent three years with Him. Here we see just being with Jesus didn't mean they had all the answers or always understood His lessons. "But the disciples didn't have a clue what he meant and were too embarrassed to ask him to explain it." (Mark 9:32)

In the preceding verses, the Bible says that Jesus didn't want anyone to know where they were because He was teaching His disciples. "The Son of Man is going to be delivered into the hands of men. They will kill him, and after three days He will rise." (Mark 9:31)

We have the vantage point of knowing the end of the story, so we "get it." They didn't understand and were afraid, even embarrassed to ask Jesus.

Often we don't want to appear "dumb" or "stupid" in front of our family, friends, or peers, so we remain quiet. The truth is just one question can open the door that leads to your breakthrough.

On our journey to Bill's healing, there were places we received a lot of information, many of it in unfamiliar medical terms. It was there that I had to ask the questions about the things I didn't know or understand. Bill's life was at stake, so looking "dumb" or "stupid" was worth the risk. There was a greater good involved than my ego.

The Glory Road also is leading me to places I do not know, to experience things I have never experienced before in both the natural and supernatural realm. Often the Lord hears my questions, or I ask someone about things I don't know. Rather than letting our embarrassment relegate us to silence, let us be bold and ask the questions and be open to receiving the answers.

Lord, we cry out for wisdom and discernment. May we not be too embarrassed or shy to ask the questions. You welcome the opportunity to teach us more about Your kingdom. May we also be gracious and willing to listen to the questions of others, and respond in love. In Jesus' name, amen.

Thank you for your encouraging words.#TheGloryRoad#Godisfaithful

Day#321 March 6

 Anchor Verse: Psalm 105:5
Don't you ever forget his miracles and marvels. Hold to your heart every judgment he has decreed. (TPT)

When amazing, life-changing things happen to us, we vow never to forget them. In that moment we say, I will always "remember."

"Don't you ever forget his miracles and marvels. Hold to your heart every judgment he has decreed." (Psalm 105:5)

Remembering God's faithfulness encourages us if we are going through a tough patch. He will see us through this valley and lead us to victory.

His time schedule doesn't always match ours because "with the Lord one day is as a thousand years and a thousand years as one day." (NJKV) When we think God is "late" in keeping His promises, He's really right on time.

On our journey to Bill's healing, there were so many miracles and marvels to remember. The Lord impressed upon me to write them down (most of them) so that I can remember and share them with you. Often Bill and I would talk about what the Lord had done and thank God for His miracles.

The Glory Road is filled with God's miracles and marvels, even though sometimes they may be camouflaged. Often our eyes need to be focused on looking for the good rather than focused on the bad. Daily, I rejoice in what the Lord is doing even when we have not seen the completion of it yet.

What are you choosing to remember in this season of your life? What memories do you play over and over again in your mind?

Philippians 4:8 reminds us where we should keep our focus, "Finally, brothers and sisters, whatever is true, whatever is noble, whatever is right, whatever is pure, whatever is lovely, whatever is admirable—if anything is excellent or praiseworthy—think about such things." (NIV)

Thank you, Lord, for Your mighty miracles and marvels in our lives. Thank you that You are a God of justice. Help us to always remember You are faithful and You are for us, not against us. In Jesus' name, we pray, amen.

Thank you for your companionship.#Godisfaithful#TheGloryRoad

Day#322 March 7

 Anchor Verse: Deuteronomy 2:7
For the Lord your God has blessed you in everything you have done. He has watched your every step through this great wilderness. During these forty years, the Lord your God has been with you, and you have lacked nothing. (NLT)

Often we live life at "break-neck" speed, going through our daily routines and quickly days, months, years fly by. Then we are old and gray, and decades have passed, what can we say about our lives at that point?

Let's stop for a moment and take inventory before we move on.

Moses in the book of Deuteronomy is recounting to the Israelites their journey and how the Lord has been with them. It's like sharing a family history and pointing out the highlights including the troubles and the triumphs.

In Deuteronomy 2:7, Moses says, "For the Lord your God has blessed you in everything you have done. He has watched your every step through this great wilderness. During these forty years, the Lord your God has been with you, and you have lacked nothing."

Look at God's faithfulness. God blessed them in "everything" they had done. God watched over "every step" through a great wilderness (an unfamiliar place). And for 40 years, you have lacked "nothing."

But God… in His love for His children provided all they needed, defeated their enemies, and bathed them in the power of His love.

That hasn't changed. God's love for you and me is still unconditional.

On our journey to Bill's healing, we learned how powerful and loving God is. He provided for us the same way He did for the Israelites on their journey. We rejoice in the God of our salvation and for His faithfulness.

The Glory Road is an unfamiliar place. Some days I face mountains or even "giants." At times, the past, present, and future collide, and I must run to my heavenly Father for comfort and instruction before I take another step.

Lord, we thank you for Your hand of protection and provision. Your banner over us is love. We surrender our past, present, and future, and say, "Have Your way, Lord." We love you, Lord, in Jesus' name, amen.

Thank you for rejoicing in my victories.#Godisfaithful#TheGloryRoad

Day#323 March 8

 Anchor Verse: Deuteronomy 5:33
Walk in obedience to all that the Lord your God has commanded you, so that you may live and prosper and prolong your days in the land that you will possess. (NIV)

"Obedience brings life." Our pastor often reminds us of this truth. Throughout the Bible, we not only "hear" God say this but we see examples of people who obeyed and those who did not.

In Deuteronomy 5, Moses is speaking to the Israelites and not only reviewing their history together and what the Lord has done, but it's Moses' farewell speech. Moses is not allowed to enter the Promised Land because of his own disobedience.

"Walk in obedience to all that the Lord your God has commanded you, so that you may live and prosper and prolong your days in the land that you will possess." (Deuteronomy 5:33)

It's a command with a promise. If you walk obedience than you will live, prosper, and prolong your days in this new place God is giving you.

On our journey to Bill's healing, we learned the power and peace that come with obeying God and walking in His ways. God blesses us in so many ways when we walk hand in hand with Him. The peace that passes all understanding will guard your heart and your mind.

The Glory Road is unfamiliar territory but I trust my heavenly guides. The Holy Spirit speaks words of direction while Jesus helps me walk with confidence to the place He has planned for me. My heavenly Father, keeps me safe and secure in His arms of love. Nobody messes with His daughter!

With each step of obedience, I am one step closer to the Promised Land. Every day, every breath is an offering of praise to the One who loves me so.

Thank you, Lord, for clearly showing us the path to life – it is the path of obedience. Give us Your strength to face the demands of this day. We know with You, ALL things are possible. We love you, in Jesus' name, amen.

Thank you for your persevering prayers.#Godisfaithful#TheGloryRoad

Day#324 March 9

 Anchor Verse: Deuteronomy 9:29
But they are your people, your inheritance that you brought out by your great power and your outstretched arm. (NIV)

Moses had his hands full as he guided the children of Israel out of Egypt to the Promised Land.

Yet, there were times when God was "done" with them. The children of Israel whined, complained, groaned, disobeyed God, and so much more. At times, Moses had to talk God out of destroying the whole lot of them.

God said to Moses, I'll just destroy them all, and give you a new nation to lead. Moses stood in the gap for the people, and reminded God of His faithfulness to not only this generation but generations past. The promises He made to Abraham, Isaac and Jacob. God's people were His inheritance.

"But they are your people, your inheritance that you brought out by your great power and your outstretched arm." (Deuteronomy 9:29)

Moses pleads with God, "God, Your reputation is the one that's on the line. These are "Your" people. You miraculously brought them out of Egypt by Your great power and Your outstretched arm, don't destroy them now."

God has mercy on them… yet, because of that generation's disobedience none of them entered the Promised Land.

I'm so grateful for the faithfulness of God and the sacrifice of Jesus who made a way for us to be brought back into right standing with God.

On our journey to Bill's healing, we have story after story of God's faithfulness. I am recounting them as I write this book about our journey. None of us can earn the gifts that God lavishes upon us. It is only His grace, mercy, and love that fill our hands, our hearts, our lives with His goodness.

The Glory Road is a place where I experience God's faithfulness daily. When my eyes are on Him, I bask in His love and His glory. If the cares of the world distract me, my feet may stumble. Because Jesus is walking beside me, He quickly comes to my rescue, and puts my feet back on solid ground.

Lord, we praise and thank you for Your faithfulness and to a thousand generations of those who love you. Forgive us where we have failed You or failed each other. Lord, renew a right spirit within us. May we walk holy before You this day, in Jesus' name, amen.

Thank you for your faithfulness.#Godisfaithful#TheGloryRoad

Day#325 March 10

 Anchor Verse: Proverbs 29:18
If people can't see what God is doing, they stumble all over themselves; But when they attend to what he reveals, they are most blessed. (MSG)

The book of Proverbs is filled with gems of wisdom to carry with us through the day. Proverbs 29:18 is one of those nuggets. We often hear it quoted as "Without a vision, the people perish."

What a blessing to live at a time in history where we have multiple translations of the Bible available to read and to study. It gives us different angles to look at God's truth and get greater revelation.

"If people can't see what God is doing, they stumble all over themselves; But when they attend to what he reveals, they are most blessed."

In the shadow of the pandemic, political conflict, division, and disharmony, many are struggling to see what God is doing. The truth is they can't see what God is doing and they are driven to despair.

"Hope deferred makes a heart sick, BUT when dreams come true at last, there is life and joy." (Proverbs 13:12 TLB)

Our society resembles Proverbs 29, people are stumbling all over themselves, because they have lost focus. Their compass has gone "haywire" and it's spinning around. They don't know where they're going.

On our journey to Bill's healing, we needed God's revelation to keep us on track. If we looked at the world or our circumstances, we would have sunk beneath the waves just like Peter when he tried to walk on water.

The Glory Road is a path where I encounter those who are facing life's challenges. Some are stumbling because they can't see what God is doing. Others are waking up from "sleep" and seeking to understand God in the midst of chaos and confusion. Lord, open our eyes to see.

Lord, we praise and thank you for who You are. Open our spiritual eyes to see Jesus. The Good Shepherd has never left you. Reach out and take His hand, and trust Him to lead you home. In Jesus' name we pray, amen.

Thank you for loving me and loving others.#Godisfaithful#TheGloryRoad

Day#326 March 11

 Anchor Verse: Mark 12:37b
The large crowd enjoyed hearing Jesus and listened to Him with delight. (AMP)

Have you ever spoken before a crowd of people?

Personally, I have spoken before small groups and very large groups. From the podium or platform, it is very interesting to watch the reaction of the crowd as you speak.

Frankly, there are times when you are greeted by "blank" faces. You wonder if they are even listening to you or if they're thinking about their next meal, last meal, or someplace else they'd rather be.

In light of my own experience, it was interesting to read Mark 12:37, "The large crowd enjoyed hearing Jesus and listened to Him with delight."

The people are focused on Jesus and His message. They aren't distracted or walking around, there's a hush over the "large" crowd as He speaks.

Mark 12:17 says, "They were amazed at him." Mark 12:34 tells us, "And from then on no one dared ask him any more questions." In other passages, we read how the crowd was hungry or angry, or they pursued Jesus even to a place He was looking for rest.

On our journey to Bill's healing, the words of Jesus were comforting and also an anchor on a windy sea. Jesus drew us in, and asked us to come and sit with Him. We found great joy there. His words are words of life and hope, filled with love and instruction. Thank you, Jesus.

The Glory Road is a path of learning and listening. Through the Bible I seek wisdom for daily living. With the Holy Spirit to guide me, I walk an unconventional path that might resemble the path of a butterfly, but in God's eyes, it makes perfect sense.

Lord, open my ears to hear, my eyes to see, my mind to understand, and my feet to walk Your path of obedience. In Jesus' name I pray, amen.

Thank you for being Jesus' hands and feet.#Godisfaithful#TheGloryRoad

Day#327 March 12

 Anchor Verse: Deuteronomy 16:17
Each of you must bring a gift in proportion to the way the Lord your God has blessed you. (NIV)

Do you have a generous heart? Do you love to give to people – gifts, your time, your energy, and/or your love?

The Bible tells us that God loves a generous giver. Why? A generous giver reflects the heart of God. God gave us His only son, Jesus, to make a way for us to spend eternity with Him. There is no greater sacrifice of love.

In verse 16, God's people are reminded that no one should appear before the Lord empty-handed. Verse 17 reminds us, "Each of you must bring a gift in proportion to the way the Lord your God has blessed you."

The Lord has blessed us in so many ways – not just financially. What are the spiritual gifts God has given you? How has God uniquely made you not only to make a living but also ways to love and serve others?

We all have 24 hours in a day with many opportunities to bless others with the gifts God has given us, not to hoard our time, talent, and energy.

On our journey to Bill's healing, it was such a blessing to see how Bill would bless others as he faced his own health challenges. Kindness, encouraging words, a grateful heart, and the word "thank you" were just some of the ways Bill greeted others. Bill gave as God blessed him.

The Glory Road is a place where I have the privilege of giving glory and honor to God. Singing praises to His name and pointing others to the source of life – God and God alone. God has given me so much, and from this treasure trove of blessing, I can generously share with you.

Lord, we come to You this morning so grateful for Your generous heart. We want to be more like our heavenly Father. Bless the Lord, O my soul, and all that is within me, bless His holy name. In Jesus' name, we pray, amen.

Thank you for your generous hearts.#Godisfaithful#TheGloryRoad

Day#328 March 13

 Anchor Verse: Mark 13:37
What I say to you I say to everyone, 'Be on the alert [stay awake and be continually cautious]!'" (AMP)

Throughout our lives, there are moments when we are called upon to be alert, to be on guard.

We are so grateful for all who work during the night in hospitals and as first responders, etc. who are willing to "go against" their natural body rhythm to make sure we are tended to as needed.

For most of us, if we need to "stay awake" past our "normal" bedtime or all night, we find it difficult to do so. Our bodies want to go to sleep.

In Mark 13, Jesus is talking about His second coming. It really stretches the disciples' understanding. Jesus who is standing before them in the flesh, is telling them that He will be crucified, buried, and rise again in three days AND that at a time in the future, Jesus will return in great power and glory.

Jesus doesn't tell them when so they can metaphorically "set their alarm clock" and be awake when He returns. Jesus says, "Be on the alert [stay awake and be continually cautious]."

On our journey to Bill's healing, every day we were on alert. Whether in the hospital or at home, when something has happened, like a stroke or heart attack, you are always vigilant, on the alert, for any symptoms. Often an illness changes the way we live our lives. We are alert and watchful, and as believers, many hours are filled with prayers asking the Lord to watch over you or your loved one to keep them from harm.

The Glory Road is a new place. It is a "foreign" place so I must be alert and watchful to my surroundings and new people and situations that I encounter. I ask for help from my heavenly Father that His angels would go before me to make my way straight and protect me. Most of all, I would see His hand at work and hear His voice and walk according to His will.

Thank you, Lord, for Your faithfulness, may You find us faithful until Jesus' return. May we light the way for others, so they too will seek you and find you when they seek you with all their heart. In Jesus' mighty name, amen.

Thank you for your companionship.#Godisfaithful#TheGloryRoad

Day#329 March 14

 Anchor Verse: Mark 14:16
The disciples left, went into the city and found things just as Jesus had told them. So they prepared the Passover. (NIV)

Jesus is making plans for what we call the "Last Supper." It was time to celebrate the Passover feast according to the Jewish tradition, and Jesus had something "extra" to add.

He knew every detail without stepping foot into the city. Jesus sent two of His disciples on an errand with detailed instructions about what they were supposed to do and where they should go, and even what they should say.

"Make preparations for us there." (Mark 14:15)

Verse 16 says, "The disciples left, went into the city and found things just as Jesus had told them. So they prepared the Passover."

They found things just as Jesus told them. We can have the same experience when we take time to listen and walk in obedience to what Jesus has planned.

On our journey to Bill's healing, we were often told to follow instructions, both from earthly advisors and our heavenly Father. There were decisions we made to make the path "easier" because we listened to a heavenly prompt through the Holy Spirit. It was just as we were told.

The Glory Road is also a place of preparation. God has a plan and purpose for my life. It is a detailed plan. My story was written before the beginning of time. I have the privilege of partnering with heaven to watch it unfold.

Lord, we are grateful Your guidance and direction. May we tune our ears to heaven's frequency. As we walk in obedience, we will receive His blessings. They are a gift from God. Thank you, Lord. In Jesus' name we pray, amen.

Thank you for your persistence in prayer.#Godisfaithful#TheGloryRoad

Day#330 March 15

 Anchor Verse: Mark 14:36
"Abba, Father," he cried out, "everything is possible for you. Please take this cup of suffering away from me. Yet I want your will to be done, not mine." (NLT)

The cup of suffering – all of us have had to "drink" from it at some point in our lives. If you haven't yet, then your time will come.

In the Garden of Gethsemane before Jesus is betrayed by Judas, He takes Peter, James, and John with Him to pray.

Jesus knew the path ahead and the suffering to come – not only a brutal death on the cross but betrayal, hatred from the angry mob, and even desertion by His own disciples.

"Abba, Father," he [Jesus] cried out, "everything is possible for you. Please take this cup of suffering away from me. Yet I want your will to be done, not mine." (Mark 14:36)

Even in those moments of such pain, Jesus says two very powerful things. Everything is possible with God. Jesus wanted God's will to be done, not His own. Even in the worst circumstances God could do the impossible.

On the journey to Bill's healing, we encountered our own "Gethsemane." In those moments, I remember crying out to God asking for Him to touch and heal Bill declaring that ALL things were possible for God. Trusting God's best was the only pathway we wanted to walk, no matter what it looked like.

The Glory Road is a path with its own challenges. There are moments of rejoicing and great joy. At times, the cup of suffering is God's path of glory for me. It's not always the "easy" choice to choose God's path. My heart cry for others is for their cup of suffering to be taken away. I have seen what God can do on our darkest nights and our deepest valleys. The sunlight of His love will pierce the darkness and His glory will be seen in us.

Thank you, Lord, even when we meet great trials, You are as close as our every breath. May we hear Your voice and walk in Your way. It is the path to life with joy in Your presence. We love you, Lord. In Jesus' name, amen.

Thank you for your kindness.#Godisfaithful#TheGloryRoad

Day#331 March 16

 Anchor Verse: Luke 18:41
"What do you want me to do for you?" "Lord, I want to see," he replied. (NIV)

There are several accounts in the Bible about Jesus healing those who were blind. From what we read, it's blindness that has been endured for years.

What a blessing to encounter men of such faith who daily lived in expectation of their healing. They didn't give up. The men believed that "one day" their sight would be restored. Why else would they choose to pursue Jesus the only one who could restore their sight?

In Luke 18, we read the account of a blind beggar who was sitting alongside the road as Jesus passed by to Jericho. As the man heard the crowd, he asked what was happening. Someone told him it was Jesus of Nazareth. The blind beggar cries out over the crowd, ""Jesus, Son of David, have mercy on me!" Twice he cried out. Jesus "stopped." Jesus asked that the man be brought to him. We read their conversation in verse 41, "'What do you want me to do for you?' (Jesus said.) 'Lord, I want to see,' he replied."

Jesus replied, "Receive your sight; your faith has healed you." And the man was immediately healed and followed Jesus. Hallelujah!

On our journey to Bill's healing, Bill encountered temporary blindness while in the hospital. For about six weeks, all he could see was gray. For a portion of that time, Bill was intubated and sedated. We didn't know Bill couldn't see. One day, just like Jesus did for the blind man, God restored Bill's sight.

The Glory Road is a place where the Lord is giving me "new" eyes to see, not just in the flesh, but in the spirit. Often we are "blind" to the truth of God, to the reality of what He is doing in our lives. Our eyes on stuck on the disaster, our old wounds, the sin of the world instead of on Jesus.

Lord, open our eyes to see. Heal us from our spiritual blindness. And heal those with physical eyesight needs. We want to "see" YOU, God, in all Your glory. ALL things are possible with You. In Jesus' name we pray, amen.

Thank you for your encouraging words.#Godisfaithful#TheGloryRoad

Day#332 March 17

 Anchor Verse: Psalm 33:3
Compose new melodies that release new praises to the Lord. Play his praises on instruments with the anointing and skill he gives you. Sing and shout with passion; make a spectacular sound of joy. (TPT)

Singing praises to the Lord is a wonderful way to shift the atmosphere, to upgrade your attitude. Maybe your attitude and countenance need an extreme makeover – only you know that for sure.

Just hearing our praises is beautiful to God's ears. Psalm 100:1-2 says, "Make a joyful noise unto the Lord, all ye lands. Serve the Lord with gladness, come before His presence with singing!" (KJV)

I still have to laugh about Bill's comment. He said, "The Bible says to make a joyful noise – but my singing is pure agony!"

Maybe some of you can identify with a voice that may not sing on-key. Your heavenly Father loves the sound of your voice, it makes Him smile.

Today is the day to release those "new" praises to the Lord. The never-before-heard songs in your heart. Whether through an instrument or your own voice, let's rock the world with that spectacular sound of joy.

On our journey to Bill's healing, there were new songs God placed in our hearts. Not just songs sung in church, but songs of praise in ICU units, in rehab hospitals, in the quietness of our apartment. We were created to praise the Lord in ALL circumstances.

The Glory Road is a new place filled with new songs. Songs I never expected to sing, songs sung by one voice instead of two blended together. They are beautiful songs I sing from the depths of my heart and soul. Some songs mixed with my tears – tears of sorrow but also many tears of joy and gratitude for such a loving Father.

Lord, we thank you for the gift of Your love. Our hearts are filled with Your praise. Your eyes are on us, O Lord. We rejoice in You, Lord. Thank you for loving us, in Jesus' name we pray, amen.

Thank you for your faithfulness.#Godisfaithful#TheGloryRoad

Day#333 March 18

 Anchor Verse: Deuteronomy 32:2

Let my teaching fall on you like rain; let my speech settle like dew. Let my words fall like rain on tender grass, like gentle showers on young plants. (NLT)

Spring is in the air. The season of spring is a time of transition and transformation. Truly, it is my favorite season of the year.

Even as nature comes alive, my heart, body, mind, and spirit come alive too. Winter can feel like we are hibernating and just making it through, one day at a time, but spring brings new hope and new life.

In Deuteronomy 32, we have the Song of Moses as he prepares the people to enter the Promised Land. Moses would not be entering that land himself because he disobeyed God. Moses wasn't told to go to "the corner" and wait for God to take him home to heaven. Rather God instructed Moses how to prepare the people to go on in the days after Moses was gone.

It takes a lot of grace and God's power at work in you to continue to do the "right thing" even when you know you will not be in a position to see the completion of a goal or dream.

"Let my teaching fall on you like rain; let my speech settle like dew. Let my words fall like rain on tender grass, like gentle showers on young plants." (Deuteronomy 32:2) Moses' words are like a healing, nourishing spring rain.

On our journey to Bill's healing, God brought gentle showers of His goodness and grace to our hearts. His teaching fell on us like rain. Like dew refreshing the grass in the morning, so God refreshed our spirits. We were tender, even broken in places, and God's words restored us.

The Glory Road is a place of new life. Coming out of the "winter season" in every respect, God is doing something new. There is new life, new hope, new purpose, new plans – all guided by His gentle hands and tender heart that desire the best for me.

Lord, thank you for Your love for us. You "water" our hearts daily through Your words of life spoken over us. Lord, may we share that nourishment with all we meet this day. In Jesus' name, amen.

Thank you for your persistent prayers.#Godisfaithful#TheGloryRoad

Day#334 March 19

 Anchor Verse: Joshua 3:5
Then Joshua said to the people, "Sanctify yourselves [for His purpose], for tomorrow the Lord will do wonders (miracles) among you." (AMP)

We understand preparation for a big event like preparing for a test, wedding, and a big corporate event. In our modern society, sanctification, purification, and dedication are not such familiar terms.

In the Old Testament, many rituals were performed according to the guidelines set out by God to purify them. We view things differently from a "New Testament" perspective because Jesus "paid the price" for our sins and shortcomings. We need to live our lives, pure and holy before God.

The Lord tells Joshua He will be with him. God will NEVER leave or forsake him on this journey. In Joshua 1, multiple times God reminds Joshua to be strong and courageous and not to be afraid.

Joshua knew what was coming. God was going to make a way through the Jordan River just as He did at the Red Sea. Joshua 3:5 says, "Then Joshua said to the people, "Sanctify yourselves [for His purpose], for tomorrow the Lord will do wonders (miracles) among you."

How are we preparing ourselves daily for God's miracles in our lives?

On our journey to Bill's healing, daily we looked to the Lord for everything. He was our Savior, Redeemer, Provider, and Friend. We lived in expectation of God's next miracle. We prepared our hearts to receive His beautiful gifts.

The Glory Road is a place of preparation and expectation. Like many of you, I have a limited view of what lies ahead. Most of the time, it's only the next step I see as I step out in faith. Believing that God will do a miracle today and tomorrow, and the day after that is like having Christmas every day.

Lord, You are the same – yesterday, today, and forever. Thank you for Your great love for us and how You fight for us. We praise you, thank you, and love you. In Jesus' name we pray, amen.

Thank you for your faithfulness. Doctor's appointment today, believing for God's favor and a good report.#Godisfaithful#TheGloryRoad

Day#335 March 20

 Anchor Verse: Joshua 6:10
"Let there be complete silence except for the trumpets," Joshua commanded. "Not a single word from any of you until I tell you to shout; then shout!" (TLB)

In military operations, a theatrical production, or even a symphony, there are times when complete silence is absolutely necessary. It is critical to the outcome of the mission. It takes discipline and obedience as you trust the person who is leading you.

We read about the Israelites' plan to "take over" Jericho.

But God had an unusual strategy. Instead of doing what they had always done, the plan God gave to Joshua was very unique. It would be a 7-day campaign. March around the city once with all the armed men. Do it for six days. Seven priests would carry trumpets of rams' horns in front of the ark. On the seventh day, they would march around the city seven times with the priests blowing the trumpets. When they heard the long blast of the trumpets, the whole army was to give a loud shout, then the wall of the city would collapse and the army would go in and take the city.

It was truly a miracle for the whole army to agree to do what their commander-in-chief told them, "Let there be complete silence except for the trumpets," Joshua commanded. "Not a single word from any of you until I tell you to shout; then shout!" (Joshua 6:10)

The Living Bible says, "Not even a whisper." God wants our immediate, complete, unquestioning obedience. It always brings life and victory.

On our journey to Bill's healing, we walked in some unconventional places as well. There were times of silence as we waited and watched God work. And in those places, God brought forth AMAZING victory! Hallelujah!

The Glory Road is a place of unconventional strategies as well. Often I do not understand why I am on the path where God is leading me, but I trust Him completely. He will never leave me or forsake me. His plans are ALWAYS the best. Obedience always brings life.

Lord, we thank you for Your work in our lives. May we be willing to quietly follow You until you tell us it's time to shout, "Victory!" We choose to wait on You, Lord, and experience the fullness of Your joy. In Jesus' name, amen.

Thank you for your faithfulness.#Godisfaithful#TheGloryRoad

Day#336 March 21

 Anchor Verse: Joshua 9:14
The Israelites sampled their provisions but did not inquire of the Lord. (NIV)

Making decisions is part of each day's fabric. No wonder we are tired by evening.

Where do we get the wisdom to make those decisions?

As believers, a trusted source is the Bible and inquiring of the Lord through prayer. We can also find wisdom in wise counsel such as our pastors or others with wisdom and experience.

In the book of Joshua, we read about the Israelites on this journey to the Promised Land. They had no knowledge of the land, it wasn't familiar.

Joshua would inquire of the Lord and God would give him directions as to how they were to move forward and what they would encounter. In Joshua 9, we read about one of their new "neighbors" who heard about "God's reputation" and tried to figure out to stay alive and not be destroyed.

The Gibeonites get dressed up as if they had come from a long distance, looking dry and worn out, and asked the Israelites to make a treaty with them. They had old moldy food and looked the part.

Joshua 9:14 says, "The Israelites sampled their provisions but did not inquire of the Lord." A big mistake, because they were really the Israelites' neighbors. When the Israelites realized their mistake, they honored the oath they made, so God's wrath wouldn't fall upon them.

On our journey to Bill's healing, we learned to inquire of the Lord first, not as our last action. The Lord is near and you will find Him if you seek Him with all your heart and soul. (Deuteronomy 4:29)

The Glory Road is unfamiliar territory to me, yet I am traveling to God's Promised Land. When I meet a new obstacle, mountain, even resting place, I must inquire of the Lord. Who wants to be in a "foreign" land if God is not there? My hope and help come in the name of the Lord.

Lord, Your heart's desire is to lead us and carry us, when necessary. May we always inquire of You first before we move forward. Forgive us when we go our own way. We love you, Lord. In Jesus' name we pray, amen.

Thank you for your companionship.#Godisfaithful#TheGloryRoad

Day#337 March 22

 Anchor Verse: Luke 1:46-47
And Mary said: "My soul glorifies the Lord and my spirit rejoices in God my Savior." (NIV)

A young woman, likely a teenager, was chosen for a holy mission by God, to be the mother of Jesus, the Son of God.

Growing up in a society where the religious laws of the day were strict, an unmarried woman who was pregnant meant trouble.

In Luke 1:39, Mary goes to visit her cousin Elizabeth, who in her "old" age was going to have a child. Elizabeth's baby jumps for joy in her womb when Mary, with child herself, enters their home.

In the midst of these circumstances of these difficult circumstances, Mary finds joy and rejoices in the Lord. Luke 1:46-47 reads, "And Mary said: 'My soul glorifies the Lord and my spirit rejoices in God my Savior.'"

When was the last time you sang a song to the Lord in the midst of difficult circumstances?

On our journey to Bill's healing, the Lord gave me a new song in my heart. When my eyes were fixed on Him, there was joy deep in my heart that just bubbled over. Even at night as I went to sleep, there was always a song of praise on my lips. Thank you, Jesus.

The Glory Road is uncharted territory as well. There are mixed emotions, challenging circumstances, yet amazing celebrations of God's goodness and grace, covered with His love and unspeakable joy.

Learning how to dance in the rain and glorify the Lord who does all things well is my heart's desire. Showing others what it looks like to walk with God and trust Him no matter what happens, He alone is worthy of our praise.

Lord, we thank you for the example of Mary, the mother of Jesus, who showed us how to rejoice in every circumstance and give honor and glory to the Lord. May Your light shine so brightly in us others may know Your love and come to You. We praise you, Lord. In Jesus' name we pray, amen.

Thank you for rejoicing in my victories.#Godisfaithful#TheGloryRoad

Day#338 March 23

 Anchor Verse: Hebrews 6:19
This hope [this confident assurance] we have as an anchor of the soul [it cannot slip and it cannot break down under whatever pressure bears upon it]—a safe and steadfast hope that enters within the veil [of the heavenly temple, that most Holy Place in which the very presence of God dwells]. (AMP)

When was the last time you cried as you prayed? As your heart was broken for yourself or others, and you couldn't find the words to speak.

My heart is stirred looking across the landscape of our nation and hearing the cries of those who mourn and lament, and don't have the words to express their pain. God is mourning with them too.

But that's not where the story ends. We have HOPE. We have Hope that is the anchor for our souls. Hope that is eternal and Hope that is rooted in the love of God that's unconditional and never ends.

"This hope [this confident assurance] we have as an anchor of the soul [it cannot slip and it cannot break down under whatever pressure bears upon it]—a safe and steadfast hope that enters within the veil [of the heavenly temple, that most Holy Place in which the very presence of God dwells]." (Hebrews 6:19)

In the Amplified version says, our anchor of hope "cannot slip and it cannot break down under whatever pressure bears upon it."

Our anchor of hope cannot slip or break down under any kind of pressure because it is rooted in the faithfulness of God.

On our journey to Bill's healing, HOPE was our lifeline. It was our hope in God, our anchor of Hope that helped us through the storms of life. When it was just Bill and me and God, it was enough. God is faithful.

The Glory Road is filled with new experiences. Not only personal tragedies, but communities of people affected by violence and injustice, a nation and a world turned upside down. Yet I have HOPE as the anchor for my soul. Jesus is the answer. He is acquainted with your sorrows. Jesus will carry you.

Lord, hear our prayer, O Lord. We pray for those whose hearts are broken and have been victims of violence and for their families. Lord, heal our land. We can't do it without Your supernatural love. In Jesus' name, amen.

Thank you for holding on to hope.#Godisfaithful#TheGloryRoad

Day#339 March 24

 Anchor Verse: 1 John 4:4
Little children, you can be certain that you belong to God and have conquered them, for the One who is living in you is far greater than the one who is in the world. (TPT)

"You can be certain" ~ when you hear words like that coming from the Bible, the Word of God, you need to stop and pay attention.

There are few guarantees that we have in life. There are many promises that are made. The truth is God's promises are the only ones we can "take to the bank" with certainty.

"Little children, you can be certain that you belong to God and have conquered them, for the One who is living in you is far greater than the one who is in the world." (1 John 4:4)

Who is the One living in us? Jesus, the risen Christ, the resurrected Savior who overcame death, hell, and the grave. That's the power we need in our lives today to overcome any obstacle that comes into our line of vision.

The one who is in the world? This would be the enemy of our souls, Satan. He comes against us in many ways, but remember what 1 John 4:4 says, Christ in us is greater than the enemy.

On our journey to Bill's healing, we often encountered this battleground. Where the "outside" forces attempted to "attack" Bill and his heavenly Father said, "I don't think so. He belongs to me." God fights for us.

The Glory Road is a battlefield where daily I encounter the opposition. In every case, I get to decide whether to believe the One who is living in me is greater than the one who is in the world.

My best choice is to let Jesus be my advocate. It reminds me of how Bill would take care of me to protect me and defend me. Even the "human" love of our life cannot do what Jesus can for us.

Thank you, Lord Jesus, You delight to love us, protect us, and encourage us to be the best we can be. Even when we face trials or mountains, Lord, You are greater and more powerful. You are our peace. In Jesus' name, amen.

Thank you for being part of my family.#Godisfaithful#TheGloryRoad

Day#340 March 25

 Anchor Verse: Luke 2:40
There the child grew up healthy and strong. He was filled with wisdom, and God's favor was on him. (NLT)

Jesus was born into the world as a little baby, just like you and me. That might be a difficult concept to grasp, that Jesus, the son of God, left the glory of heaven and was born in a manger in a stable.

Mary and Joseph took him to the temple and followed the law and tradition as other parents at that time.

"There the child grew up healthy and strong. He was filled with wisdom, and God's favor was on him." (Luke 2:40)

May the Lord stir our hearts to pray this over our children, grandchildren, and generations yet to come. God's blessings will begin to grow as our prayers are seeded across the world.

On our journey to Bill's healing, we encountered "children" of all ages. Each one of us is someone's child. Daily, I would thank God for those He brought into our lives from the doctors, nurses, techs, and therapists, to the housekeepers. Each one of them was a blessing.

The Glory Road takes me on a new path, a place I do not know, filled with new people, and those who have walked with me for many miles. We are blessed to be a blessing. Thank you, Lord, for helping us to see others through Your eyes of love and speaking life over them, no matter their age.

Lord, may Your glory be seen in us. Keep us safe in Your arms of love. Please give us health, strength, and great wisdom. May the favor of the Lord rest upon you, in Jesus' name, amen.

Thank you for speaking words of life.#Godisfaithful#TheGloryRoad

Day#341 March 26

 Anchor Verse: Joshua 23:10
Each one of you will put to flight a thousand of the enemy, for the Lord your God fights for you, just as he has promised. (NLT)

The Lord your God fights for YOU, yes, YOU. We often read the promises, the stories in the Bible like they are "stories." When we do that, we strip God's promises of their power. That's a crazy thing to do.

It's like having a stove in your house and never turning it on to cook food to feed your body. Or a refrigerator filled with food and you never open the door and you are starving.

During the middle of a storm, when we look at the size of the waves and listen to the hurricane-force winds, we can get distracted by the enemy and lose sight of the Master of the storm, Jesus.

In Joshua's farewell speech to God's people, He reminds them of the things they need to do. They must walk in obedience to God's commands, and the favor and power of the Lord will be evidenced in their lives.

"Each one of you will put to flight a thousand of the enemy, for the Lord your God fights for you, just as he has promised." (Joshua 23:10)

The MESSAGE translation starts off this section saying, "God has driven out superpower nations before you." Superpower nations bowed to the God of Israel, Lord God Almighty, Maker of heaven and earth.

On our journey to Bill's healing, God fighting for us meant so much more. It's one thing to be healthy and feel like you are walking in partnership with God. When you are knocked down by an illness or injury, and you've got nothing but your faith in God, then God is truly doing all the work.

The Glory Road has a new revelation every day of how God fights for me and how I can "put to flight a thousand of the enemy." Seeing life through God's eyes, the schemes of the enemy are exposed. We win when we stand on God's promises and do not crumble because of the enemy's lies.

Lord, thank you for the many ways You fight for us. There are so many conflicts that are resolved, battles won, without our knowledge. May Your grace, mercy, and peace be multiplied to us. In Jesus' name we pray, amen.

Thank you for your faithfulness.#Godisfaithful#TheGloryRoad

Day#342 March 27

 Anchor Verse: Luke 4:4
Jesus replied, "I will not! For it is written in the Scriptures, 'Life does not come only from eating bread but from God. Life flows from every revelation from his mouth.'" (TPT)

Many people experience decision fatigue because their brains just don't slow down, even when they are trying to sleep. You may be one of them.

In the book of Luke, chapter 4, we read that Jesus was filled with the Holy Spirit and was led into the wilderness for 40 days where He was tempted by the devil. Jesus ate nothing for those 40 days, and He was hungry.

The devil's attacks were strategic and his "darts" were designed to hit the target. His first "punch" was asking Jesus to turn a stone into bread.

When you haven't eaten in 40 days, the thought of food is likely predominant in your mind. How did Jesus respond? He quoted the scripture, the Word of God. Jesus replied, "I will not! For it is written in the Scriptures, 'Life does not come only from eating bread but from God. Life flows from every revelation from his mouth.'" (Luke 4:4)

On our journey to Bill's healing, we learned this lesson ourselves. So much was stripped away during that season, but we received so much revelation from God's heart, from the Word of God. We learned to live life a new way.

The Glory Road is a new place where many things look different. I miss Bill's commentary on daily living, but in my heart, the lessons I learned from God and Bill, help me navigate this road. It is the Word of God, the revelation of God which keeps me on the right path as my mind is on Him.

Lord, we choose to stand on Your promises. The Word of God is life and truth. May we find shelter there in the midst of life's storms. You are faithful and You will never leave us or forsake us. In Jesus' name we pray, amen.

Thank you for your persistent prayers.#Godisfaithful#TheGloryRoad

Day#343 March 28

 Anchor Verse: Psalm 118:28
You are my God, and I give You thanks; You are my God, and I praise You.
(VOICE)

When was the last time that you spent more than a few minutes praising the Lord and thanking Him for all He has done for you?

We are too often quick at our prayers. We speak a few words and then we rush on to the next "responsibility" of the day.

Just as time spent at the table together is precious and memorable, so is time spent in the Lord's presence, your heavenly Father. He loves to hear from you but God also likes to talk to you. Yes, truly it is a two-way conversation when your relationship with God is at its best.

Today in 2021, it is Palm Sunday, the beginning of the last week of Jesus' life. He was the only one who truly knew what was ahead of Him. We really can't even imagine holding all that in our heads and our hearts, but Jesus for the joy set before Him endured the cross for us.

They showered Him with praise. Psalm 118:28 is our commission too. "You are my God, and I give You thanks; You are my God, and I praise You."

On our journey to Bill's healing, we learned how powerful it was to praise the Lord. We couldn't stop praising the Lord because He did such great things for us. Just the comfort of His presence, day and night, was such a blessing. Thank you, Lord.

The Glory Road is a place of a praise and thanksgiving. Our heavenly Father watches over us day and night. God is our ever-present help.

Lord, You are great and greatly to be praised. We praise Your name. Fill us with the power of Your praise, in Jesus' name, amen.

Thank you for praising the Lord with me.#Godisfaithful#TheGloryRoad

Day#344 March 29

 Anchor Verse: Judges 7:2
The Lord said to Gideon, "You have too many warriors with you. If I let all of you fight the Midianites, the Israelites will boast to me that they saved themselves by their own strength. (NLT)

Have you ever boasted, "Look what I have done!" to everyone you know?

Where we get "led astray" is when we think we did it on our own. When we leave God out of the picture, it's the beginning of our demise.

In Judges 6, the angel of the Lord comes to visit Gideon who was threshing wheat in a winepress to keep it from the Midianites, and says, "The Lord is with you, mighty warrior." Gideon did not see himself as a "mighty warrior."

Where God saw his strength, Gideon saw weakness. By the end of the chapter, God has proven His faithfulness to Gideon and Gideon agrees to this leadership position. Their next assignment is to conquer the Midianites.

"The Lord said to Gideon, "You have too many warriors with you. If I let all of you fight the Midianites, the Israelites will boast to me that they saved themselves by their own strength." (Judges 7:2)

From the outset, God establishes He will get the glory for this victory, not Gideon and his men. There were 32,000 fighting men. God sifted them down to 10,000. Those who weren't afraid remained.

The sifting continues until only 300 men were left. With those 300 men and "God's strategy," the Midianites are defeated.

On our journey to Bill's healing, God used unconventional methods to achieve His purposes. What often seemed "crazy" to others observing our journey was God's perfect plan so He would receive all the glory.

The Glory Road is an unconventional path, and I am grateful. Normal is highly overrated. The way of man, the way of society, the "popular" route often leads to short-term gain, and long-term heartache. God's way is not only the path to victory, but the path to joy.

Lord, we are so very grateful You are El Roi, the God who sees, today, tomorrow, and all eternity. We submit today to Your unconventional plans. We say "yes" and "amen" – have Your way, Lord, in us that You might be honored and glorified. In Jesus' name, we pray. Amen.

Thank you for your faithfulness in prayer.#Godisfaithful#TheGloryRoad

Day#345 March 30

 Anchor Verse: 1 Chronicles 16:10
Glory in His holy name; Let the hearts of those who seek the Lord rejoice.
(AMP)

"Glory to God in the highest, And on earth, peace, goodwill to men." (Luke 2:14 NKJV)

This was the message the angels delivered the night of Jesus' birth to the shepherds watching their flocks in the field. The sky lit up with the glory of the God, as the Messiah was born in the city of Bethlehem.

We are to give glory to God in all things. "Magnify the Lord with me, let us exalt His name together!" (Psalm 34:3)

When we start focusing on giving God the honor and glory, it erupts from our heart and soul, and we just can't stop praising His name.

There is not a better time in history to give glory to God and rejoice in Him when the world is going through great trials. Our hope and help come in the name of the Lord, not in the name of man.

On our journey to Bill's healing, we found strength, grace, and power in the glory of God. Rejoicing and praise releases blessings. Your heart is full and overflowing with God's love and it spreads like a river of love to others.

The Glory Road is the road of blessing and seeing God's glory manifested in my life and the lives of others. A close friend prays every day for the glory of God to be released in her and over her. This is my prayer too. Remember, it's not about us, it's about God. Turn your eyes toward Jesus.

Lord, open our eyes to see You, in all Your glory. May our mouth speak forth the praise that resides deep in our soul. Our hearts be filled with Your love. Our thoughts be focused on you, the Holy One. In Jesus' name, amen.

Thank you for your persistent prayers.#Godisfaithful#TheGloryRoad

Day#346 March 31

 Anchor Verse: 1 John 4:19
We love, because He first loved us. (AMP)

Many of our actions and reactions, our likes and dislikes, are formed by those who have influenced our life from an early age.

As human beings, we often "model" the behavior of those around us. How many times have children imitated their parents' behavior much to their surprise, and sometimes embarrassment?

The good news for us, as believers, is that we have perfect examples to follow. We have God, our loving heavenly Father, and we have Jesus Christ, the Son of God who walked this earth as a man and willing laid down His life for us. We are blessed by this great gift of love.

1 John 4 describes this amazing gift of love in more detail. God loved us and so we are commanded to love one another. God loved us while we were still sinners, before we even knew "about" Him and His love, He was pouring out His love over us. "We love, because He first loved us." (1 John 4:19)

On our journey to Bill's healing, we encountered many situations where so much was stripped away. One thing never faded, God's love for us. It grew stronger, and our love for each other was multiplied and magnified.

The Glory Road is a place of great love, and often great sacrifice. Jesus gave up His home in glory to come to earth to pay the price for our sins, with His own life, that we might forever be able to spend eternity with God.

We can honor this great gift of love by loving one another. Those we know, those we don't know, those who look like us and those who are new to our world and experience – this is who we are called to love. When we love like God loved us, His love casts out all fear.

Lord, show us how to love like Jesus loves. May we take up our cross daily to follow Him. May our ears to be tuned to His voice, the still small whisper that urges us to find the lost, to encourage the hopeless, and to speak life over those who are weary. In Jesus' name we pray, amen.

Thank you for loving as Jesus loves.#Godisfaithful#TheGloryRoad

April 2021

No one who hopes in you will ever be put to shame.

~ Psalm 25:3 ~

Day#347 April 1

 Anchor Verse: Psalm 73:25
Whom have I in heaven but you? I desire you more than anything on earth.
(NLT)

We all know what it's like to be hungry. When you feel that empty feeling in the pit of your stomach, your stomach might even be "growling" right now, if you haven't eaten breakfast yet.

Psalm 73:25 reminds us about the hunger of our soul, our hunger for God. "Whom have I in heaven but you? I desire you more than anything on earth."

Are you "hungry" for God daily, hourly, minute by minute? Or has your Bible grown dusty from sitting on the shelf?

Your heavenly Father is "hungry" to be in relationship with you. His heart's desire is to walk with you and talk with you, daily, wherever you go, even when you sleep, He is watching over you.

On our journey to Bill's healing, we developed a greater desire for our heavenly Father. Many times, our only solid foundation was the fellowship, the surety we had in the Lord. Bill's math was 1+1 = 3, Bill and me and God. That's all we desired, all we needed.

The Glory Road is a solitary road. Even as the world goes on around me, I am tucked in the "cleft of the rock" where I abide with the Lord. It's more than enough. The old is gone, behold the new has come. It is a new season, a new path, a new purpose. God is the strength of my life.

What do you crave the minute you wake up? Do you hunger for the Word of God and His still small voice to show you the way to walk?

Lord, thank you for the gift of Your Presence. You love us so much. You can't imagine doing life without us. We can't imagine our lives without You. Lord, we surrender our lives to You. In Jesus' name we pray, amen.

Thank you for your companionship.#Godisfaithful#TheGloryRoad

Day#348 April 2

 Anchor Verse: Luke 23:44-45

It was now about the sixth hour (noon), and darkness came over the whole land until the ninth hour (3:00 p.m.), because the sun was obscured; and the veil [of the Holy of Holies] of the temple was torn in two [from top to bottom]. (AMP)

In history, there are recorded some life-altering moments. Moments that changed the course of the world. Today is one of those days, Good Friday 2021. It is the day Jesus was crucified to pay the price for our sins. Some may not think that sounds like a "good" day.

The Bible in detail shares the story of Jesus' final days. From His betrayal on Thursday by one of His own disciples and the events that happened through the night, to bring us to this very morning in history.

"It was now about the sixth hour (noon), and darkness came over the whole land until the ninth hour (3:00 p.m.), because the sun was obscured; and the veil [of the Holy of Holies] of the temple was torn in two [from top to bottom]." (Luke 23:44-45)

This week I heard a pastor (Pastor T.L. Rogers) share a new perspective on the temple veil being torn in two. God the Father had been silent as He watched His own son being crucified at the hands of men. Then in His great anguish, He could bear it no more, and God ripped the veil in two, just as father in that timeframe would rip His garment from top to bottom as he mourned the death of his son.

On our journey to Bill's healing, there were places where we felt moments of darkness. Even on Good Friday 2018 when Bill's heart wasn't working right, at times a 5-6 second gap. A cardiologist made a "house call" on Good Friday at the hospital, with a game plan, a pacemaker on Monday morning, Easter Monday, to remedy the situation. New hope, new life.

The Glory Road is a place of thanksgiving for Jesus' sacrifice. I, too, am called to give my best to God. To lay down my agenda, my hopes, my dreams for the "best" God has for me. God's way is always better.

Lord Jesus, we thank you for Your great sacrifice for us. You died so we might live with You forever. We choose to thank you with our lives. May our lives reflect Your love for others. In Jesus' name, we pray. Amen.

Thank you for your love.#Godisfaithful#TheGloryRoad

Day#349 April 3

 Anchor Verse: Lamentations 2:19
Rise during the night and cry out. Pour out your hearts like water to the Lord. Lift up your hands to him in prayer, pleading for your children, for in every street they are faint with hunger. (NLT)

Today we find ourselves between Good Friday and Resurrection Sunday. If you don't know the "end of the story" – this is a "tough" day.

On that day in history when Jesus was crucified and His body put in a tomb and a stone rolled in front of the entrance, the hopes and dreams of many people died with Him. They "thought" Jesus was the Messiah who came to save them – save them from the tyranny of the Roman government.

A great conquering hero wouldn't have died the death of a criminal, to be crucified – the worst death imaginable. On Saturday, which was the Sabbath for the Jews, the tone was somber, maybe even hopeless for some. There was no comfort even in the rituals which often gave them comfort.

Lamentations 2:19 reads like a page from the book of 2020-2021 – "Rise during the night and cry out. Pour out your hearts like water to the Lord. Lift up your hands to him in prayer, pleading for your children, for in every street they are faint with hunger."

We need to cry out to God for relief, because HE is our HOPE!

On our journey to Bill's healing, we encountered some desperate situations, places we cried out to God. Yes, day and night He heard our prayers. And because of Jesus' resurrection, God heard our cries and answered.

The Glory Road as it wanders through this "war zone" terrain is not devoid of hope. Jesus' love shines even brighter. Light always looks brighter in the darkness. My help (and hope) comes in the name of the Lord, the Maker of heaven and earth. (Psalm 121:2)

God, thank you that our hope comes from Jesus, our everlasting hope and our help. We lift our hands in prayer and praise to You, King of kings and Lord of lords. Hear the cry of our hearts. In Jesus' name we pray, amen.

Thank you for your faithfulness.#Godisfaithful#TheGloryRoad

Day#350 April 4

 Anchor Verse: Luke 24:1-3
But on the first day of the week, at early dawn, the women went to the tomb bringing the spices which they had prepared [to finish anointing the body]. And they found the [large, circular] stone rolled back from the tomb, but when they went inside, they did not find the body of the Lord Jesus. (AMP)

At early dawn on the first day of the week, Sunday, after their Sabbath day, the women went to the tomb to finish anointing His body for burial.

Their hearts must have been heavy, whether they walked in silence or conversed quietly of the memories they had of their friend, Jesus.

What they expected to see wasn't what they saw. The stone was rolled away from the tomb. Jesus' body was gone.

Was this an even greater pain than the first? Not only was Jesus dead but now his body had been stolen. We can only imagine their devastation.

And then… angels appeared to them to tell them the "rest of the story." "Why are you looking for the Living One among the dead? He is not here, but has risen." (Luke 24:5-6)

The words of Jesus were true. He had risen, just as He said. The women ran to tell the disciples. Peter ran to the tomb himself to check it out.

On our journey to Bill's healing, we often saw the unexpected. What was in the flesh was suddenly changed to something else. God is the God of miracles. He never lies. His promises are true.

The Glory Road has been filled with unexpected surprises. We often anticipate what today or tomorrow or five years from now will look like. God doesn't need your permission to give you His best. To turn your life what seems to be upside, to accomplish His plans and purposes in you.

Last year, Easter was April 12, 2020. Bill and I had Easter dinner with Jesus. We had no idea it would be the last Easter we celebrated together on earth. I can only imagine what Easter in heaven is like. Bill gets to experience now.

Lord, we have hope because Jesus is alive. He is risen just as He said. The tomb is empty. The cross is empty. Jesus has triumphed over death, hell, and the grave. Thank you, God, for the victory we have in Christ. Amen.

Thank you for celebrating with me.#Godisfaithful#TheGloryRoad

Day#351 April 5

 Anchor Verse: Luke 8:48
Jesus responded, "Beloved daughter, your faith in me released your healing. You may go with my peace. (TPT)

Today is the day after Easter 2021.

Now what do we do? Is it put away with your holiday decorations or has it truly changed your life, your walk, your everlasting hope?

In Luke 8, we read the account of a woman who had been pursuing her healing for a very long time. For twelve years, she had been plagued by a medical condition that the doctors couldn't heal. She had spent lots of time and money pursuing her healing, yet she had nothing to show for it.

On this particular day, the woman was in the crowd that surrounded Jesus. Her goal was to silently slip through the crowd in "stealth" mode. She believed "all" she needed to do was touch the hem of Jesus' garment and she would be healed. Touch Jesus and go, no one needed to know.

She was healed. BUT much to her dismay, she caught Jesus' attention. "Who touched me?" She came forward. The woman was willing to be seen because she had been healed, the stigma was gone.

"Jesus responded, "Beloved daughter, your faith in me released your healing. You may go with my peace." (Luke 8:48)

She is not scolded or ridiculed, instead her faith is recognized and she receives Jesus' peace. Why? Because she believed Jesus was her healer.

On our journey to Bill's healing, we encountered Jesus, the Healer too. Many times, as we faced what seemed to be the end of the road, God said "no… there is still work to do." God was able to do His mighty work in Bill because we believed He could. Faith moves mountains.

The Glory Road is a place of healing and Jesus' encounters. Not just physical healing, but healing in every area ~ mentally, physically, and emotionally. Maybe you have those needs as well. Jesus is offering you His peace.

Lord, we come in faith asking to be healed. We have run out of options. We are tired and weary. Jesus, we need You. Touch and heal us, we pray. We will be a testimony of Your goodness for all to see. In Jesus' name, amen.

Thank you for your persistent prayers.#Godisfaithful#TheGloryRoad

Day#352 April 6

 Anchor Verse: Luke 9:1-2

Jesus summoned together his twelve apostles and imparted to them authority over every demon and the power to heal every disease. Then he commissioned them to proclaim God's kingdom and to heal the sick to demonstrate that the kingdom had arrived. (TPT)

Easter Sunday ~ Resurrection Sunday is not just "one" day of the year when we celebrate the resurrected Jesus and His victory over death, hell, and the grave, we celebrate His resurrection every day.

How do we live differently because of Jesus' sacrifice and His victory?

While Jesus was still alive, He taught His disciples many things about Kingdom living. In Luke 9, we see how Jesus was preparing His disciples "before" His departure from earth.

Sometimes we have a "trial run" or a practice before a performance. We often have a coach, parent, pastor, counselor, or friend walk alongside of us as we try something new.

"Jesus summoned together his twelve apostles and imparted to them authority over every demon and the power to heal every disease. Then he commissioned them to proclaim God's kingdom and to heal the sick to demonstrate that the kingdom had arrived." (Luke 9:1-2)

On our journey to Bill's healing, we learned a lot about the power and authority we have in Jesus and through His resurrection. Praying "believing" is a good place to start. We must go out into the world to face our daily battles, not in our own strength, but in the power of Jesus.

The Glory Road is a place of commissioning. Before Bill died, God placed some dreams and visions in our hearts and minds, about the "next" things we would do. "We" will still do them together – it's just that Bill will be doing his part through supernatural resources in heaven as I walk it out here on earth. Praise the Lord for the greater things yet to come.

Lord, we come this morning confessing on our own, we can do nothing well. But with Your help, Lord, ALL things are possible. We walk in the resurrection power today, ready and willing to do ALL that You have for us to do in Jesus' name, we pray, amen.

Thank you for your bold prayers.#Godisfaithful#TheGloryRoad

Day# 353 April 7

 Anchor Verse: 1 Samuel 7:12
Then Samuel took a stone and set it up between Mizpah and Shen. He named it Ebenezer, saying, "Thus far the LORD has helped us." (NIV)

Ebenezer Scrooge was a man who was fixed on the "wrong" priorities until he had an encounter with his past that changed his future.

In 1 Samuel 7, we find Samuel and the Israelites on their journey. The Israelites would turn away from God and then turn toward God. When they were walking with God, they had victory. And when they were walking in sin, going about it their own way, they were defeated.

They cried out to the Lord because the Philistines came to attack them. The Lord heard their prayers and threw their enemy into a panic, and the Israelites defeated them.

At this location between Mizpah and Shen, Samuel set up a stone and "named it Ebenezer, saying, "Thus far the Lord has helped us." (1 Samuel 7:12) (Note that Mizpah means "outlook/watchtower" and Shen was a tooth-shaped rock – something that was a visible landmark. This is where Samuel chose to place the Ebenezer stone.)

It's important to "stop" and acknowledge the Lord's hand of direction and protection in your life. Place a memorial stone where you can visit it and remember God's faithfulness, just in your mind or in the flesh.

On our journey to Bill's healing, we took time to remember God's faithfulness. One of the ways we did this was to talk about those pivotal times in Bill's journey and write them down. These writings are now being turned into books to encourage others on their own journey.

The Glory Road is place of battlegrounds and memorial stones. I echo the words of Samuel, "Thus far the Lord has helped us." Because of God's faithfulness, I know His help will continue for as long as I have breath. God's faithfulness is not just a "one and done" event.

Lord, we come this morning with hearts filled with thanksgiving, praising you for Your faithfulness. Thank you for the power and the peace that comes in Your presence. We love you and thank you, in Jesus' name, amen.

Thank you for your faithful prayers.#Godisfaithful#TheGloryRoad

Day#354 April 8

 Anchor Verse: 1 Samuel 12:24
Only fear the Lord [with awe and profound reverence] and serve Him faithfully with all your heart; for consider what great things He has done for you. (AMP)

Samuel was a prophet, dedicated to the Lord before his birth. From a young age, Samuel committed himself to serve the Lord. "Speak, Lord, your servant is listening." (1 Samuel 3:10)

God used Samuel in a mighty way to keep the Israelites "on course" – the best he could. God would speak to Samuel and he would pass the word along to God's people.

However, the people often strayed "off" the path and went their own way. But God was faithful and He would call them back.

In 1 Samuel 12, Samuel is old and giving his farewell speech but uses this as a teaching opportunity.

"Only fear the Lord [with awe and profound reverence] and serve Him faithfully with all your heart; for consider what great things He has done for you." (1 Samuel 12:24)

On our journey to Bill's healing, often we took the time to remember what God did for us. Not only on Bill's healing journey the last few years, but all our years together. We pressed in to God as He guided us and guarded us.

The Glory Road is a place of remembrance. I have the opportunity to see God's hand at work. Not just on the days when He moves mountains but when His peace and presence fill my home. Just like a little child needs to be comforted, so my heavenly Father comforts me.

Your story is also His story about His faithfulness in your life.

Lord, this morning we sing praises to Your name. You have done great things for us. Your love extends to ALL generations. We love you and praise you in Jesus' name, amen.

Thank you for your companionship.#Godisfaithful#TheGloryRoad

Day#355 April 9

 Anchor Verse: 1 Samuel 14:7
And his armor bearer said to him, "Do everything that is in your heart (mind); here I am with you in whatever you think [best]." (AMP)

Sometimes a battle is fought alone but often it is fought with others at your side. When we enter a "battle" with God on our side, we walk in His power and authority. The battle will be won if you let God lead the way.

In 1 Samuel 14, we read of Israel's ongoing battle with the Philistines. In fact, in chapter 13, we find the Israelites hiding in caves and thickets, shaking with fear. Not exactly the picture of the "winners" in a battle.

Jonathan, Saul's son, goes on a recon mission. "Come, let's go over to the Philistine outpost on the other side." Jonathan didn't tell his father, the king. In 1 Samuel 14:6, Jonathan is speaking to his young armor-bearer, "Perhaps the Lord will act on our behalf. Nothing will hinder the Lord from saving, whether by many or by few."

"And his armor bearer said to him, 'Do everything that is in your heart (mind); here I am with you in whatever you think [best].'"

Today we still have "battles" in our lives – in the workplace, at home, in our ministries, etc. Do you have a loyal armor-bearer at your side or is God calling you to be that armor-bearer for another?

On our journey to Bill's healing, we were blessed with people (armor-bearers) God chose to walk closely beside us. In a spiritual battle, those weapons include prayer and the full armor of God. They also may include refreshment for your body, mind, and spirit.

The Glory Road is a place where the peaceful path can turn into a war zone in a single breath. God's presence hovers over me as the Holy Spirit resides in me. How blessed I am to know God has not sent me into this battle alone. Victory comes through the hands of God when we walk in obedience.

Lord, thank you for fighting for us. Thank you for heavenly helpers and those on earth too. We seek our direction from God and ask Him to be honored and glorified in all we say and do. The battle belongs to You, Lord. We love you and praise you in Jesus' mighty name, amen.

Thank you for your faithfulness in prayer.#Godisfaithful#TheGloryRoad

Day#356 April 10

 Anchor Verse: Luke 10:29
The man wanted to justify his lack of love for some kinds of people, so he asked, "Which neighbors?" (TLB)

When you find yourself "stuck" in a place, many have "come out fighting" to overcome the opposition that stands in their way.

In Luke 10, we read about an expert in the law who stood up to test Jesus. "Teacher, what must I do to inherit eternal life?"

Jesus replied, "What is written in the law?"

The man quotes the verse we know so well, "'Love the Lord your God with all your heart and with all your soul and with all your strength and with all your mind'; and, 'Love your neighbor as yourself.'"

Jesus gave him a pat on the back and said, "You have answered correctly. Do this and you will live."

Luke 10:29 says, "The man wanted to justify his lack of love for some kinds of people, so he asked, "Which neighbors?"

Jesus tells the story about the Good Samaritan who had mercy on a man he did not know, who had been robbed and beaten, and left beside the road. Many religious leaders passed by, but this man, a Samaritan, who was not like him, stopped and offered assistance. That is how we should love each other.

On our journey to Bill's healing, we encountered many God called us to love, our "new neighbors" – those who were going through valleys themselves or those who cared for Bill. Let us love one another.

The Glory Road follows a path into a foreign land. The Lord has shown me how to love people others overlook, or don't want to see. Beloved friends, we are called to love each other – no man left behind, no one tossed aside, no one left beside the road to fend for themselves.

Thank you, Lord, for the gift of neighbors, for those who walk this path of life with us. Give us spiritual eyes to see others as You see them. May we be willing to put aside our agenda, Lord, for Your agenda. We love you and praise you in Jesus' name, amen.

Thank you for your persistent prayers.#Godisfaithful#TheGloryRoad

Day#357 April 11

 Anchor Verse: 1 Samuel 17:22; 48
Then David left his provisions in the care of the supply keeper, and ran to the ranks and came and greeted his brothers…When the Philistine rose and came forward to meet David, David ran quickly toward the battle line to meet the Philistine. (AMP)

Children may be slow to move to do their chores, while they move quickly toward a meal or a fun activity. As adults, we do the same.

In 1 Samuel 17, we read the story of Goliath, the Philistine who was intimidating the Israelite army. The Israelites shrunk back in terror, because Goliath was a large man in stature (9 feet, 9 inches tall)

The youngest brother arrives sent by his father to check on his older brothers. David leaves his supplies with the supply keeper and "runs" to the battle line to greet his brothers. The wind of the Spirit of God blows in with him. It's about to change the tide of the battle.

David sees this battle differently. In verse 26, David says, "Who is this uncircumcised Philistine that he should defy the armies of the living God?"

He is willing to take on Goliath. David tells Goliath he is facing the Lord Almighty, the God of the armies of Israel, and God would deliver Goliath into his hands. David "ran quickly to the battle line to meet him." (1 Samuel 17:48) Goliath is defeated with one small stone.

On our journey to Bill's healing, we encountered "giants" in our path. We faced them with God on our side. There were days we ran to the battle line knowing God would take down Goliath, the mountain in our path.

The Glory Road is a place where giants still walk in the land. Some days I am out "tending my sheep" and God calls me to a battlefield to take on a giant. We just need to bring our willingness; God will supply the winning edge. Just as Peter ran to the tomb and found Jesus was risen, we must run to Jesus and be empowered with resurrection power for the battles we face.

Lord, thank you that with You on our side, we will not be defeated. We will not be overcome. You have written our story of victory. May we surrender to Your will and Your way. In Jesus' name we pray, amen.

Thank you for fighting the good fight.#Godisfaithful#TheGloryRoad

Day#358 April 12

 Anchor Verse: Luke 11:34
The eye is the lamp of your body. When your eye is clear [spiritually perceptive, focused on God], your whole body also is full of light [benefiting from God's precepts]. But when it is bad [spiritually blind], your body also is full of darkness [devoid of God's word]. (AMP)

When you look into the eyes of the one you love, your heart is filled with love. The same is true when a person's eyes are full of anger, fear, or joy. What is in our hearts is reflected in our eyes.

As we focus on God and the things of God, our eyes are clear and our whole body is full of light. The opposite is true as well.

"The eye is the lamp of your body. When your eye is clear [spiritually perceptive, focused on God], your whole body also is full of light [benefiting from God's precepts]. But when it is bad [spiritually blind], your body also is full of darkness [devoid of God's word]." (Luke 11:34)

Our ability to see in the natural world is impacted by how well our eyes can see the light. The same is true of our spiritual eyes. The Bible helps us to see the truth that is the guiding light of our lives. Lord, open our eyes to see.

On our journey to Bill's healing, Bill encountered a time when he was "blind" – then the Lord reversed that condition and restored his sight. At the same time, God was opening Bill's spiritual eyes to see God better, in everything that we encountered. His body and soul were filled with light.

The Glory Road is a place with opportunities to choose what I see and how I see it. God has taught me to keep my eyes on Him. When I do, my soul is filled with heavenly light and the darkness flees. God's light in us becomes a lighthouse for those who are lost.

Lord, fill us with the light and love of Jesus. He will turn your mourning into dancing. Your heavenly Father will carry you through this trial. You are loved. You are not alone. In Jesus' name, amen.

Thank you for your faithfulness in prayer.#Godisfaithful#TheGloryRoad

Day#359 April 13

 Anchor Verse: 1 Samuel 24:17, 19

He said to David, "You are more righteous and upright [in God's eyes] than I;
for you have done good to me, but I have done evil to you…For if a man finds his
enemy, will he let him go away unharmed? So may the LORD reward you with
good in return for what you have done for me this day. (AMP)

Love your enemies and pray for those who persecute you. Love and hatred are not a new thing in the 21st century.

Throughout the Bible, we see how God commands us to react in situations beyond our understanding, when the magnitude of the misdeed may not result in loving thoughts toward the person responsible.

In 1 Samuel 24, we read of an incident where Saul was sleeping in a cave and David and his men had surrounded him. David knew Saul was still God's anointed one. David refused to kill him. He only cut a piece off Saul's robe, so Saul knew David had been there and refrained from killing him.

"He said to David, "You are more righteous and upright [in God's eyes] than I; for you have done good to me, but I have done evil to you…For if a man finds his enemy, will he let him go away unharmed? So may the Lord reward you with good in return for what you have done for me this day."

Even our enemies will recognize God's hand at work in our lives, when we choose grace and mercy rather than hatred and anger.

On our journey to Bill's healing, God gave us the opportunity to let His light, hope, and love shine through us. At many crossroads, in the flesh, some would have responded in anger or frustration, but we chose God's way – the path of love and kindness. And the Lord rewarded us.

The Glory Road is a path where I get to choose my actions and reactions. To some, they won't seem "normal" – in fact, sometimes people wonder "What's wrong with you?" When you love as Jesus loves, it may not meet society's approval but it will always touch the heart of God.

Lord, show us how to love those who mean us harm rather than good. Let us show we are Christians by our love. Lord, may we reflect Your light and love everywhere we go. We live for Your glory, in Jesus' name, amen.

Thank you for your love for others#Godisfaithful#TheGloryRoad

Day#360 April 14

 Anchor Verse: 1 Samuel 26:25
And Saul said to David, "Blessings on you, my son David. You shall do heroic deeds and be a great conqueror." Then David went away and Saul returned home. (TLB)

We expect blessings and words of encouragement to flow from the mouths of family and friends, but from the mouth of our enemy? How often does that happen?

1 Samuel 26 tells us of an encounter between Saul and David. Saul is the King of Israel but God's favor has left him. David would be the next king, but it wasn't God's timing yet.

In the meantime, Saul pursues David to kill him – not just once… but relentlessly.

In the midst of this pursuit on several occasions, David has the opportunity to "take out" Saul – to turn the tables and kill his enemy. In 1 Samuel 26:12, David takes the spear and water jug near Saul's head and leaves him asleep.

David reminds Saul in verse 23 that the Lord delivered Saul into David's hands but David would not lay a hand on God's anointed. "As surely as I valued your life today, so may the Lord value my life and deliver me from all trouble." (1 Samuel 26:24)

In verse 25 it says, "And Saul said to David, 'Blessings on you, my son David. You shall do heroic deeds and be a great conqueror.' Then David went away and Saul returned home." David is blessed by his enemy.

On our journey to Bill's healing, our lives were filled with lots of "words" spoken to us, and over us, and even behind our backs. God's truth always prevailed rather than the doubt and fear of others. Bill and I held on to God's truth and it carried us through the storm.

The Glory Road is a path of many conversations. Truth and lies clash daily in our world. I chuckle at God's holy surprises. Like blessings spoken from the mouth of a person you would least suspect to speak them.

Lord, may we walk in faith, believing that ALL things work together for good to those who love You and are called according to Your purpose. (Romans 8:28) We want to be more like You. In Jesus' name, amen.

Thank you for your faithful prayers.#Godisfaithful#TheGloryRoad

Day#361 April 15

 Anchor Verse: Luke 13:18
Then Jesus said, "What is the Kingdom of God like? How can I illustrate it? (NLT)

There are some big concepts, big truths that are hard to comprehend. Quantum physics, medical terminology, mathematical equations, and the art of living and loving are just a few of the mysteries of life.

Jesus often used parables to teach God's truth, using ordinary things in life to explain what He meant. In Luke 13:18 Jesus said, "What is the Kingdom of God like? How can I illustrate it?"

"It is like a tiny mustard seed that a man planted in a garden; it grows and becomes a tree, and the birds make nests in its branches." (Luke 13:19)

The Kingdom of God blooms and grows as we walk in faith, and step out in faith, and great is the fruit. He also likens the Kingdom of Faith to yeast in dough that is spread through the whole loaf.

How is God calling us to walk out that faith – to walk in His Kingdom?

On our journey to Bill's healing, we were blessed by so many illustrations of God's Kingdom touching earth, and God's faithfulness. As we put our faith in God, He never disappointed us. As we trusted Him, the Kingdom of God grew not only in our lives but touched the lives of others.

The Glory Road is where I am called to be planted firmly in God's kingdom and let my faith shine for Him. It's about His glory, not mine. It's about His plans and purposes in my life, not mine. His desires become my desires.

Lord, we live for Your honor and glory. May we not grow weary in well doing, for in due season we will reap a harvest if we do not give up. We hold on to hope, and hold on to Your hand. You will see us through every storm. We love you and praise you. In Jesus' name we pray, amen.

Thank you for your faithful prayers.#Godisfaithful#TheGloryRoad

April 16, 2021

Bill's Graveside Service
Washington State Veterans Cemetery, Medical Lake, Washington

Only one life, 'twill soon be past, only what's done for Christ will last.

Thank you for joining me here today to celebrate Bill's life.

I am so grateful Bill chose me to be his wife... long before I understood how much I loved him.

I was a little slow at first... but once I got it... I got it. And our love continued to bloom and grow until God took him home. Our love will stay strong throughout eternity.

Today we celebrate Bill's life, Bill's legacy, but most of all, God's faithfulness.

We can do ALL things through Christ who strengthens us! All things. ~Philippians 4:13

You will do the things you think you cannot do. Truly that is the story of our journey.

My prayer for us today is that the seeds of hope and joy and faith and love that God sowed into our hearts on Bill's healing journey will take root and blossom and grow and yield a great harvest...

Not only in our lifetime, but in generations yet to come.

Thank you for all of your love and support.

I love you, Mr. Bill. Thank you for loving me!

(Paying my respects to my husband, Mr. Bill, at his graveside service.)

Day#362 April 16

 Anchor Verse: 1 Samuel 30:4
So David and his men wept aloud until they had no strength left to weep. (NIV)

When we think of those who go off into battle, often we have a mental picture of those who are stoic and strong, and seemingly without emotion. But they are human beings, just like you and me.

In 1 Samuel 30, David and his men came back from battle and discovered the Amalekites had destroyed Ziklag by fire and their wives, sons, and daughters were taken captive.

"So David and his men wept aloud until they had no strength left to weep." (1 Samuel 30:4)

Here we see the depth of their emotion, their raw grief, how much their families meant to them. Not only were they warriors, but they were husbands and fathers. They weren't afraid to show the depth of their grief.

On our journey to Bill's healing, we went through many valleys and over many mountains. Our emotions hit highs and lows. Bill once said, "I was taught that crying is a sign of weakness. Sometimes you cry on the inside deep down inside where no one can see it." What a tragedy when we teach our children that it's not okay to cry. Even Jesus wept.

The Glory Road has almost spanned a full year (2020-2021) since God took Bill home. There have been moments when tears were the language of my soul. Not always tears of sorrow, but so many times they have been tears of joy and gratitude, and tears from laughing so hard.

On the morning Bill died, April 19, 2020, my heavenly Father said to me, "Feel the emotion. Cry when you need to cry. Let others see what you are feeling." God has used what the world might try to silence to give others the freedom to mourn freely.

You may be weeping in your own Ziklag today. God will meet you there.

Lord, thank you that You are with us in our joy and our sorrow. We are not alone on our path of suffering. We are not alone in the darkest hours of our own lives. May we walk in Your victory, in Jesus' name, amen.

Thank you for your love and support.#Godisfaithful#TheGloryRoad

Day#363 April 17

 Anchor Verse: Luke 14:11
For everyone who tries to honor himself shall be humbled; and he who humbles himself shall be honored." (TLB)

What do you know about humility? The dictionary definition says, "The feeling or attitude that you have no special importance that makes you better than others; lack of pride."

Do you live like this or do you seek recognition and the praise of others?

Jesus was a humble man. He didn't live His life trying to seek the praises of others. Jesus only sought to pursue His heavenly Father's approval.

"For even the Son of Man did not come to be served, but to serve, and to give his life as a ransom for many." (Mark 10:45)

This is where our faith and our culture can run headlong into each other. Jesus tells us to be humble and advertisers urge us to be#1. Whose path will you follow?

On our journey to Bill's healing, we found that "staying under the radar" was preferable to being on center stage and seeking the limelight. Even then, there have been opportunities to share our story for God's glory.

The Glory Road is being walked out in a world where many seek notoriety and high places, and often the call to humility and serving others is only a whisper. As a follower of Jesus, I delight in the opportunity to serve rather than to be served.

Lord, we thank you for the gift of Your love. Thank you, Jesus, for leaving the mansions of glory to come to earth as a little baby for our sake. May we follow Your example to serve rather than to be served. May we be more like you, Jesus. We love and praise you, in Jesus' name, amen.

Today, April 17, 2021 would have been our 19th wedding anniversary. During our marriage, we learned the gift of serving each other. What a blessing to honor and serve Bill, not only in the last years of his life when his health challenges increased, but to love him and think of him first every day.

Please do me a favor, honor your spouse today, since I can't do that for Bill.

Thank you for all your love and support.#Godisfaithful#TheGloryRoad

Day#364 April 18

 Anchor Verse: Proverbs 4:6
Do not turn away from her (Wisdom) and she will guard and protect you; Love her, and she will watch over you. (AMP)

Wisdom doesn't come cheap. You don't purchase wisdom at the Dollar Store. For some, it takes a lifetime. For others, they won't pay the price.

Our pastor often says, "Knowledge is what we learn from our own mistakes and wisdom is what we learn from the mistakes of others."

Which path will you choose – the path of wisdom or the path of knowledge?

"And if anyone longs to be wise, ask God for wisdom and he will give it! He won't see your lack of wisdom as an opportunity to scold you over your failures but he will overwhelm your failures with his generous grace."

God is such a good, good Father. He does doesn't scold us or make fun of us when we run to Him for wisdom. He doesn't make you feel bad for not knowing the answer. God just wants us to run to Him first when we get lost.

On the journey to Bill's healing, we encountered places in the road where we desperately needed wisdom. The decisions were "above our paygrade." We had never been in those places so we didn't know what to do. We cried out for help and our gracious heavenly Father met our every need.

The Glory Road is a place where I need wisdom every day. The best decision is to ask for help instead of stumbling around until I finally get it right. I am willing to "borrow" the wisdom of others rather than get any more bumps, bruises, and scars from the journey. There are plenty of those already.

What about you? Do you hesitate to ask for help? Does your ego get in the way? Maybe you are concerned that it will affect "your image" if people think you don't have all the answers.

Lord, thank you for the gift of wisdom. We ask for an extra measure of it. Do for us what we cannot do for ourselves. And we will give You all the praise and honor and glory in Jesus' name, amen.

Thank you for your persistent prayers.#Godisfaithful#TheGloryRoad

Day#365 April 19

 Anchor Verse: 1 Corinthians 8:3
But whoever loves God is known by God. (NIV)

God is not a distant heavenly Father. Moment by moment, His eyes are upon us. We are never out of His sight.

"But if anyone loves God [with awe-filled reverence, obedience and gratitude], he is known by Him [as His very own and is greatly loved]." (1Corinthians 8:3 AMP)

Today is an important day in my life. One year ago today (April 19, 2020), God took my beloved husband, Bill, home to be with Him in heaven. In Bill's final hours, everything happened so quickly. From home to the hospital to heaven, in less than three hours ~ Bill was too soon gone from my life.

Most, if not all of us, have experienced the death of a loved one. Even as a believer whom we know is going from "glory to glory," from this life into the presence of God, our humanity feels the great loss.

Their laughter which once filled our homes and our hearts now is just an echo through time.

The MESSAGE translation of Matthew 5:4 says, "Happy are those who know what sorrow means for they will be given courage and comfort."

Jesus knew what sorrow felt like. His good friend, Lazarus, died and Jesus wasn't there. At the tomb of Lazarus, Jesus wept. Isaiah 53:3 says that Jesus was a Man of Sorrows, acquainted with grief.

On our journey to Bill's healing, we encountered places in the road where we lost loved ones. My mom died just two months before Bill. We mourned her death, but we celebrated her life because she was now free of any earthly pain. "Earth has no sorrow that heaven cannot heal."

The Glory Road, God named for me, a road filled with His glory, leading to His glory. This is the road I have invited you to walk with me.

You are the God who knows us, in our joy, in our sorrow, in our failures, and our victories. Lord, lead us on our journey to Your glory. We love you, Lord. In Jesus' name we pray, amen.

Thank you for all your love and support.#Godisfaithful#TheGloryRoad

Day#366 April 20

 Anchor Verse: Luke 15:32
But it was fitting to celebrate and rejoice, for this brother of yours was [as good as] dead and has begun to live. He was lost and has been found. (AMP)

The "prodigal son" is a familiar story. There are two brothers, one decides he wants to see the world and asks his father for his share of his inheritance. His father gives it to him. The young man heads out into the world and spends it all. Finding himself penniless, the young man hires himself out to a farmer to tend to his pigs. The pigs have food and he is starving.

The son decides to humble himself, go home to his father and admit he sinned and was no longer worthy to be called his son, "but at least hire me as your servant so I can eat."

His father sees him coming from a distance. The young man's father runs to him, embraces him, and asks for a celebration. The older brother wasn't very happy. Then his father reminds the older son why they are celebrating.

"But it was fitting to celebrate and rejoice, for this brother of yours was [as good as] dead and has begun to live. He was lost and has been found." (Luke 15:32)

God does the same for each one of us when we choose to go our own way and veer off the path. His arms are always open to receive us.

On our journey to Bill's healing, we were blessed by our heavenly Father's love time and time again. When Bill found himself in the land of pain and suffering, and even chaos and confusion, His heavenly Father came running and gathered Bill in His arms of love.

The Glory Road is a place of God's love. So many people are lost right now. People who have chosen to run the wrong way. We should not be quick to judge or condemn, because the truth is in our own hearts – whether in thought, word, or deed, we too have sinned and fallen short of God's glory.

Lord, forgive us when we have wandered away from Your presence. You are always being willing to draw us into Your arms of love – anytime and anywhere. You alone are our help and our salvation. In Jesus' name, amen.

Thank you for your persistent prayers.#Godisfaithful#TheGloryRoad

Day#367 April 21

 Anchor Verse: Lamentations 3:40
Let's take a good look at the way we're living and reorder our lives under God.
(MSG)

When life is spinning out of control, do you take a moment to stop and figure out the cause?

There's good news. When God is the captain of ship, we will stay on course. The wind and the rain will come, but the ship will not sink.

The book of Lamentations is filled with many hard things and difficult circumstances. It is filled with lament, and sorrow, and "how did we get here?" moments. Jeremiah, the author, inserts nuggets of hope and truth.

"Let's take a good look at the way we're living and reorder our lives under God." (Lamentations 3:40)

On our journey to Bill's healing, there was a lot of examination. Not only by the medical folks, but God helped us shine His light on our spiritual lives too. Our faith in God was tested and strengthened through every circumstance. As for me and my household, we will serve the Lord.

The Glory Road is a place of reflection. Am I leading with God's love? Am I trusting God no matter what the circumstances look like around me? Do I believe without a shadow of doubt that God is for me and not against me? The answers are found in a life reordered under God as I am filled with His love, His joy, and His peace.

Lord, we run to You asking for help where there are holes in our lives. You will not allow our ship to sink. When we cry out to You, You promised to help us. Lord God Almighty, Maker of heaven and earth, thank you for rescuing us in our distress. You are our faithful guide. In Jesus' name, amen.

Thank you for your love and support.#Godisfaithful#TheGloryRoad

Day#368 April 22

 Anchor Verse: Luke 17:16
He fell flat on the ground in front of Jesus, face downward in the dust, thanking him for what he had done. This man was a despised Samaritan. (TLB)

When God does something miraculous in your life, beyond your understanding, how do you show your gratitude to the King of kings and the Lord of lords?

Luke 17 tells the story of Jesus traveling to Jerusalem along the border between Samaria and Galilee. As He went into the village, ten men with leprosy met Jesus. They stood at a distance and called out in a loud voice, "Jesus, Master, have pity on us!"

Jesus saw them, and told them to go show themselves to the priests. "And as they went" ~ they were cleansed. It was their act of faith that healed them.

One of them when he saw he was healed, came back, praising God in a LOUD voice. In Luke 17:16 it says, "He fell flat on the ground in front of Jesus, face downward in the dust, thanking him for what he had done. This man was a despised Samaritan."

There is nothing dignified about lying flat on the ground in the dirt and dust, but I believe the former leper's heart was so filled with gratitude a little dirt didn't faze him. That's how we need to praise the Lord for the life He gives us every day.

On our journey to Bill's healing, there were many times when Bill was like the "leper" who needed to be healed. We sang praises to His name in the doctor's office or hospital room. We reached out to heaven as we were so grateful for God's love ~ with tears of joy and gratitude.

The Glory Road is a place of joy and healing. Remember how David danced before the Lord and his wife found that to be undignified? God deserves our gratitude and praise regardless of whether others understand.

Lord, thank you for the gift of being seen by You. There is healing in Your hands. May we receive it as an act of faith, and walk in it. May we be Jesus' hands and feet to the outcasts and the strangers. In Jesus' name, amen.

Thank you for your perseverance.#Godisfaithful#TheGloryRoad

Day#369 April 23

 Anchor Verse: 2 Samuel 18:33
The king was stunned. Heartbroken, he went up to the room over the gate and wept. (MSG)

Our lives are filled with a mixture of emotions. There is joy and sorrow, mourning and dancing, hope and despair, also enthusiasm and apathy.

There is a yearning in our hearts to know the comfort and the love of our heavenly Father. Our spirit desires peace even while our mind and emotions are in turmoil.

Absalom, King David's son, is trying to kill his father and take over the kingdom. This is a prodigal son who is seeking to not only harm his father, but boldly go against God, his heavenly Father.

That never ends well. Rebellion never brings life; rebellion brings grief, to the rebel and to those who surround him.

In 2 Samuel 18, the battle rages on. Absalom riding on his mule gets his long hair caught in the tree, and Joab kills him. The king, his father, has asked his troops, "Be gentle with the young man Absalom for my sake."

Absalom from a strategical standpoint was his father's enemy, but David's heart as his father grieved for his son's soul. His love for his son was greater than Absalom's ambition.

When King David is informed of his son's death, it says, "The king was stunned. Heartbroken, he went up to the room over the gate and wept."

On our journey to Bill's healing, we encountered those who didn't know God's love and those who had walked away. Our hearts were grieved. We loved them and showed them the love of God shining in and through us.

The Glory Road winds its way through the land where many have run from the Lord. Those who are not friends of God are His enemies. God weeps for those who are lost. We weep as well, not just for our birth children, but all children – no matter their age. God's heart is not one soul should perish.

Lord, this morning we praise and thank you that You love us with an everlasting love. You are our Redeemer, Savior, and Friend. Lord, we bring the prodigals to You. Good Shepherd, find them and bring them home. We know nothing is impossible for You, nothing. In Jesus' name we pray, amen.

Thank you for your faithful prayers.#Godisfaithful#TheGloryRoad

Day#370 April 24

 Anchor Verse: Proverbs 13:3
The one who guards his mouth [thinking before he speaks] protects his life; The one who opens his lips wide [and chatters without thinking] comes to ruin. (AMP)

"God gave us two ears and one mouth for a reason – to listen more than we speak." This was often a phrase that my husband spoke, and most of all, what he practiced.

Bill said he learned a lot more by listening than by talking all the time. It's true. Careless words spoken can get us into big trouble,

When King Solomon the book of Proverbs, there wasn't social media or texting, where a quick response can inflame thousands.

"The one who guards his mouth [thinking before he speaks] protects his life; The one who opens his lips wide [and chatters without thinking] comes to ruin." (Proverbs 13:3)

Do you think before you speak or do your emotions or opinions cause you to open your mouth before it passes through the filter of your brain?

In Proverbs, it says that we should "guard" our mouth – to think before we speak, and it will protect our life. Do you find this to be true?

As a writer, speaker, and book editor, words are the tools of my craft. Each word matters. Each word is carefully chosen like a beautiful gem and rightly put in its place. Words have the power to encourage or inflame. The choice is ours.

On our journey to Bill's healing, I observed how Bill chose his words wisely. When he spoke, I listened and continue to treasure his words in my heart.

The Glory Road is place where words matter – a lot. We have seen the power of the media and words spoken through the use of the internet. Lives have been enhanced and ruined by hastily spoken words.

O Lord, may I be a better steward of my words, knowing when to speak and when to be silent. Holy Spirit, guard my mouth that I may not lead myself to the path of destruction. In Jesus' name, I pray, amen.

Thank you for your faithful prayers.#Godisfaithful#TheGloryRoad

Day# 371 April 25

 Anchor Verse: 2 Samuel 22:17

But me he [God] caught—reached all the way from sky to sea; he pulled me out of that ocean of hate, that enemy chaos, the void in which I was drowning. (MSG)

When was the last time you found yourself in a battle, trial, conflict or confrontation bigger than your own ability or strength?

For many of us, we wouldn't have to look too far. We live in a world where the battle rages daily. We read of casualties in the war between good and evil. In fact, you may be one of the wounded ones this morning.

If we look at the context of this story, once again the Philistines and the Israelites are engaged in another battle. David became exhausted and one of his men slew the enemy who vowed to kill him.

Second Samuel 22 is entitled "David's Song of Praise" in my Bible. As David often did during his lifetime, he sang praises to the Lord for what God had done. The book of Psalms is filled with David's songs.

Verse 17 describes poetically what God did for David. "But me he caught—reached all the way from sky to sea; he pulled me out of that ocean of hate, that enemy chaos, the void in which I was drowning."

In verse 20, it describes David's reaction to God's rescue. "He stood me up on a wide-open field; I stood there saved—surprised to be loved!"

On our journey to Bill's healing, God was our shield and defender. He lifted us up and out of our battles and stood us in His presence. We sang praises to His name because of God's indescribable love for us.

The Glory Road is a battlefield, not only externally but internally. Those words "ocean of hate, that enemy chaos" describe the world today. But the good news is still the same ~ God reached down and rescues me – and you.

Lord, we praise you. Your love is greater than the ocean of hate where we live and the enemy chaos that threatens our stability, our security in You. Thank you for the gift of Jesus and His power to overcome sin, death, and the grave. Because He lives, we live also. We will give You, Lord, all the praise, honor, and glory in Jesus' name, amen.

Thank you for your encouraging words.#Godisfaithful#TheGloryRoad

Day#372 April 26

 Anchor Verse: Luke 19:10
For the Son of Man came to seek and to save the lost. (NIV)

When was the last time you lost something? You may not need to think long to remember. How much effort did you put into finding it?

When Jesus came into the world, His primary mission was to seek and save the lost – not a lost object or possession, but to find you and me.

In Luke 19, we read about a man who was a wealthy tax collector. Tax collectors didn't have the best reputation. Zacchaeus wanted to see Jesus but he was too short to see over the crowd. He climbed up into a sycamore tree.

When Jesus came along, He looked up at Zacchaeus in that tree and told him to come down immediately because Jesus was coming to his house. Zacchaeus came down at once and welcomed Jesus. As you can imagine, there was grumbling in the crowd, "He has gone to be a guest of a sinner."

Zacchaeus's response to Jesus was he would give half of his possessions to the poor, and if he had cheated anyone, he would pay them back four times the amount. Salvation came to his house that day.

The moral of the story: "…the Son of Man came to seek and to save the lost." Jesus came to save you and me.

On our journey to Bill's healing, Jesus saw Bill wherever he was. There were times when his illness put Bill in a foreign place, a place he did not know. Jesus met him there, and the lost was found. The sick man was given new life – both physically and spiritually.

The Glory Road is a place of new experiences, places I do not know. Without a doubt, I know Jesus has gone ahead of me to make my pathway straight. Even when I can only see one step ahead, it's enough, because I know the one who holds my hand. He is always with me.

Lord Jesus, we are so grateful You came to save us, the lost sheep. Your left Your home in glory to come into the world to find us and rescue us. We ask for Your hand of protection over us. We are safe in the hollow of Your hands. We praise you, Lord. In Jesus' name, amen.

Thank you for your persistent prayers.#Godisfaithful#TheGloryRoad

Day#373 April 27

 Anchor Verse: John 16:22
You have sorrow now, but I will see you again and then you will rejoice; and no one can rob you of that joy. (TLB)

Jesus, as He walked this earth, was acquainted with all of our emotions. He knew joy and sorrow, the thrill of a sunrise, the joy of a sunset, the satisfaction of a good meal, and the blessing of a good night's sleep.

He also carried the heavy burden of what awaited Him – His death on the cross. It was why God sent into the world; Jesus must die so we could live.

We really can't comprehend the struggle. You and I know what it's like to receive bad news – a difficult diagnosis, the loss of a job, the loss of a loved one, but to bear the weight of the sins of the world is beyond understanding.

In John 16:22, Jesus says, "You have sorrow now, but I will see you again and then you will rejoice; and no one can rob you of that joy." In another translation, it uses the illustration of a woman giving birth to a child. The pain of childbirth is great, but the joy of the new baby held in her arms is even greater.

That is the great joy that we will know when we are reunited with Jesus when our life here on earth ends. In heaven, no one can rob us of that joy.

On our journey to Bill's healing, we experienced walking through difficult places. Trying to explain to others what was happening, while experiencing the joy we found in the Lord. Many did not understand. One day we will be reunited with those who have entered glory and our joy will be complete.

The Glory Road is a place of opposites– where joy and sorrow are the flip sides of the coin. Jesus' life helps us understand it's okay to have the struggle and not be able to fix it. We will have sorrow now as our loved ones die, but greater still will be the joy when we are reunited.

Lord, thank you for not only knowing our grief but the greater joy which comes in the morning. Walk with those with heavy hearts. Fill them with the fullness of Your joy. We lift our hands in praise. In Jesus' name, amen.

Thank you for your encouragement.#Godisfaithful#TheGloryRoad

Day#374 April 28

 Anchor Verse: 1 Kings 4:29
God gave Solomon wisdom and very great insight, and a breadth of understanding as measureless as the sand on the seashore. (NIV)

If we are honest with ourselves, there are so many places that we walk in this world that are beyond our understanding. We may feel ill-equipped for the task. There are circumstances beyond our control that seem daunting. There are challenges that come in the darkness of the night that block out the light.

Solomon was King David's son who took the throne after his father's death. In those last moments of David's life, there was a competition about who would succeed him. God has His way, and Solomon took his rightful place, the son of David, David whom the Lord called a "man after His own heart."

The Lord came to Solomon in a dream in 1 Kings 3:5, and said, "Ask for whatever you want me to give you." Solomon acknowledged God's faithfulness to his father, David, because David was faithful to God and righteous and upright in heart. God's kindness extended to Solomon.

In verse 9, Solomon says, "Give your servant a discerning heart to govern your people and to distinguish between right and wrong."

God granted his prayer as we read in 1 Kings 4:29, "God gave Solomon wisdom and very great insight, and a breadth of understanding as measureless as the sand on the seashore."

On our journey to Bill's healing, there were many places in the road where we ran to God and asked for His help, wisdom, and provision. In ourselves, we didn't have the wisdom we needed, but God did.

The Glory Road is a new space. Daily, I run to my heavenly Father and ask for His help to navigate life. God is never stingy in His provision. He is Jehovah Jireh, our Provider. He is Jehovah Shalom, our Peace.

Lord, we come asking for Your help, acknowledging we cannot do it on our own. Lord, open our eyes to see and our ears to hear your still small voice. May we receive the fullness of Your joy. In Jesus' name we pray, amen.

Thank you for your faithfulness.#Godisfaithful#TheGloryRoad

Day#375 April 29

 Anchor Verse: Isaiah 42:3
He will not break the bruised reed, nor quench the dimly burning flame. He will encourage the fainthearted, those tempted to despair. He will see full justice given to all who have been wronged. (TLB)

God has many attributes, qualities, ways in which He moves, but this morning, we're going to look at God's tenderness, His gentleness, and His role as encourager.

In Isaiah 42:3 it says, "He will not break the bruised reed, nor quench the dimly burning flame. He will encourage the fainthearted, those tempted to despair. He will see full justice given to all who have been wronged."

Some of you needed to hear this encouragement this morning, because frankly, that's not what you are seeing manifested in your physical surroundings. It might not be what people are speaking over you, or to you, or even about you.

God's truth is what we need to hold on to today. What God speaks is life and hope and joy. Even if you are feeling like a "bruised reed," like grass that's been trampled, or water has been thrown on the fire in your heart and soul, God is there to help you up and breathe new life into you. He will rekindle the flame in your heart and encourage you.

On our journey to Bill's healing, we found God was all of these things and more. When we were "on the ropes" and to the medical community it looked like Bill had been "knocked down and out" by an illness, down for the count, God said, "No way! Bill Hollace has much more life in him because I said so."

The Glory Road is filled with life. It has crossroads where conflicts occur, train wrecks and conundrums, but always God says, "Follow Me! I will show you the way to life. It may be narrow and even a hard climb, but with My help, you're going to make it!"

Lord, we praise and thank you this morning You see everything that happens in our lives. You are near to us in our times of trouble and in our rejoicing. You also set us on the rock, the solid rock of Jesus, where we will stand and not fall, or fail. Your love knows no boundaries. Do what only You can do, Lord. In Jesus' name we pray, amen.

Thank you for speaking life over me.#Godisfaithful#TheGloryRoad

Day#376 April 30

 Anchor Verse: 1 Kings 8:24

You have kept your promise to your servant David my father; with your mouth you have promised and with your hand you have fulfilled it—as it is today. (NIV)

God is not just a God of today, but history is filled with many ways God moved in the lives of ordinary people – kings and queens, and heads of state.

In 1 Kings 8, we read Solomon's prayer of dedication for the temple as he stands before the altar of the Lord. This is Solomon's prayer to God and the rest of us. We get to listen as Solomon recounts God's faithfulness.

"You have kept your promise to your servant David my father; with your mouth you have promised and with your hand you have fulfilled it—as it is today." (1 Kings 8:24)

By the end of his prayer, Solomon was on his knees before the Lord with his hands spread out toward heaven.

What a powerful image and great reminder. With God's mouth, He makes promises, and with His hand, God fulfills them. We lift our hands in praise to give Him glory.

On our journey to Bill's healing, we were so blessed to see God make promises, not only for healing but for provision, and to do it. We sang praises to God's name – in the waiting and fulfillment of His promises.

The Glory Road is a beautiful canvas on which God's promises and the fulfillment of them are illustrated. Every step is an opportunity to see God move. Every crisis is an opportunity to trust in God's faithfulness. Every victory is an opportunity to sing praises to His name.

Lord, we praise you for the gift of this day. Your promises are true for a thousand generations. Your grace is sufficient and Your power is made perfect in our weakness. We trust You, Lord, to do what we cannot do and You will get all the glory. We love you, Lord. In Jesus' name we pray, amen.

Thank you for your faithful prayers. Today is a doctor's appointment with the oncologist. Praising God in advance for His faithfulness and mighty miracles.#Godisfaithful#TheGloryRoad

May 2021

For you have been my hope, Sovereign Lord, my confidence since my youth.

~ Psalm 71:5 ~

Day#377 May 1

 Anchor Verse: Luke 21:4
For they have given a tiny part of their surplus, but she, poor as she is, has given everything she has. (NLT)

Many of the miracles Jesus performed were for those who had faded into the landscape – the lepers, the blind, the deaf, and those that society didn't want to associate with like the Samaritan woman, the tax collectors, etc.

In Luke 21, Jesus is in the temple watching people put their money in the "offering basket" or as they called it, the "temple treasury." Rich and poor alike passed by. One particular woman caught Jesus' attention. She was a poor widow. The woman put in a few copper coins, sometimes referred to as the "widow's mite."

Jesus took a moment to teach His disciples a lesson. In verses 3-4, it says, "I tell you the truth," Jesus said, "this poor widow has given more than all the rest of them. For they have given a tiny part of their surplus, but she, poor as she is, has given everything she has."

Was Jesus talking just about the money the people were giving? Or was His reference to giving our lives and everything we have – time, talent, and resources to God? Since Jesus gave His all to us, can we give Him anything less?

On our journey to Bill's healing, we learned so much about God's provision and putting God first in our lives including our finances. Tithing and giving offerings to the Lord bring blessings to both those who give and those who receive.

The Glory Road is the place where I am a widow. God is asking me to give "all" my resources to Him so they can be used in His kingdom for His glory. When we put God first, we will lack nothing. He will not withhold one good thing from His children. God continues to bless me daily.

Lord, we come with grateful hearts. God, we can't out give You. Today we commit to give not out of our surplus, but we give you the first fruits of the harvest. We pledge to give you our lives, our love, our finances, and our talents. We love you, Lord. In Jesus' name we pray, amen.

Thank you for your love and support.#Godisfaithful#TheGloryRoad

Day#378 May 2

 Anchor Verse: Luke 22:28
You are those who have remained and have stood by Me in My trials. (AMP)

When the difficulties in life come, some fall away. It's like the parable of the Sower and the different kinds of soil – rocky soil, soil along the path, thorny places, and good soil. It's only the seed planted in the good soil that takes root and yields a great harvest.

Jesus teaches His disciples that the greatest among them is the one who serves, not the one who is seated at the table. Jesus (the Son of Man) didn't come into the world to be served, but to serve, and give His life as a ransom for many. (Matthew 20:28)

In Luke 2:28, Jesus says, "You are those who have remained and have stood by Me in My trials." Jesus promises them a reward in heaven when His kingdom comes.

Have we remained with Jesus during the good times and the trials? Have we been faithful?

On our journey to Bill's healing, quickly the Lord set our priorities. There were so many places on the path where it was God and Bill and me. He stood by us and we stood with Him during the darkest nights and the deepest valleys. We didn't run away, we remained and stood with Jesus.

The Glory Road is a place where I am also called to remain and stand with Jesus. In the chaos of the world, Jesus is our only solid rock. We won't dodge trials and temptations on our path. It means we choose wisely and at every intersection we choose Jesus, and the path to life. God always rewards our obedience and our faithfulness.

Lord, we thank you for the gift of Your love and Your faithfulness. We choose to answer the call to remain and stand with You even when the world calls us to a different path. You are our first love, our only love. Lord Jesus, may You find us faithful. We love you. In Jesus' name we pray, amen.

Thank you for your friendship.#Godisfaithful#TheGloryRoad

Day#379 May 3

 Anchor Verse: 1 Peter 1:3
Celebrate with praises the God and Father of our Lord Jesus Christ, who has shown us his extravagant mercy. For his fountain of mercy has given us a new life — we are reborn to experience a living, energetic hope through the resurrection of Jesus Christ from the dead.

When was the last time you celebrated the gift of life ~ eternal life? And gave thanks to God because of His extravagant mercy?

There are things in our lives we take for granted. "Simple" things like our heart beating, our lungs breathing, the sun rising and setting, even the gift of gravity so we don't fly off into space.

Maybe today is a good day to thank God for your many blessings – big or small. The gift of gratitude blesses us and touches the heart of God.

In 1 Peter 1:3, we read that Peter is calling people to remember and celebrate with praises God's mercy which gives us new life. "Celebrate with praises the God and Father of our Lord Jesus Christ, who has shown us his extravagant mercy. For his fountain of mercy has given us a new life – we are reborn to experience a living, energetic hope through the resurrection of Jesus Christ from the dead."

We are reborn to experience a "living, energetic hope!" Is that the kind of hope you have today?

On our journey to Bill's healing, we were blessed to be given eyes of faith to see and experience this living, energetic hope. Often what you "see" through your spiritual eyes cannot be adequately conveyed to those around you. Bill and I were able to experience that living, energetic hope together.

The Glory Road is a place of living, energetic hope because of God's mercy. It's not just a "shower" of mercy, but a "fountain" of mercy that never runs dry. Because Jesus was raised from the dead, we now have that resurrection power living in us. Great is our victory over the obstacles we encounter.

Lord, we sing praises to Your name. We put all our gifts, talents, resources, our very lives on the altar, and ask You to use us where we best fit. Lord, may we reflect Your love. In Jesus' name, amen.

Thank you for your faithfulness.#Godisfaithful#TheGloryRoad

Day#380 May 4

 Anchor Verse: 1 Kings 18:3-4
*The man in charge of Ahab's household affairs was Obadiah, who was a devoted
follower of the Lord. Once when Queen Jezebel had tried to kill all of the Lord's
prophets, Obadiah had hidden one hundred of them in two caves – fifty in each –
and had fed them with bread and water. (TLB)*

God is a great strategist – the best ever! This world may have engineers,
scientists, great educators, and business strategists, but all of their knowledge
cannot compare to the wisdom of God.

Time after time, throughout both the Old and New Testament, we read of
how God put people in particular places to achieve His purposes.

In 1 Kings 18, we read about Obadiah, a devoted follower of the Lord, who
was serving a wicked, evil king. It's sort of ironic that such an evil man has a
devoted follower of the Lord (equivalent of a Christian, a believer, in our
time) in charge of Ahab's household affairs.

Obadiah has a key role in God's plans. Ahab's wife, Queen Jezebel, is trying
to kill all the prophets in the land, and Obadiah, who is working by God's
instruction in 1 Kings 18:4 says, "Once when Queen Jezebel had tried to kill
all of the Lord's prophets, Obadiah had hidden one hundred of them in two
caves – fifty in each – and had fed them with bread and water."

God is hiding these 100 prophets and feeding them essentially out of King
Ahab and Queen Jezebel's household. Only God… What the enemy meant
for evil God will use for the good. (Genesis 50:20)

On our journey to Bill's healing, God placed us in places of death and
darkness where we were called to be the light. There we spoke life, hope, and
joy, and peace, where in the flesh, it looked the exact opposite.

The Glory Road is a place of the unusual. We are living in a season where
things are still turned upside down. God has a plan and He is working it out,
as we walk it out. This isn't the end – it's a new beginning.

Lord, open our eyes to see You, know You, and be led by You, Holy Spirit.
Let our light shine as You fulfill Your purpose in us. In Jesus' name, amen.

Thank you for your persistent prayers.#Godisfaithful#TheGloryRoad

Day#381 May 5

 Anchor Verse: Proverbs 30:5
Every word of God is tested and refined [like silver]; He is a shield to those who trust and take refuge in Him. (AMP)

The words of God – gathered in the Bible – are the most powerful words in the world. They are greater than any book on the New York Times bestseller list.

Life-giving words come from the heart of God. Anything less than life-giving is not from God.

Proverbs 30:5 says, "Every word of God is tested and refined [like silver]; He is a shield to those who trust and take refuge in Him."

We should not expect anything less for ourselves. It is in the refining in our own lives that God burns out the dross – the junk, the sin, the self-centeredness and makes us more like Him.

Then it goes on to say, "He [God] is a shield to those who trust and take refuge in Him."

Trusting God involves putting our lives in His hands, as well as those of our loved ones, and believing that everything that happens will be for our good and for His glory. When the storms of life come, we can take refuge in Him.

On our journey to Bill's healing, we learned the truth of Proverbs 30:5. God's words of truth and life were powerful and effective, sharper than a two-edged sword. (Hebrews 4:12) He was our shield as the arrows of the enemy sought to wound us and we took refuge in Him during the storms.

The Glory Road is where the Word of God guides my path. It is the sure foundation on which I stand. My hope, help, peace, and joy are found there. This powerful gift from God gives me new revelation every day.

Lord, we praise and thank you for the gift of You. The gift of Your love, Your life, Your powerful words. We can't do life without You. Come and walk with us. Direct our path. Keep our feet from falling. We will give You all the praise and honor and glory in Jesus' name, amen.

Thank you for your persistent prayers.#Godisfaithful#TheGloryRoad

Day#382 May 6

 Anchor Verse: John 15:15
I no longer call you servants, because a servant does not know his master's business. Instead, I have called you friends, for everything that I learned from my Father I have made known to you. (NIV)

The Word of God is so powerful. It is the living, breathing power of God. They are not just "words" on a page, they contain God's pneuma breath.

"I no longer call you servants, because a servant does not know his master's business. Instead, I have called you friends, for everything that I learned from my Father I have made known to you." (John 15:15)

Go back and read the verse again. (I'll wait for you.)

What words or phrases stand out to you?

The words "no longer" stood out to me. What I was, I no longer am that person. In this case, Jesus calls me friend and "everything" that Jesus learned from His Father He has made known to me.

What a blessing. To be known and recognized as a friend of Jesus rather than a servant who doesn't know his master's business.

On our journey to Bill's healing, Bill learned more deeply, more intimately what it meant to be a friend of God. In his nighttime dreams, Bill walked with Jesus along the shores of Galilee. Walking and talking, learning more about Jesus and God the Father.

The Glory Road is a place where I walk with Jesus. A friend of Jesus is one who takes the time to sit in silence with Him. When we are with those we love the most, silence is not awkward. Our love in the silence speaks louder than words. The Spirit of God inhabits the place where we abide with Christ.

Thank you, Lord Jesus, You call us Your friends. All the Father has revealed to You, You share with us. Thank you for the fruit that abides because of our relationship with You. May You be glorified, in Jesus' name, amen.

Thank you for your companionship.#Godisfaithful#TheGloryRoad

Day#383 May 7

 Anchor Verse: Luke 24:21
We had thought he [Jesus] was the glorious Messiah and that he had come to rescue Israel. (TLB)

Our expectations don't always match up to what actually happens. We can either run to God, or run away from Him. The choice is ours.

Just three days after Jesus died, there were two men walking on the road to Emmaus when Jesus, the risen Christ, encounters them.

Cleopas responds, "Are you the only one visiting Jerusalem who does not know the things that have happened there in these days?" (Luke 24:16)

Jesus responds, "What things?"

They describe Jesus as a prophet, powerful in word and deed before God and all the people. "We had thought he was the glorious Messiah and that he had come to rescue Israel." (Luke 24:21)

Jesus hadn't met their expectations. It was three days since His crucifixion and they tell how the women had found an empty tomb. Jesus responds by saying, how foolish you are that you are slow to believe all that the prophets have spoken about the Messiah. Their eyes were opened after Jesus sat at the table and broke bread with them.

On our journey to Bill's healing, we encountered the risen Christ. We saw evidence of His handiwork in Bill's life daily. Bill was blessed with heavenly encounters in dreams and visions the last few years of his life.

The Glory Road is a place where Jesus walks with me. There are times I am slow to understand the path and how the pieces fit together. I continue to learn more about Jesus. It is not only what I see with my eyes in the flesh, but what the Lord reveals in my spirit.

Lord, thank you that You are for us and not against us. You see the end from the beginning. Open our eyes to see what You would have us see. Jesus, please encourage us, instruct us, and break the chains that bind us. We love you. In Jesus' name we pray, amen.

Thank you for your persistent prayers.#Godisfaithful#TheGloryRoad

Day#384 May 8

 Anchor Verse: Luke 24:48
You are witnesses of these things. (NIV)

What is a witness? The Merriam-Webster dictionary defines witness as "attestation of a fact or event: testimony or one that gives evidence specifically: one who testifies in a cause or before a judicial tribunal."

Throughout the Bible, we read account after account of many miracles in the lives of ordinary people. From the events of the Old Testament, like the parting of the Red Sea when the Israelites walked through on dry ground to the many healing miracles that Jesus performed in the New Testament.

God still does miracles today in our lives and we are called to be witnesses of those miracles. We are to go and tell the story of what Jesus did for us.

On our journey to Bill's healing, we were blessed in so many ways to see God's hand at work. Not only the many times that Bill was healed miraculously, but even other things like finances, supplies we needed, people to help Bill, etc. All of those were places where we could bear witness to the power of God at work in our lives.

The Glory Road is also an opportunity to bear witness to God's mighty hand at work. The world is rather chaotic these days but as we shift our focus toward heaven and what God is doing, we can see amazing miracles.

When we see the good, the glorious, and God's hand at work in our lives, even what shouldn't have happened, happens. We are called to be "His witnesses" just as Jesus told His disciples to go into the world and tell His story, about the things He had done.

Lord, we praise and thank you for the gift of Jesus. We thank you for the opportunity to share with others what You have done in our lives. May we share our story for Your glory. Be honored and glorified in our lives, O Lord. In Jesus' name we pray, amen.

Thank you for your faithfulness.#Godisfaithful#TheGloryRoad

Day#385 May 9

 Anchor Verse: John 1:14
The Word became flesh and made his dwelling among us. We have seen his glory, the glory of the one and only Son, who came from the Father, full of grace and truth. (NIV)

In the beginning was the Word, and the Word was with God, and the Word was God. (John 1:1) And the Word was Jesus Christ, God's son, who came into the world, so that we might be saved.

God had a rescue plan from the creation of the world, a way for us to be brought back into fellowship – right relationship with God.

Our focus today is on verse 14, about Jesus becoming human like us and living here on earth. For some, this might be difficult to comprehend how the Son of God could come from heaven to earth, live as a man, and yet be the Savior of the world. That is where the gift of faith comes in, and revelation that comes from God, when we seek Him and the truth.

"The Word became flesh and made his dwelling among us. We have seen his glory, the glory of the one and only Son, who came from the Father, full of grace and truth." (John 1:14)

We have seen His glory – and now Jesus wants His glory to be seen in us.

On our journey to Bill's healing, one of our prayer warriors shared with me how both her and her husband prayed every night that the glory of the Lord would be released in them and that their minds would be sanctified – holy to the Lord. They prayed for Bill, and me. This is the key to how we become more like Jesus. That's what I want to do.

The Glory Road is the road where God's glory is seen in me. Jesus was full of grace and truth, and that is what we are called to be filled with too. On this path we walk, may our words and actions, and reactions, be filled with grace and truth. Lord, be honored and glorified in me.

Heavenly Father, thank you for the gift of Jesus, so that our relationship with You could be restored. May Your love, heavenly Father, flow in us, and through us, and around us, and out of us. May we live for Your glory. Let the beauty of Jesus be seen in me. In Jesus' name we pray, amen.

Thank you for loving me.#Godisfaithful#TheGloryRoad

Day#386 May 10

 Anchor Verse: John 1:41
He first looked for and found his own brother Simon and told him, "We have found the Messiah" (which translated means the Christ). (AMP)

When you have good news to share or have made an incredible discovery, who is the first person you tell?

Often it is those closest to you, and for many of us, it would be family members – a brother or sister.

John the Baptist announced the coming of the Messiah. He baptized Jesus with water, and the Spirit came down from heaven, and rested on Jesus. This was the beginning of Jesus' ministry.

A short time later, Jesus passes by the place where John and some of his disciples were sitting. John announces, "Look, the Lamb of God!" When two of his disciples heard this, they followed Jesus. They spent the day with Jesus. One of them was Andrew, Simon Peter's brother. In verse 41 it tells us, "He [Andrew] first looked for and found his own brother Simon and told him, "We have found the Messiah" (which translated means the Christ)."

Andrew went looking for his brother, it's the very first thing he did. Andrew didn't want Simon to miss out on this opportunity. In verse 42, it tells us, Andrew brought Simon to Jesus. Then Jesus upon meeting, Simon, looked at him and said, "You are Simon the son of John. You shall be called Cephas (which is translated Peter)."

On our journey to Bill's healing, we were blessed to share our story of what God was doing first with family and close friends, and then others. You can't keep it to yourself!

The Glory Road is a place of sharing about Jesus and His mighty miracles. Taking the opportunity weekly to share what Jesus is doing in my life so my family can hear and see, and be invited into that inner circle with Jesus. And I continue to find my new identity in Jesus. He calls me by name and I belong to Him. (Isaiah 43:1)

Lord, we will not keep the good news of Jesus to ourselves but share it with our brothers and sisters, those in our sphere of influence. Have Your way in us today. Lord, be glorified in all that we do and say, in Jesus' name, amen.

Thank you for your encouraging words.#Godisfaithful#TheGloryRoad

Day#387 May 11

 Anchor Verse: John 2:11
Jesus performed this miracle, the first of His signs, in Cana of Galilee. They did not know how this happened; but when the disciples and the servants witnessed this miracle, their faith blossomed. (VOICE)

Can you imagine being at a wedding which is a time of celebration and the refreshments run out? Poor planning on someone's part, or people were extremely thirsty on a hot day, or more people came than expected, we don't know the cause. We do know the solution~ Jesus.

Jesus' mother, Mary, sees Him as the solution. Jesus tells her that His "hour hasn't come." But just like a mom, she goes to the servants and prepares them, "Do whatever he tells you." Mary was confident Jesus had the solution, and knew He would act. Is that our posture today? It should be.

In John 2:11 it says, "Jesus performed this miracle, the first of His signs, in Cana of Galilee. They did not know how this happened; but when the disciples and the servants witnessed this miracle, their faith blossomed."

It was through this miracle that Jesus' own disciples believed Jesus was who He said He was, and their faith blossomed.

On our journey to Bill's healing, we were so blessed not only by the power of God's presence but to see His miracles. Healing that happened without explanation. Praise the Lord for the reality of miracles.

The Glory Road is also a path filled with miracles, not only in my life but in the lives of others. There are places in the road where there are no human solutions. Mountains are just opportunities for the mighty power of God to move and for His children to praise and worship Him.

Today you might be standing at the foot of a mountain, at the bedside of a loved one, looking at the empty chair where your loved one should be, and you are discouraged, because your eyes can't see the solution.

God, thank you for calling us to look higher. May we look to the hills where our help comes from, it comes in the name of the Lord, Maker of heaven and earth. We have victory in Jesus' name, today, and tomorrow, and every day of our life. Stand and see the deliverance of the Lord. Hallelujah, amen.

Thank you for your perseverance.#Godisfaithful#TheGloryRoad

Day#388 May 12

 Anchor Verse: Psalm 19:7
The law of the Lord is perfect (flawless), restoring and refreshing the soul; The statutes of the Lord are reliable and trustworthy, making wise the simple. (AMP)

There is nothing flawless in this world – I'm not flawless, you're not flawless.

Psalm 19:7 is a powerful verse, "The law of the Lord is perfect (flawless), restoring and refreshing the soul; The statutes of the Lord are reliable and trustworthy, making wise the simple."

In the English language, we use descriptive words (adjectives) to amplify the message we are trying to convey.

Psalm 19:7 uses the words: restoring, refreshing, reliable and trustworthy. This is God's heart for us this morning. Soak it in.

The law of the Lord is perfect and what does it do? It restores and refreshes our soul ~ it's a continuous process for all of our lives. It's not a "pill" you take once and you're done. Instead, it's new life and breath that comes every moment of every day. Thank you, Lord.

The statutes of the Lord are reliable and trustworthy – just like the strong foundation of a house and the sturdy walls and supports that hold it up. And the purpose of the statutes is to make even the simple, wise.

On our journey to Bill's healing, God came to us in new ways. He opened our eyes to see things we had never seen before. We heard God's voice and chose to walk in His way. Daily, our souls were restored and refreshed. And yes, God continued to make us wiser as we listened and obeyed.

The Glory Road is a place where the Word of God is mighty and powerful. It is my compass and my blueprint for living. It is a path of learning, and unlearning. It is a path of receiving and releasing. It is God's path to glory not only for me, and for you. Lord, have Your way in me.

Lord, thank you for the gift of this new day. Your Word is alive and full of power. Thank you for new revelation. We are not alone on this journey called life. You will never leave us or forsake us. This is the day the Lord has made and we will rejoice and be GLAD in it. In Jesus' name, Amen.

Thank you for your faithfulness.#Godisfaithful#TheGloryRoad

Day#389 May 13

 Anchor Verse: 2 Kings 17:14

But Israel wouldn't listen. The people were as stubborn as their ancestors and refused to believe in the Lord their God. (TLB)

When we use the word "stubborn", what picture comes to your mind? Is it a person or an animal? We often think about donkeys being stubborn. Each one of us has times in our lives when we are stubborn and obstinate.

Another word (synonym) that is used in this passage is "stiff-necked" which is not a common word used today. The Jews were used to the ox as a familiar useful domestic animal to plow the land.

They used a team of oxen and had an "ox-goad" to prod them along when they were moving too slow or to keep them on course. If an ox was hard to control, and wanted to deviate off the path, it was called "hard of neck" – stiff-necked, because it wouldn't respond to his master's correction.

In 2 Kings 17, God's people – the people of Israel are like these oxen. "But Israel wouldn't listen. The people were as stubborn as their ancestors and refused to believe in the Lord their God."

They were stubborn, prideful, and instead chose their own way rather than walking in the path that God had for them. God's people refused to believe in the Lord their God and they were punished accordingly.

On our journey to Bill's healing, we encountered some people who were stiff-necked, stubborn, and walking in darkness rather than the light of God's love. God often used Bill, even in the midst of his illness, to be a light for Him. Many times, Bill's words filled with love and grace gave hope and joy to those God put in his path.

The Glory Road has its own oxen blocking the path because of their stubbornness. God calls us to respond in love. The Holy Spirit is God's "ox-goad" relentlessly pursuing them and inviting them to fellowship with Him.

Lord, we thank you for the gift of Your love. You loved us before we even knew You. You love us, even when we are stubborn, and stiff-necked. Soften our hearts. May the oil of joy flow over the dry, cracked places in our souls so we can better love You and each other. Lord, we love you and praise you this morning in Jesus' name, amen.

Thank you for your encouragement.#Godisfaithful#TheGloryRoad

Day#390 May 14

 Anchor Verse: Job 3:26
I have no peace, no quietness; I have no rest, but only turmoil. (NIV)

Job was a man who knew the highs and lows of life.

Job is tested. All his children die, his livestock are stolen, and his servants killed. Job lost it all. Yet in verse 20 Job's response is, "The Lord gave and the Lord has taken away; may the name of the Lord be praised."

Job gets to a low point in his life. Here in chapter 3, Job makes a speech, and he expresses the anguish of his soul. In verse 26 it says, "I have no peace, no quietness; I have no rest, but only turmoil."

Maybe you have been in that place yourself, maybe you are there today. There is trouble to your left, trouble to your right.

God is there. He not only exists in the eye of the storm, but your heavenly Father will shelter you in the storm. Seek shelter in His peace.

"The Lord gives strength to his people; the Lord blesses his people with peace." (Psalm 29:11)

On our journey to Bill's healing, we encountered many storms ~ not only health storms, but life storms. There were places in the road where the enemy came with all he had to steal our peace, yet we chose to rest in the arms of the Prince of Peace.

The Glory Road is a place of storms. Sometimes they come suddenly, without warning. At other times, you can see them forming on the horizon. In either case, my peace is anchored on the solid rock of Jesus Christ. When the wind and the waves of life are so intense, no matter how much water is pouring into my boat (life), I know the captain of my ship will get me to a safe harbor, if I just hold on.

Lord, we praise you for Your faithfulness. We are so grateful that no storm is bigger than You are. We rest in Your faithfulness. Praise the Lord, You are our peace. Our power, our hope, and our joy come and remain when we abide in You. We love you and praise you in Jesus' mighty name, amen.

Thank you for your persistent prayers.#Godisfaithful#TheGloryRoad

Day#391 May 15

 Anchor Verse: John 4:50
Then Jesus told him, "Go back home. Your son is healed!" And the man believed Jesus and started home. (TLB)

Throughout Jesus' journey on earth, He not only shared the good news with people, but many were healed.

In John 4, we read the story of a man, a royal official whose son lay sick in Capernaum. (Jesus was in Cana a little over 16 miles away.) The man went to Jesus and "begged" him to come and heal his son, who was dying.

Jesus commented that unless people saw signs and wonders, they wouldn't believe. That is why many were drawn to Jesus, is it the same for us today?

The man was not distracted from his mission. Again, he said to Jesus, "Sir, come down before my child dies." In verse 50 Jesus replies, "'Go back home. Your son is healed!' And the man believed Jesus and started home."

The man did not hesitate. He didn't say, "The only way my son will be healed is if you come to my house." The royal official believed Jesus, and took action. On his way home, his servants met him, and they told him his son was alive. He inquired of the time, and it was at the exact moment Jesus said, "Your son is healed."

On our journey to Bill's healing, we learned to trust the word of God. Not only the words spoken in the Bible, but the specific words, direction, and truth that God spoke to us individually. There is healing when God speaks. His words are full of life and power.

The Glory Road is filled with encounters with those who believe in Jesus and those who do not know Him as Savior, Lord, and Friend. When we bring our cares to the feet of Jesus, we must come in faith, even if it is faith the size of a mustard seed. By choosing to believe, we activate God's power, plans, and purpose in our lives.

Lord, there is nothing too hard for You, absolutely nothing. We run to the throne room of grace and fall on our knees before You. We sing praises to Your name and worship You as King of kings and Lord of lords. Boldly, we approach Your throne to find help in our time of need. We believe and we receive the gifts from Your hands. In Jesus' name we pray, amen.

Thank you for believing in miracles.#Godisfaithful#TheGloryRoad

Day#392 May 16

 Anchor Verse: John 5:3
Hundreds of sick people were lying under the covered porches—the paralyzed, the blind, and the crippled—all of them waiting for their healing. (TPT)

Sickness is not new to the 21st century. Today, we may be battling some illnesses and viruses we have not seen previously, but people have been in search of healing for centuries.

In Jesus' time, there was a place where those who had various conditions gathered. It was called Bethesda ~ translated house of mercy or house of grace. In some manuscripts, it was said that from time to time an angel of the Lord would come down and stir the waters. The first one into the pool after each disturbance was completely healed.

"Hundreds of sick people were lying under the covered porches—the paralyzed, the blind, and the crippled—all of them waiting for their healing."

Jesus hearing of this place decided to stop by for a visit. Of all the people lying there, Jesus approaches a man who had been an invalid for thirty-eight years. Jesus just had one question, "Do you want to get well?" The man responds to Jesus that he can't get into the water fast enough to be healed, no one is there to help him.

The man only knows one way to be healed, but Jesus knows the man is face to face with the Healer Himself.

At Jesus' word, "Get up! Pick up your mat and walk" …the man is healed!

On our journey to Bill's healing, Bill met Jesus the Healer too. And in that encounter, Bill's miraculous healings were testimony to God's power today.

The Glory Road is a place where the Healer still walks today. Not only in my life, but in the lives of others, we hear testimonies of His healing power. Many who have been burdened for years find comfort, solace, and healing in the presence of Jesus. The Bible says by His stripes we are healed.

God, You are our healer, Jehovah Rapha. In Your kingdom, delay is not denial. We pray for those who have become weary in the wait. Lord, may today be the day of their healing ~ body, mind and spirit. Let us rejoice in the God of our salvation. In Jesus' name we pray, amen.

Thank you for believing in miracles.#Godisfaithful#TheGloryRoad

Day#393 May 17

 Anchor Verse: Habakkuk 3:18
Yet I will [choose to] rejoice in the Lord; I will [choose to] shout in exultation in the [victorious] God of my salvation! (AMP)

Life is about choices – every moment of every day. We choose to be happy or sad. We choose to see the cup as half full or half empty. We choose to make good choices or poor choices.

When you choose to rejoice in the valleys because you remember God's goodness and faithfulness and love, it is even sweeter. Your songs of praise have an added anointing, that pierce the darkness that surrounds you.

Habakkuk 3:18 speaks of this powerful position, "Yet I will [choose to] rejoice in the Lord; I will [choose to] shout in exultation in the [victorious] God of my salvation!"

"Yet" is a powerful word with only three letters. It means in spite of everything that was spoken ahead of this statement, we choose to rejoice in the Lord and shout in exultation in the victorious God of our salvation.

These are the circumstances that are highlighted in Habakkuk 3:17. "Though the fig tree does not blossom and there is no fruit on the vines, though the yield of the olive fails and the fields produce no food, though the flock is cut off from the fold and there are no cattle in the stalls…"

On our journey to Bill's healing, God gave us a choice, every moment of the day and night. We could choose to praise Him in the storm or allow the rain to flood our boat and sink us. We chose joy and to rejoice in our salvation.

The Glory Road meanders through land that is often troubled. There are fewer still waters and green pastures (like those mentioned in Psalm 23) and more battlegrounds and rough waters. Yet…I will trust Him no matter what my earthly eyes see. I choose to put my hand in the hand of Jesus who not only stills the stormy waters, but His nail-scarred hands remind me that through Calvary, I am victorious in Jesus' name.

Lord, thank you for the gift of Your powerful words through the Bible. We praise you in the middle of the storm. You do all things well. God, You hold our lives in Your hands, and we are grateful. May Your praises never leave our lips. In Jesus' name, we pray, amen.

Thank you for being my companion.#Godisfaithful#TheGloryRoad

Day#394 May 18

 Anchor Verse: John 6:12

When the people had eaten their fill, he said to his disciples, "Gather the leftovers so nothing is wasted." They went to work and filled twelve large baskets with leftovers from the five barley loaves. (MSG)

Stewarding the miracle… that's our call. In God's Kingdom, nothing is ever wasted. Even these leftovers after a big feast had a purpose.

Wherever Jesus went, people followed Him. In John 6, Jesus took His disciples up on a mountainside, as He often did. This is where the disciples got more "schooling" ~ private tutoring on the things of the Kingdom that they would need to fulfill their commission.

The crowds continued to come. As Jesus looked up and saw the people coming, He said to Philip, "Where shall we buy bread for all these people to eat?" (Jesus had an idea in mind but wanted to see how His disciples would respond.) Philip responded in a practical way. "We don't have enough money to buy food for all these people; it would take more than a half year's wages to feed them."

Andrew spoke up and told Jesus of the little boy who had five small barley loaves and two small fish. It didn't seem like enough to feed all the people but Jesus had a plan. After all the people sat down, the disciples distributed the food until all were fed. Then in John 6:12 it says, "When the people had eaten their fill, he said to his disciples, 'Gather the leftovers so nothing is wasted.' They went to work and filled twelve large baskets with leftovers from the five barley loaves."

On our journey to Bill's healing, we learned a lot about God's economy. God's provision for us in every area of our lives, was not just adequate, it was abundant. No matter the need, God had more than enough for us.

The Glory Road is a place of signs, wonders, and miracles. It starts from the heart of God, a place of overflowing abundance. What we might consider "leftovers" in the flesh, God sees as seeds for the next miracle.

Lord, may we be good stewards of not only the physical resources God has given us, but our spiritual heritage. God wants to use our gifts, talents, resources to be the seed for a miracle in the lives of others. We love you, Lord, and praise you in Jesus' name, amen.

Thank you for being good stewards.#Godisfaithful#TheGloryRoad

Day#395 May 19

 Anchor Verse: 1 Chronicles 9:27
They would spend the night stationed around the house of God, because they had to guard it; and they had charge of the key for opening it each morning. (NIV)

Each of us has an assignment, a place we are called to serve, a place where we are gifted to serve.

1 Chronicles 9 talks about those chosen to be gatekeepers. They were in charge of guarding the gates of the house of the Lord. There were 212 of them and four principal gatekeepers were Levites, entrusted with the responsibility for the rooms and treasuries in the house of the Lord.

In verse 27 it tells us what they did, "They would spend the night stationed around the house of God, because they had to guard it; and they had charge of the key for opening it each morning." They had the night watch.

As believers in the 21st century, Jesus is the key that opens the door to the Kingdom of God. Jesus opens the door to the untold, unimaginable blessings that God has for His children. We just need to say "yes" to Him.

On our journey to Bill's healing, we learned a lot about those who had the night watch, and those who opened up the day, the morning routine (especially those who came for a blood draw in the pre-dawn hours.) But greater than what we saw in the flesh, was the Spirit of God at work throughout the night, and day. He opened doors that no man could shut, and closed doors that no man could open.

The Glory Road is filled with God's gatekeepers. Not only those in positions of authority in our churches but we, you and me, are given a place to stand watch. In those places, we not only guard the blessing, wisdom, and potential God has given to us, but in our hands, we hold the key to unlock the door that has held many captive to old thoughts, old ways, old lies.

Heavenly Father, thank you for the gift of Jesus Christ. In Him, we can experience freedom. Your steadfast love never changes ~ day or night, You are faithful. May we walk in that new freedom, in Jesus' name, amen.

Thank you for persevering.#Godisfaithful#TheGloryRoad

Day#396 May 20

 Anchor Verse: John 6:68
Simon Peter answered, "Lord, to whom shall we go? You [alone] have the words of eternal life [you are our only hope]." (AMP)

Where do you look for answers to life's questions? Do you turn to human sources – people, the internet, Google, or do you turn to God? The source of your wisdom will determine the path of your life.

When Jesus walked the earth, many were drawn to the signs, miracles, and wonders that He performed.

Not everyone would be a faithful follower. They would come to a place in the road when the glamor faded and the hard work of being a believer would begin. It wouldn't always be fun and filled with miracles, there would be persecution as well.

Jesus knew many followers had walked away. In verse 66 it says, "'You do not want to leave too, do you?' Jesus asked the Twelve." Peter replies, "Lord, to whom shall we go? You [alone] have the words of eternal life [you are our only hope]." (John 6:68)

On our journey to Bill's healing, we were quickly reminded that Jesus was Bill's only hope, my only hope. Jesus is the bread of life, not just bread to feed our physical bodies but also our souls. Our hope is fixed on Jesus, the Solid Rock on which we stand, He is unshakeable.

The Glory Road is a place where many are turning away from Jesus, their only true hope. While walking through this pandemic season, many have turned their eyes away from heaven to the things of this world, the chaos and confusion, and been filled with darkness. Our help (and hope) comes from the Lord, the Maker of heaven and earth. (Psalm 121:2)

Lord, I pray for those who are lost, those who have wandered off the path and are stuck in the weeds, the muck and mire of life. Thank you, Holy Spirit, You are there to speak life, hope, and wisdom to them. Thank you, Jesus, the Good Shepherd who is willing to leave the 99 behind to pursue the one sheep that is lost. Bring the wandering ones back home. You are our only hope. In Jesus' name we pray, amen.

Thank you for your faithfulness.#Godisfaithful#TheGloryRoad

Day#397 May 21

 Anchor Verse: Psalm 107:13-14
Then they cried to the Lord in their troubles, and he rescued them! He led them from the darkness and shadow of death and snapped their chains. (TLB)

This psalm starts out by reminding us to give thanks to the Lord for He is good; His love endures forever. These should be the first words out of our mouth in the morning, "Thank you, Lord. I praise you, Lord!"

There is a vivid word picture painted in verses 13-14, "Then they cried to the Lord in their troubles, and he rescued them! He led them from the darkness and shadow of death and snapped their chains."

This is the story of the redeemed – this is the story of the children of God – you and me. When we cry out to Him in our troubles, God not only rescues us, but leads us out of darkness and the shadow of death. And then ~ He snaps the chains that have held us back from ALL that God has for us.

On our journey to Bill's healing, God rescued us many times. Our "boat" was being tossed around on the sea of life ~ in the storm of health issues. God rescued Bill and took him from a place of darkness into the light of God's love. Bill found healing there in every area of his life.

The Glory Road is a beautiful picture of God rescuing me and so many others within my view. That's the cool thing about God. His love is so abundant, His heart is so big, that God wants to rescue each one of us and pull us into His arms of love and shelter us there.

Hear God's words, "I love you, My child. Come to Me, and you will find peace. Come to Me, and you will find the strength you need to take the next step. Come to Me, and my love will heal the broken places in your heart and in your life. Come to Me, and receive My rest. I am enough. You are enough when you partner with Me. Today is your day of freedom as I snap the chains that bind you." Amen.

Thank you for persevering.#Godisfaithful#TheGloryRoad

Day#398 May 22

 Anchor Verse: John 7:16
So Jesus told them, "My message is not my own; it comes from God who sent me." (NLT)

People become experts in their field often through long years of study under teachers who have also invested years in research.

"Students are not greater than their teacher. But the student who is fully trained will become like the teacher." (NLT) (Luke 6:40)

John 7 says it was time for the Jewish Festival of Tabernacles. Jesus' brothers urged Jesus to go so Jesus' disciples might see His work. "No one who wants to become a public figure does so in secret." They didn't understand or believe Jesus was the Messiah. His time hadn't come yet.

Halfway through the Festival, a week-long celebration, Jesus goes into the temple courts to teach. The Jews were amazed at His teaching. "How did this man get such learning without having been taught?" (John 7:15 NIV)

Jesus points them to the source of His wisdom, of the things being taught. "My message is not my own; it comes from God who sent me." (John 7:16)

Where does our wisdom come from today?

On our journey to Bill's healing, we learned how to separate words spoken from a person's own heart and experience and those which were the truth of God. When we ask for wisdom, God will provide. When we believe we are great in our own eyes, great will be the fall.

The Glory Road is a place of learning and teaching. Bill and I were commissioned by the Lord Himself to tell our story for His glory. It's not for our glory, or my glory, I share what we learned in our walk with God through difficult places. The only truth worth sharing and repeating is the truth of God. I will forever be a student in His classroom.

Lord, we seek to do Your will, Your way. We recognize all our wisdom comes from You, and You alone. May we not boast about what we know, but just like Jesus may we humbly share the message from God who sends us into a world of darkness. May we be the light which draws others to You. We love you and praise you, in Jesus' name we pray, amen.

Thank you for your faithfulness.#Godisfaithful#TheGloryRoad

Day#399 May 23

 Anchor Verse: Psalm 107:31
Let them give thanks to the Lord for his unfailing love and his wonderful deeds for mankind. (NIV)

A heart filled with thanksgiving is a heart that has no room for selfish endeavors. A heart filled with gratitude for what the Lord has done looks toward heaven with arms held high and sings glory to God's name.

Earlier this week we looked a passage from Psalm 107, and were reminded this psalm tells the story of the redeemed. The redeemed are those God has delivered from the hand of the enemy.

"Let them give thanks to the Lord for his unfailing love and his wonderful deeds for mankind." (Psalm 107:31)

We are to celebrate God's unfailing love and recount His wonderful deeds for mankind. What are the wonderful deeds the Lord done for you in your lifetime? Tell us the story of God's unfailing love in your life.

On our journey to Bill's healing, God was so good to us. His love grew stronger with every day. Day or night, His arms of comfort and courage surrounded us. The many ways God touched our lives will fill many books.

The Glory Road is a place of remembrance and rejoicing. During a season of loss, the enemy of our souls would have us believe we are all alone. Our loss is so great, joy is far away. That's not what God says. God promises that He will never leave us or forsake us.

Today is Pentecost Sunday 2021, the day the Holy Spirit came, the Comforter Jesus promised. They were given power to go tell their story. Out of their obedience, you and I heard the good news of Jesus, and made the decision to become part of the family of God.

Lord, thank you for Your unfailing love. You have saved us from destruction without our knowledge and kept our feet on solid ground. With grateful hearts, we bow to the King of kings and the Lord of lords. We rededicate our lives to You. We love you and praise you, in Jesus' name, amen.

Thank you for your persistent prayers.#Godisfaithful#TheGloryRoad

Day#400 May 24

 Anchor Verse: 1 Chronicles 22:19
Now devote your heart and soul to seeking the Lord your God. (NIV)

There are times and seasons in our lives when God has a specific task for us. When we put God first, everything else falls into place. It's God's math and it works every time.

In 1 Chronicles 22, we read of King David and his desire to build the house of the Lord. David started bringing together resources and skilled craftsmen.

Since David was a man of war and much blood was shed during his reign as king, God determined Solomon, David's son, would build the house to honor God. Solomon means peace.

In verse 19, David is addressing the leaders of Israel, and reminding them God is with them. He commissions them with these words, "Now devote your heart and soul to seeking the Lord your God." They would only find success as they devoted their hearts and souls to seeking God.

On our journey to Bill's healing, in the midst of the storm, God called both of us to devote our heart and soul to seeking Him. It was only when our eyes were fixed on heaven this peace like a river filled our souls.

The Glory Road is a path with a purpose. Its purpose is not what Barb Hollace wants for her life ~ it is what God's plans are for her. Sometimes they are different. In every case, I would gladly lay down my plans for His plans. He knows the way that I take, the best way.

It has been 400 days since God took Bill home to heaven, and sometimes it feels like it was just yesterday. This one thing I know, God will never leave me or forsake me, never! In I Chronicles 22:13, we hear David encourage Solomon with these words, "Be strong and courageous. Do not be afraid or discouraged." These words are also meant for us today just as they were spoken to Joshua in Joshua 1:9 as he began to follow a new path.

Lord, we thank you Your plans for us are always good. You delight in seeing your children grow up and step into all You have for them. Our heart's desire is to know You more and walk in ALL You have for us. Lord, we surrender all this morning – our successes, our failures, our hopes and dreams. We live for Your glory. In Jesus' name we pray, amen.

Thank you for your faithful prayers. Today I have an MRI to check on the tumor's shrinkage. Believing for the miracle God has in mind. Thanks for standing with me.#Godisfaithful#TheGloryRoad

Day#401 May 25

 Anchor Verse: John 9:5
As long as I am with you my life is the light that pierces the world's darkness.
(TPT)

Light and darkness are two guarantees that happen every day. At creation, the light God called day and the darkness He called night.

When Jesus came into the world, He said to the people, "I am the Light of the world. So if you follow me, you won't be stumbling through the darkness, for living light will flood your path." (John 8:12)

In John 9, Jesus encountered a man blind from birth. Jesus' disciples asked, "Rabbi, who sinned, this man or his parents, that he was born blind?" Isn't it interesting Jesus' own disciples associated this health problem with sin.

Are we guilty of doing the same today?

Jesus sets the record straight, "Neither this man nor his parents sinned," said Jesus, "but this happened so that the works of God (God's power) might be displayed in him."

"As long as it is day, we must do the works of him who sent me. Night is coming, when no one can work. As long as I am with you my life is the light that pierces the world's darkness." (John 9:4-5 NIV)

On our journey to Bill's healing, we were surrounded by God's army of angels and found comfort in the words of Jesus and the arms of our heavenly Father. What looked bleak in the eyes of the world was turned into something beautiful.

The Glory Road is a place where darkness and light often collide. Just as a lightning strike lights up the darkness, and it looks like noonday. Jesus, the light of the world, is a 24/7, 365 days a year kind of light. It never grows dim; it gets stronger the more we know Him.

This account of the blind man being healed was one of the first stories/promises God brought to mind after my cancer diagnosis. This illness came so the glory of God could be seen in my life. That's what has happened, and will continue until my healing is completely manifested.

Lord, we thank you that You sent Jesus into the world to light up the darkness. We thank you for that light shining into every situation we face today. You are great and greatly to be praised. In Jesus' name we pray, amen.

Thank you for your faithful prayers.#Godisfaithful#TheGloryRoad

Day#402 May 26

 Anchor Verse: 1 Chronicles 29:17
I know, my God, that you examine our hearts and rejoice when you find integrity there. (NLT)

What is the meaning of the word "integrity"? The Cambridge English Dictionary defines it as "the quality of being honest and having strong moral principles that you refuse to change."

This is the mirror we can hold up daily to examine our lives and our actions.

In 1 Chronicles 29, King David is speaking, praying, and praising the Lord for what He has done. Solomon, King David's son, is now on the throne and it is Solomon who will build the new temple for the Lord.

"Lord our God, all this abundance that we have provided for building you a temple for your Holy Name comes from your hand and all of it belongs to you." (1 Chronicles 29:16)

David goes on to say in verse 17, "I know, my God, that you examine our hearts and rejoice when you find integrity there."

Is your heart filled with integrity ~ the quality of being honest and having strong moral principles that you refuse to change?

On our journey to Bill's healing, we re-discovered the truth about integrity. It is good to examine what's in your own heart but also to weigh the actions of others against this standard. God rewards those who walk uprightly and are filled with integrity. God rewards our faithfulness.

The Glory Road is filled with people whose motives aren't always good. Not everyone walking on this planet is a person of integrity. We need wisdom to navigate those places of interaction. Most of all, we are called to pray for those who act with a heart of deception.

Thank you, Lord, for the gift of Your love, peace, power, and multiplied blessings. We pray for those who walk in the darkness of lies and deception. May the sunshine of Your love penetrate those dark places. Thank you, Lord, all are welcome at Your table. May You be honored and glorified in our lives, in Jesus' name, we pray, amen.

Thank you for your prayers.#Godisfaithful#TheGloryRoad

Day#403 May 27

 Anchor Verse: John 10:11
I am the Good Shepherd. The Good Shepherd puts the sheep before himself, sacrifices himself if necessary. (MSG)

Sheep and shepherds were common in the days of Jesus.

Jesus is that Good Shepherd and He puts us, His sheep, before Himself. The Son of God sacrificed His own life at Calvary so we might live.

In the earlier verses, we read sheep will only listen to the voice of their shepherd and follow him. They will not follow a stranger ~ they will run away because they don't recognize his voice.

As believers, followers of Jesus, we know His voice and follow where He leads us. Psalm 23 is a beautiful psalm describing the Good Shepherd. Psalm 23:1 says, "The Lord is my shepherd, I lack nothing." Jesus cares for us, refreshes us, and defends us against our enemies. Do you know Jesus as the Good Shepherd?

"A hired man is not a real shepherd. The sheep mean nothing to him. He sees a wolf come and runs for it, leaving the sheep to be ravaged and scattered by the wolf. He's only in it for the money. The sheep don't matter to him." (John 10:12-13 MSG)

I am so grateful that Jesus does not run at the sign of danger, but instead draws us closer to defend us.

On our journey to Bill's healing, we were guided by the Good Shepherd wherever we went. Jesus was there to fiercely defend Bill and to lay down His own life for him. There were many times Jesus carried Bill when he was too worn out from the battle to walk alone.

The Glory Road is a place where Jesus, the Good Shepherd guides and protects me. When I sleep at night, I know Jesus is watching over me and will defend me from the wiles and strategies of the enemy. By day, I am blessed to listen to His voice. I have no fear when Jesus walks with me.

God, thank you for the gift of Jesus who willingly laid down His life for us. Thank you, Jesus, when danger comes, You rise up to defend us and neutralize the enemy who comes to steal, kill, and destroy. Your gentle voice comforts us in the midst of the storm. We praise you, in Jesus' name, amen.

Thank you for your faithful prayers.#Godisfaithful#TheGloryRoad

Day#404 May 28

 Anchor Verse: 2 Chronicles 6:19
Then hear their prayers and their petitions from heaven where you live, and uphold their cause. Forgive your people who have sinned against you. (NLT)

Are you an intercessor, someone who prays for others?

In 2 Chronicles 6, we hear (read) the words of King Solomon's prayer of dedication, as he prays to God on behalf of the people God has called him to lead. Solomon's prayer also includes the needs of foreigners asking God to touch their lives too.

Solomon's prayer is not just about God's faithfulness in generations past, but also God's work in their lives in the present and going into the future.

It is powerful to hear the prayers of the leader of a nation on behalf of his people. We don't often see that in public today.

In Solomon's prayer, as he speaks to God, he basically says, I know these people will sin against you, because there is no one who doesn't sin, and You will get angry, God, and turn them over to their enemies. But if they have a change of heart, and turn back to You with their heart and soul and cry out to You, please hear their prayers.

"Then hear their prayers and their petitions from heaven where you live [your dwelling place], and uphold their cause. Forgive your people who have sinned against you." (2 Chronicles 6:19)

On our journey to Bill's healing, the power of our prayers was magnified. Your prayers mixed with our prayers went up to heaven as a beautiful aroma and God heard us and His favor rested upon us. God has a heart of compassion and is filled with forgiveness and grace.

The Glory Road is a place of prayer. I'm so grateful for God's daily presence and the ability to reach out to Him in prayer, with your needs and mine. God is not a faraway God; He is as close as our next breath.

Lord, this morning we pray heaven would touch earth as we cry out to You. We pray for healing miracles, for souls to be set free, and restoration in families. Lord, do what only You can do and we will give You ALL the honor and the glory. In Jesus' name we pray, amen.

Thank you for your persistent prayers.#Godisfaithful#TheGloryRoad

Day#405 May 29

 Anchor Verse: 2 Chronicles 7:15
My eyes will be open and my ears attentive to every prayer made in this place.
(NLT)

"In my trouble I cried to the Lord, and He answered me." (Psalm 120:1 AMP) We have all been there, in those places where God was our only hope. God needed to rescue us or we were lost, done, finished.

God loves us so much He is not deaf to our cries; they move His heart. God listens attentively to His children and then is moved to action.

In 2 Chronicles 7, as we continue to read about the dedication of the temple, in verse 12, we read that the Lord appeared to Solomon with a message.

We read that often-quoted verse, 2 Chronicles 7:14, reminding us that even in our most desperate circumstances (including a pandemic) God says, "If my people, who are called by my name, will humble themselves and pray and seek my face and turn from their wicked ways, then I will hear from heaven, and I will forgive their sin and will heal their land."

We often stop reading here but 2 Chronicles 7:15 says, "My eyes will be open and my ears attentive to every prayer made in this place."

On our journey to Bill's healing, God's eyes were on us and His ears were attentive to our cries – in church, ICU, our home – even in the grocery store or Panera. God loved Bill so much He was as attentive to Bill's needs as a mom is to her newborn baby. Every move Bill made God knew about.

The Glory Road is watched over by El Roi, the God who sees. My heavenly Father is attentive to every detail of my life's journey. He hears every conversation that I have with Him or with others. God delights to be part of my victory celebrations and walk with me through the fire of adversity.

Lord, we praise you because You are near to the broken-hearted and save those who are crushed in spirit. You rejoice with those who rejoice and mourn with those who mourn. We surrender all to You, and ask for Your blessing upon our path and all those we love, in Jesus' name we pray, amen.

Thank you for being my companion.#Godisfaithful#TheGloryRoad

Day#406 May 30

 Anchor Verse: Acts 3:6-7

Then Peter said, "Silver or gold I do not have, but what I do have I give you. In the name of Jesus Christ of Nazareth, walk." Taking him by the right hand, he helped him up, and instantly the man's feet and ankles became strong. (NIV)

The New Testament is filled with stories of people who had been sick or had a disability for a long time. People who must have been discouraged.

In Acts 3, we read the story of Peter and John who are going to the temple to pray at three in the afternoon. They encounter a man who had been lame since birth, he couldn't walk. In fact, the man was being carried to the temple to beg, because that's how he got money to meet his needs.

When he sees Peter and John, he asked them for financial help, just like he did with everyone else. This time, the man received an unexpected answer.

"Then Peter said, "Silver or gold I do not have, but what I do have I give you. In the name of Jesus Christ of Nazareth, walk." (Acts 3:6)

Peter tells the man he won't give him money, but instead he has the power through Jesus to heal him. There are action steps put to Peter's words, "Taking him by the right hand, he helped him up, and instantly the man's feet and ankles became strong."

What God has given us ~ our gifts and talents, both natural gifts and supernatural gifts are to be shared with others.

On our journey to Bill's healing, Bill encountered Jesus in a mighty way. Miracles happened! You saw them with your own eyes. God gave both of us the gift of faith to share with others, the gift of encouragement. We are called to mobilize it and use it for God's kingdom and His glory.

The Glory Road is a place of miracles against the backdrop of the darkness of this world. There is no mountain too high God cannot move it. There is no valley too deep He cannot fill it with His love and power. There is no desert too hot and dry God cannot water it with His healing rain.

Thank you, Lord, You are the God of miracles. Thank you for the invitation to open our hands and hearts to be used by You. We are willing to be all You want us to be. In Jesus' name we pray, amen.

Thank you for believing in miracles.#Godisfaithful#TheGloryRoad

Day#407 May 31

 Anchor Verse: Psalm 108:4
For great is your love, higher than the heavens; your faithfulness reaches to the skies. (NIV)

There are not enough words in the English language to describe the love and faithfulness of God. Even if we combined all the languages in the world, they would fall short of describing the One who created us and loves us.

King David wrote many of the psalms we still read today. As you read the book of Psalms, you read psalms that describe both joys and sorrows. Most of all, they give praise and honor and glory to God throughout David's life.

David is committed to praising and worshiping the Lord, not only in private, but among all the nations. He delights to share his relationship with God and tell of God's mighty deeds and His lovingkindness.

Psalm 108:4 says, "For great is your love, higher than the heavens; your faithfulness reaches to the skies." The same is true today. Lord, Your love is higher than the heavens and Your faithfulness reaches the skies… and more.

On our journey to Bill's healing, God's love and faithfulness were not just traits we read about in the Bible, but they were real to us in our own lives. We experience love from family and friends, but it pales in comparison to God's love. Truly it is beyond description and such a precious gift.

The Glory Road is a place saturated with God's love and faithfulness. It often brings me to tears, tears of gratitude and thanksgiving. God loves me – as I am, with my faults and failures. He rejoices in my victories and carries me over the rough places in the road.

What about you? Can you describe the magnitude of His love and grace, His power and His peace? There is nothing that can compare to the sweetness of His presence. Great is the Lord and worthy of our praise.

Lord, we praise and thank you this morning for who You are, Lord God Almighty, maker of heaven and earth, and our heavenly Father, who loves us with an everlasting love. Nothing in my hands I bring, simply to the cross I cling. Thank you for loving us so well, we dedicate our lives to loving You today and every day of our lives. In Jesus' name, we pray, amen.

Thank you for your faithfulness.#Godisfaithful#TheGloryRoad

June 2021

May the God of hope fill you will all joy and peace as you trust in him. So that you may overflow with hope by the power of the Holy Spirit.

~ Romans 15:13 ~

Day#408 June 1

 Anchor Verse: John 12:43
For they loved the praise of men more than the praise of God. (NKJV)

Who is the audience you play to every day? Who is it you live to please or to hear their praise?

There are some lessons we learn quickly in life and others that take us a lifetime to master. One of those lessons is~ whose approval do we seek?

The answer may roll off your tongue or it may take a moment of silent reflection. But truly, it is an important question to ask yourself.

In John 12, we read that many of the leaders of Jesus' day believed in Him, but because of the Pharisees they would not openly acknowledge their faith for fear they would be put out of the synagogue. John 12:43 says, "For they loved the praise of men more than the praise of God." Are we doing the same thing today?

On our journey to Bill's healing, Bill was surrounded by a team of many people who helped him recover from his many physical challenges. His "performance" or "progress" was measured in their eyes. But the only praise worth hearing was the praise of his heavenly Father as he navigated life's path to healing and restoration.

The Glory Road is filled with many voices – those crying out for my attention. The voice I long to hear is the voice of my heavenly Father and His praise, and the voice of the Holy Spirit directing my steps on this path to life. Jesus walked this earth and leaned in to hear the voice of God, who directed His path. Shouldn't we do the same? Listen for the praise of heaven.

Today as you go through the day, be aware of your actions. Are you doing them to seek the praises of men or the praise of your Father in heaven?

Lord, thank you for a heart check this morning. You come not to condemn us or criticize us but to lift us up, and encourage us so we might be more like You. May we reflect Your honor and glory, in Jesus' name, amen.

Be blessed as you are a blessing to others.

Thank you for seeking the praise of God.#Godisfaithful#TheGloryRoad

Day#409 June 2

 Anchor Verse: John 13:15
I have given you an example to follow. Do as I have done to you. (NLT)

A pattern to follow, an example to repeat ~ it makes it so much easier to do the right thing, to live life the right way.

We have heard the expression, "Don't do as I do, do as I say." That's something we say as human beings, but what Jesus spoke, Jesus did. There was no difference, no double standard between His speech and His actions.

In John 13, after dinner, Jesus got up from the meal, wrapped a towel around His waist, and after pouring water into a basin began to wash His disciples' feet, and dry them with the towel.

When Jesus got to Peter, Peter asked, "Lord, are you going to wash my feet?" Jesus told Peter that he wouldn't understand what was happening, but later Peter would.

"Now that I, your Lord and Teacher, have washed your feet, you also should wash one another's feet. I have set you an example that you should do as I have done for you." (NIV) (John 13:14-15)

If we faithfully lived out the example of what Jesus did when He walked this earth, the world would be transformed. The change begins in us.

On our journey to Bill's healing, we learned so much about following Jesus and listening to the voice of the Holy Spirit directing our path. When "normal" is stripped away, God doesn't leave a big hole. He fills the gap with Himself ~ His love, His power, His grace, His peace.

The Glory Road is a place of revelation and repetition. We are often content remaining in our "kindergarten" understanding of whom God is but our heavenly Father wants to elevate us far beyond that to higher places. When we are willing, there are no limits to what God can do in us and through us.

Lord, thank you where You call us, You equip us. There is no lack in Your kingdom or in our lives to do what You want us to do. Holy Spirit, may we hear Your voice as You direct our steps. Let Your light shine brightly in us, O Lord. May others be drawn to You. In Jesus' name, amen.

Thank you for speaking words of life.#Godisfaithful#TheGloryRoad

Day#410 June 3

 Anchor Verse: 2 Chronicles 20:12
We do not know what to do, but our eyes are on You. (AMP)

Have you ever been in a place when it seems like the whole world is against you and it looks like nothing is going your way?

You are not alone. In fact, people throughout time have come to places of being overwhelmed, seemingly overpowered, outnumbered, and have wondered why God is so long in moving. Does that sound like your life?

In 2 Chronicles chapter 20, there was a vast army coming against them. Jehoshaphat stood up in the temple, "Lord, the God of our ancestors, are you not the God who is in heaven? You rule over all the kingdoms of the nations. Power and might are in your hand, and no one can withstand you."

The king reminds God he knows who God is. God rules over the nations and God's track record of defeating the enemy on their behalf is stellar.

2 Chronicles 20:12, "For we have no power to face this vast army that is attacking us. We do not know what to do, but our eyes on you." All the people stood there before the Lord, with their eyes on heaven, waiting for God to do what only He could do.

On our journey to Bill's healing, there were many places where we faced multiple "enemies" ~ things that were out of our control or we didn't the resources to "defeat" them. We learned quickly that when we didn't know what to do, we kept our eyes on God. He always came through.

The Glory Road is also a place where situations come and go and I am powerless on my own to overcome them. With my eyes fixed on heaven, day or night, I know where my help comes from, it comes in the name of the Lord. He will lead me to victory, not in my own strength, but in His.

Lord, there are things we face that are bigger than us. As we stand firm, we will see the deliverance of the Lord. We praise and worship You this morning as King of kings and Lord of lords. In Jesus' name we pray, amen.

Thank you for not giving up.#Godisfaithful#TheGloryRoad

Day#411 June 4

 Anchor Verse: John 14:15-16
If you love me, obey me; and I will ask the Father and he will give you another Comforter, and he will never leave you. (TLB)

"If you love me, obey me." These are the words of Jesus to His disciples. These are also Jesus' words to us today.

Obedience is something we teach our children early in life. They are taught obedience from a place of love; the same way Jesus was teaching His disciples. It wasn't because He was a harsh taskmaster. Jesus knew the reward that was coming because they obeyed.

Jesus spent three years with His disciples and they learned much and saw many miracles. His time on earth was coming to an end, but God had a plan so His children would not be left as orphans.

"And I will ask the Father and he will give you another Comforter, and he will never leave you." (John 14:16)

The Holy Spirit, the Spirit of truth, was the gift His disciples would receive after Jesus returned to heaven. He would be their Comforter and remain with them for all of their lives.

On our journey to Bill's healing, we learned about the joy of obedience and how it opened up the floodgates of God's blessings. It's not like a treasure chest or a trip to the candy store. God's blessings aren't measured by human standards. Our joy is far greater than anything we can ever imagine.

The Glory Road is a path where Jesus walks with me and talks with me. The Holy Spirit, the Comforter, guides my way. There is no greater love than the love of our heavenly Father. His heart's desire is to give good gifts to His children as we learn to walk in obedience to His commands.

Lord, You are the God of truth and Your promises never fail. Thank you for the gift of the Comforter, the Holy Spirit, who guides our way. In the good times and the challenges, Your word is truth. Your word is life. May we enter into the joy of walking with You as You uphold us in Your powerful, victorious right hand. In Jesus' name, amen.

Thank you for your persistent prayers.#Godisfaithful#TheGloryRoad

Day#412 June 5

 Anchor Verse: John 15:11
My purpose for telling you these things is so that the joy that I experience will fill your hearts with overflowing gladness! (TPT)

Joy transcends happiness… by miles! Joy is a gift from the Lord that can be present even in difficult circumstances. Joy cannot be stolen by the enemy of our souls or by anyone else. Joy is magnified in the presence of the Lord.

There's a song we often sing at church about "joy unspeakable that won't go away." Do you know that kind of joy? If not, let me tell you about the source of that joy – Jesus.

In John, chapter 15, Jesus continues to speak to His disciples. "I am the vine, you are the branches." The disciples could get a mental picture of exactly what this looked like – daily they saw an example of this in their lives.

Jesus shares with them about the pruning process, the cutting away of some of the good branches so that the tree would bear better fruit. Many of you know what that looks like in your own life.

"My purpose for telling you these things is so that the joy that I experience will fill your hearts with overflowing gladness!" (John 15:11)

Jesus wants His disciples to experience the joy Jesus experiences which is found in His connection with God, our heavenly Father, and then their hearts will be filled with overflowing gladness. That's His promise to us too.

On our journey to Bill's healing, Jesus invited Bill, and me, to experience His true joy, and we both said, "yes" … definitely yes. In the process, we experienced His indescribable joy in some of the most difficult places a human being can face. God's presence was always with it as well as His joy.

The Glory Road is a place of joy. Yes, there are times and places where there are tears and grieving too, but the joy of the Lord is greater, truly it is my strength. (Nehemiah 8:10)

Lord, thank you for the joy that comes from Your heart. Joy is a fountain that flows from the depths of our soul. Thank you, Lord, for Your goodness and grace, Your mercy, and Your peace. Great are You, Lord, and most worthy of our praise. We love you, Lord. In Jesus' name we pray, amen.

Thank you for sharing your joy with others.#Godisfaithful#TheGloryRoad

Day#413 June 6

 Anchor Verse: Psalm 150:1
Praise the Lord! Praise God in his sanctuary; praise him in his mighty heaven! (NLT)

Did you wake up with praise for the Lord on your lips this morning? Was your heart so full of thanksgiving to God that you said, "I just can't stop praising His name."?

With all God has done for us, we should be praising God every day – all day, and all night.

The psalmist, David, who wrote many of the psalms, throughout this book in the Bible spends a lot of time praising the Lord for who He is, His wonders throughout creation, and the amazing ways God rescued David.

David's songs of praise are not merely words but they come from the depth of his heart and soul.

When you sing, does it come from a heart full of praise for who God is and His wonders? Or do you merely pay "lip service" to the King of kings and the Lord of lords?

Have you discovered this truth that our praise fills our hearts, souls, and lives with the joy of the Lord and it sends negativity, anxiety, darkness, and even our enemy running the other direction? Praising the Lord fills you up to full and overflowing, so the light and love of Jesus Christ radiates out of you.

On our journey to Bill's healing, we learned the power of praising the Lord. It didn't matter the geographical location – home, hospital, doctor's office, or the local park, God got all the glory for our victories. Things that were impossible for man (us) were possible with God. (Matthew 19:26)

The Glory Road is a path that is filled with praise – morning, noon, or night; it's always a great time to praise the Lord. The Bible says to make a joyful noise unto the Lord. It doesn't say you have to sing with perfect pitch or with the voice of a professional singer, it's your attitude that matters.

Lord, we come with hearts filled with praise and adoration. We lift our hands high in praise, and say, "Worthy are You, Lord, to receive all our praise." May it be not only our mouths, our words, which proclaim it but that our lives would testify of Your faithfulness. In Jesus' name we pray, amen.

Thank you for praising the Lord with me.#Godisfaithful#TheGloryRoad

Day#414 June 7

 Anchor Verse: John 17:18
Just as You commissioned and sent Me into the world, I also have commissioned and sent them (believers) into the world. (AMP)

What does it mean to be commissioned? When a person is commissioned, they are given a task and the authority to carry it out. You are entrusted with an assignment.

Many are familiar with the "Great Commission" that Jesus gave His disciples and that has been passed down to you and me today. (Matthew 28:18-20)

The assignment is clear as well as the authority to carry out the mission. Jesus tells His disciples that ALL authority in heaven and on earth had been given to Him. Then Jesus commands them to go and make disciples of all nations, not just the people in the area where they currently resided. And then to baptize them, and teach them what Jesus had taught His disciples.

"Just as You commissioned and sent Me into the world, I also have commissioned and sent them (believers) into the world." (John 17:18)

When Jesus left the glory of heaven, His heavenly Father had a mission for Him. Jesus was commissioned and sent by His heavenly Father. Now Jesus is commissioning and sending His disciples (believers) into the world to do the same thing. God has a plan and a purpose for each one of us.

On our journey to Bill's healing, we learned that no matter your physical condition, God can use every person. God loves to use vessels in all shapes and sizes, ages, geographical locations~ to share His love and joy. You and I have a message to share in thought, word, and deed.

The Glory Road is walked out where it's even more imperative to let my light shine for Jesus. The darkness is darker, but the light is even brighter. What an honor to share our story for God's glory. God's message is for the whole world and I am a small, and important, piece of that puzzle.

Lord, thank you for the commission, the instructions You have given are to go and tell our story about what God has done for us. We are blessed to be Your children. Let our light shine for You today in Jesus' name, amen.

Thank you for your persistent prayers.#Godisfaithful#TheGloryRoad

Day# 415 June 8

 Anchor Verse: 2 Chronicles 31:20
This is what Hezekiah did throughout Judah, doing what was good and right and faithful before the Lord his God. (NIV)

Every moment of every day we have a choice – to do the right thing or the wrong one. Every decision is a crossroad to follow God or to go our own way. Which way will you choose? Which path will I choose?

An individual, family, church, community, city, state, or nation who chooses to follow the Lord will be blessed according to God's standards, not the standards of man. God's blessings are always greater.

In 2 Chronicles 31, we read about Hezekiah and the choices he made while leading his people. As King Hezekiah gave generously from his own resources, the people followed their leaders' example and also gave generous donations. And the Lord blessed the people.

2 Chronicles 31:20 says, "This is what Hezekiah did throughout Judah, doing what was good and right and faithful before the Lord his God."

Today is my birthday and reading this passage, I was drawn to the words "good and right and faithful." This is our goal, this is the place where we give from a generous heart, and greater still are the blessings. Not only to those who receive the gift, but in God's economy, He also blesses the giver.

On our journey to Bill's healing, we saw God multiply our blessings, time and time again. God always rewards our faithfulness. Even in Bill's most challenging moments on this journey, I witnessed Bill's choice to do what was good, right, and faithful to God. So many were blessed, even in Bill's weakness, because Bill chose God to be His strength.

The Glory Road is a path filled with decisions – daily. It is a path that is shaped by the decisions we make, not only individually but also corporately as a nation, and as the family of God. There is no greater adventure, nothing more rewarding than being led by the Holy Spirit on a God adventure.

Lord, reveal to us Your joy, Your peace, Your power, Your presence ~ not for our glory but for Your glory. You are so faithful and always reward our faithfulness. May You find us faithful. In Jesus' name, amen.

Thank you for your encouraging words.#Godisfaithful#TheGloryRoad

Day#416 June 9

 Anchor Verse: 2 Chronicles 32:8
With him there is only an arm of flesh, but with us is the Lord our God to help us and to fight our battles. (AMP)

Battles ~ we all have them. In fact, some of the most defining moments in our lives have a battle at the core of them.

Whether that battle involves an achievement, like earning a degree, or a health challenge, or a personal goal like running a race, or a battle involving someone you love, God is with you in the beginning, middle, and end of it.

As a believer, a follower of Jesus, you will never fight another battle in your life alone – never! The world will tell you otherwise, the devil, the enemy of our souls, will spout some "trash talk" saying you are alone and not good enough, but they are lies from the pit of hell itself.

"With him there is only an arm of flesh, but with us is the Lord our God to help us and to fight our battles." (2 Chronicles 32:8)

Our enemies, those who oppose us in battle ~ whatever form they may take, "only" have an arm of flesh… but WE have the Lord our God to help us and to fight our battles.

On our journey to Bill's healing, we learned about the power of God and how much greater it is than any human power (arm of flesh) or illness. With God on our side, we are more than conquerors, overcomers, victorious sons and daughters of the King of kings and the Lord of lords.

The Glory Road is littered with battles. Every battle I face God is with me. I am never alone. When I am weak, He is strong. When I am weary, He is even stronger. God will fight my battles. I just need to ask for His help.

Lord, we praise and thank you that we are victorious in Jesus' name. There is nothing we face, no giant like Goliath, no sea too deep like the Red Sea, no decision too big, and no circumstance too daunting, that You, our heavenly Father are unable to make a way through it, or over it, or around it. We come with our mustard seed-sized faith this morning and say, "Lord, do it again." We praise You, Lord, for Your faithfulness, in Jesus' name, amen.

Thank you for your faithful prayers.#Godisfaithful#TheGloryRoad

Day#417 June 10

 Anchor Verse: 2 Chronicles 34:3
When he [Josiah] had been king for eight years—he was still only a teenager—he began to seek the God of David his ancestor. (TLB)

An eight-year-old becoming king of a nation is something we can't imagine in modern times. Josiah became King of Judah at the age of eight after his father, King Amon, a wicked king, was assassinated.

The most important part is found in 2 Chronicles 34:3, "When he [Josiah] had been king for eight years—he was still only a teenager—he began to seek the God of David his ancestor."

Yesterday (6.9.21), I had the blessing of attending the eighth-grade graduation of my second cousin, a young man with great potential. As we sat in the school parking lot watching these teenagers graduate and begin the next phase in their lives as high school students, my thoughts were drawn in opposite directions ~ both looking forwards and backwards.

The key to Josiah's success was that at the age of 16, he began seeking the God of his fathers (his ancestors). God gave Josiah wisdom to lead wisely and the courage to take action and carry out God's plans.

On our journey to Bill's healing, although he was no longer a teenager, gained great wisdom as he sought the Lord, and took action. God's favor was upon Bill and others were blessed because of Bill's obedience.

The Glory Road is the path of wisdom. When your life changes abruptly, it's an opportunity to seek God's face and ask Him to supply what you lack. We lack nothing when we turn to God first, last, and always.

Heavenly Father, even though most of us are no longer teenagers, please use us to bless and teach younger generations. Use me, Lord, wherever You want me to go so I might be ALL that You have created me to be. We speak life and blessings over our youth today. In Jesus' name we pray, amen.

Thanks for your love and prayers.#Godisfaithful#TheGloryRoad

Day#418 June 11

 Anchor Verse: John 19:35
And he (John, the eyewitness) who has seen it has testified, and his testimony is true; and he knows that he is telling the truth, so that you also [who read this] may believe. (AMP)

Finding the truth and knowing the truth is not only a noble goal, it's absolutely necessary for the survival of a nation.

Compare it to building a house. The first thing a builder does is establish a strong foundation using concrete. We all have seen a house, barn, storage shed, or skyscraper in its infancy as the building takes shape.

The book of John was written by John, Jesus' beloved disciple. In John 19, John establishes the credibility of what has been written. John 19:35 says, "And he (John, the eyewitness) who has seen it has testified, and his testimony is true; and he knows that he is telling the truth, so that you also [who read this] may believe."

John shared all this information for only one purpose ~ that we might believe in Jesus, who came to give us eternal life so we might be restored in our relationship with God.

On our journey to Bill's healing, we experienced many amazing things ~ miracles from the hand of God. We were eyewitnesses to the power and truth of God. What a blessing to share our story for His glory.

The Glory Road is a path filled with encounters with God and others who have shaped my life. I have been through the refining fire, multiple times. What I do know is this, not one moment, not one circumstance has taken place outside of God's reach or His view. All of this is for my good and for His glory. God wastes nothing. Because of His love, we are more than conquerors, victorious in Jesus' name.

Lord, we praise and thank you for the gift of Your love. Your love is founded on truth, because You are truth. May we walk in ALL You have planned for us. Let our hearts and minds be set on the truth of God. May the words of our mouth and the meditation of our hearts be acceptable in Your sight, O Lord, our strength and our redeemer. In Jesus' name, amen.

Thank you for your words of life.#Godisfaithful#TheGloryRoad

Day#419 June 12

 Anchor Verse: John 20:8
Then the other disciple who had reached the tomb first went in, and after one look, he believed! (TPT)

Seeing and believing ~ there's a lot of that happening, not only today but throughout history.

Has life in this pandemic season created more mistrust in us, in others, and in institutions?

Believing is a choice. It may take a thimble full of faith or a Pacific Ocean-sized vat of faith. Are you willing to take the first step as God fills the void?

John 20 tells us about Mary approaching the tomb of Jesus, three days after his crucifixion, and finding it empty. She runs to tell the disciples. Peter and John (the disciple Jesus loved) then ran to the tomb to verify what Mary said.

John looked into the tomb and saw it was empty except for the grave clothes lying there. Peter went in and examined all the evidence of Jesus' disappearance. In John 20:8, it says, "Then the other disciple who had reached the tomb first went in, and after one look, he believed!"

On our journey to Bill's healing, there were many intersections where seeing and believing met a leap of faith. Often God called us to leap, trusting that God alone would catch us. Bill and I with hands joined in faith said, "God, we trust you!" And jumping, He caught us every time.

The Glory Road is a walk of faith. Often it is others that require, or even demand, to see the evidence of healing or proof of another truth, before they will believe. With childlike faith, I am willing to take God's hand and trust Him even when I cannot see.

Lord, we praise you for who You are. You do not require we show proof of our faith or good works in order to be loved by You. Great is Your faithfulness, O Lord, to ALL generations, including our generation. Forgive us, Lord, when we demand proof before we are willing to believe. We step out in faith this morning with only one goal, may You would be honored and glorified in our lives. In Jesus' name we pray, amen.

Thank you for taking a leap of faith.#Godisfaithful#TheGloryRoad

Day#420 June 13

 Anchor Verse: Ezra 7:28
Because the hand of the Lord my God was on me, I took courage and gathered leaders from Israel to go up with me. (NIV)

With school coming to an end for many students, summer activities are about to begin. It's time for vacation travels which involve planning.

Circumstances may arise that necessitate traveling quickly without much warning or preparation but usually there is time to make a plan. Here in the book of Ezra, we see another facet of the preparation plan – the mental and spiritual part of the trip.

"Because the hand of the Lord my God was on me, I took courage and gathered leaders from Israel to go up with me." (Ezra 7:28)

The hand of the Lord was on Ezra. God was not only guiding his steps but protecting Ezra. All that we need the Lord will provide.

Ezra took courage because the hand of the Lord was on him. He had no fear or anxiety because God gave him courage. God was fighting for him.

He gathered up leaders from Israel to go with him. Because the Lord was with Ezra, not only did he have courage for himself, but to lead others. As a leader, there is a greater responsibility but with God's help you can lead well.

On the journey to Bill's healing, the hand of the Lord was with us. We couldn't have navigated those places of life well without God's help. God gave us courage and we received blessings from His hands and from yours.

The Glory Road is a beautiful path because the hand of the Lord is with me. Daily, my heavenly Father gives me courage to take the next step to accomplish the plans and purposes He has for me. Without Him, I can do nothing but with God ALL things are possible.

Lord, we thank you for Your tender care. We declare God, You are for us and not against us. Thank you for the never-ending supply of courage which comes from Your heart and Your hands. May we walk out the plans You have for us in Jesus' name, amen.

Thank you for your faithful prayers.#Godisfaithful#TheGloryRoad

Day#421 June 14

 Anchor Verse: Acts 1:3

After the sufferings of his cross, Jesus appeared alive many times to these same apostles over a forty-day period, proving to them with many convincing signs that he had been resurrected. During these encounters, he taught them the truths of God's kingdom. (TPT)

"Jesus is alive!" This was Mary Magdalene's declaration after finding the empty tomb and having an encounter with Jesus.

But the story didn't end there. After Jesus was resurrected from the dead, He appeared to His apostles and others over a forty-day period.

In the opening pages of Acts 1, we read in verse 3, "After the sufferings of his cross, Jesus appeared alive many times to these same apostles over a forty-day period, proving to them with many convincing signs that he had been resurrected. During these encounters, he taught them the truths of God's kingdom."

Jesus proved to His disciples (the eleven apostles) with many "convincing" signs He had been resurrected. In many ways, this illustrates the kindness of Jesus and the goodness of our heavenly Father. How gracious Jesus was to erase any doubts which might have lingered after His death. His resurrection was not merely a possibility, but the truth.

On our journey to Bill's healing, we were blessed with the peace of Jesus' presence and the power of the Holy Spirit to guide us through the obstacles we faced. We were never alone. Jesus walked with us, and often with Bill through dreams and visions.

The Glory Road is a place of revelation and multiplied power and peace. Jesus walks with me daily and reminds me that in this world we will have tribulation and trials, but to be of good cheer, for He has overcome the world. Because He lives, I can face today, and tomorrow, and the days to come filled with His resurrection power.

Lord, we praise and thank you for Your goodness and grace. You have not left us alone to navigate this life. We have the Bible for instruction for living according to Your plan and the gift of the Holy Spirit to guide us. Lord, we surrender our lives anew to You today, in Jesus' name, amen.

Thank you for being prayer warriors.#Godisfaithful#TheGloryRoad

Day#422 June 15

 Anchor Verse: Nehemiah 2:18
Then I told them about how the gracious hand of God had been on me, and about my conversation with the king. They replied at once, "Yes, let's rebuild the wall!" So they began the good work. (NLT)

Nehemiah was the cupbearer to King Artaxerxes when he heard the news that the wall of Jerusalem was broken down and its gates had been burned.

As Nehemiah appeared before the king, his grief was evident, it couldn't be hidden. Not only was the favor of God upon Nehemiah, but the king's favor was heaped on top of God's favor.

Even in his grief, God placed a plan of action in Nehemiah's heart. When the king asked him what he needed, Nehemiah had a ready answer.

This is a strategy we need to follow. God honors our grief but also has a plan and a way out of it to do the good work God has called us to do.

Nehemiah 2:18 says, "Then I told them about how the gracious hand of God had been on me, and about my conversation with the king. They replied at once, "Yes, let's rebuild the wall!" So they began the good work."

On our journey to Bill's healing, we found favor in the eyes of God when we ran to Him in the middle of the storms of life. God's favor continued to flow through the medical team and others chosen to help us, and through you all, with your prayers and encouraging words.

The Glory Road is a place with a plan and purpose. Bill and I navigated the storms of life together until God called Bill home in 2020. As I walk this path alone, I know God's hand is upon me. There is favor. There is hope. God's power is at work to break through any opposition standing in the way of His plans. I sing praises to His name in the middle of the storm as God reveals His plans to repair the broken places in my life.

Lord, we praise for You are El Roi, the God who sees. You are Jehovah Jireh, our Provider. You are Jehovah Shalom, our Peace. You are Jehovah Nissi, our banner. You are El Shaddai, God Almighty. Thank you for Your plans and purpose for our lives. We ask for Your hand of protection over us as we walk in Your way, doing Your will, so You would be honored and glorified. In Jesus' name we pray, amen.

Thank you for your faithfulness.#Godisfaithful#TheGloryRoad

Day#423 June 16

 Anchor Verse: Nehemiah 6:16
When all our enemies heard about this, all the surrounding nations were afraid and lost their self-confidence, because they realized that this work had been done with the help of our God. (NIV)

When God is fighting for you, nothing can stop you.

In the book of Nehemiah, Nehemiah is leading the effort to rebuild the wall around Jerusalem. He has enlisted the help of the people and each family is rebuilding a section of the wall. Together, they have taken on this task even as the naysayers are giving them a hard time.

The wall was completed in fifty-two days. Only God could do that through the willingness of His people to give their all.

Half of the men were builders, while the other half were equipped with spears, shields, bows, and armor. Some carried materials in one hand and held a weapon in the other. They would not be kept from their mission, their holy mission to rebuild the wall.

"When all our enemies heard about this, all the surrounding nations were afraid and lost their self-confidence, because they realized that this work had been done with the help of our God." (Nehemiah 6:16)

On our journey to Bill's healing, we were called to stand up against Bill's health issues with faith in God. We saw God move on his behalf because of God's love and His power at work. Bill was victorious, the Miracle Man, because God was for him and not against him.

The Glory Road is a place of battles and victories won with God's help. I can't take one step on this Glory Road in my own strength. As I continue to lean into the healing God promised, the Sword of the Spirit (the Word of God) is in one hand and my other hand is doing God's work for me.

Lord, thank you for what You are doing in our lives. We pray for the broken-down walls You are calling us to repair. No weapon formed against us will prosper. May we fight the good fight of faith, knowing we will be victorious because You're on our side. In Jesus' name we pray, amen.

Thank you for your bold prayers.#Godisfaithful#TheGloryRoad

Day#424 June 17

 Anchor Verse: Nehemiah 9:19a
Because of your great compassion you did not abandon them in the wilderness.
(NIV)

Today let us rejoice in the grace and mercy and compassion of God. Bless the Lord, O my soul, and ALL that is within me, bless His holy name.

We have such a good, good Father. God gives us so much more than we deserve. He loved us before we first loved Him, and God keeps on loving us. It's hard to comprehend the depths of His love.

In Nehemiah chapter 9, we read the Israelites gathered together fasting and confessing their sins to the Lord. Out of their heart cry, they remember God's goodness, even when they complained and sinned in the wilderness.

God's faithfulness continued to bless them. "Because of your great compassion you did not abandon them in the wilderness." (Nehemiah 9:19) They are talking about their ancestors who, as it says in verse 16, became "arrogant and stiff-necked, and they did not obey your commands."

Yet, "by day the pillar of cloud did not fail to guide them on their path, nor the pillar of fire by night to shine on the way they were to take."

This wasn't just for a minute God showed them His compassion, but for the 40 years they were in the wilderness. God's love and kindness isn't just for today, He's in it for the long haul with us.

On our journey to Bill's healing, we were blessed by God's great compassion. God didn't leave Bill alone for even one moment, even one breath. The Spirit of God hovered over Bill and filled him with hope, joy, endurance, and a heart filled with gratitude. God will do the same for you.

The Glory Road is the path walked out with El Roi, the God who sees me. Jehovah Jireh is my provider. Jehovah Shalom is my peace. He abides with me, in the day or the night. His love NEVER fails.

Thank you, Lord, for Your grace. Your love covers our sins and Your forgiveness wipes the slate clean. May Your example inspire us to be more like You. Let the love of Jesus shine through us. In Jesus' name, amen.

Thank you for your love and kindness.#Godisfaithful#TheGloryRoad

Day#425 June 18

 Anchor Verse: Acts 4:18
They called them back and warned them that they were on no account ever again to speak or teach in the name of Jesus. (MSG)

When you have an encounter with Jesus, your life is transformed forever. After Pentecost (Acts 2), Peter and John went out among the people to speak the message Jesus had given them that many would come to know Jesus and follow Him, just as Jesus' disciples had done.

In Acts 3, as Peter and John are going into the temple to pray, a lame beggar is healed, and the people were filled with wonder and amazement.

Peter is quick to point out that it is not by their own power or godliness this man is able to walk, but "it is Jesus' name and that faith that comes through him that has completely healed him." (Acts 3:16)

The religious leaders were so upset with Peter and John they are arrested. After spending the night in jail, they are brought before the religious leaders. "They called them back and warned them that they were on no account ever again to speak or teach in the name of Jesus." (Acts 4:18)

"But Peter and John spoke right back, "Whether it's right in God's eyes to listen to you rather than to God, you decide. As for us, there's no question—we can't keep quiet about what we've seen and heard." (Acts 4:19-20)

On our journey to Bill's healing, we couldn't stop telling the story of what Jesus did for Bill. We shared not only the victories but how with heaven's intervention, we walked through the deep valleys. If we had stopped sharing the story, I think we would have exploded.

The Glory Road is a place of testimony ~ sharing our story for God's glory. As Bill was recovering, we thought God's plan was for us to travel and share our story and plant seeds of hope. When God called Bill home, God's plan wasn't altered. I am commissioned to continue on this road. Bill is with me in spirit, as I continue our miraculous story of God's many miracles.

Lord, give us the courage to fearlessly share the gospel, the miracles, and the transformational work of God in our lives. Lord, give us holy boldness to share our story for Your glory in Jesus' name, amen.

Thank you for believing in miracles.#Godisfaithful#TheGloryRoad

Day#426 June 19

 Anchor Verse: Acts 4:32
All the believers were one in mind and heart. Selfishness was not a part of their community, for they shared everything they had with one another. (TPT)

From birth, often our lives revolve around us, and what we want or what we need. As we begin to grow up, we are taught that life isn't just about "us."

"Me" turns into "we" as God's love penetrates our hearts and shows us a better way to live. There is greater joy when you no longer consider yourself to be the center of the universe.

We read about Peter and John as they led the people, but also the attitude and actions of those who were following Jesus. Not only were they filled with the Holy Spirit but they spoke the Word of God boldly.

"All the believers were one in mind and heart. Selfishness was not a part of their community, for they shared everything they had with one another." (Acts 4:32)

Selfishness was not a part of their community. Can you imagine living in a community where no one was selfish? This is a picture of what the family of God ~ the church should look like and how we should act.

On our journey to Bill's healing, God brought unselfish people into our lives willing to share their time and resources. We were also willing and able to share what God had done in us and through us. This is nothing more powerful than the hearts and minds of those who are surrendered to Jesus and what can be accomplished through them.

The Glory Road is a landscape filled with those who are self-centered and those who share themselves with others. What a blessing I have been given to selflessly share my life, my time, and resources with those God brings across my path. What a blessing to love like Jesus loves.

Thank you, Jesus, for Your example of how to live our lives seeking the best for others. Everything we have is a gift from Your hands. Direct us to the places where our resources can be multiplied for Your kingdom. In Jesus' mighty name we pray, amen.

Thank you for your generous hearts.#Godisfaithful#TheGloryRoad

Day#427 June 20

 Anchor Verse: Esther 2:11
And every day Mordecai paced in front of the court of the women's quarters, to learn of Esther's welfare and what was happening to her. (NKJV)

In the book of Esther, we read the story of Hadassah, also known as Esther, who was raised by her cousin Mordecai after her parents died.

When the edict was sent out by King Xerxes that he was looking for a new queen, many young women were invited to the palace to compete for this position. Esther was one of the young women who were brought to Susa. Mordecai instructed her not to reveal her nationality or family background.

Esther found favor with Hegai, who was in charge of the harem, and God put Esther on the path to win favor with the king.

In the meantime, Mordecai, who was an attendant in the king's court, watched over Esther. "And every day Mordecai paced in front of the court of the women's quarters, to learn of Esther's welfare and what was happening to her." (Esther 2:11)

Reading about Mordecai's watchful care reminds us of how a father watches over his children. The greatest example of all is how God watches over us, as our heavenly Father.

On our journey to Bill's healing, we did not walk the path alone. God was in charge of Bill's care and brought people into our lives to assist us on this journey. As Bill's wife, I am so grateful for the honor and privilege of walking beside him on this journey. What a blessing from the heart of God.

The Glory Road is not a path I walk alone. God is always with me and His angels surround me, both heavenly angels and earthly angels. The enemy may try and deceive you to believe you are alone, but that is a lie. As children of God, we never walk alone.

Lord, we thank you for the gift of companionship on this road of life. You never leave us alone, heaven and earth move at Your command to guard us, guide us, and protect us. We love you, Lord. In Jesus' name we pray, amen.

Thank you for your faithfulness.#Godisfaithful#TheGloryRoad

Day#428 June 21

 Anchor Verse: Esther 4:16
Then I will go in to [see] the king [without being summoned], which is against the law; and if I perish, I perish." (AMP)

Today people in general are more accessible than in previous times in history.

In the book of Esther, we read of King Xerxes' empire in Persia and the inaccessibility of the king unless a person was summoned to come into his presence.

Haman has a plot to destroy the Jews across the Persian Empire because Mordecai wouldn't kneel and pay honor to him. Haman's heart was bent not only on Mordecai's destruction but ALL the Jews in the kingdom.

Queen Esther hears Mordecai is in distress and sends a messenger to find out what's happening. Mordecai tells her she must take action to save her people. Esther was brought to the kingdom for such a time as this.

If she went to the king without being summoned, the king could have her killed. Protocol was protocol, and the king held absolute power in his hands. Esther is moved by the request, and tells Mordecai to call for a three-day fast among the Jews. At the end of that time, she would approach the king, and "if I perish, I perish." (Esther 4:16)

Are you willing to do whatever it takes to obey God's command for you?

On our journey to Bill's healing, we learned the necessity of listening to God's voice and following His commands. We were willing to risk being misunderstood rather than disobey our heavenly Father. Our actions may not have saved a nation, but God used Bill's journey to impact many lives.

The Glory Road is a place of absolute commitment to God. There are times when my actions may not make sense to others, but God has brought me here for such a time as this. Instant obedience is God's call to all of us.

Thank you, Lord, for Esther who was willing to put it all on the line, even face death for a greater mission than her own life. Jesus also laid down His life so we might be saved. We recommit our lives to follow where You lead us. May You be honored and glorified today in Jesus' name, we pray, amen.

Thank you for your faithful prayers.#Godisfaithful#TheGloryRoad

Day#429 June 22

 Anchor Verse: Esther 8:16
For the Jews, it was a time of celebration. Darkness had turned to light. Sadness to joy. Shame to honor. (VOICE)

God loves to surprise us. He delights to turn the most horrible experiences of our lives into places of victory and celebration.

Joseph is sold into slavery and is elevated from the pit to prison to the palace. Joseph's brothers come to Egypt to get food so they don't starve. Joseph reveals himself to them, and they are afraid.

"You intended to harm me, but God intended it for good to accomplish what is now being done, the saving of many lives." (NIV) (Genesis 50:20)

Haman was seeking revenge, and his mission was not only to get rid of Mordecai, but all of the Jews in the Persian Empire. God's plan was to save the lives of many (the Jews) and see the destruction of their enemies.

"For the Jews, it was a time of celebration. Darkness had turned to light. Sadness to joy. Shame to honor." (Esther 8:16)

Where does God want to do this in your life?

On our journey to Bill's healing, we encountered places where it looked bad in the natural, but God had the final word. Where it looked like the end of the road, it was just a curve and God had more running room for Bill. Our tears were replaced with shouts of joy. God turned our tests and trials into a testimony of His goodness and grace.

The Glory Road is filled with God's holy surprises. The "facts" may lead us to anxiety or even despair BUT the truth of God puts us on the path to victory. It's not over until God says it's over. He delights in parting the Red Sea, in bringing dry bones back to life, and replacing the blindness of our human eyes with eagle eye vision in the spiritual realm.

Lord, we praise you for the places You have brought new hope and new life. We bring our broken parts and broken places to You and ask for an extra measure of hope, love, grace, and faith. Thank you for the dreams You want to accomplish – even those we have put on the shelf. In Jesus' name, amen.

Thank you for your persistent prayers.#Godisfaithful#TheGloryRoad

Day#430 June 23

 Anchor Verse: Acts 7:3
"Leave your country and your people," God said, "and go to the land I will show you." (NIV)

When God came to Abram (later called Abraham), He challenged him in many ways. God promised Abram he would be the father of many nations. Only one problem, Abram and his wife Sarai had no children. In fact, they were advanced in years (old by human standards), beyond what would normally be seen as child-bearing age. Yet, that did not faze God.

God didn't seen dreams dashed – He saw an opportunity to do the miraculous. Not just a miracle for this couple, but a miracle that we still stand in awe and wonder reading about thousands of years later.

This was the first step of faith Abraham had to accept and walk in. The second one we find here, recounted by Stephen in Acts 7:3 – "'Leave your country and your people,' God said, 'and go to the land I will show you.'"

Do you trust God enough to follow Him without reservation?

On our journey to Bill's healing, we were led on a journey to a place we did not know. For those not familiar with our story, my husband's health journey started in 5 hospitals in 2 states for 5.5 months as he fought for his life. Faith was the bridge that kept us connected to God and His plans. From January 10, 2018 to April 19, 2020, we learned the joy which comes in fully surrendering your life, hopes, dreams, and loved ones to God.

The Glory Road is a place of faith. Two months after my husband died, I was unexpectedly diagnosed with breast cancer. It set in motion a whole new journey of faith, and finding joy in every moment. God continues to lead me through the Holy Spirit to a land I do not know, through things I have never previously experienced. In Him, I find unspeakable joy.

Lord, we praise you for Your faithfulness. We submit ourselves to You and Your authority. We trust You to lead us through our challenges and our victories. For that we rejoice this morning. In Jesus' name we pray, amen.

Thank you for your faithfulness.#Godisfaithful#TheGloryRoad

Day#431 June 24

 Anchor Verse: Acts 7:29-30
At this, Moses fled the country and lived in the land of Midian, where his two sons were born. Forty years later, in the desert near Mount Sinai, an Angel appeared to him in a flame of fire in a bush. (TLB)

In Acts 7, we step into Stephen's speech to the Sanhedrin as he reviews some highlights from Israel's history.

Beginning in verse 20 and moving forward, we read the story of Moses from his extraordinary birth into his leadership position in Israel. Moses took justice into his own hands and killed an Egyptian and hides the body in the sand. When two Israelites are fighting and Moses steps in, the man responds, "Are you going to kill me like you killed that Egyptian yesterday?"

Moses knows he is in big trouble. He begins tending sheep on the backside of the desert, seemingly forgotten. His routine was the same every day. You might wonder if Moses thought about those days in Egypt.

"Forty years later, in the desert near Mount Sinai, an Angel appeared to him in a flame of fire in a bush." (Acts 7:30)

God hadn't forgotten Moses. He was being schooled ~ raised up for the leadership position God had in mind. You have not been forgotten either.

On our journey to Bill's healing, we walked into our own wilderness. Everyone else's life was moving forward, good things were happening, and we were "stuck" in the hospital fending off attacks from the enemy. Just like Moses, God hadn't forgotten us. He was always there to give wise counsel.

The Glory Road is a place of hope and healing, of wisdom and holiness. I walk on holy ground because it is the path of His choosing. My path is different from the mainstream, there is great joy in my walk with God.

Lord, You are our rearguard and You redeem our lives from destruction. You crown us with lovingkindness and tender mercies. We are not forgotten; we are right in the center of Your will as we seek Your face. May it be done this day according to Your will in Jesus' name, amen.

Thank you for your persistent prayers.#Godisfaithful#TheGloryRoad

Day#432 June 25

 Anchor Verse: Isaiah 66:1-2
This is what the Lord says: "Heaven is my throne, and the earth is my footstool. Could you build me a temple as good as that? Could you build me such a resting place? My hands have made both heaven and earth; they and everything in them are mine. I, the Lord, have spoken!" (NLT)

Even the most beautiful painting by the world's most revered artist, pales in comparison to God's creation. The colors of nature found in sunrises and sunsets, the intricate colors painted on birds, and flowers that blossom bright and tall are testimony to God's creativity.

In our "infinite wisdom," we try and capture God's holiness in a building using our own hands. God must laugh when our feeble attempts to look important fall short compared to this stunning world He created.

"This is what the Lord says: "Heaven is my throne, and the earth is my footstool. Could you build me a temple as good as that? Could you build me such a resting place? My hands have made both heaven and earth; they and everything in them are mine. I, the Lord, have spoken!" (Isaiah 66:1-2)

On our journey to Bill's healing, we quickly learned about God's power and His tender mercies. There was nothing we could make or offer that hadn't already come from His hands. One thing we could do was surrender our lives to Him, and give Him first place in our lives. We could choose to trust God even when our eyes couldn't see the outcome. That's what we did.

The Glory Road is a place where I can see with new eyes old truths that might have been hidden. Yesterday (6.25.21) the eye doctor announced my vision had only changed a smidgen in over 2.5 years and my eye health was great. The Holy Spirit reminded me my spiritual vision had improved by leaps and bounds. When we walk through difficult places and choose to keep our eyes on heaven, God opens our eyes to see Him in a new way.

Lord, You are the Creator of heaven and earth. As Your creation, we bow before You this morning and declare Your faithfulness. Today we want to walk in freedom with You and in all You have in mind for us. May Your glory be magnified in us, O Lord. In Jesus' mighty name we pray, amen.

Thank you for believing in miracles.#Godisfaithful#TheGloryRoad

Day#433 June 26

 Anchor Verse: Acts 8:4
Although the believers were scattered by persecution, they preached the wonderful news of the word of God wherever they went. (TPT)

As human beings, we tend to prefer being together rather than scattered apart. We live in communities where we have easy access to resources.

The first century church found themselves scattered by persecution. In Acts 7, we read of the stoning of Stephen. What followed was an intense persecution of those who had chosen to follow Jesus. In Acts 8:3 it says, "But Saul began to destroy the church. Going from house to house, he dragged off both men and women and put them in prison."

"Although the believers were scattered by persecution, they preached the wonderful news of the word of God wherever they went." (Acts 8:4)

Hope coming out of hopelessness, persecution producing life, and the church thriving instead of dying, these were the marks of the early church. What does that look like in our lives today?

I am reminded of a dandelion gone to seed. A dandelion only takes 9 to 15 days to come to full maturity. The dandelion produces 110 -150 seeds (white fluffy ones) that become airborne and are "scattered" by the wind. Most don't go far only about six feet from the parent but seed have been documented as going 100 km (62+ miles). And the root can be 3 ft. deep.

If our roots are deep in the Lord, the good news of Jesus can be spread hundreds or thousands of miles wherever His love is scattered.

On our journey to Bill's healing, we went to many places. Everywhere we went, the love of God was with us and His glory was seen in us. We preached the good news of Jesus, not just with words but how we lived.

The Glory Road is a place of gathering and scattering. Just like dandelion fluff is scattered by the wind, so the good news of Jesus can reach places we could never imagine. When we speak, write, and share what God has done in our lives, the seed is planted in the hearts of others. May new life take root.

Lord, may the good news of Jesus spread like dandelion fluff. May it be magnified and multiplied as the church shares what You have done in our lives. Release Your glory in us we pray, in Jesus' name, amen.

Thank you for your faithfulness.#Godisfaithful#TheGloryRoad

Day#434 June 27

 Anchor Verse: Job 8:10
But those who came before us will teach you. They will teach you the wisdom of old.
(NLT)

What a blessing that we can learn from previous generations. History records the wisdom of our elders. We can choose to follow the path of wisdom and be willing to learn from them.

In the book of Job, Job is being tested by the devil himself, and God is allowing it happen. The first seven days Job's friends came and sat in silence and now they have started to speak. Some of their words are good advice and others are not.

"Just ask the previous generation. Pay attention to the experience of our ancestors. For we were born but yesterday and know nothing. Our days on earth are as fleeting as a shadow. But those who came before us will teach you. They will teach you the wisdom of old." (Job 8:8-10)

The wisdom of old reminds me of my paternal grandfather who was a wise man, wisdom born of age. Many discussions on Sunday afternoon were filled with his wit and wisdom.

On our journey to Bill's healing, we were blessed with advice from others. Some of it was relevant, and some, not so much. The best advice we found was in the Bible and the heart of our heavenly Father. All wisdom flows from the throne room of grace. Run to God in your time of need.

The Glory Road is a place where I need wisdom to navigate life daily. Not only for today but as I look toward tomorrow and the Jeremiah 29:11 plans God has for me, I must seek His face and His wisdom. Learning from the mistakes of others and listening to what has worked for them only makes sense. Lord, lead us on the path to victory and restoration in Jesus' name.

Heavenly Father, we praise you for Your excellence and Your wisdom. Thank you that all that we need Your hand will provide. We run to You and lay our concerns at Your feet. We open our ears to hear, our eyes to see, and our minds to understand the plans You have for us and the strategy to walk them out. We love you and praise you, in Jesus' name, amen.

Thank you for your persistent prayers.#Godisfaithful#TheGloryRoad

Day#435 June 28

 Anchor Verse: Acts 9:3-4
As he [Saul] neared Damascus on his journey, suddenly a light from heaven flashed around him. He fell to the ground and heard a voice say to him, "Saul, Saul, why do you persecute me?" (NIV)

As Acts chapter 9 begins, we are told that "Saul was still breathing out murderous threats against the Lord's disciples." He was a man on a mission, and the mission was to destroy the church.

Saul is on his way to Damascus to find more believers and take them as prisoners to Jerusalem, when something big happens.

"As he neared Damascus on his journey, suddenly a light from heaven flashed around him. He fell to the ground and heard a voice say to him, 'Saul, Saul, why do you persecute me?'" (Acts 9:3-4)

And Saul responds, "Who are you, Lord?"

"'I am Jesus, whom you are persecuting,' he replied."

Isn't it interesting that Saul addresses Jesus as "Lord"? Even those who have gone so far astray have within them the knowledge of who God is. And the reverence that is due His name.

On our journey to Bill's healing, we encountered those who were walking in darkness far from the love of God. They were "blind" to God's love, even as Saul was blind for those three days after his encounter with Jesus. We were given the opportunity to sow seeds of God's love and light into their lives.

The Glory Road is filled with people from all different walks of life, with many different beliefs and opinions. Many of them are followers of Jesus, some do not know Him, and others have turned away from the truth.

There are souls I have prayed for that God would choose to meet them through a Damascus Road experience and there would be a radical change as they met Jesus face to face. Maybe that person is you.

Lord, You do not let us wander in darkness alone. Your presence is always with us as you "knock" on the door of our heart. Thank you for choosing Saul to be an ambassador for the gospel of Christ. He became a fierce defender of the faith. May we do the same. In Jesus' name, amen.

Thank you for choosing Jesus.#Godisfaithful#TheGloryRoad

Day#436 June 29

 Anchor Verse: Acts 9:26
When he [Paul] arrived in Jerusalem, he tried to join the disciples; but they were all afraid of him, not believing that he really was a disciple. (AMP)

Many of us have heard the expression, "A leopard can't change his spots." It actually comes from the Bible, Jeremiah 13:23.

We may look at those around us and think, or even say, "He or she will never change." Maybe we've even said it about ourselves. It's our "excuse" not to do better, love better, or walk away from the path of destruction and the vices we have chosen to find comfort in our lives.

Saul, now Paul, is a good example. The reports of Saul (now Paul) spread throughout the region, and when Paul arrives in Jerusalem, Jesus' disciples are not convinced he's a different man. They see the leopard's spots, the old man, not this new creation in Christ.

"When he arrived in Jerusalem, he tried to join the disciples; but they were all afraid of him, not believing that he really was a disciple." (Acts 9:26)

Jesus' disciples are afraid of Paul. This man had been persecuting many believers and hauling them off to jail. Could they trust him?

Maybe this is your story. Once you were in the world, and did as the world did, now you walk with Jesus, but people aren't sure you have really changed.

On our journey to Bill's healing, Bill met Jesus in a new way. He was invited to walk and talk with Jesus and his heavenly Father, in dreams and visions. There was a new intimacy cultivated in the darkest nights and through the deepest valleys. Not everyone got to see what I saw – some may have only seen the old man. That is their loss and heaven's gain.

The Glory Road is the path to freedom, a path of greater intimacy with God. It may have its challenges but often what others don't see is the blessing, the beautiful tapestry God is weaving in and through my life.

Lord, may we believe for the impossible in our lives and embrace those who have left the old life behind, and chosen to walk with You. May we not doubt the old is gone and the new has come. Just as You have faith in us, may we have faith in others. In Jesus' name we pray, amen.

Thank you for believing in miracles.#Godisfaithful#TheGloryRoad

Day#436 June 30

 Anchor Verse: Acts 10:4b
The angel said, "Your prayers and neighborly acts have brought you to God's attention. (MSG)

What have you done that has brought you to God's attention?

In Acts 10, we read of a man named Cornelius who was a centurion in the Italian Regiment. He and all his family were devout and God-fearing people. Cornelius gave generously to those in need and prayed to God regularly.

One afternoon (at 3 pm) Cornelius has a vision and sees an angel of God sent to him with a message. "The angel said, 'Your prayers and neighborly acts have brought you to God's attention.'" (Acts 10:4)

The angel gave him instructions about what to do next. Cornelius obeys and sends two of his servants and a devout soldier to get Peter as the angel said.

Some of you may doubt God sees and knows what you are doing daily. You believe God is a distant God who sits on His throne in heaven and rules like an earthly king distant from the hearts and minds of his people. The truth is God cares about each and every part of your life.

On our journey to Bill's healing, we learned so much more about God's intimate love. Every detail of Bill's journey was important to God. Every kindness shown to Bill, and by Bill to others, was recorded in heaven. The prayers prayed for us, by you, and how Bill interceded for us came up as a praise offering before the Lord.

The Glory Road is a place of accounting. Often when we are called to serve others, it is done from a place of love. We don't count the cost; we just do what needs to be done. Sometimes God wants to remind us our labor is not in vain. God is keeping a record of those prayers and kindnesses shown to others. This isn't a works thing but rather an offering of love.

Heavenly Father, thank you for Your love for us. Thank you for the moments when heaven touches earth and we are reminded that You are El Roi, the God who sees, loves, and cares. Nothing is done outside of Your view. Thank you for Your amazing grace in Jesus' name we pray, amen.

Thank you for your persistent prayers.#Godisfaithful#TheGloryRoad

July 2021

There is surely a future hope for you and your hope will not be cut off.

~ Proverbs 23:8 ~

Day#438 July 1

 Anchor Verse: Acts 10:30
Cornelius replied, "Four days ago I was fasting and praying here in my home at this very hour, three o'clock in the afternoon, when a man in glistening clothing suddenly appeared in front of my eyes. (TPT)

Details are important. You know that, right?

In Acts 10, when Peter and Cornelius meet, God sends an angel to give the details and directions to both men separately, and because of their obedience they come together. This is a historic moment. God breaks down the "wall" between the Jews and the Gentiles.

Let's look at a couple more details. Acts 10:30 says, "Cornelius replied, "Four days ago I was fasting and praying here in my home at this very hour, three o'clock in the afternoon, when a man in glistening clothing suddenly appeared in front of my eyes."

When Cornelius invited Peter, a follower of Jesus, a man who devoutly followed the Jewish protocol, to come to his house, and Peter accepted, the wall is torn down between the Jews and the Gentiles. This event paved the way for you and me to enter in.

On our journey to Bill's healing, we were often surprised and delighted by the lengths God went to put details in place. There were no coincidences only aligned paths to the throne room of grace where we found help in our time of need. The right people, right places, right time ~ holy synchronicity… that's how God loves to move and show Himself to us.

The Glory Road is a place where I see God in every detail. I rejoice He loves me so much that He goes to such great lengths to arrange holy surprises for me. Thank you, Lord. Even in the last few days of June, I saw God move in a mighty way. Praise the Lord!

Lord, You are great and greatly to be praised. We lift our hands and hearts to you in praise. Worthy is the Lamb that was slain to pay the price for our redemption. We open our hands and hearts to receive the gift of Your love and mercy this morning in Jesus' name, amen.

Thank you for your faithfulness.#Godisfaithful#TheGloryRoad

Day#439 July 2

 Anchor Verse: Job 22:22
Listen to his instructions, and store them in your heart. (NLT)

People learn information in many different ways. Educators have created categories for these ways to help them help understand their students and how they best learn.

The Bible is filled with great examples of God communicating with us. Sometimes it is via the written word (Bible). Other times an angel is sent to deliver a message or God sends a message through a dream or a vision, to just name a few.

Eliphaz, one of Job's friends, has this advice for Job, "Listen to his instructions, and store them in your heart." Eliphaz is speaking of God's instructions. (Job 22:22)

This is good advice. When we memorize scripture verses, they are readily accessible, "weapons" we can use to fight the battles we face in our lives.

There are many great Bible verses that reinforce this. "The law of his God is in his heart; Not one of his steps will slip." (Psalm 37:31). "Place these words on your hearts. Get them deep inside you." (Deuteronomy 11:18) "I desire to do your will, my God; your law is within my heart." (Psalm 40:8)

On our journey to Bill's healing, we listened to God's instructions and let them direct our path. The truth we learned from His lips is what kept us afloat through the storms of life. God was, and still is, our refuge and strength, an ever-present help in time of trouble.

The Glory Road is a path of new instruction, or maybe I listen differently now. A lot has been stripped away out of my life. These last couple of years even though the loss has been great, I believe in God's Kingdom the gain has been greater. I'm so grateful for God's instruction and His words of power, comfort, and peace imprinted on my heart.

Thank you, heavenly Father, for the gift of Your Word, the Bible. Thank you that You still speak with us today. Your mercies are new every morning and great is Your faithfulness. We lift our hands in praise, in Jesus' name, amen.

Thank you for your persistent prayers.#Godisfaithful#TheGloryRoad

Day#440 July 3

 Anchor Verse: Job 28:12-13
"But where can wisdom be found?
And where is the place of understanding? Man does not know its value, Nor is it found in the land of the living. (NKJV)

Wisdom and understanding are not something we think about daily like food and water. But on the other hand, they are guiding forces in our lives.

In the book of Job, we learn much about life and wisdom and what they look like. Job 28, 12-13 says, "But where can wisdom be found? And where is the place of understanding? Man does not know its value, Nor is it found in the land of the living."

True wisdom and understanding come from God. Wisdom is a capacity of the mind that allows us to understand life from God's perspective.

Understanding is something that comes from the mind of man. It is a synonym for intelligence and discernment.

Often we try and muddle through our lives and figure out our problems with our own understanding and perspective. Many times, it doesn't turn out very well. But when we turn our eyes on Jesus and look to God's Word for heavenly wisdom, He will make our paths straight.

On our journey to Bill's healing, we were reminded of the vastness of God's wisdom and understanding. God had all the answers we needed to navigate the tight turns and mountain terrain whose only guardrails were the heavenly host that formed an impenetrable shield.

The Glory Road is uncharted territory. Wisdom and understanding are in God's hands and He gives it to me liberally as I seek His face. "Let us then approach God's throne of grace with confidence, so that we may receive mercy and find grace to help us in our time of need." (Hebrews 4:16)

God, You are a good, good Father. We praise and thank you for the gift of this day. We do not face it alone. Everything we need can be found in You. All wisdom and understanding flows from heaven to us, Your children, here below. Lord, walk with us today. Make our rough places smooth and the crooked places straight. In Jesus' name we pray, amen.

Thank you for your faithfulness.#Godisfaithful#TheGloryRoad

Day#441 July 4

 Anchor Verse: Psalm 118:5
Out of my distress I called on the Lord; The Lord answered me and set me free.
(AMP)

Today is the 4th of July, Independence Day, a day that we celebrate freedom in the United States of America.

There may be difficulties in your life today, mountains that loom before you – finances, illness, difficult situations or relationships. In fact, some of them look so big they fill your vision field and it's all you can see.

When you are in that place of being "stuck," there is only place to turn which will get you any real results and that is to God, your heavenly Father.

As we celebrate freedom on the horizontal plane today, let's turn our eyes to the greater freedom that can be ours ~ freedom through Jesus Christ.

In Psalm 118, David begins by giving thanks to the Lord for God's love endures forever. How long? Forever!

Throughout the psalm, he describes the tug-of-war happening in his life. The battles David faces and the people who are coming against him. David declares the Lord is his helper and he will look in triumph on his enemies.

That's God's promise to you today. Psalm 118:5 says, "Out of my distress I called on the Lord; The Lord answered me and set me free."

On the journey to Bill's healing, we encountered many battles. What God made abundantly clear was He was for us, and would fight for us. When God is on your side, you can shout the battle cry of victory in Jesus' name.

The Glory Road has moments when mountains loom large in my path, torrential rainstorms threaten to wash out the road where I stand. Then my heavenly Father lifts me up with His powerful right hand and places me on the solid ground. The storm passes, and I come out of the cleft in the rock where He shields me. There I raise my hands in praise.

Lord, thank you for the gift of freedom and for Your hand of protection over this nation. Lord Jesus, thank you for purchasing our spiritual freedom on Calvary. Whom the Son sets free is free indeed. In Jesus' name, amen.

Thank you for your faithfulness.#Godisfaithful#TheGloryRoad

Day#442 July 5

 Anchor Verse: Hebrews 12:11
Now all discipline seems to be painful at the time, yet later it will produce a transformation of character, bringing a harvest of righteousness and peace to those who yield to it. (TPT)

Parents discipline their children to teach them right from wrong. Teachers show their students which the right answer and the wrong answer so they learn the correct foundations of truth for the rest of their lives. God disciplines and corrects His children to keep us on the right path.

Discipline isn't always pleasant unless you have God's perspective. In 2 Corinthians 4:17 Paul says, "For our light and momentary troubles are achieving for us an eternal glory that far outweighs them all." Do you have that kind of perspective when you are going through the refining fire?

"Now all discipline seems to be painful at the time, yet later it will produce a transformation of character, bringing a harvest of righteousness and peace to those who yield to it." (Hebrews 12:11)

Discipline transforms our character. Those who are training for a sports event spend a lot of time in training and it can be very painful.

On our journey to Bill's healing, God made course corrections all the time, always for our good and for His glory. God was doing something bigger than we could see. And the heat of the refining fire… it was the warmth of God's love because He saw "the more" in us. It could only shine brighter after the fire consumed the clumps of debris that kept the treasure hidden.

The Glory Road is a place of discipline. Not being taken to the woodshed kind of discipline but the steady gentle hand of God teaching me right living so I may be transformed into His image.

Lord, we praise and thank you for the gift of Your love manifested in discipline when we get off track. Your love never changes it only grows stronger. May we be transformed into the likeness of Jesus. We praise you and thank you in Jesus' name, amen.

Thank you for your faithful prayers.#Godisfaithful#TheGloryRoad

Day#443 July 6

 Anchor Verse: Job 32:9
But it is not mere age that makes men wise. Rather, it is the spirit in a man, the breath of the Almighty that makes him intelligent. (TLB)

Wisdom is not just reserved for those who have gone around the sun many, many times. God is the giver of wisdom and He decides which vessels are filled with it.

Paul says to Timothy in 1 Timothy 4:12, "Don't let anyone think less of you because you are young. Be an example to all believers in what you say, in the way you live, in your love, your faith, and your purity." (NLT) Paul was teaching Timothy in the New Testament that wisdom and right living should be seen in his life, even though he was young. Timothy needed to be an example to others. So do we.

In today's passage from Job 32:9, Elihu speaks up, the youngest of Job's friends, "But it is not mere age that makes men wise. Rather, it is the spirit in a man, the breath of the Almighty that makes him intelligent."

When we see people through God's eyes, we can see wisdom in our little children and young adults, in those who are younger than we are and older as well. Wisdom isn't just about a number, it's about our relationship with God and the revelation that comes from heaven, as God breathes wisdom into us.

On our journey to Bill's healing, we were blessed by those who had wisdom, some beyond their years. It wasn't always those with the most education or experience who were able to comfort or help Bill but those with tender hearts who had been blessed with wise counsel, knowledge, and understanding. Gratitude still fills my heart for them today.

The Glory Road intersects both earth and heaven. If I could see what a day looked like from God's view, there would be moments where heaven and earth touched and godly wisdom and understanding were released into my mind and the minds of others. It is not the number of my years that brings wisdom but the moments I have spent in God's presence.

Lord, we live for Your glory. Fill us with the resurrection power that raised Jesus from the dead. Give us the mind of Christ so we can see things rightly and love unconditionally. Make we not walk in judgment but be clothed with Your holiness and righteousness. We love you in Jesus' name we pray, amen.

Thank you for being a prayer warrior.#Godisfaithful#TheGloryRoad

Day#444 July 7

 Anchor Verse: Job 34:3
For the ear tests words as the tongue tastes food. (NIV)

The Lord is in the calm and in the storm. He is present in the valleys as well as the mountaintop experiences.

Even this morning as I write this (7.4.21), a thunderstorm can be heard in the distance. The rumbling, the occasional lightning strike as I pray for the land and no fires being started, as the land is parched just as we are without a word from the Lord.

Job 34:3 says, "For the ear tests words as the tongue tastes food."

When we eat, our taste buds help us decipher what the food is and how good, or bad, it tastes to us. It might be sweet or salty or spicy. Sometimes what we crave varies from one moment to the next.

As believers, we test the words we hear and how they line up with the truth of God found in the Bible. We test what goes into our spirit. We run away from what is evil and harmful and embrace the good and holy.

On our journey to Bill's healing, Bill walked through deep valleys. After his brain bleed, many parts of his body were affected. His brain created new neuro pathways including reclaiming words and thoughts. His ability to eat was impacted, and for a time had a feeding tube, but God changed all that.

The Glory Road is a place where I am learning these truths in a new way. His word as it takes root in my heart gives me new understanding and revelation. I test the words of others to make sure they align with His truth and discard those words which do not. After chemo in 2020, there are still some foods I'm learning to eat. It takes time to recover from an assault on your body.

Lord, we praise and thank you that You are greater than anything we face. You are greater than our biggest challenge. God is greater than our worst nightmare and even bigger than our biggest dream. We rest in Your arms of love this morning, in Jesus' name we pray, amen.

Thank you for your persistent prayers. It was one year ago today that I was diagnosed with breast cancer. Today I celebrate God's faithfulness and His continued healing power at work in me.#Godisfaithful#TheGloryRoad

Day#445 July 8

 Anchor Verse: Job 37:5
God's voice thunders in marvelous ways; he does great things beyond our understanding. (NIV)

Do you believe that God speaks to us?

In Job 37:5, Elihu says, "God's voice thunders in marvelous ways; he does great things beyond our understanding."

Our sense of hearing tells us a lot about what is happening around us. The piercing whine of a siren, a loud train whistle, or even the sound of screeching tires, cause our brains to quickly go on alert.

Just as these "outside" voices tell us of things to come, the quiet voice of the Holy Spirit reminds us who we are and whose we are.

God also does things beyond our understanding. That's part of the wonder, majesty, and mystery of God – it makes God, God. We can't define Him. We can't fit God in a box. We stand in awe of Him daily and what He has done and what He still plans to do in our lives.

On our journey to Bill's healing, we heard God's voice thundering in difficult places and also His still small whispers in the darkness of the night. His voice reminds us of the power of His presence. Even in the silence, we can know the comfort of His love and the restrained power of Lord God Almighty.

The Glory Road is a path filled with many sights and sounds ~ noises that seek our attention when it is God's voice alone our heart and soul desire to hear. When the Lord speaks to us in the storms of life in His thunderous voice, may we stop and linger in His presence as the thunder echoes in the distance. Let us not turn away from His fierce love and majestic power that paves a way for righteousness and justice to touch the earth.

Thank you, Lord, for communicating with us. You are not a faraway God; You are as close as our next breath. Heavenly Father, You long to be in communion with us, in fact, You call to us daily. May we find strength and power in You. We love you and praise you in Jesus' name, amen.

Thank you for your persistent prayers. I received a great report from the doctor yesterday. God is so good.#Godisfaithful#TheGloryRoad

Day#446 July 9

 Anchor Verse: Job 38:28-30
And who do you think is the father of rain and dew, the mother of ice and frost? You don't for a minute imagine these marvels of weather just happen, do you? (MSG)

In the last few chapters of Job, God has been listening to the conversations between Job and his friends, and Job's conversation with God. Now it's God's turn to speak and powerful is His message.

"And who do you think is the father of rain and dew, the mother of ice and frost? You don't for a minute imagine these marvels of weather just happen, do you?" (Job 38:28-30)

Have you ever thought about where the rain, dew, ice, frost, lightning, hail etc. come from when they touch the earth? They don't just appear on their own. They can't "will" themselves into being.

They were formed by the hand of God just like we were formed. God wrote a book about your life before you drew your first breath, and God created the heavens and earth at His command.

On our journey to Bill's healing, we learned so much about the amazing way God created our bodies and the intricate ways they are woven together. How our heart and lungs are connected and how the blood flows and how it stops when a blockage occurs – it is so amazing to see God's creative hand at work. When things are broken, God can restore, recreate, and renew us.

The Glory Road is a place of discovery. Looking at things through God's eyes rather than being self-centered. Thank you, Lord, for revelation about our lives, our bodies, and how Your ways are so much better than our ways.

Lord, thank you for the mystery of who You are. You can't be contained in a box limited by our small understanding. You are nature's conductor in the symphony of life. May we listen closely for Your voice when it thunders or in the quiet whisper of a gentle breeze. In Jesus' name, amen.

Thank you for your encouraging words.#Godisfaithful#TheGloryRoad

Day#447 July 10

 Anchor Verse: Job 42:5
'I had heard of You [only] by the hearing of the ear, But now my [spiritual] eye sees You. (AMP)

There are many things in our life we have only heard about or read out, but when we see it for ourselves, it's totally different.

It's the difference between hearing about Mt. Rushmore, Grand Canyon, or Lincoln Memorial, or other such wonders, and basking in the grandeur with a personal visit.

When it comes to spiritual matters and having an encounter with God, our lives are forever changed, our spiritual eyes are opened. Once we have "seen" God and His mighty hand at work, we are no longer blind.

In this last chapter of Job, Job has a personal encounter with God. Job has talked about God, he has thrown his words and questions at God, but a new revelation of who God is has sprung up in him. Maybe you understand Job's experience, because it has been your experience too.

On our journey to Bill's healing, Bill encountered God in a new way. There was a moment between life and death, where God and Bill had a conversation and it changed Bill's perspective of God forever. Bill was ready to go home to heaven, the pain was great, the battle was difficult, but God said it wasn't time. After that encounter, Bill's spiritual eyes were opened and his understanding and relationship with God grew deeper.

The Glory Road has been an eye-opening experience. Even once our spiritual eyes are opened and we see God for the "first" time, it doesn't stop there. Our walk with God just grows deeper as we spend time in His presence. Praise the Lord for new depths of understanding.

Lord, we praise and thank you for the gift of life lived in Your presence. We do not face this world alone. We lean into You and share our greatest desires and needs. Thank you for unspeakable joy. In Jesus' name, amen.

Thank you for walking with me.#Godisfaithful#TheGloryRoad

Day#448 July 11

 Anchor Verse: Psalm 1:3
But they delight in doing everything God wants them to, and day and night are always meditating on his laws and thinking about ways to follow him more closely. (TLB)

What do you think about day and night? What are the things that catch your attention and monopolize your time?

Is it God and the Bible? Or in the alternative, is it social media, the news, video games, YouTube, TikTok, worries, or work? There are so many things in this world which compete for our attention. But there is only one thing worthy of our all ~ that is God and God's teachings.

As we step into the book of Psalms, one of the first topics that grabs our attention is where we focus our time and attention?

The person who is describes here in Psalm 1 is the one who "delights" ~ finds great joy in doing everything God wants them to do. Does that describe you?

Our days and nights are filled with many activities, many responsibilities, and many people. This is where the psalmist says our attention should be focused ~ "and day and night are always meditating on his laws and thinking about ways to follow him more closely." (Psalm 1:3)

On our journey to Bill's healing, learning where to focus our time and attention was important. Focusing on God and how to follow Him more closely changes the whole course of your life. Your thoughts, attitude, reactions, and focus are transformed when you put God first. When we practiced this, peace filled our mind, hearts, and home.

The Glory Road is a place of new beginnings. It is a new path that is anchored in the Word of God and His ways. Without Him, I can do nothing well. With God, ALL things are possible as He opens new doors of possibilities before me.

Lord, You are great and greatly to be praised. We choose to come into Your presence and experience the fullness of Your joy. Our hearts yearn for Your truth and righteousness. We love you and praise you in Jesus' name, amen.

Thank you for your faithfulness.#Godisfaithful#TheGloryRoad

Day#449 July 12

 Anchor Verse: Psalm 5:12
For you bless the godly man, O Lord; you protect him with your shield of love.
(TLB)

As we walk through this world, we encounter trials and tribulations in a world that is filled with war in both the physical and spiritual realm. As believers, we know God fights for us… and we always win.

Psalm 5:12 says, "For you bless the godly man, O Lord; you protect him with your shield of love." Some translations use the word "righteous" to describe the man the psalmist is addressing.

What does righteous mean? One who is in right relationship with God, who seeks to follow God with all of his heart in every area of his life. God blesses those who diligently seek Him. (Hebrews 11:6)

What does a shield of love look like to you? In describing the full armor of God Paul speaks of in Ephesians 6, we have the "shield of faith" that protects us from the fiery darts of the enemy. What size of shield do you imagine in your mind? The shield I see is big.

The shield of love described here in Psalm 5:12 is not a small, round shield. The word here is tsin'nāh, which refers to a "standing shield"—a massive barrier, like a door, which covered a soldier's entire body. That is how big God's shield of love and favor is around you as you walk in righteousness.

On our journey to Bill's healing, the shield of God's love was around us. It was like that massive barrier described here in Psalm 5:12. Day and night, the Lord was vigilant in His care of Bill. God's love never fails.

The Glory Road is a place of God's favor and protection. He never leaves me alone to wander aimlessly on this road. God has a plan and a purpose for my life. And I delight to follow Him, as God raises His protective hand as a shield of love to protect me and surround me to defeat the enemy at every turn. God is great and greatly to be praised.

Lord, thank you for Your presence. You are a shield about us. You are the One who lifts my head when life is difficult and I am weary. You carry us when the load is heavy and our strength is small. In Jesus' name, amen.

Thank you for your faithful prayers.#Godisfaithful#TheGloryRoad

Day#450 July 13

 Anchor Verse: Psalm 8:2
You have built a stronghold by the songs of children. Strength rises up with the chorus of infants. This kind of praise has power to shut Satan's mouth. Childlike worship will silence the madness of those who oppose you. (TPT)

Have you ever watched little children praising and worshiping the Lord? It's beautiful. It's like heaven touches earth in that moment.

On the 4th of July weekend, the children from our church's Sunday School classes sang a couple of songs in honor of Independence Day.

The best part was what happened before they went on stage. The worship team was praising the Lord inviting the Holy Spirit to dwell with us. Watching those little children praising the Lord reminded me they know their heavenly Father's voice, and they praise His holy name.

"You have built a stronghold by the songs of children. Strength rises up with the chorus of infants. This kind of praise has power to shut Satan's mouth. Childlike worship will silence the madness of those who oppose you."

Our children – infants and toddlers, all our children as they grow up in the knowledge of the Lord are a weapon God uses to shut the mouth of the enemy. Their faith is not tainted by disappointment or the opinions of others. Their faith and worship are powerful and pure.

On our journey to Bill's healing, after Bill was out of the hospital and we were able to return to church, some of the children would come to "check" on Bill. It was beautiful. It was like an angel visitation. Praise the Lord for our children and for those with childlike faith.

The Glory Road is filled with the prayers of the saints and often those saints are less than three feet tall. Only God would use what the world overlooks as His carriers of light, love, hope, and joy. Children are truly a gift from God.

Lord, thank you for the gift of our children and their faith. Jesus asked the children to be brought to Him. May we do the same. Lord, we also understand our responsibility as their elders to guide, guard, and protect them as they walk in all You have for them. In Jesus' name, amen.

Thank you for your companionship.#Godisfaithful#TheGloryRoad

Day#451 July 14

 Anchor Verse: Acts 19:11
God kept releasing a flow of extraordinary miracles through the hands of Paul.
(TPT)

Often among believers we talk about "surrendering" our lives to God. What does that mean?

We may see surrendering as a defeat, not a victory. The truth is when we surrender to God, we have just opened up the doors of blessing into the Kingdom of heaven.

God takes the ordinary in our human world and turns it upside down.

In Acts19, we continue to read about Paul and his traveling adventures for God and spreading the good news. His story is one of the most powerful stories about surrendering to God. Paul has a radical conversion on the Damascus Road. God stops him in his tracks, he's blinded by the light, and after three days, his sight is restored and with new "spiritual" eyes, Paul walks a new path spreading the good news of Jesus.

We read God is doing extraordinary miracles through the hands of Paul. (Acts 19:11) Yes, the hands that once held letters to round up the Christians to be put in jail and persecuted are now the hands God is using to heal others through God's mighty power.

On our journey to Bill's healing, Bill was so blessed to be the recipient of many miracles which came from the heart of God. Your prayers moved the hand of God. Bill and I daily surrendered our lives, our hopes and dreams into God's hands trusting Him to do what was best for us.

The Glory Road is a place of surrender to God alone. I don't bow to my circumstances. I will only kneel to the King of kings and the Lord of lords. God is a God of miracles. Every breath is a testimony to His faithfulness.

Lord, we surrender our lives anew to You today. We pray that You would use our hands to carry out the miracles You have in mind. That might be a hug, a written note, a phone call, a meal, the gift of our presence ~ we trust You to waste nothing in our lives. In Jesus' name we pray, amen.

Thank you for your daily prayers.#Godisfaithful#TheGloryRoad

Day#452 July 15

 Anchor Verse: Psalm 15:5b
Those who do these things will never be shaken; they will stand firm forever.
(TPT)

In this world, the news is filled with structures, people, governments, ethical boundaries that fall apart daily. But in the Bible, we meet the unshakeable, unchangeable, unstoppable God.

"Lord, who may dwell in your sacred tent? Who may live in your holy mountain?" (Psalm 15:1)

In Psalm 15, David is wondering who can come near to the Lord and live in His presence.

This person's walk is blameless (passionate and wholehearted. He does what is righteous (sincere). They speak the truth from their heart (always). Their tongue utters no slander (doesn't insult others). She doesn't do any wrong to her neighbor (doesn't listen to gossip or rumors). He casts no slur on others (never harms a friend with his words.)

They will despise a vile person (evil and evil workers) but honor those who fear the Lord (commends the faithful ones who follow the truth). They keep an oath even when it hurts, and does not change their mind (makes firm commitments and follows through no matter the cost). They lend money to the poor without interest (never crushes others with exploitation) and doesn't accept a bribe against the innocent (can't be bought).

On our journey to Bill's healing, we learned how to be unshakeable as we aligned ourselves with God. Not only can good flow to others, but we are filled up with the joy of the Lord and live in the overflow.

The Glory Road is filled with opportunities to do the "right" thing and live in right relationship with others. We need to adopt God's way of doing things and not our own ways. What a joy it is to live life in communion with God and to walk in His way of blessing for ourselves and others.

Thank you, Lord, for the gift of Jesus. Jesus put others first but was constantly running back to You, heavenly Father, to have his tank filled up with Your goodness and grace to pour out into others. Lord, may we learn from Jesus' example. May we remain unshakeable, unstoppable, and unchangeable. In Jesus' name we pray, amen.

Thank you for your encouraging words.#Godisfaithful#TheGloryRoad

Day#453 July 16

 Anchor Verse: Psalm 16:1
Keep and protect me, O God, for in You I have placed my trust and found refuge.
(AMP)

Where do you run for refuge in the storms of life?

In our area, with the hot temperatures and virtually no rain for a very long time, fire danger is high. There are thousands of acres burning in our state right now (2021). The threat is not only from the fire, but from the smoke as the wind blows it here and there.

More than the physical storm challenges we may face, the storms of greater magnitude are the ones affecting our mind and spirit. The attacks from the enemy can be intense when we are engaged in spiritual warfare.

"Keep and protect me, O God, for in You I have placed my trust and found refuge." (Psalm 16:1)

David knows he needs God to protect him. David's trust is not in his possessions, the fighting men that surround him, his arsenal of weapons or even his keen mind, David's trust is in God and God alone. It is there David finds refuge in the cleft of the rock, the only unshakeable place.

On our journey to Bill's healing, we quickly learned that God was our only strong refuge. From the first morning when the ambulance took Bill to the hospital until the day he drew his final breath, God was our refuge and strength, a mighty help in time of trouble. There were many days of trouble. We lived in the peace of His presence under the shelter of His wings.

The Glory Road is a place of hope, a place of warfare, and a place of peace. With faith as my wraparound shield, the double-edged sword of the Spirit in my hand, which is the word of God, and the belt of truth strapped around my waist, I go into battle knowing God is with me and He is for me.

Lord, victory comes in Your name. When the arrows of the enemy are flying around us, we just need to tuck ourselves in with You. We choose not to worry or be anxious. May we rest in Your arms of love and fight to win another day. We love you and praise you, in Jesus' name we pray, amen.

Thank you for your persistent prayers.#Godisfaithful#TheGloryRoad

Day#454 July 17

 Anchor Verse: Acts 20:36
When Paul had finished speaking, he knelt down with all of them and prayed. (NIV)

There were many "congregations" ~ groups of believers that were established on Paul's missionary journeys. Much of the New Testament was written as Paul's letters (teachings) to them.

In Acts 20, Paul is visiting the believers in Ephesus and it's time to say goodbye to the elders at the church. Farewells are difficult. It was as difficult for Paul as it was for the people there.

"And now, compelled by the Spirit, I am going to Jerusalem, not knowing what will happen to me there. I only know that in every city the Holy Spirit warns me that prison and hardships are facing me." (Acts 20:22-23)

In obedience, Paul was leaving Ephesus and facing the unknown, but the Holy Spirit warned Paul that His path would not be pleasant.

At the end of Paul's farewell speech, Paul shows us his humility. "When Paul had finished speaking, he knelt down with all of them and prayed."

He came out of the "pulpit" from a place of position and authority, and knelt down with them, a position of humility, and prayed. I can imagine there were many tears shed.

On our journey to Bill's healing, God taught us about that posture of humility. Not speaking or acting from a "higher place" but coming alongside those who are hurting and "kneeling" with them, if not in the flesh, definitely in the Spirit. God's peace and presence fill the place where that happens.

The Glory Road has been filled with many opportunities to serve others rather than to be served. I have been so blessed by those who have surrounded me to lift up my arms and serve me in the flesh. In return I can stand with them, or kneel with them, as they go through their own hardships.

You are not a distant God, but God, You come and walk with us. You carry us when we cannot walk on our own. Kneeling with us when we are weary and You wrap Your arms around us when we mourn. May we be humble leaders like Paul, and kneel and pray with others as we seek Your face and walk in Your way. We praise you, Lord. In Jesus' name we pray, amen.

Thank you for your faithfulness.#Godisfaithful#TheGloryRoad

Day#455 July 18

 Anchor Verse: Psalm 22:4
In You our fathers trusted [leaned on, relied on, and were confident]; They trusted and You rescued them. (AMP)

Often the lessons we learn are learned through repetition. God is a good teacher and there are lessons so important He repeats them over and over again. Not just in words but in actions.

Many of the psalms were written by King David. Often the psalms are filled with his raw emotions ~ joy, sorrow, triumph, defeat, frustration, and more. He was a human being just like you and me, but because of David's relationship with God there were many epiphanies.

Often it happens quickly... something "clicks" in your brain and now you have the answer, you know the meaning or have learned the lesson.

David cries out to God because he is in a difficult situation. In the opening verses, it seemed like God abandoned him. "My God, my God, why have you forsaken me?"

In Psalm 22:4, David has an epiphany moment, "In You our fathers trusted [leaned on, relied on, and were confident]; They trusted and You rescued them." David remembers the faithfulness of God through past generations.

On our journey to Bill's healing, we were constantly reminded of God's faithfulness. Every morning we received His new mercies. Every evening, we counted our blessing. Yes, absolutely we leaned on, relied on, were confident in and trusted God, and time after time He rescued Bill. Thank you, Lord.

The Glory Road is a place of contrasts. There are moments of calm followed by stormy waters. Just like a storm can arise quickly at sea, that is also true in our lives. The good news, God is faithful. He will help you patch the leak in your boat or send someone alongside of you to help with the repairs. The storm will come but God has an escape route planned for you.

Lord, we praise you for Your faithfulness to all generations, and to us. May we not be afraid but rest in Your arms of love in Jesus' name, amen.

Thank you for trusting in God.#Godisfaithful#TheGloryRoad

Day#456 July 19

 Anchor Verse: Psalm 25:4
Direct me, Yahweh, throughout my journey so I can experience your plans for my life. Reveal the life-paths that are pleasing to you. (TPT)

In the book of Psalms, on many occasions, we read about David crying out to the Lord for instruction, protection, and guidance.

Putting our trust in God is the first step. We need to know how to live according to God's commands to live a good and righteous life. A life lived on the narrow road not the road which wanders through the wilderness, brambles, and brokenness.

"Direct me, Yahweh, throughout my journey so I can experience your plans for my life. Reveal the life-paths that are pleasing to you." (Psalm 25:4)

The Passion translation expands on that in a beautiful way. David is asking for direction throughout his life's journey so he can experience God's plans for his life that will be pleasing to Him.

On our journey to Bill's healing, our eyes and ears were turned toward heaven. Our heart's desire was to hear God's voice and to walk in a way which pleased Him. It is only in the presence of God we receive and experience the fullness of His joy and the amazing plans He has for our lives.

The Glory Road is a place of instruction. Yes, there have been trials. Yes, there have been places of grief. But this particular tapestry God is weaving together is a new design. My ears are attentive to His voice. My eyes are open to see, not only in the natural but the supernatural (with my spiritual eyes). My mouth seeks to speak only His words of life, not words that wound.

Lord, show us Your ways and teach us Your path, so You alone would be honored and glorified. Keep our feet from falling. May we hear Your voice and walk in Your way. We love you, Lord. In Jesus' name we pray, amen.

May your eyes be opened to see the wonders of His love. May your ears hear His voice and walk in obedience. May your mouth speak words of life to all who cross your path, words of life that come from the heart of God.

Thank you for your companionship.#Godisfaithful#TheGloryRoad

Day#457 July 20

 Anchor Verse: Psalm 26:3
I will never lose sight of your steadfast love for me. Your faithfulness has steadied my steps. (TPT)

Troubles will come... and troubles will go. Storms will arise and the rain and the wind and even the thunder and lightning may make us tremble, but God is our refuge and strength there. He is our ever-present help. (Psalm 46:1)

In Psalm 26, David is pouring out his heart to the Lord. He makes a pretty bold statement in the first verse, "Vindicate me, Lord, for I have led a blameless life; I have trusted in the Lord and have not faltered."

Not many would be so bold as to say we have lived a blameless life. David's life was not without its trials and temptations, and he didn't always do the right thing. But God said, "He is man after my own heart." (Acts 13:22) David might have messed up and made mistakes but he went running back into God's presence, where God could make things right.

"I will never lose sight of your steadfast love for me. Your faithfulness has steadied my steps." (Psalm 26:3)

On our journey to Bill's healing, we never lost sight of God's steadfast love. In the darkness of the night in ICU with monitors beeping around us, with life and death only a breath apart, God's love and faithfulness lit up the room with His glory. God's faithfulness steadied our steps when we walked on high mountains where there was no guardrail except Jesus.

The Glory Road is not without its trials and potholes, and even detours, because of trouble on the road ahead. With every step, I can hear the voice of the Holy Spirit, my Comforter, speaking words of life and words of hope as the Prince of Peace holds my hand reminding me that I am an overcomer.

Thank you, Lord, for Your faithfulness. Your love is unconditional and so very powerful. Your love, heavenly Father, raised Jesus from the dead so we might have life forever with You. Your promises will NEVER let us down. Steady us today, O Lord, so we might walk uprightly with You, and You will receive all the praise and honor and glory in Jesus' name, amen.

Thank you for your faithful prayers.#Godisfaithful#TheGloryRoad

Day#458 July 21

 Anchor Verse: Psalm 29:4
The voice of the Lord echoes through the skies and seas. The Glory-God reigns as he thunders in the clouds. So powerful is his voice, so brilliant and bright— how majestic as he thunders over the great waters! (TPT)

Thunderstorms ~ not everyone's favorite event. Dogs run and hide. Children find refuge in their parents' arms. Adults either love them or tremble like their children. In this season of dryness, even drought, thunder and lightning are dreaded because of the danger of fires being ignited.

David offers a different perspective as we see God moving through nature.

"The voice of the Lord echoes through the skies and seas. The Glory-God reigns as he thunders in the clouds. So powerful is his voice, so brilliant and bright— how majestic as he thunders over the great waters!" (Psalm 29:4)

Sometimes God uses His "outside" voice… the one that thunders, that can't be missed, as He calls out for us to pay attention.

When God speaks to us through nature, it is in our best interest to pay attention. He's got something to say. God's voice is brilliant and bright, and yes, majestic as He thunders over the great waters.

On our journey to Bill's healing, we witnessed the power of God in the storm, when His voice thundered over our lives. There were times God's voice echoed through the hospital corridors as He declared, "This child is mine. Enemy, you cannot have him. You cannot touch him."

The Glory Road goes through quiet places but also stretches of the road are filled with God's thundering voice, and as it says in Psalm 29:7, "The voice of the Lord strikes with flashes of lightning." May we stop and listen and pay attention to what He is speaking to our hearts and minds.

Lord, we praise because You are not one dimensional but multi-dimensional. Thunder and lightning convey Your message and get our attention. Lord, protect us we pray through the storms of our lives. We turn our eyes toward You and declare Your faithfulness to ALL generations in Jesus' name, amen.

Thank you for your faithful prayers.#Godisfaithful#TheGloryRoad

Day#459 July 22

 Anchor Verse: Psalm 32:9
Don't be ornery like a horse or mule that needs bit and bridle to stay on track.
(MSG)

"As stubborn as a mule" ~ have you heard that expression? Said about you or someone else?

A mule's parents are a male donkey and a female horse. Mules do not like to be pushed or prodded to go your way right now. They might come around to the idea, and walk forward at their own pace or not move at all.

We all see the beauty of a horse in motion as its rider guides it with a bit and bridle. The power of its being is released under a skillful hand.

"Don't be ornery like a horse or mule that needs bit and bridle to stay on track." (Psalm 32:9)

Do you have difficulties in staying on track? Do you wander off into the bramble bushes and sinkholes of life because you want to go your own way?

On our journey to Bill's healing, we needed to follow a course God had ordained. There were places in the road that were difficult especially as Bill was recovering from his brain bleed and a host of other complications. As God was healing his brain and his body, Bill had to trust God to lead him through unknown places, terrain that was dark and dangerous at times. We trusted God to lead us by the light of His love even through dark valleys we did not know to the mountain of victory, the pinnacle of His peace.

The Glory Road is a place to exercise my faith and put my trust in my heavenly Father who knows the way. I don't need to be skittish or stubborn. I just need to trust God to direct my path to the destination that He alone knows, the path of righteousness and right living. May I trust You more.

Lord, we praise you in the storms of our lives. We will praise you in the darkness and the light. We praise you at midnight and at the dawning of the day. Instead of being ornery like a mule or a horse, we choose to trust in You, our heavenly Father, that You will lead us in paths of righteousness for Your name's sake. (Psalm 23:3) In Jesus' name, amen.

Thank you for your perseverance. Please pray for my dad who is having knee revision surgery next Wednesday (7.28.21) and for me as I travel to help him, and be with my family.#Godisfaithful#TheGloryRoad

Day#460 July 23

 Anchor Verse: Psalm 34:12-13
Do you want a long, good life? Then watch your tongue! Keep your lips from lying. (TLB)

Life is not a free ride. The Christian life is not a free ride where God does everything and we do "nothing."

Jesus paid the price so we might have eternal life with Him, but we need to start living with high standards now. We hear terms like living a "godly" life or a righteous life. What does that mean?

It means that not only is it our heart's desire to be more like Jesus on the inside, but our actions reflect our intentions.

You may have heard the expression about a tree being known by its fruit. (Matthew 7:20, Luke 6:44) We are also known by the words coming out of our mouths.

"Do you want a long, good life? Then watch your tongue! Keep your lips from lying." (Psalm 34:12-13) Life flows out of our mouth but our words can also lead to our demise.

The MESSAGE translation says, "Guard your tongue from profanity, and no more lying through your teeth." Profanity and lying are not the fruit of a godly heart. Jesus, make us more like you and cleanse our heart and mouth.

On our journey to Bill's healing, we learned about the power of our words. Words spoken to others and words spoken to ourselves have the power to bring life or to crush a spirit. May we choose words of life… so the trail we leave behind is filled with a beautiful bouquet of His love and His presence.

The Glory Road is a path filled with words. There are some words I don't take into my spirit because they are words that crush and destroy. The words my heavenly Father speaks over me are words of life and love. When I let His words take root in my heart, my words are full of life and power.

Lord, may we choose You today. As our heart desires a long, good life, may we watch the words that form in our spirits and come out of our mouths. As a man thinks in his heart so is he. (Proverbs 23:7) Lord, purify our thoughts and words so You alone, will be honored and glorified in Jesus' name. Amen.

Thank you for speaking words of life.#Godisfaithful#TheGloryRoad

Day#461 July 24

 Anchor Verse: Psalm 36:7
How priceless is your unfailing love, O God! People take refuge in the shadow of your wings. (NIV)

Priceless~ in a world where everything has a price, a priceless item is a rare commodity. It's exactly the right word to describe God's unfailing love.

In a world that is mixed-up and messed-up at times, often we see what we're missing, what we may not have the resources to purchase. In those moments, we are reminded priceless treasures come from God's heart.

Time in God's presence, revelation from God's Word (the Bible), listening to the gentle waters of a stream, feeling a cool breeze on your face, or hearing the laughter of a child ~ these are the priceless moments of our lives.

David captures this moment, "How priceless is your unfailing love, O God! People take refuge in the shadow of your wings." (Psalm 36:7)

Scripture reminds us of this place of refuge. "And in the shadow of Your wings I will take refuge until destruction passes by." (Psalm 57:1) "He shall cover you with His feathers, And under His wings you shall take refuge; His truth shall be your shield and buckler." (Psalm 91:4)

On our journey to Bill's healing, we experienced the priceless, unfailing love of God every day. Not only His new mercies every morning but love that knew no boundaries. Day or night, God swooped down, wherever we were and provided refuge in the shadow of His wings. Just like a mother bird protecting her babies, we knew that no harm would befall us there.

The Glory Road is where I find refuge under the shadow of His wings. Some days the battle is fierce, and other days, I need to find rest there. His love never fails. There are no words to describe God's love, from the mountains He moves in my life to the sweet sound of His whispers of encouragement.

Lord, we praise and thank you for the gift of Your unfailing love. Words cannot express our gratitude. Fight the battles we cannot fight. Give us the rest we so desperately need. With our songs and our lives, we will give You all the praise, honor, and glory in Jesus' mighty name. Amen.

Thank you for your love and support.#Godisfaithful#TheGloryRoad

Day#462 July 25

 Anchor Verse: Psalm 37:18-19
Day by day the Lord watches the good deeds of the godly, and he prepares for them his forever-reward. Even in a time of disaster he will watch over them, and they will always have more than enough no matter what happens. (TPT)

Our God is not a faraway God who put the universe in motion and then walked away. He doesn't slumber or sleep. God is preparing us for the days ahead when we will be with Him forever.

As a world, we have been living through an extended season of trials and tribulations. We have been stretched to what seemed like our breaking point. So many changes, so much loss, so many "new" things, "new" ways, when it's the "old" ways that we long for and hope will return.

"Day by day the Lord watches the good deeds of the godly, and he prepares for them his forever-reward. Even in a time of disaster he will watch over them, and they will always have more than enough no matter what happens." (Psalm 37:18-19)

When we walk in obedience to God and His commands, He will reward our steps. God watches over us in the midst of disasters, whether they are physical, emotional, mental, spiritual, or even financial. He will make sure we have more than enough to meet our needs no matter what happens.

On our journey to Bill's healing, we learned of the greater depths of God's faithfulness. Even as the coronavirus shut down many places, God provided for our needs. What we had was multiplied. It was always enough. Although we may not understand God's math, we just need to give God our praise.

The Glory Road is passing through new terrain. It has its ups and downs, new mountains, beautiful valleys with sweet scents, but also some "stinky" places. But through it all, God is faithful. All that I have needed His hand has provided. My wants can wait for His perfect timing.

Lord, we praise and thank you for the gift of this day. We thank you that You are a 24/7 God through every season of our lives. Even if we stumble and fall, you will pick us up and move us forward on the path You have called us to walk. Great is Your faithfulness. In Jesus' name we pray, amen.

Thank you for your persistent prayers.#Godisfaithful#TheGloryRoad

Day#463 July 26

 Anchor Verse: Psalm 40:16
But may all who seek you rejoice and be glad in you; may those who long for your
saving help always say, "The Lord is great!" (NIV)

Is your heart filled with gladness and rejoicing this morning? I hope so. If
not, why not?

Maybe you are longing for God's saving help because you are buried under
life's cares and troubles. There has been a lot going on in the world lately.
Many people even in my circle of influence are facing health issues and
traumatic situations, either for themselves or others. But that is NOT the
end of the story.

The storm is the place where God wants to rewrite the story of your life. The
storm isn't the end, it's a new beginning. It's the place where we see God's
faithfulness shining most brightly.

"But may all who seek you rejoice and be glad in you; may those who long
for your saving help always say, "The Lord is great!" (Psalm 40:16)

In Psalm 40:16, we see the use of the word "always." Note two things: 1.
The use of the word "always": Not just once in a while but ALWAYS, they
say, "The Lord is great!" 2. These are the people that long for God's help…
not those who have already seen it happen. Is this you?

On our journey to Bill's healing, we were witnesses to God's great
faithfulness. Day after day, week after week, month after month, God was
GREAT and FAITHFUL. We had the opportunity to share this testimony
with you. Our prayer is you would rejoice and be glad because of what God
had done for you. And what He longs to do for you, greater things.

The Glory Road is marked with memories and monuments to God's
faithfulness not only in my life, but in the lives of others. As I join with many
of you to pray, we see miracles happen. People healed and delivered, and
others set free. Why? Because that's who God is, "The Lord is great!"

Lord, we praise you for who You are this morning. You are the one our
hearts long for. You are faithful in the sunshine and the rain. We keep our
eyes on You and we trust in You, O Lord. In Jesus' name we pray, amen.

Thank you for your persevering prayers.#Godisfaithful#TheGloryRoad

Day# 464 July 27

Anchor Verse: Psalm 44:3

They did not conquer the land with their swords; it was not their own strong arm that gave them victory. It was your right hand and strong arm and the blinding light from your face that helped them, for you loved them. (NLT)

The powerful imagery God used as He wrote the Bible through the hands of men often magnifies the impact of the written word.

When it comes to God and His ways, our words cannot describe the magnitude of His power, His presence or His peace.

"They did not conquer the land with their swords; it was not their own strong arm that gave them victory. It was your right hand and strong arm and the blinding light from your face that helped them, for you loved them." (Psalm 44:3)

Scripture is so powerful in how it gives us an "attitude adjustment" and changes our perspective to focus on God and not ourselves. We are not the heroes of our story, God is.

It was not because of the great swordsmanship of the children of Israel or their great military strategy, or strong arm, or military might that gave them victory, it was the favor of God and His mighty power.

God's right hand is a symbol of God's expertise to achieve victory over anything in our lives. God's strong arm has the power to carry out what He has designed. The favor of the Lord rests upon us.

On our journey to Bill's healing, the power, favor, and lovingkindness of God rested upon us. There was nothing lacking. Some days this was walked out as Jehovah Gibbor, the Lord Mighty in battle, or Jehovah Shalom, our Peace, or Jehovah Jireh, our Provider, or El Elyon, the Lord Most High. God was all we needed. He was always enough.

The Glory Road is a place of war and a place of peace. It is the intersection where faith and fear meet and faith always wins. It is where Jesus set me free. Nothing has a hold on me except the power of God's love.

Lord, may we rejoice in You, the God of our salvation. He is great and greatly to be praised. He is all we need. In Jesus' name we pray, amen.

Thank you for your faithfulness.#Godisfaithful#TheGloryRoad

Day#465 July 28

 Anchor Verse: Psalm 46:5
God is in the midst of his city, secure and never shaken. At daybreak his help will be seen with the appearing of the dawn. (TPT)

There is something so powerful about the word of God ~ not only the words that are spoken but the power of the Spirit that is woven into the tapestry of its message.

"God is our refuge and strength, an ever-present help in time of trouble." (Psalm 46:1)

Read that again. He is an "ever-present" help... not just once in a while... but ever-present, never failing, always ready and willing and able to help you with great love and lots of joy.

In verse 4, it tells us of the river that makes "glad" the city of our God, the holy place where the Most High dwells. A city that is glad... not always the picture we have of our cities on earth today. We are seeing a lot of sadness and violence here on earth in our cities.

"God is in the midst of his city, secure and never shaken. At daybreak his help will be seen with the appearing of the dawn." (Psalm 46:5)

On our journey to Bill's healing, we were blessed to see God's hand at work, daily. We heard His voice and chose to walk in His way. His help was always present at the appearing of the dawn, often after a long dark night. But in His presence, we see light. We have hope. We are filled with His joy.

The Glory Road is the place where my feet are planted firmly on the foundation of the Lord, in a city that is secure and never shaken. At daybreak, His help is seen. Even this morning (7.28.21) as my dad has surgery to fix his knee where the replacement part broke, God's peace is covering us and we see God's help even in the pre-dawn hours.

Lord, may we find rest in You today, You who are unshakeable, unstoppable, and unmovable. We cast all our cares on you. We stand in Your presence and cry out, "Holy, holy, holy is the Lord God Almighty! The whole earth is filled with His glory... the WHOLE earth. (Isaiah 6:3) Lord, fill us anew with Your power and presence, in Jesus' powerful name, amen.

Thank you for your faithfulness and praying for my dad's knee surgery.#Godisfaithful#TheGloryRoad

Day#466 July 29

 Anchor Verse: Psalm 50:1
The God of gods, the mighty Lord himself, has spoken! He shouts out over all the people of the earth in every brilliant sunrise and every beautiful sunset, saying, "Listen to me!" (TPT)

Does a morning sunrise still fill you with awe and wonder when the first rays of light command the darkness to flee in Jesus' name? How about the peace and beauty of a sunset, God's final word of shalom over the busy day that's left you weary? Then God exchanged your weariness with His peace.

There is power in the name of Jesus. At God's word, the world came into being. At His word, every morning we are given the gift of a new day. Great is His faithfulness! There is nothing too hard for Him, nothing.

"The God of gods, the mighty Lord himself, has spoken! He shouts out over all the people of the earth in every brilliant sunrise and every beautiful sunset, saying, 'Listen to me!'" (Psalm 50:1)

There is something that happens in a conversation with a person we love and who loves us. More than words are exchanged. There is a heart connection. Their hope, love, joy, peace is passed along to us. What a blessing to leave a person's presence feeling more blessed than when we met them.

On our journey to Bill's healing, we were encouraged by the sound of God's voice. Some days it was a still, small whisper, and in other cases, there were shouts of joy or warning or His peace and power as He spoke into Bill's life. God is a master communicator.

The Glory Road has held new sights, new sounds, and new experiences. Through it all, I have been blessed by an awareness of His presence. I have seen His face in the sunrise or the power of His voice in the rolling thunder. Lord, I stand in awe of You this morning. There is no one like you, Lord.

Lord, this morning we lift our hands in praise. We praise and thank you that no weapon formed against us will prosper. At Your command, all nature bows to You, and every knee will bow and every tongue confess that Jesus Christ is Lord to the glory of God the Father.

Thank you for your prayers of faith. My dad is doing great after surgery yesterday.#Godisfaithful#TheGloryRoad

Day#467 July 30

 Anchor Verse: Romans 2:9-10
Anyone who does evil can expect tribulation and distress…But when we do what pleases God, we can expect unfading glory, true honor, and a continual peace…
(TPT)

There is a law of nature that says, "You reap what you sow." If a farmer plants corn, he doesn't expect to see wheat when it comes to maturity. Apples don't appear on a cherry tree, and onions don't turn into beets.

What God implemented in the laws of nature is also true in our lives.

"Anyone who does evil can expect tribulation and distress—to the Jew first and also to the non-Jew. But when we do what pleases God, we can expect unfading glory, true honor, and a continual peace…" (Romans 2:9-10)

God is not a respecter of persons, what He does for one, He does for another. The rain falls on the just and the unjust. (Matthew 5:45)

When we do what pleases God, the reward is "unfading glory, true honor, and continual peace." Why would we want to do anything "but" what pleases God? It seems like a no-brainer. Read those rewards one more time, "unfading glory, true honor, and continual peace." That's my goal.

On our journey to Bill's healing, we encountered people and situations where good and evil were real. And the results were just as evident. Bill and I were grateful to be blessed with God's reward of unfading glory, true honor and continual peace. What a blessing to be a child of God.

The Glory Road is all about making good choices, and walking in obedience to God's commands. His way is the best way. I live for His honor and glory. As His daughter, my heart's desire is to be more like my heavenly Father.

Lord, we thank you for the gift of free will to choose to do what is right. You reward our obedience when we do the right things. We pray for those who are walking in darkness that they might know the protection of Your love. Today we choose You, O Lord. In Jesus' name we pray, amen.

Thank you for your persevering prayers for my dad. The "plan" is he will come home from the hospital today.#Godisfaithful#TheGloryRoad

Day#468 July 31

 Anchor Verse: Psalm 55:12
But as for me, I will call upon the Lord to save me, and I know he will!

Words are so powerful on their own, but when they tell a story, their power is magnified.

Psalm 55 tells us the story of David's enemies and the trouble David is encountering. "Fear and trembling have beset me; horror has overwhelmed me." (Psalm 55:5) Not a very pretty picture of David's circumstances.

That's not the end of the story. In the midst of this psalm, there are two places David infuses new hope as God breathes new hope into his life.

David says, "All this might be happening in my life, my enemies, my suffering, my pain, my troubles, let me tell you how it's different for me."

In Psalm 55:12, David points out the difference for the man who walks with God. "But as for me, I will call upon the Lord to save me, and I know he will!" and also in the last verse of Psalm 55, verse 23, "… But as for me, I trust in you."

Is that your story? "But as for me, I trust in you." That's a bold prayer.

On our journey to Bill's healing, we walked through the refining fire, the furnace of affliction, and the wilderness of wandering, but all of it with our heavenly Father at our side. Bill called on the name of the Lord to save him, spare his life, and God did.

The Glory Road is filled with new opportunities to trust God ~ wherever He leads me and often for reasons beyond my understanding. What an amazing honor to be trusted by God with a task bigger than yourself because the only way you can succeed is with His help.

Lord, we praise and thank you for the gift of this day. You alone are worthy of our praise. As we turn our holy hands toward heaven, You will hear our cries for mercy. Intervene in the lives of those who need You. Lord, You are faithful and NOTHING is too hard for You, Lord. In Jesus' name, amen.

Thank you for your bold prayers. Dad is home and the healing continues.#Godisfaithful#TheGloryRoad

August 2021

*Therefore since we have such a hope,
we are very bold.*

~ 2 Corinthians 3:12 ~

Day#469 August 1

 Anchor Verse: Psalm 59:9-10a
You are my strength; I wait for you to rescue me, for you, O God, are my fortress. In his unfailing love, my God will stand with me. (NLT)

Watching and waiting are a part of our lives. Even a baby waits to be born until God says it's time.

What do we do in the waiting? Is our energy wasted in worry and anxiety or do we choose to wait on the Lord?

Psalm 59 reminds us of the best place to place our hope. It is not in the things of this world, but in God, our heavenly Father.

"You are my strength; I wait for you to rescue me, for you, O God, are my fortress. In his unfailing love, my God will stand with me." (Psalm 59:9-10a)

Throughout the Bible, we are reminded that God is our strength.

"God is our refuge and strength, an ever-present help in time of trouble." (Psalm 46:1)

"The joy of the Lord is my strength." (Nehemiah 8:10)

God is the only one on whom we can rely. He will be found faithful in every circumstance and situation.

On our journey to Bill's healing, God was Bill's strength daily. God stood with Bill even when in the flesh Bill could barely stand on his own. God rescued Bill again and again because God is faithful. He loved Bill so much.

The Glory Road may be unfamiliar territory to me but it is not unfamiliar territory to God. His love never fails, His glory never fades. His light shines brightly in the darkness, rain, clouds, hurricanes and the storm. He is a strong tower and I can run to Him and be safe.

Lord, we love you and praise you. You are our shelter in the storm. You are our peace. I pray for those who are lost and need to find their way back to You. For those who are weary, be their strength; uphold them with Your powerful right hand. In Jesus' mighty name, amen.

Thank you for your persevering prayers.#Godisfaithful#TheGloryRoad

Day#470 August 2

 Anchor Verse: Romans 5:2
... rejoice in hope of the glory of God. (NKJV)

What does it mean to rejoice?

The dictionary defines rejoice in this way, "To rejoice is to feel great happiness or joy, or to take great pleasure in something."

There is only place, one solid rock where we can find eternal joy, eternal hope… and that is in God, our heavenly Father.

Romans 5:2 tells us to "rejoice in the hope of the glory of God." The Amplified version expands on that to say, "the manifestation of His excellence and power."

We really can't even comprehend the full magnitude of His excellence and power. There are moments in our day, in our lives, where we get a peek of His glory, His excellence, and His power, whether in nature or in relationship with others.

On our journey to Bill's healing, we saw glimpses of the glory of God. There was a pure and holy light streaming from God's face and it touched our hearts and lives. Our hope in God brought us through the darkest nights and the places where others didn't see any hope. God knew the whole story and we trusted Him to write the perfect ending.

The Glory Road is a path where I get new revelation of His excellence and power. Daily I watch for God's hand at work in the details of my life or the lives of others. His glory and majesty are as beautiful in the first light of dawn as in the laughter of a child or His answer to our prayers. Often, I turn my head and heart toward heaven and say, "Thank you, Lord."

Lord, thank you for the gift of Your love. You call us to be holy and to choose You over anything this world has to offer ~ first, last, and always. Lord, may we be Your hands and feet. May Your honor be seen in us. May Your glory rest upon us and be a beacon of light to those walking in darkness. You are great and greatly to be praised. In Jesus' name. Amen.

Thank you for your companionship.#Godisfaithful#TheGloryRoad

Day#471 August 3

 Anchor Verse: Psalm 63:2
I have seen You in Your sanctuary and have been awed by Your power and glory.
(VOICE)

"Seeing is believing" ~ it's a phrase that we often speak, and truthfully, many people operate from this place. They walk by "sight" and not by "faith."

What we see is determined by where we focus our eyes.

Psalm 63 is a powerful psalm. The imagery is powerful but the spirit behind it is even stronger.

In the early verses the psalmist says, "I have seen You in Your sanctuary and have been awed by Your power and glory." (Psalm 63:2)

Are you in awe of the power and glory of God? Each day the Lord gives me life, I stand in awe of His might and power. At the same time, the power of His mercy and grace fills me with such joy and hope.

The Passion translation says, "I'm energized every time I enter your heavenly sanctuary to seek more of your power and drink in more of your glory."

On our journey to Bill's healing, we lifted our eyes away from the chaos of the world into the face of Jesus who sits at the right hand of God. The resurrection power that raised Jesus from the grave lived in Bill, it lives in me and you. When we fall short of the glory God intended for us, it's not because of lack on His part, but that we refuse to drink from the cup of suffering so that we might experience the greater glory God has for us.

The Glory Road is a place of contrasts, what the enemy intended for evil, God uses for good. Daily, as I help my dad is his recovery from knee revision surgery, I am brought to tears by God's love and faithfulness. He releases not only the spirit of joy but showers of His blessings.

Lord, we long to see Your face and walk in Your ways. Our eyes are set on You, King Jesus, who conquers the enemy of death. Our ears are attentive to Your voice. We are filled with joy in Your presence so we might go out and spread this joy to others. In Jesus' mighty name, amen.

Thank you for your faithfulness.#Godisfaithful#TheGloryRoad

Day#472 August 4

 Anchor Verse: Psalm 66:20
I will forever praise this God who didn't close his heart when I prayed and never said no when I asked him for help. He never once refused to show me his tender love. (TPT)

How many of you are praying people? For some of you, it is a daily discipline. For others, it may be a "foxhole" prayer in time of trouble. Regardless of the frequency of your prayers, one thing I know, God will never turn a deaf ear to you. He will not ignore you. In fact, your heavenly Father rejoices when you rejoice and weeps when you weep.

Many of you could bear testimony to this truth. In fact, many of you, or your loved ones, are still alive today because God is a God of love and mercy.

In the Message translation, Psalm 66:16-20 gives us the context for today's anchor verse, "All believers, come here and listen, let me tell you what God did for me. I called out to him with my mouth, my tongue shaped the sounds of music. If I had been cozy with evil, the Lord would never have listened. But he most surely did listen, he came on the double when he heard my prayer. Blessed be God: he didn't turn a deaf ear, he stayed with me, loyal in his love."

On our journey to Bill's healing, we lived in a place of prayer. We may not have literally been on our knees in prayer, but our spirits were always bowed before the King of kings and the Lord of lords. God heard the cries of Bill's heart. His heart was attentive to Bill's every breath and heartbeat.

The Glory Road is filled with my prayers as I walk forward into this unknown land. Some places may look familiar but I see them with new eyes, without Bill's commentary on the surroundings. I am so grateful that God comes "on the double" when He hears my prayer. Sometimes my prayer is as simple as just the name of Jesus. There is power in the name of Jesus.

Lord, we praise and thank you for the gift of this new day. Your mercies are new every morning and great is Your faithfulness. We choose You over anything this world might offer. Great, great, great are You, Lord. Thank you for being our anchor in the storms of our lives. You are faithful. You are faithful. In Jesus' mighty name, we pray, amen.

Thank you for your love for Jesus.#Godisfaithful#TheGloryRoad

Day#473 August 5

 Anchor Verse: Psalm 69:29
I am burdened and broken by this pain. When your miracle rescue comes to me, it will lift me to the highest place. (TPT)

There are moments and places where people feel they are invisible, unseen by others, even those really close to them.

Many of you deal with pain and affliction daily and often go unnoticed. You may have a chronic health condition where daily you battle fatigue, pain, immobility, isolation, even anxiety, or depression. Often the enemy of our souls will use our weakness, our difficult places to plant seeds of doubt and fear in our mind and spirit.

You are not invisible to God. The Holy Spirit is hovering over you. Jesus is walking with you, hand in hand. Your heavenly Father is speaking love, life, and blessings through His authority into your body, mind, and spirit.

In our journey to Bill's healing, there were places where we felt invisible to the world. Everyone has their own life, responsibilities, challenges, joys, etc. People need to tend to their own "stuff" and sometimes we find ourselves keeping company with God alone. It's a great place. Everything we need can be found in His presence where we find the fullness of His joy.

The Glory Road is filled with opportunities to be Jesus' hands and feet. It's a place of contrasts ~ being alone and together, vulnerability and strength, tears of sorrow and tears of joy and gratitude. For some of you, it's a time of pain that turns into a place of healing. Healing isn't always physical. Sometimes God speaks words of life to our spirit, or anoints us with the Balm of Gilead to heal our souls. Receive that healing today.

Lord, even as I walk my own journey to healing, I see my dad walking out his own journey. We lift up those in pain, those who are afflicted. You are the God of their salvation. I pray for healing in the innermost places. Lord, make us deaf to the lies of the enemy. You are the Lord, our healer, and we praise You! Be blessed. Be at peace. You are loved in Jesus' name, amen.

Thank you for your prevailing prayers. My dad continues to walk in his healing.#Godisfaithful#TheGloryRoad

Day#474 August 6

 Anchor Verse: Psalm 71:18
Now that I am old and gray, do not abandon me, O God. Let me proclaim your power to this new generation, your mighty miracles to all who come after me. (NLT)

It is not just in the vigor of our youth God has plans for us but at every stage of our lives, even our old age.

The psalmist was speaking of God's faithfulness but also of his own duty, responsibility, and commission from God to tell his story for God's glory.

"Now that I am old and gray, do not abandon me, O God. Let me proclaim your power to this new generation, your mighty miracles to all who come after me." (Psalm 71:18)

As God does mighty things in our lives, we are blessed with the opportunity to share our experience with others. We are quick to tell of our own exploits, but the pleasure is even greater to share God's power.

On our journey to Bill's healing, we found joy and hope in God's presence. With every God encounter, there were mighty miracles to share with you. Bill never let an opportunity pass to share his story for God's glory.

The Glory Road was named by my heavenly Father. The day after Bill died, in His still small voice, the Lord directed me to begin a new path with Him. He called it the Glory Road. Why? Because my grief would be overcome by His glory. Others would see God's fingerprints as I walked with Him through this valley of grief to the greater things God has planned for me.

As you have seen in these 474 days, God has been faithful. O the joy that has been mine to abide in God's presence, to be fed at His banqueting table, to be comforted in my grief and share our story for His glory.

Lord, thank you we are not alone in our journey here on earth. You are an ever-present help in time of trouble. We will praise you in the sunshine and the storm. We will proclaim Your name on high. In Jesus' name, amen.

Thank you for your fervent prayers.#Godisfaithful#TheGloryRoad

Day#475 August 7

 Anchor Verse: Psalm 73:23
Yet, in spite of all this, I still belong to you; you hold me by my right hand. (TPT)

Life has ups and downs, joy and sorrow, expansion and loss... just "stuff." Our lives are not lived in a straight line. They are like a symphony with soft and loud places.

The one constant for us as believers is that God is with us. He will never leave us or forsake us.

In the first 72 psalms, David has shared the cries of his heart and the faithfulness of God. Asaph is the author of Psalm 73 and he talks about his life and his struggles. But the constant theme is God's faithfulness.

In Psalm 72:21-22, Asaph comments how his heart was grieved and his spirit embittered. He was senseless and ignorant, a brute beast before God.

"Yet, in spite of all this, I still belong to you; you hold me by my right hand." (Psalm 72:23)

Yet in spite of all this" ~ each one of us has a "yet, in spite of all this" story of our lives.

On our journey to Bill's healing, we encountered many difficult places. Life was a mixture of emotions, situations, people, and pleasures. One thing we could always count on was God's faithfulness. He would hold on to our hands and walk us through each place triumphantly.

The Glory Road is also a place of "yet, in spite of all this" moments. Not only in my own life, but in the lives of those I know, love, and encounter. Even on my way home (8.6.21) from visiting my family on the other side of the state, there was a fatal accident on the highway ahead. Delayed by 2.5 hours while they cleared the accident site, it was a great opportunity to pray.

Lord, we praise and thank you for the gift of Your presence. Great is Your faithfulness that extends to ALL generations. May we hold on to Your right hand as You guide us through stormy waters, as we lie down in green pastures, and as You speak peace to our souls. In Jesus' name we pray, amen.

Thank you for your faithful prayers. I'm back home again (8.7.21) and my dad continues to get stronger.#Godisfaithful#TheGloryRoad

Day#476 August 8

 Anchor Verse: Romans 8:24
We are saved by trusting. And trusting means looking forward to getting something we don't yet have—for a man who already has something doesn't need to hope and trust that he will get it. (TLB)

As believers, we place our hope in God. We trust Him with our past, present, and future. The Bible reminds us we can trust Him with our very lives. We can't change the past but we can surely trust God with the future.

In Romans 8, the apostle Paul wrestles with the topic of living our life according to the flesh (our sinful nature) and choosing to walk according to the Spirit, God's best for us.

Paul puts the battle in proper perspective, "I consider that our present sufferings are not worth comparing with the glory that will be revealed in us." (Romans 8:18)

In verse 24, Paul talks about trusting God and about hope ~ unseen hope, not hope that has already come to pass. It's anticipating what is to come, not what you already hold in your hands.

Hope that is seen is no hope at all. Who hopes for what he already has? The Living Bible uses the term "trusting" ~ we are saved by "trusting." We trust in God to do what He says He will do and to reward those who diligently seek Him. (Hebrews 11:6)

On our journey to Bill's healing, we had many opportunities to trust God and to hope for what we didn't already see. It took time and trusting God's faithfulness to see the outcome of Bill's healing, his transformation. We believed God's promises were true. We trusted in God's nature. We declared God's faithfulness as we waited in hope. God did not disappoint us.

The Glory Road is the path to victory. Daily, I choose to trust in God to carry out His best plans for me. I choose to walk in obedience. I choose to step out in faith to do what I cannot do on my own but only by His grace and His strength, the Holy Spirit at work in me.

Lord, we entrust you with our lives. God, You are for us and not against us. Our present sufferings are nothing compared to the joy set before us. We have hope because of Jesus' victory at Calvary. In Jesus' name, amen.

Thank you for your encouraging words.#Godisfaithful#TheGloryRoad

Day#477 August 9

 Anchor Verse: Psalm 78:53
He kept them safe, so they were not afraid. But the sea closed in upon their enemies and overwhelmed them. (TLB)

Safety ~ it's one of the things we long for from the time of our birth. When we are safe, we have no fear. We can walk through difficult and dangerous places and not be afraid.

It stretches our imagination to picture the children of Israel as they left Egypt fleeing from a harsh ruler, Pharaoh, in massive numbers and wandering through the wilderness for 40 years. Moses, as their leader, was following the instructions of God as he led hundreds of thousands of people to a destination he did not know. This is a great picture of a walk of faith.

Psalm 78 tells us about what God did as He led His people and how those stories are passed along from one generation to the next.

In verse 53 we find the psalmist's message about the safety of God's people. "He kept them safe, so they were not afraid. But the sea closed in upon their enemies and overwhelmed them."

Being safe and not being afraid are two different things. A child can be safe in his parent's arms and still be afraid. Safety is a physical reality while fear is mental and emotional.

Psalm 78:53 reminds us God kept them safe and they were not afraid.

On our journey to Bill's healing, God kept us safe even through difficult places where life and death were only a breath apart. We were not afraid. Fear had no hold on us because our trust was placed in God who holds the world and everything in it in the hollow of His hands.

The Glory Road is a path of victory, through deep waters and lofty peaks. There are enemies who seek to harm me but I am not afraid because I am safe in my heavenly Father's arms of love.

Lord, we praise and thank you for the safe haven You are. You are our shelter in the storms of life. God is our refuge in times of trouble. We don't need to be afraid because You are fighting for us. We lift our arms in praise this morning. In Jesus' name we pray, amen.

Thank you for your faithfulness.#Godisfaithful#TheGloryRoad

Day#478 August 10

 Anchor Verse: Psalm 79:8b
May your mercy come quickly to meet us, for we are in desperate need. (NIV)

We are familiar with the acronym "ASAP" which means "as soon as possible." It means to drop whatever you are doing and do this one thing… right now. There's urgency to the tone, there's no time for delay.

In Psalm 79, the psalmist conveys this urgency in his words. God's people have been overrun by their enemies; Jerusalem has been invaded and left in rubble. "How long, Lord? Will you be angry forever?" (Psalm 79:3)

God, pour out Your wrath on the nations that don't acknowledge You. The psalmist continues to look for the answer to this endless trouble. Is it the sins of past generations that are causing this problem?

Psalm 79:8 says, "May your mercy come quickly to meet us, for we are in desperate need."

Reading this passage, it sounded like our heart cry in our nation and around the world, in August 2021. Lord, we are in desperate need, we need Your mercy.

A couple of other translations use this verbiage. "We are devastated beyond belief." (TPT) "We are on the brink of despair." (NLT)

On our journey to Bill's healing, we hit some difficult places, places where we knew God was the only answer; our hope didn't lie in human hands or medical solutions. Our eyes and hearts were turned toward heaven as our hearts yearned for resolution and healing. Hope always comes from God.

The Glory Road is walked out in a world where God's compassion and mercy are desperately needed. God is our only hope because others are relegated to their own corner as we wait out the storms in our own lives. God's faithfulness has been a brilliant beacon of light for me.

Lord, we praise and thank you for the gift of life, the gift of Your love. Our eyes are on You, Lord, and we will not be moved. Go before us this day. Lift our heads. Lift up our eyes. Our hope comes in the name of the Lord, and we will praise you until our final breath. In Jesus' name we pray, amen.

Thank you for your persevering prayers. Today my dad goes to see the surgeon's PA-C for his first check-up post-surgery. (2021) Thanks for walking with us.#Godisfaithful#TheGloryRoad

Day#479 August 11

 Anchor Verse: Psalm 81:13
If my people would only listen to me… (NIV)

Throughout the Old Testament we read stories about how the children of Israel disobeyed God and the consequences that followed. One of the greatest examples is instead of the 11-day journey from Egypt to the Promised Land, God took them through the wilderness for 40 years.

That's a pretty vivid example of what "not" to do unless you prefer the long way to your destination. Those who disobeyed died in the wilderness and never reached the Promised Land. Obedience brings life. Disobedience is the path to destruction.

Several times in this psalm we hear the words of God lamenting over His people. It breaks God's heart when His people do not listen to Him. Psalm 81:13 says, "If my people would only listen to me…"

God knows the heartbreak, the hard times avoided if we listen to Him and walk in His ways rather than wander off the path and into trouble.

On our journey to Bill's healing, we encountered places where we had a choice to follow God's way or our way. We chose God's way because it was the path to life. Life is too hard to navigate without God at your side.

The Glory Road is a place of peace in the midst of a world in turmoil. When I keep my eyes on Jesus, and my ears tuned to the still, small voice of God, my path is steady and my heart is at peace. I long to hear God's voice. Without Him, I would lose my way. God's way is the path of life.

Lord, we come before you on our knees, asking for forgiveness for the times we have chosen our own way rather than Your way. Lord, show us the path to life. Lead us by Your powerful right hand. Keep us safe under the shadow of Your wings. May we choose You in the sun at noonday and in the darkness of the night. In Jesus' name, we pray, amen.

Thank you for your companionship. My dad got the staples out of the incision in his leg yesterday (8.10.21).#Godisfaithful#TheGloryRoad

Day#480 August 12

 Anchor Verse: Romans 12:21
Do not be overcome and conquered by evil, but overcome evil with good. (AMP)

Good and evil ~ and the battle between them has been a longstanding feud since the beginning of time. Throughout history, we see the places where good has "won" and also where evil has had its way.

Romans 12 is filled with so many powerful truths and instruction for Christian living. We start out the chapter being called to present our bodies as a "living sacrifice", holy and pleasing (acceptable) to God, which is our reasonable service (true and proper worship). Our lives are to be lived for the glory of God. Nothing less is what He asks of us.

Beginning in verse 9 to the end of the chapter, in my Bible it has the heading, "Love in Action." We are instructed by Paul in this letter to the Roman church how to overcome evil. Through our continuous acts of love evil's path is blocked and God has the final victory in our lives and in our world.

The chapter ends with this exhortation, "Do not be overcome and conquered by evil, but overcome evil with good."

On our journey to Bill's healing, we saw evil raise its ugly head more than once. We fought back the darkness of evil by choosing to respond in love and spread acts of kindness. Yes, we overcome evil with good.

The Glory Road is a path filled with God's light and love. Daily, I choose to walk with God and walk in the light of His love. I run into His presence so my cup is filled to overflowing so I can pour love, joy, and goodness into the lives of others. That is how we conquer evil.

Where have you chosen to pitch your tent? In the land of evil or on holy ground ~ where God abides? Together we can overcome evil with good.

Lord, we thank you there is an antidote to evil and it is the love of God. Lord, fill us up to full and overflowing as we choose the path of love and kindness so we will not be conquered by evil but goodness will triumph once again. In the face of chaos, we declare victory in Jesus' mighty name. Amen.

Thank you for your persistent prayers.#Godisfaithful#TheGloryRoad

Day#481 August 13

 Anchor Verse: Psalm 88:13
Lord, you know my prayer before I even whisper it. At each and every sunrise you will continue to hear my cry until you answer. (TPT)

Prayer is one of the most powerful gifts God has given us.

Psalm 88 is the psalmist's heart cry as he goes through a difficult time in his life. At times the struggle seems so hard, he begins to wonder where God is in all of the darkness he is facing.

Even in the darkness, his heart knows there is only one place to run, the only one who can save him, Lord God Almighty, Maker of heaven and earth.

"Lord, you know my prayer before I even whisper it. At each and every sunrise you will continue to hear my cry until you answer." (Psalm 88:13)

Your struggle may be long, my friend, but at some point, it will come to an end. God is a good, good Father.

On our journey to Bill's healing, our hearts and minds were filled with prayers to the Lord. In hospitals, doctor's offices, rehab facilities, our home or our church, our prayers rose like incense before the throne of grace. It was there, Bill found help in his hour of need. I found comfort when the air seems stripped of oxygen as we fought for Bill's life.

The Glory Road is filled with prayer day and night. "At each and every sunrise you will continue to hear my cry until You answer." My prayers will be relentless for those I love going through the fires of adversity. Heavenly Father, greater still is Your power and love and ability to deliver us.

Lord, thank you for not leaving us alone. You are closer than our next breath. You have a plan and a purpose even in the midst of our suffering. We lean into Your presence this morning and trust You with the path that lies ahead. Lord, You are faithful. In Jesus' name we pray, amen.

Thank you for your faithfulness. Dad's healing and recovery from PT yesterday (8.12.21) continues. Lord, strengthen his bones, body, mind and spirit in Jesus' name.#Godisfaithful#TheGloryRoad

Day#482 August 14

 Anchor Verse: Psalm 89:8
O Jehovah, Commander of the heavenly armies, where is there any other Mighty One like you? Faithfulness is your very character. (TLB)

When was the last time you pondered the character of God? Have you thought about the amazing qualities that we attribute to God who loves you and me unconditionally?

Our heavenly Father is not distant, nor does He rule from heaven like a puppet master. He is involved in our daily lives. God loves us so much daily He watches over our coming and going, rejoices in our victories, mourns when we mourn, and encourages us with every breath.

In Psalm 89, there are many descriptive passages about God, but in verse 8, we stop for a moment to ponder this question. "O Jehovah, Commander of the heavenly armies, where is there any other Mighty One like you? Faithfulness is your very character."

Jehovah is the Commander of the heavenly armies, the angels that move at His command. We have witnessed military precision and prowess throughout the history of the world, both used for good and for evil. There is none other like Jehovah, the Commander of angel armies.

Faithfulness is His very character. We talk about faithfulness a lot in our lives. We are drawn to those who are faithful. We can count on them when life gets difficult. My friends, how faithful are you?

On our journey to Bill's healing, the faithfulness of God was like a golden thread running through Bill's story. Day after day, night after night, God's faithfulness was our refuge and strength, and His faithfulness kept us from perishing under the weight of the load.

The Glory Road is a path where I not only see God's faithfulness but declare His faithfulness, not only to you, but to future generations. It is so important to share what God has done in our lives. It is through our declaration of faith others are made aware of the hope within us.

Lord, thank you for Your unconditional love. You never leave us alone in the battles we face daily. Faithfulness is Your character and I pray we would be just like our heavenly Father. May others say we are faithful, faithfulness is part of our character. We love you and praise you, in Jesus' name, amen.

Thank you for your faithfulness.#Godisfaithful#TheGloryRoad

Day#483 August 15

 Anchor Verse: Psalm 92:14
[Growing in grace] they will still thrive and bear fruit and prosper in old age; They will flourish and be vital and fresh [rich in trust and love and contentment]. (AMP)

Moses encountered God at the burning bush when he was 80 years old, and God called him to lead the children of Israel out of Egypt to the Promised Land. Abraham (originally Abram) was 75 years old when God called him from his father's house to go to a place he did not know.

At 99, God told him, "I am God Almighty; walk before me and be blameless. I will confirm my covenant between me and you and will greatly increase your numbers… As for me, this is my covenant with you: You will be the father of many nations." (Genesis 17:1-2, 4)

"[Growing in grace] they will still thrive and bear fruit and prosper in old age; They will flourish and be vital and fresh [rich in trust and love and contentment]." (Psalm 92:14)

What a great promise! Take this to heart and insert your name here. "_____ will still thrive, bear fruit and prosper in old age. _____ will flourish, be vital and fresh [rich in trust, love and contentment.]"

On our journey to Bill's healing, we learned the blessing of growing in grace as we both grew older. Bill learned how you can thrive and prosper spiritually even when you are walking through challenges in your flesh and your health. May we all learn to thrive in grace every year of our lives.

The Glory Road is a path that leads me into my older years. My white hair is a crown of glory. God has entrusted me with some life trials to make me stronger for His honor and glory. So blessed by the saint surrounding me.

Lord Jesus, You are the resurrection and the life. As we follow You, we too will experience the joy of the Lord which is our strength. Nothing is too hard for You and as we put our hand in Your hand, nothing will be too hard for us either. We love you, Lord, in Jesus' mighty name we pray, amen.

Thank you for your companionship. Last night (8.14.21) was Dad's first night "solo" without a caregiver. The angels of the Lord stood guard over him.#Godisfaithful#TheGloryRoad

Day#484 August 16

 Anchor Verse: Romans 15:33
And now may God, who gives us his peace, be with you all. Amen. (NLT)

The apostle Paul often spoke of God's peace, the God of peace when he wrote letters to the many churches he visited. Paul knew the power of God's peace and the difference between peace and turmoil (chaos).

When you come from a life filled with chaos, bad decisions, conflict, and confusion, you can really appreciate the peace God offers. Abiding there is truly like heaven on earth.

Romans 15:33 says, "And now may God, who gives us his peace, be with you all. Amen."

Paul uses the word "all" ~ why is that significant? Paul doesn't differentiate between Jews and Gentiles, or any other classification. Paul is speaking this blessing of God's peace over all of us.

On our journey to Bill's healing, God liberally bestowed upon us the gift of His peace. Our heavenly Father was with us every step. Truly, He never left us nor did He forsake us. He is our peace even in the chaos.

The Glory Road is a place of peace in a weary land, turned upside down at the whim of others. In God, and God alone, His peace passes all understanding and guards my heart and my mind through Christ Jesus.

Lord, thank you for the gift of Your peace. Your love never runs out. There is a river of life that flows from the throne room of grace and it is accompanied by God's peace that passes all understanding. There is only one measure of peace for all mankind. There is no distinction between us when it comes to Your peace. Lord, may we be bathed in Your peace wherever we go. May we extend Your peace to all we meet. In Jesus' name, amen.

Thank you for your prayers of faith.#Godisfaithful#TheGloryRoad

Day#485 August 17

 Anchor Verse: Romans 16:3
Tell Priscilla and Aquila hello. They have been my fellow workers in the affairs of Christ Jesus. In fact, they risked their lives for me, and I am not the only one who is thankful to them; so are all the Gentile churches. (TLB)

In the former days, writing a letter took time, it was an investment. Sometimes a letter wasn't written in one day, it might have been over a course of time depending on its length.

The book of Romans is a letter written to both the Jewish Christians and the Gentile Christians in Rome who were gathering in house churches. As we read chapter 16, in his heart, mind, and spirit, Paul is thinking about people who have meant so much to him and done so much for the body of Christ. It's like a list of Academy Award winners.

Priscilla and Aquila were Jewish Christians who met Paul in Corinth after they had to flee Rome because of their faith. They were also tentmakers and at times traveled with Paul. Paul knew of their hospitality and how they encouraged other Christians, and also did so much for him. This couple was a powerful example to Paul about what it looked like to serve the Lord and be willing to risk their lives for the gospel of Christ.

On our journey to Bill's healing, we encountered many people who lived life in the trenches, on the front line, where spiritual warfare abounds. Many reached out to us not only in the flesh, but day after day, they bombarded the gates of heaven with prayers for Bill. They are heroes of the faith God will welcome when they claim their eternal reward.

The Glory Road is a path where many Christians shine brightly for the Lord in a world that's been plunged into darkness. The stars in a dark night sky shine brightly for God's glory and we are called to do the same. Your acts of love and kindness can change the trajectory of a person's life.

Lord, thank you for those You have brought into our lives to help us on our life's journey. We thank you for fellow believers who have risked their lives or reputations to walk with You, Lord, and to walk with us. May we be found faithful in all we do and speak. In Jesus' name we pray, amen.

Thank you for your encouraging words.#Godisfaithful#TheGloryRoad

Day#486 August 18

 Anchor Verse: Psalm 101:7
He who practices deceit will not dwell in my house; He who tells lies and half-truths will not continue [to remain] in my presence. (AMP)

There are places in the Bible where the author doesn't "pull any punches" ~ they hit the target square on… and if they hit the mark, so be it.

In Psalm 101, the psalmist, David, is pretty blunt. He begins Psalm 101 speaking of singing of God's love and justice. David chose to conduct the affairs of his house with a blameless heart. "I will have nothing to do with what is evil." (Psalm 101:4) David is drawing the line.

Psalm 101:7 says, "He who practices deceit will not dwell in my house; He who tells lies and half-truths will not continue [to remain] in my presence."

On our journey to Bill's healing, there were some places we didn't have a choice about where we would go, because Bill's illness took us there. We did have a choice about who we would listen to and whether we allowed their words or life choices to impact our lives. We chose to listen to God.

The Glory Road is a place where great wisdom and discernment are needed. Without Bill at my side, the path looks different. I can't ask him a question or hold his hand as I walk through tough places. What I have learned is to trust in God's faithfulness, His wisdom, knowledge, and understanding and those who have chosen to walk in His truth, not deceit. I choose to draw the line. As for me and my house, we will serve the Lord.

What about you? Are you willing to draw the line when it comes to your friends and colleagues? Which camp are you choosing ~ the Lord's side or the enemy's side? We can't straddle the fence. We're either with God or against Him ~ it's that simple.

Lord, we praise and thank you that You are the absolute representation of truth and justice and righteousness. It is who You are. You have drawn the line and You call us to draw the line as well. Lord, I pray for those walking in darkness. Please draw them into the light of Your love where they will receive the fullness of Your joy. Lord, we need Your help in a world that is reeling in chaos and confusion. We ask You to fight for us, just as You promised. We love you and praise you in Jesus' name, amen.

Thank you for your encouraging words.#Godisfaithful#TheGloryRoad

Day#487 August 19

 Anchor Verse: Psalm 104:33
I will sing to the Lord as long as I live. I will praise my God to my last breath!
(NLT)

Do you like to sing? Singing from the heart is what counts, not whether you sing like an angel. My husband used to say making a joyful noise unto the Lord was painful to those around him because he sang off-key.

Somehow I think that once the notes leave our mouth and reach heaven they sound like a beautiful melody to our heavenly Father.

"I will sing to the Lord as long as I live. I will praise my God to my last breath!" (Psalm 104:33)

Do you praise God "all" the time ~ even through your trials?

The psalmist loves God so much that he says he will praise the Lord until his last breath. With my mouth will I make known Your faithfulness, O Lord.

On our journey to Bill's healing, at every intersection we got to choose our reaction to circumstances. Would we choose joy and sing praises to God in the storm, or in the alternative, would we be sucked into the pit of despair and grumble and complain? You and I get to make that choice every day.

The Glory Road is filled with joy, praises and singing, even in the nighttime hours when the things of the day call for our attention. In the past, I shared that on Bill's journey to healing God gave me a song to sing as I would lie down for the night. "I sing praises to Your name, O Lord!" I praised God no matter how well or how challenging the day.

Lord, thank you for the gift of this day. Your love never fails, and Your mercies are new every morning, great is Your faithfulness. Lord, we choose to praise you in the storm and in the calm. We align ourselves with Your plans for us and for this world. We will sing praises to You until our final breath. Amazing grace, how sweet the sound! Thank you for Your grace, mercy, and peace. In Jesus' mighty name we pray, amen.

Thank you for your faithfulness.#Godisfaithful#TheGloryRoad

Day#488 August 20

 Anchor Verse: 1 Corinthians 3:8
He who plants and he who waters are one [in importance and esteem, working toward the same purpose]; but each will receive his own reward according to his own labor. (AMP)

Teamwork is a powerful example of how people with diverse gifts can work together for a common goal. It's not about competition but working together to win the prize.

When you watch the Olympics, a high-level competition of amazing physical talent, we catch a glimpse of how a team works together. It's more than individual talent, if they don't come together, they will lose the competition.

In 1 Corinthians 3, Paul has an extended discussion about building a strong foundation and bringing new believers into the kingdom of God. The Lord has assigned each one of us a task. "I planted the seed, Apollos watered it, but God has been making it grow." (I Corinthians 3:6)

Paul gives us a little dose of humility in verse 8, "He who plants and he who waters are one [in importance and esteem, working toward the same purpose]; but each will receive his own reward according to his own labor."

On our journey to Bill's healing, we were aware of the roles each person had in our lives. Even Bill as a patient was used to encourage those who took care of him; they loved to come into his room. What a blessing to be Jesus' hands and feet wherever we go.

The Glory Road offers many opportunities to walk together as a team to spread the good news of Jesus. My path includes many amazing people who give without counting the cost. What they do is not for credit or reward. All for His glory is our battle cry. Lord, have Your way in me.

Lord, thank you for the gift of a new day. We keep our eyes on You, Lord, and ask for Your kingdom to come, Your will to be done on earth as it is in heaven. You will reward each one of us as we walk in obedience to Your will. Be exalted, O Lord. In Jesus' name, amen.

Thank you for your companionship.#Godisfaithful#TheGloryRoad

Day#489 August 21

 Anchor Verse: 1 Corinthians 4:20
For the Kingdom of God is not just a lot of talk; it is living by God's power.
(NLT)

"Talk is cheap" is a phrase commonly used in our world. A person can talk a good talk but what do those words produce? What is the fruit that can be seen?

The MESSAGE translation puts it this way, "I know there are some among you who are so full of themselves they never listen to anyone, let alone me. They don't think I'll ever show up in person. But I'll be there sooner than you think, God willing, and then we'll see if they're full of anything but hot air. God's Way is not a matter of mere talk; it's an empowered life." (1 Corinthians 4:18-20)

Are we guilty of these actions ourselves? Do we believe we know everything and consequently don't listen to anyone else? Saying someone is full of hot air is a pretty bold statement.

Living an empowered life is what God has called us to do. The only way that can happen is if we are listening to God and walking according to His truth as set out in the Bible. That is our goal. That is our high calling.

On our journey to Bill's healing, we heard a lot of "talk" and we needed God through the Holy Spirit to help us filter out what was true and what was just "hot air." We were mindful that our own talk was in alignment with God's Word so we bore fruit that honored Him.

The Glory Road is a path filled with much talk. The world right now is full of noise ~ like a beehive and trying to sort out the truth from the gibberish is a full-time job. Praise the Lord for the wisdom and discernment that comes from heaven so we might walk uprightly before Him.

Lord, thank you the gift of Your Word, the Bible. It's the truth of God preserved over generations. Heaven itself partners with us to bring truth and light to our lives. May our words reflect the light of God's truth and hope and not the counterfeit words of the world. We are children of the King of kings and the Lord of lords, in Jesus' name we pray, amen.

Thank you for your faithful prayers.#Godisfaithful#TheGloryRoad

Day#490 August 22

 Anchor Verse: Psalm 107:21
So lift your hands and give thanks to God for his marvelous kindness and for his miracles of mercy for those he loves! (TPT)

There are so many things in our lives that we take for granted. Not only our homes, our jobs, our families, but often the gift of each breath we breathe.

"So lift your hands and give thanks to God for his marvelous kindness and for his miracles of mercy for those he loves!" (Psalm 107:21)

When was the last time, you worshiped the Lord with all your heart and mind and body and spirit?

"His miracles of mercy for those he loves" ~ exactly describes what God did for Bill during his journey to healing. Because of God's love, so many times God said, "It's not the end of the road; it's just a new beginning."

On our journey to Bill's healing, we experienced the love of God in a new way, in a dimension we had never experienced in our lifetime. Bill's encounters with God were powerful, not only for Bill, but for all of us who surrounded him. One moment it looked like Bill's life was coming to an end and instead God breathed new life into him, and we praised God's name.

The Glory Road is a path where miracles of mercy happen daily, not only in my life, but those around me. Day or night, we have the opportunity to raise our hands toward heaven and praise the Lord, for His goodness and grace.

"The steadfast love of the Lord never ceases; his mercies never come to an end; they are new every morning; great is your faithfulness. (Lamentations 3:22-23)

Lord, we thank you for the gift of this new day. Thank you for Your hand of protection over us. No weapon formed against us will prosper. We raise our voices to heaven this morning and thank you for Your miracles of mercy. Lord, You deserve all our praise. In Jesus' name, amen.

Thank you for your faithfulness.#Godisfaithful#TheGloryRoad

Day#491 August 23

 Anchor Verse: Psalm 113:3
From sunrise-brilliance to sunset-beauty, lift up his praise from dawn to dusk.
(TPT)

Nature is filled with many wonders but there are few that compare to the beauty of a sunrise or a sunset. Whether you are a morning person or evening person determines whether a sunrise or sunset is your favorite view.

The sunrise today isn't a rerun from October 15, 1865 ~ God doesn't work like that… He is original all the way.

Our desire to praise the Lord starts in our heart, not externally. Nature's beauty might add a little more crescendo to the symphony of praise. If your heart isn't set on praising the Lord, no joy-filled words will come out of your mouth.

The psalms are filled with page after page of praise to the Lord in good times and hard times. Let all that is within me bless His holy name.

What about you? Is your heart filled with praise this morning? Or have the things of the world seeped into your boat and you're about to go under?

On our journey to Bill's healing, we welcomed each new day as a gift and thanked the Lord as the day came to an end for our many blessings. Every day God was faithful. Every day He gave us a reason to rejoice and be glad.

The Glory Road follows a new trail to new places. Some of the places have familiar terrain and others represent a brand-new landscape. What remains the same is my trust in the Lord that He will never leave me or forsake me. Daily, I give Him thanks for His tender care and new mercies.

Lord, thank you for the gift of this day. We thank you for the beauty of this morning's sunrise and look forward to the closing of the day with another hand-painted sunset to bless Your people. We choose to praise you wherever we walk, wherever we rest, wherever we gather with others. Our hearts are filled with praise because You have a plan that is greater than what we can see with our human eyes. Thank you for help and hope that come in the name of the Lord, in Jesus' name we pray, amen.

Thank you for your persistent prayers.#Godisfaithful#TheGloryRoad

Day#492 August 24

 Anchor Verse: Psalm 118:7
For you stand beside me as my hero who rescues me. I've seen with my own eyes the defeat of my enemies. I've triumphed over them all! (TPT)

We do not face the challenges of life alone. It's not just me against the world. God is on my side. The Lord is not only my helper; He's my healer and hero.

"For you stand beside me as my hero who rescues me. I've seen with my own eyes the defeat of my enemies. I've triumphed over them all!" (Psalm 118:7)

Growing up you might have had a childhood hero, whether that was a real person or a cartoon character or superhero. The best hero ever is Jesus. He will never let us down. In fact, He gives us victory over every enemy who crosses our path.

We don't triumph over just a few of them, but all of our enemies. Enemies aren't necessarily people but also our thoughts and emotions. When we trust in anything but the truth of God, we can easily be defeated. However, the truth is we are victorious in Jesus' name. Thank you, Lord.

On our journey to Bill's healing, we encountered some difficult places, situations beyond our comprehension, even places that left us at a loss for words. But even on the darkest nights or the brightest days, God's faithfulness lit the way. Jesus was Bill's hero again and again.

The Glory Road is a pathway through uncharted territory. Some places are similar to former experiences but the last time I passed through those places Bill was at my side. The road looks different as a solo traveler rather than in the company of others. But with Jesus at my side, I need not fear or doubt or stumble or hesitate to take the ground He has for me.

Lord, we praise and thank you we have victory in Jesus. He overcame death, hell, and the grave and because Jesus was victorious, so are we. Today we choose to trust in You, Lord. We ask You to keep our feet from falling as we take new territory. We love you, Lord, in Jesus' name, amen.

Thank you for your faithfulness. Thank you for your prayers that started in January 2018 as Bill began his health journey. Your prayers have sustained me through the darkest nights as well as the places of victory. The truth still rings loudly ~ nothing is impossible with God... absolutely nothing. #Godisfaithful#TheGloryRoad

Day#493 August 25

 Anchor Verse: Psalm 119:30
I have chosen the way of faithfulness; I have set my heart on your laws. (NIV)

Decision-making for most of us is just part of the landscape of our lives; it has become such a habit. In 2020, there was a study done about how many decisions the average person makes in a day, the number they arrived at was 35,000 decisions a day. No wonder we are tired by the end of the day.

Psalm 119:30 speaks of a specific decision. "I have chosen the way of faithfulness; I have set my heart on your laws."

The psalmist says that he has chosen to walk in the way of faithfulness to God. And he stays faithful to God because he sets his heart on God's laws.

The only path to peace in this life, in this world is to abide in God's presence and to hold on to His promises and to walk in faithfulness to His commands. This is truly the path to life.

On our journey to Bill's healing, we relied on our faith at every turn. Yes, there were some days it felt like we made 35,000 decisions and other days, God might have trimmed that number a little. But it was our faithfulness to God and God's faithfulness to us that sustained us and allowed us to be triumphant every day.

The Glory Road is a place where God walks with me daily. With my hand in His hand, we walk along life's path and He holds me up in the difficult places and we dance through the joyful places. He is such a good, good Father. God showed Himself faithful during Bill's journey to healing and He has done the same for me on this new pathway. I trust Him even when my eyes can't see the way ahead because I know that He is trustworthy.

What about you? Have you chosen the way of faithfulness? It's the only way to find true happiness as you navigate the storms of this world.

Lord, we praise and thank you for the gift of a new day. Your mercies are new every morning and great is Your faithfulness. Lord, thank you for being our guide and our guard. As we trust in You and choose to walk the path of faithfulness, You reward our faithfulness with abundant blessings. Lord, we choose You today and every day in Jesus' name, amen.

Thank you for your persistent prayers.#Godisfaithful#TheGloryRoad

Day#494 August 26

 Anchor Verse: Psalm 119:136
When I witness the rebellious breaking your laws, it makes me weep uncontrollably! (TPT)

As we survey our nation, it's such a chaotic storm. Right is called wrong, and wrong is called right. There is much confusion and fear. Jesus must be weeping over what He sees in our nation today.

"When I witness the rebellious breaking your laws, it makes me weep uncontrollably." (Psalm 119:136)

Have you ever wept like that? There are times these days when my heart is so broken by what's happening to good people, I do weep uncontrollably. And I hear Jesus weeping at my side as well.

What can we do in this midst of this time of lawlessness?

We can let the light and love of Jesus shine all the more brightly. Loving like Jesus loves will be a ray of hope in the darkness. In Romans 12:21 it says, "Do not be overcome and conquered by evil, but overcome evil with good." (AMP) This is where we take our stand. This is where we are triumphant in Jesus' name.

On our journey to Bill's healing, just as Bill was battling his own illness, the world was having its own battles. There were times when Bill was in ICU where I would sit still in God's presence and pray and intercede not only for Bill but for the nation. It can be a lonely journey to stand in the gap for others but God always hears the cries of our hearts.

The Glory Road is a place where daily new skirmishes pop up. Moments when believers come together and pray and ask for heaven's help and believe for the miracles we need. Weeping may endure for the night, but joy comes in the morning, hallelujah! (Psalm 30:5)

Lord, You are a God who is close by. You are not distant. You are not deaf to our cries. You are very much actively working on our behalf. We thank you and praise you that You fight for us, every day in every way. With you on our side, we always win. Our hope and help come in the name of the Lord. Lead us onward today, O King Eternal, to victory in Jesus' name.

Thank you for your encouraging words. Yesterday (8.25.21) was four weeks since my dad's knee surgery and he continues to make good progress.#Godisfaithful#TheGloryRoad

Day#495 August 27

 Anchor Verse: Psalm 122:1
I was glad when they said to me, "Let us go to the house of the Lord." (AMP)

In the modern age in which we live, there are some things we take for granted. Most people have smartphones to be connected to information instantly, where years ago, letters were written to tell of an event and it might take weeks or months to hear the news.

Travel is another aspect of life that has changed so much, not just long distances but going to the grocery store. Hopping in your car to go rather than walking or taking a horse and buggy.

As we walked through the Covid season starting in 2020, we discovered what we thought were "rights" were really "privileges." For our own safety and the safety of others, we had to stay home from work, school, even church.

Reading Psalm 122:1 with that lens, it has a different perspective, "I was glad when they said to me, "Let us go to the house of the Lord."

Yes, I was "glad" when they said let's go the house of the Lord, and to see those we know and love. Community means coming together. We need each other. Isolation is not good for any of us.

On our journey to Bill's healing, through the months Bill was in the hospital, God created our own private "house of the Lord." Bill, me and God ~ there we were able to abide in His presence. As soon as Bill got out of the hospital, one of his first requests was to go back to church.

The Glory Road is a place of new realities, where we don't take for granted what we hold in our hands. Daily, we need to praise God for the gift of this day and the blessings in 24 hours. We don't live in fear but with a new appreciation for the many gifts that God has given to us.

Lord, thank you for the gift of this day. Every day is filled with gifts of love from Your hands. We lift our hands in praise this morning and we ask that You would bring order to a world filled with storms and chaos. Take whatever's wrong and please make it right. We will give you all the praise and honor and glory in Jesus' name, amen.

Thank you for your faithful prayers.#Godisfaithful#TheGloryRoad

August 28, 2021

Bill's Celebration of Life Service
Spokane Dream Center, Spokane Valley, Washington

It's been 497 days since God took Bill home to heaven. None of us ever expected it would take this long to come together to have Bill's celebration of life service. These are unprecedented times in which we live.

But the most defining moment for me happened just a couple of days after Bill died. There was a knock on my apartment door. When I opened the door, I found a mutual friend who lived in our apartment community. Tears were streaming down her face as we embraced.

She began to tell me her story, but the phrase that stood out was this, "Bill saw the good in others that no one else could see." This is how she will remember Bill. Yes, this is the man I knew and loved, a good man.

No matter your resources, your health circumstances, your position in life, you get to choose every day how to treat others. May we choose wisely.

Today, Mr. Bill passes the torch on to you and to me… to find the good in others that no one else can see. This is the greatest tribute we can pay to Mr. Bill today and the rest of our lives.

To speak life and hope and encouragement into each other rather than words that tear down and destroy.

Together we can make the world a better place to live once again.

Thank you, Mr. Bill, for showing us the way.

I love you!

(An excerpt from my remarks at Bill's celebration of life service.)

Day#496 August 28

 Anchor Verse: Psalm 123:2b
...our eyes look to the Lord our God, till he shows us his mercy. (NIV)

When we walk on a new path, a new trail especially if the ground cover is less than stable, we tend to go more slowly, hesitantly, so we don't fall.

What is true for walking in the flesh is also good practice for walking in the spirit. The psalms are filled with great wisdom about how to navigate life and overcome adversity and remember to walk in peace with the Lord.

"Our eyes look to the Lord our God, till he shows us his mercy."

How do we keep our peace in the middle of the storm?

The answer: keeping our eyes on the Lord our God until He shows us His mercy. That's our only hope and the only hope we need.

On our journey to Bill's healing, we were so grateful for the Lord's mercies that were new every morning. Every day His faithfulness was as sure and secure as the rising of the sun and its setting at the end of the day. With our eyes fixed on heaven, everything else fell into place.

The Glory Road is a place where my priorities focused on heaven lead the way. When I encounter a logjam, I hesitate for a moment while the path is cleared and then move on. I praise the Lord for the lesson learned at that juncture. We don't always go around the mountain, sometimes we have to go over it or through it.

Lord, we praise and thank you for heaven's help in our lives. Thank you, Lord, that Your love never ceases and Your mercies never come to an end. They are new every morning and great is your faithfulness.

Thank you for the thousands of prayers you have prayed on our behalf. Today (8.28.21) we celebrate Bill's celebration of life service on what would have been his 78th birthday. Mr. Bill, you are Always Loved, Never Forgotten. Thank you for your love.#Godisfaithful#TheGloryRoad

Day#497 August 29

 Anchor Verse: Psalm 126:2
Our mouths were filled with laughter, our tongues with songs of joy. Then it was said among the nations, "The Lord has done great things for them." (NIV)

What we are going through our lives on the inside is reflected on the outside too. People who are in good health look healthy. Those who are uncertain about life or filled with fear move forward cautiously or sometimes don't move at all.

When we hear someone's mouth filled with laughter telling stories of great joy about what the Lord has done for them, we stand up and pay attention.

People are drawn to the good. People desire good things to happen to them, they don't like to be caught in the pit of despair. When good things are happening to us, we invite others to join the party.

Psalm 126 is a psalm about rejoicing. In verse 2 it says, "Our mouths were filled with laughter, our tongues with songs of joy. Then it was said among the nations, 'The Lord has done great things for them.'"

When we are going through deep waters, we hold on to God's hand and we are grateful for how He leads us and provides for us and saves us.

On our journey to Bill's healing, we experienced places of great joy. Our mouths were filled with laughter, and our tongues with songs of joy. People around the world said, "The Lord has done great things for them."

The Glory Road is a path filled with God's faithfulness and favor. God gives me joy in some of the darkest circumstances and my tongue is filled with songs of joy because God has been so good to me.

Lord, thank you for the gift of this day. You have blessings for us we cannot imagine. We pray for those going through deep valleys. Give them songs of joy and fill their mouths with laughter. We love you, in Jesus' name, amen.

Thank you for all who attended Bill's celebration of life service yesterday (8.28.22) – either in person or online. Truly the presence of the Lord was with us. It was a beautiful tribute to a life well lived and a man well-loved.#Godisfaithful#TheGloryRoad

Day#498 August 30

 Anchor Verse: Psalm 130:2
Hear my cry, O Lord. Pay attention to my prayer. (NLT)

Often our prayers are not filled with flowery words and long phrases. They come straight from our heart, the core of our being. They are direct. They are precise. They are the cry of our heart.

Just like an arrow honed in on the bull's eye of the target so are the prayers we offer to our heavenly Father.

As a parent, when your child is sick and you don't know what to do, you cry out to the Lord.

When your loved one is in the hospital, husband or wife, and the battle has been long, and the progress is like a snail's pace, yet you continue to believe because God promised a victorious healing, you cry to the Lord, the one who keeps His promises.

Our words are simple just as the psalmist says it here in Psalm 130:2, "Hear my cry, O Lord. Pay attention to my prayer."

Pay attention to my prayer among the millions that are prayed to You daily, Lord. I need your help. I need your mercy. I need an extra measure of grace today. I can't make it without you.

On our journey to Bill's healing, God often gave me specific prayers to pray and how to instruct others to pray. God knew the plans He had for Bill…plans to give him hope and a future and to bless so many on his own healing journey. Together we boldly entered the throne room of grace and there we found hope in our time of need.

The Glory Road is a path filled with opportunities to pray for others. As I pull my life back together after Bill's memorial service (8.28.21) and celebrating his birthday, I ask the Lord to hear my cry for mercy and to pay attention to my prayer. There will be potholes of grief (grief bombs) in the days ahead but now my mission is to live for the Lord as He sees fit.

Lord, we praise and thank you that You have plans for us for they are good. You ask us to walk together with You on this path called life. We will encounter places where we don't have the answers, but You do. We love you and trust you. We rely on You, Lord. In Jesus' name we pray, amen.

Thank you for your continued prayers.#Godisfaithful#TheGloryRoad

Day#499 August 31

 Anchor Verse: Psalm 132:1
Lord, please don't forget all the hardships David had to pass through. (TPT)

Everyone has a "past" ~ some with better parts than others. It's like a patchwork quilt. The good news as a child of God is God makes all things beautiful. He is weaving together a beautiful tapestry out of our lives so ALL of it ultimately is for His glory.

Have you ever considered our hardships are part of our victory story?

Sometimes God allows a few loose strings for a reason, because it is a connection to our humanity and also God's divinity.

Psalm 132:1 says, "Lord, please don't forget all the hardships David had to pass through. "Other translations use phrases like, "don't forget his sufferings, his afflictions, the hardships that he endured."

The rest of the chapter goes on to share how committed David was to finding a dwelling place for the Lord. David was willing to sacrifice everything including rest. God rewarded David's faithfulness.

What heavenly assignments has the Lord given you that move you to action?

On our journey to Bill's healing, there were hardships we passed through. But we passed through them, we didn't camp there. God had a plan and purpose for each portion of the terrain ~ all for His glory.

The Glory Road is a place where each step is a step of significance. There is not one moment of suffering, not one tear shed that doesn't have a greater purpose in the Kingdom of God. I live for His glory and His glory alone. This life is not about me, it's all about Him. Lord, have Your way in me.

Lord, thank you that You have written a book about our lives before we were born. Each line, every page, every chapter has one theme…for the honor and glory of God. We trust You when our eyes can't see. What we see right now is not the end of the story, it's just part of the journey. We lift our hands in praise. In Jesus' name we pray, amen.

Thank you for your faithful prayers. Today is my MRI to see what the Lord has been doing below the surface. Praise the Lord for the healing that is still on its way.#Godisfaithful#TheGloryRoad

September 2021

Guide me in your truth and teach me for you are my God, my Savior, my hope is in you all day long.

~ Psalm 25:5 ~

Day#500 September 1

 Anchor Verse: Psalm 136:13
Praise the Lord who opened the Red Sea to make a path before them, for his loving-kindness continues forever. (TLB)

Often praise is not the first order of business as we open our eyes.

There is only one who deserves all our praise and our attention, our heavenly Father. God is the only one who ALWAYS has time for us. He is never in a rush. His words are always full of wisdom and compassion.

Psalm 136 leads us through recounting what the Lord has done and it is spotlighted by this refrain, "His love endures forever."

"Praise the Lord who opened the Red Sea to make a path before them, for his loving-kindness continues forever." (Psalm 136:13)

The children of Israel were being pursued by Egyptian troops, and in front of them was the Red Sea without any means to cross over ~ it looked like certain death. What would they do? Without God's help, it was over. But God split the Red Sea in two, and the people passed through on dry ground. The Egyptian troops drowned. Their enemies were no more.

On our journey to Bill's healing, we faced some Red Sea moments. Moments that without the Lord's intervention Bill would have died. God had a plan where He would be honored and glorified and Bill would be given a second chance at life (more than once.) Praise the Lord whose love endures forever.

The Glory Road is a path filled with His love which endures forever. Daily, I am a blessed when God makes a way when I don't see a way. His thoughts are higher than my thoughts and His plans are way better than mine.

Lord, we surrender anew to You today. We trust you. We believe in you and we say, "Have Your way in us, O Lord." May Your glory be seen in us in Jesus' mighty name, amen.

Thank you for your persistent prayers.#Godisfaithful#TheGloryRoad

Day#501 September 2

 Anchor Verse: Psalm 137:1
By the rivers of Babylon we sat and wept when we remembered Zion. (NIV)

There is order in God's world. There are fun things, there are hard things. We will laugh and we will cry. We will be silent and talk, but in the end, everything is still under God's control. We may have to look hard for the meaning, but there is one.

In Psalm 137:1, the Jewish exiles sat along the rivers of Babylon and wept because they were in captivity far from their homeland.

"By the rivers of Babylon we sat and wept when we remembered Zion."

Our life isn't always filled with laughter; there are times we weep. There are times we mourn the loss of the ones we love, but as believers, we can rejoice they are in heaven with God for eternity.

Life is not easily sorted out. Sometimes our emotions have us walking quite a difficult route. I have several friends who have long-term health issues and every day is a roller coaster ride for them. May we remember to lift up those around us walking through difficult places and even let them know that they are not alone, even when it feels like it.

On our journey to Bill's healing, there were times we stopped and remembered when life was different. What life looked like and felt like prior to that ambulance ride on the morning of January 10, 2018, when hospitals were something you drove by, not where you lived your life.

God's goodness, grace, mercy, and peace were our companions. We never doubted His love for us. Life might have changed, but God's love did not.

The Glory Road is a place of remembering. As I continue the healing process after Bill's memorial service, I am reminded that love and life's emotions are complicated creatures. Just because the service is finished and the box is "checked", we are not instantly transported to a place of no more sorrow or pain. Daily, the Lord continues to heal our hearts.

Lord, we praise and thank you for the gift of remembering. Thank you for the gift of walking through difficult places with You at our side. Let us offer an extra measure of Your grace to all we encounter today. May You be honored and glorified in our lives every day, in Jesus' name we pray, amen.

Thank you for your faithfulness.#Godisfaithful#TheGloryRoad

Day#502 September 3

 Anchor Verse: Psalm 140:7-8
*O Lord, you are my God and my saving strength! My Hero-God, you wrap
yourself around me to protect me. For I'm surrounded by your presence in my day
of battle. Lord Yahweh, hear my cry. May my voice move your heart to show me
mercy. (TPT)*

In a world where daily the headlines are filled with wars and rumors of wars,
and we recount problems past and problems yet to come, it's easy to become
overwhelmed.

As we face troubles, we run back to this solid rock of truth and we talk to
God and ask Him to restore our peace as we linger in His presence.

In Psalm 140:7-8, the psalmist paints a picture of God coming to save us. "O
Lord, you are my God and my saving strength! My Hero-God, you wrap
yourself around me to protect me. For I'm surrounded by your presence in
my day of battle. Lord Yahweh, hear my cry. May my voice move your heart
to show me mercy."

On our journey to Bill's healing, God was our saving strength. He covered
our heads in the day of battle and wrapped Himself around us to protect us.
Bill was protected night and day, not just when he was in ICU, but in our
home, God's hand of protection was a ring of fire around him.

The Glory Road is a place where God protects me from the fiery darts of the
enemy. When the battles come, which they still do, God is ready to defend
me. His angels stand guard around me and they speak songs of deliverance
over me. They are available day or night; they do not slumber or sleep.
Thank you, Lord, for hearing my cry for mercy and always being willing to
listen to my heart cry. I am victorious in Jesus' mighty name.

Lord, we run to this morning and lift our hands in praise. There is nothing in
this world that is greater than my God. I trust You, Lord, even when my eyes
can't see the path ahead. I trust you, Lord, to do what is best for me and
believe You are the God of miracles. In Jesus' name we pray, amen.

Thank you for your companionship.#Godisfaithful#TheGloryRoad

Day#503 September 4

 Anchor Verse: Psalm 145:8a
The Lord is gracious and compassionate. (NIV)

Our goal in life is to be more like Jesus~ to love as Jesus loves, to speak words of truth and life, to be His hands and feet. It's a lofty goal but Matthew 19:26 says, "With man this is impossible, but with God all things are possible."

Psalm 145 lists two of God's attributes. He is gracious and compassionate.

We should be so grateful for God's grace because He does not reward according to our sins but because of Jesus' sacrifice we are no longer sinners in God's eyes, we are His children.

The root of compassion in Latin means "co-suffering." God does this as we walk through difficult places. He suffers with us and more than the suffering, He bathes us in His love and helps us to rise above the storm.

Pastor Dave, our senior pastor, has the gift of compassion. As the shepherd of our flock, we are such a blessed people to have a leader who has the heart of Jesus and is touched by the things that touch Jesus' heart.

On our journey to Bill's healing, the grace and compassion of God were multiplied. Not only from God's heart, day and night, but also from the hearts of others. Both family and friends and also professionals who do their work with great expertise but also hands and hearts filled with compassion.

The Glory Road is a path filled with God's grace and compassion. Some days I am the one offering it to others, and other days, I am the recipient.

"Praise be to the God and Father of our Lord Jesus Christ, the Father of compassion and the God of all comfort, who comforts us in all our troubles, so that we can comfort those in any trouble with the comfort we ourselves receive from God. For just as we share abundantly in the sufferings of Christ, so also our comfort abounds through Christ." (2 Corinthians 1:3-5)

Thank you, Lord, for comforting us in all of our troubles so we can comfort others. Lord, as Your children, we want to be more like You and be filled with Your love, grace, mercy, peace, and a heart filled with compassion. May we love like You love others. In Jesus' name, we pray, amen.

Thank you for your encouraging words.#Godisfaithful#TheGloryRoad

Day#504 September 5

 Anchor Verse: Psalm 147:8
He fills the sky with clouds, sending showers to water the earth so that the grass springs up on the mountain fields and the earth produces food for man. (TPT)

How often do you actually think about the sun rising unless you've had a long sleepless night and you look forward to the night finally being over? (Or your best sleep coming just before dawn…)

As children, we are often captivated by the shapes of the clouds in the sky, and sometimes as adults as well, when our eyes are drawn heavenward.

For those who are living through drought-like conditions in the United States and around the world, the forecast of rain showers and then "actual" rain fills our hearts with joy. Dancing in the rain takes on a whole new meaning. Even the grass of the field that spring up so nature's creatures can be fed is a marvelous work from God's hands.

The psalmist brings all these details to our attention because they are important. They are a sign of God's love for us ~ His tender care. It's not just the creation of the world at the beginning of time that fills us with awe and wonder but the fact that daily God takes care of our every need.

On our journey to Bill's healing, daily we became more aware of God's gifts. We took the time to stop, look, listen, and then open our mouths with thanksgiving to God who loves us so much. Many things you take for granted until they are taken away. Let us be filled with joy daily.

The Glory Road is filled with daily blessings. I am more aware of the details of God's handiwork in my life. A good night's sleep, a good meal, the laughter of a child, and a conversation and prayer with a friend ~ these are all gifts from God's hands. Even the chair you are sitting in right now as you read this is a gift of support from your loving heavenly Father.

Lord, we praise and thank you for the gift of clouds, rain, and green grass. We thank you for gifts, both big and small, and the opportunity to share those gifts with others. Lord, may our hearts be filled with gratitude. We love you and praise you in Jesus' name we pray, amen.

Thank you for your faithful prayers.#Godisfaithful#TheGloryRoad

Day#505 September 6

 Anchor Verse: Psalm 150:2
Praise him for his mighty miracles! Praise him for his magnificent greatness! (TPT)

What fills your heart with praise? What gets your eyes on heaven rather than the troubles of this world? A song? A conversation? Reading the Bible?

"Praise him for his mighty miracles! Praise him for his magnificent greatness!" (Psalm 150:2)

When was the last time you praised God for His mighty miracles in your own life or the lives of others? It's good to praise the Lord.

On our journey to Bill's healing, he was given the title "Miracle Man" because of the many times God saved Bill's life ~ not just once or twice. Every time it looked like a health challenge would "take him out" God said, "It's not time. I still have work for Bill to do. I need him to shine with My glory and let others be encouraged and have their hope restored." Thank you, Lord, for the gift of Mr. Bill's life. God is the God of mighty miracles.

The Glory Road is also a place of miracles ~ in my life and yours. Every breath, every heartbeat, every step we take is a blessing from the heart of God. It was Albert Einstein who once said, "There are two ways to live your life. One is as though nothing is a miracle. The other is as though everything is a miracle." This is the way to walk in joy daily and to experience life the way God wants us to live. We are more than conquerors in Jesus' name.

Choose joy! Choose to see the miracles in your life and in the lives of others.

Lord, we praise and thank you for the gift of Your mighty miracles. We praise you for Your magnificent greatness. Even as we go through deep waters may our eyes be focused on You and Your excellence and Your love for us. May our hearts be filled with praise today. In Jesus' name, amen.

Thank you for your faithful prayers.#Godisfaithful#TheGloryRoad

Day#506 September 7

 Anchor Verse: Proverbs 1:3
Their purpose is to teach people to live disciplined and successful lives, to help them do what is right, just, and fair. (NLT)

Being a teacher is a difficult position. You may have a message, a lesson to share but without cooperation, you will not get the results you are seeking.

The book of Proverbs is filled with the words of Solomon, the wisest man who ever lived. They are lessons we can apply to our own lives.

When Solomon becomes king, God asks Solomon what he wants to receive from God. "Ask for whatever you want me to give you." (1 Kings 3:5)

That's quite an offer coming from the Creator of the universe. Whatever Solomon wanted God would have given to him. Solomon responds in a way that pleases the heart of God.

"Therefore give to Your servant an understanding heart to judge Your people, that I may discern between good and evil. For who is able to judge this great people of Yours?" (1 Kings 3:9 NKJV)

God is so pleased with Solomon's request that not only does God give him the wisdom to govern God's people but also wealth and honor, and a long life. (1 Kings 3:12-14)

On our journey to Bill's healing, Bill was given wisdom beyond his years. Not only in the days prior to his illness, but during his illness, God blessed those of us who were in Bill's presence and learned from his walk of faith. Just like Jesus, Bill looked for the good in others that no one else could see.

The Glory Road is a path where I need God's wisdom, not only for myself, but for those God has called me to speak into their lives. We are not called to positions of authority and wisdom for our own ego but for God's glory.

Lord, we praise and thank you for Solomon's example that instead of asking for worldly gain we would ask for wisdom and understanding. Thank you for Your hand that guides us through the Bible and its wisdom. May we learn how to walk uprightly before You, Lord, so You would be honored and glorified in our lives. We love you, Lord, in Jesus' name, amen.

Thank you for choosing to be wise.#Godisfaithful#TheGloryRoad

Day#507 September 8

 Anchor Verse: Proverbs 4:12
Your progress will have no limits when you come along with me, and you will never stumble as you walk along the way. (TPT)

At every intersection of our lives, every decision we make, we have a choice. We can walk according to wisdom's path (direction) or we can choose the other road where we end up in the ditch, wilderness, or desert

King Solomon in Proverbs wants to be clear about the benefits and the pitfalls when it comes to choosing the way of wisdom.

In the Message translation it says, "Dear friend, take my advice; it will add years to your life. I'm writing out clear directions to Wisdom Way, I'm drawing a map to Righteous Road. I don't want you ending up in blind alleys, or wasting time making wrong turns. Hold tight to good advice; don't relax your grip. Guard it well—your life is at stake!"

Take my advice. There are many in the world who say to us "take my advice" from infomercials to family members, people in authority in our lives, and pastors, friends, and teachers. But we need to weigh their words of wisdom against the Word of God.

"Your progress will have no limits when you come along with me, and you will never stumble as you walk along the way." (Proverbs 4:12 TPT)

On our journey to Bill's healing, we discovered the benefits of being wholly committed to God and His ways. Doors opened up before us as we choose to walk with our hands in God's hand. It doesn't mean the trials won't come; it just means that we are never alone.

The Glory Road is a path where we desperately need wisdom, every single one of us, even those who think they know it all. My heart's desire is to know God more and to walk in rhythm with His heartbeat which is filled with the fullness of joy. Lord, we want to know You more.

Lord, thank you that wisdom is not beyond our grasp. With Your help, we can walk and not fall. We also pray for our leaders. May our lives be anchored to the truth of the gospel of Jesus Christ. There is no shadow of turning with You, Lord. We love you, Lord. In Jesus' name we pray, amen.

Thank you for your persistent prayers.#Godisfaithful#TheGloryRoad

Day#508 September 9

 Anchor Verse: 2 Corinthians 2:9
For this was my purpose in writing, to see if you would stand the test, whether you are obedient and committed to following my instruction in all things. (AMP)

In days gone by when a person wrote a letter to another person, there was a reason for the letter. It was a "big deal" to send a letter to another country or even to another state. Our words had a purpose, something important to share. It also meant we cared enough to take the time to sit down and write a letter ~ yes, with pen in hand ~ to someone we loved.

Much of the New Testament was written by Paul and were "letters" written to a specific church in a specific location. It was written in response to a question that had arisen there or a person or situation Paul was aware of and needed to address. Paul was the founder and pastor of many of churches.

In 2 Corinthians 2:9, Paul has a message for the church in Corinth, "For this was my purpose in writing, to see if you would stand the test, whether you are obedient and committed to following my instruction in all things."

Paul is upfront about his purpose… and it's about passing a test. Maybe as the church in Corinth read this letter they thought, "Test? I didn't know there would be a test!" Yes, it was a test to see if they would be obedient and committed to the instructions of Jesus through Paul's words.

We are asked to pass the same test. The question is, will you pass the test?

On our journey to Bill's healing, God had a purpose for everything we experienced. God doesn't just "do stuff" without a purpose. We learned invaluable lessons about following Jesus through good times and difficult times. We were so blessed by His love, grace, mercy, and peace.

The Glory Road is a place I am tested daily. I am a called to walk in obedience to the teachings of Jesus even when I don't understand the reason, the purpose, or even the overall mission. But faith is like that, we believe without seeing because we trust Jesus. Lord, find me faithful.

Lord, You have a plan and a purpose for our lives. The Bible is for instruction, the Holy Spirit is our Comforter, and Jesus is our example of how to live life in an often-weary land. Our hope is in You. We give You all the praise and honor and glory due Your name. In Jesus' name, amen.

Thank you for your prayers of faith. #Godisfaithful#TheGloryRoad

Day#509 September 10

 Anchor Verse: 2 Corinthians 3:3
Clearly, you are a letter from Christ showing the result of our ministry among you. This "letter" is written not with pen and ink, but with the Spirit of the living God. It is carved not on tablets of stone, but on human hearts. (NLT)

We often talk about the fruit that comes from a tree is evidence of the kind of tree that it is. Pears don't grow on an apple tree and ripe juicy peaches are not found on a cherry tree. God created each tree with a purpose and with the intentional purpose of the fruit it would bear.

In 2 Corinthians, Paul is speaking to the believers there and conveying an image of how their lives reflect what Paul and others have poured into them. Not only what has been taught to them, but what they have taken into their spirits and how they have chosen to live their lives ~ bearing good fruit.

"Clearly, you are a letter from Christ showing the result of our ministry among you. This "letter" is written not with pen and ink, but with the Spirit of the living God. It is carved not on tablets of stone, but on human hearts." (2 Corinthians 3:3)

What a beautiful image. You are a letter from Christ. Did you know that?

On our journey to Bill's healing, God changed our perspective about so many things. When God is part of the equation, what is "bad" can become "good" and an opportunity to become more like Jesus and let our light shine so others can see God's good work in us.

The Glory Road is a new chapter in my life. There are many facets to the story, some joyful, other places are difficult, and all of them are infused with new life and hope coming from the heart of God.

Thank you, Lord, we are a letter from Christ, not just with pen and ink which will fade away, but written on human hearts by the Spirit of the living God. We want to know Your heart and to seek Your path and trust You every day. We choose You to be our companion and guide. May fresh revelation of who You are fill our hearts and minds in Christ Jesus. We love you and praise you in Jesus' name, amen.

Thank you for your fervent prayers. Dad goes to see the surgeon (9.10.21) for a follow-up. Expecting a good report.#Godisfaithful#TheGloryRoad

Day#510 September 11

 Anchor Verse: Proverbs 12:20
Deception fills the hearts of those who plot harm, but those who plan for peace are filled with joy. (TPT)

Today is September 11, 2021. Twenty years ago, our nation was rocked by those who plotted harm against us as planes were flown into the Twin Towers in New York City, the Pentagon, and another crashed in Pennsylvania. We sat in front of our T.V. in disbelief of what was unfolding before us. The magnitude of the tragedy is still echoing through our hearts, minds, and lives twenty years later.

We saw the "best" and the "worst" side by side. There were so many heroes that rose up that day and in the days that followed. We also saw a side of evil that this country had never previously experienced. Our bubble of protection was pierced as well as our hearts.

In the days following 9/11, there was unity and rebirth of patriotism and love for our country and others that we hadn't seen in a very long time. God bless America rang through our city streets and across the countryside.

Reading Proverbs 12:20 reminded me of 9/11. "Deception fills the hearts of those who plot harm, but those who plan for peace are filled with joy."

Those who plot harm today are filled with deception, their motives are evil and they do not seek the good of others. While those who plan for peace, who seek peace, who are counselors of peace are filled with joy.

On our journey to Bill's healing, as we fought for Bill's life, we were living in a world of chaos. The battle between good and evil has existed since the beginning of time and will continue until the day of the Lord's return.

The Glory Road is a place of opposites. We can choose to be part of the solution rather than the problem as the love of Jesus flows through us. My prayer is that you choose wisely today and teach the next generation to choose what is right.

Lord, thank you for Your love for us, for this country. Lord, we ask for Your hand of protection over us. Lord, we choose You and to be ambassadors of hope today and every day of our lives. We love you in Jesus' name, amen.

Thank you for choosing joy. Dad's appointment went great. His surgeon is happy.#Godisfaithful#TheGloryRoad

Day#511 September 12

 Anchor Verse: Proverbs 15:30
Light in a messenger's eyes brings joy to the heart, and good news gives health to the bones. (NIV)

The book of Proverbs is filled with precious gems. Not diamonds, emeralds, rubies, sapphires, pearls, but the most expensive gem, God's wisdom.

Part of my study every morning includes looking at multiple translations of the verse God chooses for us. Reading through the different translations of Proverbs 15:30, the Passion translation says, "A twinkle in the eye means joy in the heart, and good news makes you feel fit as a fiddle."

When a person has a twinkle in their eyes, we know they have good news in their heart, something that fills them up with great joy. So much joy, they can't wait to share it with others.

Some of you have gone through deep valleys physically and there are days it's hard to be positive when you are hurting so much. I'm so grateful for the Great Physician who heals us and the Holy Spirit, our Comforter, who helps us through our times of weakness.

On our journey to Bill's healing, I rejoice in remembering the light in Bill's eyes, the twinkle of mischief when he was feeling good. And when we received a good report or Bill conquered a "mountain," there was great joy that filled his body, mind, and spirit, and mine too.

The Glory Road is a place where I encounter those with a twinkle in their eye, especially those who have been touched by the joy of the Lord. Many miracles happen daily ~ amazing stories of God's faithfulness and healing power. What a blessing to be able to share the joy of Jesus wherever we go.

Lord, Your joy is our strength. We thank you for health and healing. Please comfort those going through dark valleys who are wrestling with hard questions and difficult situations. May Your comfort and revelation change their course. We praise you, Lord, in Jesus' name, amen.

Thank you for your faithfulness.#Godisfaithful#TheGloryRoad

Day#512 September 13

 Anchor Verse: Proverbs 17:27
*A truly wise person uses few words; a person with understanding is even-tempered.
(NLT)*

In looking at the book of Proverbs, there are many verses that speak about words, and what we say, and how what we say reflects what is in our hearts. Today's verse reminds us how much our words line up with our character.

"A truly wise person uses few words; a person with understanding is even-tempered." (Proverbs 17:27)

When a truly wise person uses few words to express their thoughts, we know that they have weighed their response in their heart before it ever rolled off their tongue. On the other hand, there are those who speak almost instantly, without giving their words much, if any, thought, often their words are not sweet to the soul, but bitter to our ears.

The second part of the verse says a person with understanding is even-tempered. Even-tempered means not easily annoyed or angered, doesn't speak with rash words or have a hasty temper. We're back to controlling our tongues that can quickly get us in trouble.

On our journey to Bill's healing, and even prior to that, Bill learned the powerful lesson about speaking less and listening more. He learned more by listening. When Bill spoke, people listened. Even as he was hospitalized, on his worst days, Bill had a kind word for those who assisted him.

The Glory Road has daily opportunities to weigh my words before I share them out loud. We should bring our thoughts and words to our heavenly Father. He is the best judge about what we should say and what should be "deleted" from our thoughts, social media posts, and text messages. We need the Holy Spirit's help to guard our words and keep us even-tempered.

Lord, You are a fountain of wisdom. Lord, please filter the words that come out of our mouths. Please guard our thoughts, the seeds that are planted in our minds that quickly bear fruit. We want to be holy and righteous before You. May our walk reflect Your attributes. Let love lead the way. May peace be the fruit of our walk. We love you and praise you in Jesus' name, amen.

Thank you for your encouraging words.#Godisfaithful#TheGloryRoad

Day#513 September 14

 Anchor Verse: 2 Corinthians 7:7
We were relieved not only to see him [Titus} but because of the report he brought us of how you refreshed his heart. He told us of your affection toward me, your deep remorse, and how concerned you were for me. This truly made my heart leap for joy! [TPT]

Today's passage focuses on Titus and the joy he brought to Paul and his companions when Titus came to visit them. When they arrived in Macedonia, they had no rest but were harassed at every turn – conflicts on the outside, fears within. (2 Corinthians 7:5)

2 Corinthians 7:7 says, "We were relieved not only to see him [Titus} but because of the report he brought us of how you refreshed his heart. He told us of your affection toward me, your deep remorse, and how concerned you were for me. This truly made my heart leap for joy!"

Not only was Paul encouraged by the visit from his friend Titus, but Paul was blessed because Titus had been encouraged by those who refreshed his heart and their concern for Paul.

Encouragement and kind words refresh your heart.

On our journey to Bill's healing, we were refreshed by others. Even though in-person visitors were kept to a minimum since Bill spent most of his hospital time in ICU, cards, emails, phone calls, text messages from others refreshed and encouraged both of us. An encouraging word can rekindle a flickering flame. Thank you for blessing and refreshing us.

The Glory Road is a place where I have not only given blessings but received them. The love of God sustains us. Just like Titus did for Paul, you have the ability, responsibility, and honor of being "Jesus with skin on" to others. Show us who we need to bless today.

Lord, thank you for the gift of friends and family. Our actions can restore hope in another. Thank you for kind words, encouraging words, that lift us up out of the pit of despair and place us on the solid ground of faith. Lord, use us where we can best be Your hands and feet. May we build each other up and not tear each other down. Lord, You are our only hope.

Thank you for your persistent prayers. Doctor's appointment for me (9.14.21) ~ asking for God's favor.#Godisfaithful#TheGloryRoad

Day#514 September 15

 Anchor Verse: 2 Corinthians 8:5
And they exceeded our expectations: They gave themselves first of all to the Lord, and then by the will of God also to us. (NIV)

In the body of Christ, the church, we are called to work together to spread the good news. We come in all shapes and sizes with many different talents. Just like a human body, we all have our function and we fit perfectly in the place God has for us.

In this passage, 2 Corinthians 8, Paul is talking about "the grace that God has given the Macedonian churches" and the actions they took. In verse 2 it says, "In the midst of a very severe trial, their overflowing joy and their extreme poverty welled up in rich generosity." They gave without counting the cost, they were eager to share in Paul's ministry.

And next comes great words of praise from Paul but also how we should pattern our lives, "And they exceeded our expectations: They gave themselves first of all to the Lord, and then by the will of God also to us."

On our journey to Bill's healing, it was so powerful to see how Bill exceeded the expectations of medical staff as well as family, friends, and strangers. It was the power of God at work in him and also Bill's willingness to submit to the Lord and let God lead the way. Mighty things happen when God is in charge and we are willing to do what He commands.

The Glory Road is filled with opportunities to exceed the expectations of others because God is in control of my life. My allegiance is first of all to Him ~ my time, my talents, my finances, all of it is His to use wherever, however, whenever. All for His glory is my battle cry.

Lord, we thank you for opportunities to serve. You have called us by name and we belong to You. Nothing is too hard for You; all things are possible with You by our side. Give us willing hearts to give of our finances, but also our time and our talents. You have choreographed and places we can be Jesus' hands and feet. May we be cheerful givers. In Jesus' name, amen.

Thank you for your faithfulness. Good report from the surgeon. Keep praying, God is listening.#Godisfaithful#TheGloryRoad

Day#515 September 16

 Anchor Verse: 2 Corinthians 9:8
And God will generously provide all you need. Then you will always have everything you need and plenty left over to share with others. (NLT)

As a child growing up did you hear the phrase "sharing time is a happy time" from the adults in your life?

Children aren't always excited about sharing, and truthfully, there are times adults aren't thrilled about sharing their resources either.

We can give because God is continually pouring into us. His love never ends. His resources have no boundaries. All that we need His hand will provide.

In 2 Corinthians 9:8, we learn about what God will supply and the "more." "And God will generously provide all you need. Then you will always have everything you need and plenty left over to share with others."

God "generously" provides all we need. God is not stingy. We don't have to beg, in fact, God often answers our prayers before we even pray them. We will have everything we need plus plenty left over to share with others.

Have you given without "counting the cost" and seen how God not only supplied your needs but filled your hands to full and overflowing?

On our journey to Bill's healing, God multiplied our blessings. We were also able to sow into the lives of others. My eyes fill with tears as I remember God's faithfulness and how our cups ran over with joy and blessings.

The Glory Road explores new terrain. So many opportunities to love others and to share what the Lord has given to me. It's not just about sharing our financial blessings, but sharing our faith, our hope, our joy ~ the world desperately needs faith, hope, joy, and peace. All of these gifts God supplies in abundance to His children. Share what the Lord has given you.

Lord, we praise and thank you for the gift of Your love. You supply ALL our needs from a heart filled with love. Shift our perspective from one of scarcity to abundance. It's not about the resources we can count or We love you and praise you, O Lord. In Jesus' name we pray, amen.

Thank you for being a cheerful giver.#Godisfaithful#TheGloryRoad

Day#516 September 17

 Anchor Verse: 2 Corinthians 10:17-18
For the one who boasts must boast in the Lord. So let's be clear. To have the Lord's approval and commendation is of greater value than bragging about oneself. (TPT)

As children, we often compare what we have to others. "My dad's stronger than your dad." "My toy is better than your toy." And on it goes…

Somehow we think that when we compare ourselves, or what we have to others, and we have "more" or a better quality "in our own eyes" that we have something to brag about.

In Matthew 20:28 it says, "…the Son of Man did not come to be served, but to serve, and to give his life as a ransom for many." (NIV) Jesus stepped down from the glory of heaven to be born as a little baby in a stable and walk this earth as a man who endured all the things we endure, and then went to the cross and died for us, and rose from the dead, and now is in heaven. If Jesus came to serve, we should follow His example.

We are called to "boast in the Lord" and what God has done, not that we are so "stunning." Because the truth is that all the "good" we do is because of God's goodness in us. We love others because God loved us first. We are called to love and to serve, not to brag about how great we are.

On our journey to Bill's healing, we were able to continually boast in the Lord. Bill was willing to submit to God's leading and His plan for healing, even in the tough places. Bill's victories were God's victories.

The Glory Road is a place where God is honored and glorified in the mess of daily living. I am grateful for the opportunity to partner with Him as I walk this walk. Serving others is an honor and a blessing. We are here to do Your will, Lord, in Your way for Your purpose.

Lord, we stand in awe of You. We kneel before You and sing, "Holy, Holy, Holy are You, Lord." Lord, we are so grateful for the opportunity to serve others and let You receive all the honor and glory. Lord, adjust our sights today. Be glorified today. In Jesus' name we pray, amen.

Thank you for your companionship.#Godisfaithful#TheGloryRoad

Day#517 September 18

 Anchor Verse: Proverbs 31:17
She equips herself with strength [spiritual, mental, and physical fitness for her God-given task] And makes her arms strong. (AMP)

Most of us are familiar with the Proverbs 31 woman. As we read through the list of her qualities, somehow it doesn't really match up with the assets we see in ourselves. We are equipped for every task He calls us to do.

We are like a gold mine that has deep treasures still waiting to be mined. When the time is right, God brings those gifts to the forefront. You are still a package waiting to be unwrapped.

"She equips herself with strength [spiritual, mental, and physical fitness for her God-given task] And makes her arms strong." (Proverbs 31:17)

What does spiritual, mental and physical fitness look like for you? Does that look like a work-out at the gym or walking with a friend? Mental fitness means we continue to learn and grow and gain wisdom from others about the amazing way God has put our world together. Spiritually, we spend time with the Lord daily ~ listening for His voice, asking to be led according to His plan for us, and reading the Bible and learning from His wisdom.

On our journey to Bill's healing, Bill worked on restoring his strength with God's help. Bill continued to get strong because of God's strength in him. When we are weak, then we are strong because of Jesus' resurrection power in us. The joy of the Lord is my strength. (Nehemiah 8:10)

The Glory Road has so many opportunities to build my spiritual, mental, and physical fitness. Honestly, I'm probably better at the spiritual and mental fitness than the physical fitness. I'm really not a "gym" girl... but the Lord continues to show me creative ways to build my strength. I want to be at my highest and best so I can serve Him with all I have ~ every part of me so He is honored and glorified.

Lord, we thank you for the ways You equip us so we might serve You. May we continue to press into You and learn more about ourselves and who You have called us to be. We love you and praise you in Jesus' name, amen.

Thank you for your faithful prayers.#Godisfaithful#TheGloryRoad

Day#518 September 19

 Anchor Verse: Ecclesiastes 2:23b
… even at night his mind does not rest. (AMP)

In this book of Ecclesiastes, written by King Solomon, the wisest man who ever lived, we see a lot of wrestling with life and life's issues. God not only gave Solomon wisdom but wealth and honor, and the promise of a long life if Solomon followed the Lord's commandments. (1 Kings 3:13-14)

Despite what Solomon had, which looks like "everything", the man is struggling with understanding life and what Solomon is seeing in the world. "Utterly meaningless! Everything is meaningless." (Ecclesiastes 1:2)

We come back to Solomon's sleepless nights, "…even at night his mind does not rest." Other translations say, "Restless, bitter nights" or "even in the night his heart takes no rest."

Elsewhere in the Bible we find God's promises about how He will sustain us through the night hours.

"In peace I will lie down and sleep, for you alone, O Lord, will keep me safe." (Psalm 4:8)

I lay down and slept, yet I woke up in safety, for the Lord was watching over me. (Psalm 3:5)

On our journey to Bill's healing, sleep was a necessity for healing. Bill needed lots of rest for his body to heal. Sometimes we had middle of the night conversations, but always before we went to sleep, we prayed together. After anointing our pillows and foreheads with anointing oil, we asked the Lord to protect us and give us good rest.

The Glory Road is filled with lots of daytime activities and sometimes the "leftovers" of the day spill into the night. Not always worries, but chasing the unknown, chasing God's best for me. Other nights I'm on "prayer duty" ~ on assignment at my heavenly Father's request. I am honored to give up sleep to stand in the gap for you, and others who need God's help.

Lord, You have created night and day. When we surrender our thoughts, questions, concerns, even our worries to You, You are faithful to hold them safe in Your hands of love and answer our call. We never get Your voicemail; we always have Your listening ear. Lord, I ask for a good night's rest for all those reading this today. In Jesus' name we pray, amen.

Thank you for your faithful prayers.#Godisfaithful#TheGloryRoad

Day#519 September 20

 Anchor Verse: Ecclesiastes 5:3a
A dream comes when there are many cares. (NIV)

How did you sleep last night? Was it a sweet sleep without dreams or good dreams? Or was your night restless as in your dreams you sorted out the things weighing on your heart?

Solomon, the author of the book of Ecclesiastes is talking about wisdom, our words, and our relationship with God and with others. What we think about and what we say are really important. Many words or few words are the mark of a wise man or a fool.

In Ecclesiastes 5:3, it says, "A dream comes when there are many cares." A couple of other translations say it this way: "Too much activity gives you restless dreams" and "Just as being too busy gives you nightmares." For all of us, there are times in our lives when we are juggling a lot of activities or many cares. If they aren't resolved during our waking hours, often our brain decides to work on them at night… when we should be sleeping.

This is the wisest man in the world, who is the King of Israel, making the statement. We can only imagine what his cares look like and his restless dreams. How do we "lie down and sleep in peace?"

On our journey to Bill's healing, Bill had some restless nights, and occasionally nightmares. The next morning, we would talk through the nightmare and then speak the truth about what God tells us in the Bible.

The Glory Road is a new path. There are mountains and valleys, sheer cliffs, green pastures, and every kind of terrain. Many of them are unfamiliar, especially on a solo flight. At the end of the day, I am learning to drop my cares at Jesus' feet and take some time to release the cares of my day before I lie down to sleep. When I try to "rush" from awake to asleep, it doesn't always work so well.

Lord, we praise and thank you for who You are. You created the world and everything in it. Today, I choose to put my cares in Your hands. Even as I walk through this day, I invite You, Lord Jesus, to walk with me. Show me what to take up and carry and what burden is not mine to bear. Lord, give us wisdom and insight today. In Jesus' name we pray amen.

Thank you for your persistent prayers.#Godisfaithful#TheGloryRoad

Day#520 September 21

 Anchor Verse: Proverbs 16:24
Pleasant words are like a honeycomb, Sweet and delightful to the soul and healing to the body. (AMP)

A pastor recently shared that the words we speak are more like an arrow than a sword. When a sword is used as a weapon, there is time for the intended target (person) to cry out for mercy, and the sword can be stopped and a life saved.

Once the archer pulls back the bow and the arrow is released, he cannot stop it. Even if the person cries out for mercy, he no longer has control of the arrow. Once our words come out of our mouths, we don't know the depth they will hit, wound they will make, or damage they will cause.

On the flip side of that scenario, if we speak words of life, words of encouragement, they are seeds deposited in a person's heart, soul, and mind that will forever blossom and grow. Their life, their perception of who they are is shaped by the encouraging words, words of truth you speak over them.

In Proverbs 16:24, we are reminded of the power of pleasant, kind, gracious, and life-giving words. "Pleasant words are like a honeycomb, Sweet and delightful to the soul and healing to the body." Words that heal ~ may those be the words spoken from our mouths today.

On our journey to Bill's healing, we encountered both kinds of words. With the armor of God in place, especially the shield of faith, we used it to deflect the arrows (words) of the enemy. Even people with good intentions can speak words that wound us. Lord, guard the words we speak.

The Glory Road is often filled with many words, words that can weigh you down. Daily, we must sort through those words and only choose to receive into our spirit words that bring life. My prayer is the words I speak reflect the love of Jesus and are filled with joy and hope and life.

Lord, we praise and thank you for the words of life spoken over us by You. The Bible is filled with Your promises and declarations of how beloved we are. May we hold our words on our tongues a little bit longer before we release them and only release words that are as sweet as honey and filled with truth. We love you and praise you in Jesus' name amen.

Thank you for your companionship.#Godisfaithful#TheGloryRoad

Day#521 September 22

 Anchor Verse: Ecclesiastes 11:10
…banish anxiety from your heart. (NIV)

Most of us would agree that "banishing" something is often easier said than done especially when it comes to our thoughts, actions, and reactions.

According to the dictionary, it has two meanings: to "forbid, abolish, or get rid of (something unwanted)" or also to "send (someone) away from a country or place as an official punishment."

The Bible talks about anxiety. One of those verses is Philippians 4:6, "Do not be anxious about anything, but in every situation, by prayer and petition, with thanksgiving, present your requests to God."

God knew His children would be anxious but He doesn't leave us there. God says run to Him, to cast our cares on Him because He cares for us.

There are situations where anxiety and depression in a person's life need more help than just prayer. If you need more assistance, seek help. God didn't call us to walk this path alone.

Solomon in Ecclesiastes 11:10 says, "Banish anxiety from your heart." Why? Because our thoughts come from what has captivated our hearts. Declare this morning, "Anxiety, I am banishing you from my heart."

On our journey to Bill's healing, there were moments and situations which were difficult. When your life is hanging in the balance between life and death, only God can keep you in peace. Bill shared his choice of peace and having a positive outlook with me.

The Glory Road is a place where I view the turmoil of the world, yet I can choose to walk on the path of peace. Often that means stopping and sitting at the feet of Jesus. When I choose not to engage in the chaos or the crazy chatter, my soul can stay at peace.

Lord, You have not left us alone. You are as near as our next breath. I pray for those who are wrestling with anxiety this morning, or even depression. We say to anxiety, you are not welcome here. My heart belongs to the Prince of Peace. Keep our eyes watchful for those who are struggling so we can speak an encouraging word to them. In Jesus' mighty name we pray, amen.

Thank you for your persistent prayers.#Godisfaithful#TheGloryRoad

Day#522 September 23

 Anchor Verse: Romans 4:21
Being fully persuaded that God had power to do what he had promised. (NIV)

If you could measure how much you believe God is able to do what He promises, how full would your measuring cup be? Would it be filled to the top, halfway, a quarter… or empty?

We must believe that God can do what He promised~ that's our part… believing.

In Romans 4, Paul shares the story of Abraham, a man who in his old age (100 years old) is still waiting for God's promise for a son. "Against all hope, Abraham in hope believed and so became the father of many nations, just as it had been said to him, "So shall your offspring be." (verse 18) Do you have that kind of faith?

Abraham was strengthened in his faith and gave glory to God. The key is holding on to our faith and giving God the glory.

"Being fully persuaded that God had power to do what he had promised." (Romans 4:21) Fully persuaded ~ Abraham had no doubt, no disbelief, even at 100 years old that he could father a child and Sarah at 90 years old would be the mother. This is God's territory.

On our journey to Bill's healing, there were many intersections where we chose faith, where we chose to believe when our eyes couldn't see beyond the crisis in front of us. With our eyes firmly fixed on Jesus, and our hand in His hand, we walked the path of faith, the path of life, and we saw miracles happen. Thank you, Lord, for unshakable faith in an unshakable God.

The Glory Road is where I walk by faith daily, hourly, minute by minute. So much is new, even the "old" looks different. I speak out loud the faith in my heart so that the enemy knows I am not afraid. I choose to be strong and courageous because I am the daughter of the King of kings and the Lord of lords. Lord, You are my shield and my defender.

Lord, we thank you for the gift of faith, power of faith, and weapon of faith. The shield of faith is part of the armor of God and it deflects the fiery arrows of the enemy. May Your love take root in us. In Jesus' name, amen.

Thank you for believing in miracles.#Godisfaithful#TheGloryRoad

Day#523 September 24

 Anchor Verse: Galatians 3:9
So those who rely on faith are blessed along with Abraham, the man of faith.
(NIV)

Relying on faith rather than relying on our own skill and independence is such great advice. Our independent "I can do everything" spirit can get us in trouble... every time. What we think we can do and what we can actually do (without God's help) is in reality not very much and not very impressive.

I'm not saying you aren't skilled and can't do amazing things, but when God is part of the equation our possibilities soar.

In Galatians 3, Paul is having a deep discussion with the church about faith and the works of the law. "So those who rely on faith are blessed along with Abraham, the man of faith." (Galatians 3:9)

Sometimes looking at other translations broadens the scope of our understanding.

The Message translation says, "Anyone who tries to live by his own effort, independent of God, is doomed to failure." And to that we say, "Amen!"

The Passion translation magnifies the promise, "And so the blessing of Abraham's faith is now our blessing too!" This is our inheritance too.

On our journey to Bill's healing, we relied on our faith in God to lead us through every valley and over every mountain. It was not the works of our hands that would heal Bill or give us the strength to stand through the trial, but only the grace of God. Bill's faith in God continued to soar as he walked his path to healing. God was the first place Bill ran in time of trouble. Bill's heavenly Father met him there.

The Glory Road has many facets ~ fast, slow, valley, and mountain terrain, but all of it under the view of God's eyes. God knows the end of my story ~ and all the parts in-between. Each step is choreographed to bring God glory.

Lord, thank you for the gift of Your love. You make a way where there doesn't seem to be a way. We lean into You today. Our attempts are feeble compared to the strength we need. We love you, Lord. In Jesus' name, amen.

Thank you for your encouragement.#Godisfaithful#TheGloryRoad

Day#524 September 25

 Anchor Verse: Galatians 4:28
Now you, brothers and sisters, like Isaac, are children of promise. (NIV)

Today the Lord wants to remind us we are children of God's promise, our birth, our life and our future are filled with miracles.

Abraham was chosen by God to be the father of many nations. Yet Sarah, his wife, did not conceive any children, even into her old age. For years, God's promise was burning in Abraham's heart but he didn't see the fulfillment of it. Yet, he believed.

When the fulfillment of the promise was long in coming, Sarah, Abraham's wife, told him to take her servant, Hagar, and bear a child with her, maybe this was the way God would give Abraham an heir. When humans try to orchestrate God's promise "their" way, it doesn't turn out very well.

In Galatians 4:28 it says, "Now you, brothers and sisters, like Isaac, are children of promise." Today you and I are the children of God's promise. In the Amplified version it says, we are not only born by physical descent but we are children born miraculously. You are a miracle.

On our journey to Bill's healing, God shifted our perspective about many areas in our lives. When so much is stripped away, even as many are experiencing in this season, God and God's promises are like precious gems. They are what gets us through the hard times and are our hope for the future. Quickly, we began to appreciate the miracle of life and its blessings.

The Glory Road is a road of revelation, not just about who I am, but who God is. God's plans are so much bigger than what I can comprehend. When I choose to walk by faith and not by sight, my eyes are opened and I have a greater understanding of whose I am, the beloved daughter of the King of kings and the Lord of lords. My life bears fruit of my miraculous beginnings.

Lord, thank you for the gift of who You are. Your love never changes, it just grows stronger. Help us to understand the reality of who we are, your children, miracles created through Your hands. Lord, we lift up our hands to worship You. We love you, Lord, in Jesus' name we pray, amen.

Thank you for your persistent prayers.#Godisfaithful#TheGloryRoad

Day#525 September 26

 Anchor Verse: Galatians 5:7
You were running the race so well. Who has held you back from following the truth? (NLT)

Life is like running a race. Our lives resemble a marathon, not a sprint. A race is not easy but the reward is worth it.

I'm not much of a "runner" as a sport but for years my husband and I did a lot of walking. One of the things we learn is our boundaries. How far can we push ourselves before our bodies push back? A little pushback expands our boundaries, but pushing too hard… our bodies always win.

In Galatians 5, Paul uses the analogy of running a race to describe to the believers in the church at Galatia, how they were walking out their faith. "You were running the race so well. Who has held you back from following the truth?" (Galatians 5:7)

Other translations use words like, "who deceived you?" or "who led you astray?" or "who cut in on you?" or "who stopped you?"

Paul is talking about interference from an outside force, another person, another "runner" in the race. We do not live this life alone. We are surrounded by many people ~ those who are running the race with the Lord and those who have chosen to walk in the darkness of the world.

On our journey to Bill's healing, we had a two-track course. Our first priority and commitment were our walk with God. The second track was the physical battle we faced in Bill's body. There was input we received from his medical team and the Lord helped us navigate our decisions.

The Glory Road is a road race. There are many people on this path going at their own speed to their own destination. Daily, I get to choose who influences me. Will I listen to God's still small voice and the truth I read in the Bible or will my walk, my race be hindered by the voices and opinions of others around me? I choose the Lord and His ways.

Lord, we praise and thank you for the gift of Your love. We do not run this race of life alone. Lord, we ask for Your divine protection and provision as we finish the course You have for us. Lord, may we keep our eyes on You. We love you and praise you in Jesus' mighty name, amen.

Thank you for your companionship.#Godisfaithful#TheGloryRoad

Day#526 September 27

 Anchor Verse: Galatians 6:7
Do not be deceived, God is not mocked; for whatever a man sows, that he will also reap. (NKJV)

Paul is reminding the believers about God's character. He encourages the believers to do good to each other, and to test their own actions and make sure they are living a life pleasing to the Lord.

"Do not be deceived, God is not mocked; for whatever a man sows, that he will also reap." (Galatians 6:7) Paul boldly speaks the truth to them. Don't be deceived, don't let the enemy or anyone else try and persuade you God does not stand for justice. God's justice always prevails.

The Amplified version says, "Do not be deceived and deluded and misled; God will not allow Himself to be sneered at (scorned, disdained, or mocked by mere pretensions or professions, or by His precepts being set aside.) [He inevitably deludes himself who attempts to delude God.]"

God's truth is God's truth and it will not change. Many have tried to go their own way and have crashed because just like a brick wall, or something more impenetrable, God cannot be moved or shaken.

"For whatever a man sows, that he will also reap." If you plant an apple tree, it will bear apples. If you plant carrot seeds, you will not harvest onions, but rather carrots. This will never change.

On our journey to Bill's healing, we gained a greater understanding and reverence for God. When you sow love into the lives of others, you will see love take root in them. Words of life bring life, and words that are hurtful are destructive. Speak life, hope, and joy into the lives of others.

The Glory Road is painted with bold colors and vivid scenes. The contrast between light and darkness is greater every day. All around us we see the "harvest" of what others have planted in their lives. We, ourselves, are seeing the fruit of our own actions. Our prayers bear much fruit.

Lord, You are a God of justice but also mercy. Without Your mercy, we would surely perish. We pray for those who are sowing to their own destruction. Open their eyes. We confess we don't always do what is right or speak what is holy, forgive us. We love you, Lord, in Jesus' name, amen.

Thank you for your persevering prayers.#Godisfaithful#TheGloryRoad

Day#527 September 28

 Anchor Verse: Ephesians 1:19-20
I pray that you will begin to understand how incredibly great his power is to help those who believe him. It is that same mighty power that raised Christ from the dead and seated him in the place of honor at God's right hand in heaven. (TLB)

The longer I walk with the Lord, the more I learn, the more I love Him. And yet, you and I only understand a small fraction of His love for us, His power at work in us. Every day the revelation grows, if we press in and wait in His presence to know Him more.

Paul wrote letters to the churches he established when he couldn't make it there in person. His letters are not "fluff" they are powerful words of truth and sometimes admonition. What we can read not only in his words but the spirit that goes with it, is Paul's love for God and how much he wants them to understand and claim that resurrection power which is available to them.

"I pray that you will begin to understand how incredibly great his power is to help those who believe him. It is that same mighty power that raised Christ from the dead and seated him in the place of honor at God's right hand in heaven." (Ephesians 1:19-20)

We live so far beneath what God has for us because of our lack of understanding of His power that is "available" to those who trust Him.

On our journey to Bill's healing, our eyes were opened to new revelation. Bill was invited to walk with Jesus in dreams and visions those last two years of his life. We saw God's mighty power as He touched and healed Bill. All praise and honor and glory go to the King of kings and the Lord of lords.

The Glory Road is a place of greater revelation. I walked by Bill's side and saw His power at work. Now God wants me to have a deeper revelation of His power in my own body, mind, and spirit. My heart's desire is the "more" God for me. May God do that for you, too.

Thank you, Lord, for who You are. We stand in awe of You. Your heart's desire is to fill us to full and overflowing so we can share that gift with others. Fill us now, O Lord. We are thirsty and only You can quench our thirst. We are hungry for the Bread of Life ~ Jesus. Equip us for the assignments You have for us in Jesus' name, amen.

Thank you for your faithfulness.#Godisfaithful#TheGloryRoad

Day#528 September 29

 Anchor Verse: Ephesians 2:17
For the Messiah has come to preach this sweet message of peace to you, the ones who were distant, and to those who are near. (TPT)

Peace ~ it's something our soul longs for, and our minds too. You won't find peace in the media or social media, even on our streets, and sometimes not even in our homes.

Even before Jesus was born, the scriptures declared that He would be the Prince of Peace in Isaiah 9:6. "For to us a child is born, to us a son is given, and the government will be on his shoulders. And he will be called Wonderful Counselor, Mighty God, Everlasting Father, Prince of Peace."

Do you know Jesus as the Prince of Peace? Maybe you know Jesus as your savior and even as the Lord of your life. But to find true rest and peace, you need to invite Him into your life as the Prince of Peace.

In Ephesians 2:17, we read that the Messiah (Jesus) came to bring peace to us. "For the Messiah has come to preach this sweet message of peace to you, the ones who were distant, and to those who are near."

This passage is about you and me. Jesus knows those who are walking with Him and being loved by Him. He also sees the lost sheep who have wandered away and those who haven't even been born yet. His peace is bountiful and available for generations yet to come.

On our journey to Bill's healing, we learned the blessing of receiving Jesus' peace in the middle of the storm. Knowing His joy and peace in the midst of a difficult diagnosis and frailty of your own body is truly a gift from God.

The Glory Road has a path of peace carved out of it. It is a narrow place where Jesus calls me to walk with him. Just as Jesus beckoned Peter to get out of the boat and walk with Him on the water, Jesus will help us through our challenges as we keep our eyes on Him. Hold on to Jesus' hand no matter what you face and His peace will flow into your life.

Thank you, Jesus, You are the Prince of Peace. We trade our chaos, worry, anxiety, and turmoil for Your peace. Lord, we trust you to lead us on paths of righteousness for Your name's sake. In Jesus' name we pray, amen.

Thank you for your companionship.#Godisfaithful#TheGloryRoad

Day#529 September 30

 Anchor Verse: Ephesians 3:7
By God's grace and mighty power, I have been given the privilege of serving him by spreading this Good News. (NLT)

Some people may think of serving as an unwanted job. Maybe you think that sitting at the table and being served means you have a greater stature, a higher position than those serving. Jesus shattered that misconception.

"For even the Son of Man did not come to be served, but to serve, and to give His life a ransom for many." (NKJV) (Mark 10:45)

"For I have given you an example, that you should do as I have done to you. Most assuredly, I say to you, a servant is not greater than his master; nor is he who is sent greater than he who sent him. If you know these things, blessed are you if you do them." (John 13:15-17 NKJV)

In Ephesians 3:7, Paul talks about the privilege of serving God by sharing with others. "By God's grace and mighty power, I have been given the privilege of serving him by spreading this Good News."

Our commission is the same~ to serve the Lord by spreading the Good News. And you will be equipped for the mission, for the task by "God's grace and mighty power."

On our journey to Bill's healing, we were bathed in God's grace and mighty power. Even in Bill's deepest valleys, the light of God's love and power were seen in Bill. Bill would tell you he had the privilege of sharing what God had done for him. Bill was ready to go to the ends of earth to share the Good News. His story will live on through his words and books.

The Glory Road is a path of amazing opportunities to serve the Lord by serving His people. There is no task too big or too small when God calls you to be His hands and feet. All that we need Jehovah Jireh will provide. It's beautiful. And so exciting. Serving the Lord by serving others brings me great joy. May we all know the joy of serving, every day, everywhere we go.

Lord, thank you for the gift of Jesus. You have assignments where we can be Your hands and feet. All we need to do is to say "yes." You are a creative God. May we be a reflection of Your creativity. In Jesus' name, amen.

Thank you for bringing joy to others.#Godisfaithful#TheGloryRoad

October 2021

Be strong and take heart all you who hope in the Lord.

~ Psalm 31:24 ~

Day#530 October 1

 Anchor Verse: Ephesians 4:31-32
Lay aside bitter words, temper tantrums, revenge, profanity, and insults. But instead be kind and affectionate toward one another. Has God graciously forgiven you? Then graciously forgive one another in the depths of Christ's love. (TPT)

Our words and our actions are a reflection of the state of our hearts. What is brewing deep inside of us in our soul and spirit comes out of our mouths.

Paul is reminding the believers in Ephesus that our words and actions impact our witness. If we "say" we are followers of Jesus, but we do things that are not very Christ-like, what message does that send to the unbeliever? Are we sending a mixed message?

In Ephesians 4:31-32, Paul lays it out, "Lay aside bitter words, temper tantrums, revenge, profanity, and insults. But instead be kind and affectionate toward one another. Has God graciously forgiven you? Then graciously forgive one another in the depths of Christ's love."

Paul doesn't leave us feeling condemned by our actions. He reminds us that God has forgiven us for all our sins ~ in thought, word, and deed. Because this is true, we must "graciously" forgive one another in the "depths" of Christ's love. His love has no boundaries ~ there is no "top" or "bottom" to the love of Jesus. That's good news, my friend.

On our journey to Bill's healing, we walked many places. We were often caught in the crossfire of the volley of the words and actions of others. Some of them turned the air "blue" as the expression goes. Other words hit our shield of faith and bounced off, and some of them grazed our flesh. The never-ending love of Jesus washed away what the enemy meant for evil.

The Glory Road is navigated in a season where there is much warfare ~ in the spirit and the flesh. There are places I choose not to go so I will not be exposed to things that will not nourish my body and soul. With the wisdom of God to guide us, may we remember to stay on the narrow path.

Lord, we praise and thank you for who You are, a God of love. Please guard our mouths as we are ambassadors of our heavenly Father. Forgive us for the times we have let You down. Restore us and cleanse our lips and our hearts. We love you and adore you, in Jesus' name we pray, amen.

Thank you for your faithfulness.#Godisfaithful#TheGloryRoad

Day#531 October 2

 Anchor Verse: Ephesians 5:2a
Live a life filled with love, following the example of Christ. (NLT)

Love ~ it's something we talk about, it's flashed on movie screens and featured in romance novels, and millions of greetings cards have been given in the name of love. But is that really love? Or it is only a "cheap" imitation of what "true love", "pure love" really is?

There is no greater example of love than what Jesus Christ did for you and me. He was willing to die for us so that we might be brought back into relationship with God. That might sound like a lot of mumbo jumbo to someone who doesn't know Jesus.

In Ephesians 5:2, Paul reminds his audience of the importance of love, not just to talk about it, but to put action to their words. "Live a life filled with love, following the example of Christ."

When we are trying to learn a new skill, it's helpful to follow a pattern. That's what Paul does here. We are to live "our life" filled with love, but the good news, we can follow Jesus' example to help us learn the ropes.

Note it says "our life" not just a couple of places like church or home or when we're by ourselves, but our whole life should be filled with loving others like Jesus loved them.

On our journey to Bill's healing, we encountered many people, both those who walked in love and those who were still walking in the darkness of self-centeredness. Bill had the opportunity to live a life filled with love even from a hospital bed. The medical staff loved to come into Bill's room. Bill loved well with the love of Jesus in his heart. His actions reflected Jesus' love.

The Glory Road follows a path through a land where people are in desperate need of the love of God. Many are filled with fear and confusion. May the light and love of Jesus break through the darkness. Every opportunity I have, my heart's desire is to plant seeds of love in the lives of others.

Lord, You are love. May we love without counting the cost. "Greater love has no one than this, that someone lay down his life for his friends." (John 15:13) May we love as You love us. Let that be our mission today and every day. Thank you for helping us to love the unlovable. In Jesus' name, amen.

Thank you for your persistent prayers.#Godisfaithful#TheGloryRoad

Day#532 October 3

 Anchor Verse: Ephesians 5:19b-20
*Sing and make music from your heart to the Lord, always giving thanks to God
the Father for everything, in the name of our Lord Jesus Christ. (NIV)*

The Bible is full of scripture verses that challenge us and stretch us to
become more like Jesus. We have Jesus as an example to walk as He walked,
love as He loved, and speak as He spoke with words of kindness and
encouragement.

"He has shown you, O mortal, what is good. And what does the Lord
require of you? To act justly and to love mercy and to walk humbly with your
God." (Micah 6:8)

In Ephesians 5, Paul is talking to the believers in Ephesus about how they
should live – "not unwise but as wise making the most of every opportunity
for the time is short." (Ephesians 5:16)

Paul offers a "new" way to think and to act, maybe differently than they had
ever considered. "Sing and make music from your heart to the Lord, always
giving thanks to God the Father for everything, in the name of our Lord
Jesus Christ." (Ephesians 5:19b-20)

Do you sing and make music from your heart to the Lord and give thanks to
God for EVERYTHING? Everything. That's a tall order, isn't it?

On our journey to Bill's healing, our perspective was changed about life and
giving thanks for everything. God opened our eyes to see the good in every
situation ~ a Romans 8:28 revelation. From our hearts we could praise the
Lord, and sing that He was worthy of our praise, worthy of it all.

The Glory Road has challenged my perspective and cadence. The world is in
a mess right now but God calls us apart from the world, into His presence.
In His presence, I sing and make music in my heart to the Lord and sing
praises to His name.

Lord, we praise and thank you this morning that You are our heavenly
Father. You ALWAYS desire Your best for us. You do not hesitate to move
heaven and earth to achieve Your purposes for us and to protect Your
children. Life may not always be easy but we know Lord, You are always
faithful. We rest in Your arms of love this morning and listen to You sing
songs of deliverance over us. In Jesus' name we pray, amen.

Thank you for your friendship.#Godisfaithful#TheGloryRoad

Day#533 October 4

 Anchor Verse: Ephesians 6:24
Grace to all who love our Lord Jesus Christ with an undying love. (NIV)

Love ~ we talk about it a lot in our world, media, churches, and families. One expression from years ago is that "love makes the world go round." Not sure that's true "literally" but love is a strong motivator and very powerful.

The Bible tells us that God loved us before we even knew Him. "We love because He first loved us." (1 John 4:19)

God's love is unconditional and lasts forever… it has no end.

That might be a difficult concept to wrap your head around because many things in this world wear out or run out. Not God's love.

As we come to the end of this letter Paul is sending to the church in Ephesus, we find his final response, word of encouragement, and exhortation. "Grace to all who love our Lord Jesus Christ with an undying love." (Ephesians 6:24)

Those who love Jesus Christ with an "undying" love. Is that you?

Undying love ~ love that never ends. Some translations use the words "incorruptible, never gets weak, never ends, and never dies." "Undying love" may seem like a lofty goal but great is the reward.

On our journey to Bill's healing, our love for Jesus became stronger every day. Our love for each other was multiplied and magnified through our trials. God's grace ~ His unmerited favor flowed like a river in every place

The Glory Road is a place of great grace. Grace is not only something we receive from God's heart but something we can freely give to others. As I walk this path alone, Jesus' love for me takes on new meaning. When we read God's Word and spend time in His presence, we get to know Him more. Your heart's desire is to love others as God loves you.

Lord, words cannot quantify Your love for us. We pray for those who have not opened the gift of love You have for them. You still love them and always will. May today be the day they open their hearts to receive Your never-ending love. We love you and praise you in Jesus' name, amen.

Thank you for your love and support.#Godisfaithful#TheGloryRoad

Day#534 October 5

 Anchor Verse: Philippians 1:27a
Whatever happens, keep living your lives based on the reality of the gospel of Christ. (TPT)

Whatever happens…

We are living in a time when we don't know what will happen next ~ good or challenging. It is a time in our history where things are being shaken. Not only in our own lives, but systems, structures, the status quo, even things that we thought were unshakable.

Whatever happens…God will not fail us. He is unshakable, unstoppable, and unmovable.

In the context of Philippians, the first chapter, Paul is writing to the church there to encourage them. Even if he doesn't come to visit them, his exhortation is no matter what happens, they should keep living their lives based on the reality of the gospel of Christ.

The full verse says, "Whatever happens, keep living your lives based on the reality of the gospel of Christ. Then when I come to see you, or hear good reports of you, I'll know that you stand united in one Spirit and one passion—celebrating together as conquerors in the faith of the gospel."

We are in this together. Believers worldwide are called to unite under the banner of Christ and be united in one Spirit and to celebrate we are conquerors (more than conquerors) in the faith of the gospel.

On our journey to Bill's healing, our faith in God was the tap root that kept us centered and sturdy through the storms of life. "Whatever happens" ~ God is faithful. "Whatever happens" ~ He is Lord. "Whatever happens" ~ we are safe in the hollow of His hands. "Whatever happens" ~ He will never leave you or forsake you.

The Glory Road is a place of greater revelation and more episodes of "whatever happens." With God on our side, we don't need to walk in fear. We hold on to Jesus' hand and trust Him to guide us on the narrow path of faith. There's no greater place to be than in the center of His will.

Thank you, Lord, for the gift of this day. Whatever happens, You will be right by our side. The best is yet to come. In Jesus' name we pray, amen.

Thank you for your faithfulness.#Godisfaithful#TheGloryRoad

Day#535 October 6

 Anchor Verse: Philippians 2:20-21
Timothy is like no other. He carries the same passion for your welfare that I carry in my heart. For it seems as though everyone else is busy seeking what is best for themselves instead of the things that are most important to our Lord Jesus Christ. (TPT)

The apostle Paul spoke his mind. He was not afraid to talk about tough topics or address difficult situations. Paul was also quick to commend those who were doing the "right thing" and living a life that reflected Jesus.

Timothy was a vital member of Paul's missionary team. There were times when Timothy went as Paul's representative and also was Paul's scribe and co-author. Paul was Timothy's mentor.

"Timothy is like no other. He carries the same passion for your welfare that I carry in my heart. For it seems as though everyone else is busy seeking what is best for themselves instead of the things that are most important to our Lord Jesus Christ." (Philippians 2:20-21)

This is high praise from Paul; it would be high praise for any of us. To carry "the same passion for your welfare as I carry in my heart" ~ to catch the vision from the leader of the ministry you support, that's powerful.

Are we busy seeking what is best for ourselves rather than the things that are most important to our Lord Jesus Christ?

On our journey to Bill's healing, we learned about "busyness" and how quickly circumstances can strip it away. What remains is only what is important in God's eyes. There is great joy and blessing when you choose to have a great passion in your heart for the welfare of others.

The Glory Road is a road filled with passion in my heart for the welfare of others, because I know what it's like to be in need. Prayer and a caring heart will impact many lives as we love as Jesus loves. You are important to me.

Lord, thank you for the gift of Your example. May we lay down our busyness and take up the mantle of peace and passion for those who are in need. In Jesus' name we pray, amen.

Thank you for your companionship.#Godisfaithful#TheGloryRoad

Day#536 October 7

 Anchor Verse: Philippians 3:13
But one thing I do… (NIV)

In a world that applauds results and rewards ambition, the pressure to do multiple things, build your resume, build "bigger storehouses" is staggering. There is a subliminal melody about doing more that infiltrates every nook and cranny of our very being. But it doesn't have to be that way.

The apostle Paul had been given many "sheep" to look after, to advice, to mentor, to shepherd, yet, we find great wisdom in his choices.

Reading this passage in Philippians 3, when my eyes fell on these words, "But one thing I do" my spirit was caught just like a fish on a hook. God's reminder that only one thing is important, only one thing is needed…only one… that is our pursuit of God.

The full text of Philippians 3:13-14 says: "Brothers and sisters, I do not consider myself yet to have taken hold of it. But one thing I do: Forgetting what is behind and straining toward what is ahead, 14 I press on toward the goal to win the prize for which God has called me heavenward in Christ Jesus." (NIV)

On our journey to Bill's healing, we learned the lesson of the "one thing." Holding one thing in your hand, your heart, your mind, is sufficient. When we hold up our pursuit of life to the Lord, and place it at His feet, and ask Him to guide us, guard us, and protect us as we seek His face, that is where we find the blessing. Hallelujah for the lesson of the "one thing."

The Glory Road is a place of exploration of new things and remembering the lessons of the past and nuggets of wisdom I have gleaned. Yet, as I live today, as I look ahead to tomorrow, there is one thing I seek, and that is my Lord Jesus Christ. Nothing else matters if Jesus isn't in the center of who I am and what I do. All for Your glory, Lord. I live for Your glory.

Lord, thank you for the reminder there is only one thing to seek and that's You. Refine us, prune us, burn away the dross, so we may be vessels of honor for You, Lord. May our lives reflect Your glory and not the results of our own ambitions. In Jesus' name we pray, amen.

Thank you for your persistent prayers.#Godisfaithful#TheGloryRoad

Day#537 October 8

 Anchor Verse: Isaiah 30:19
How compassionate he will be when he hears your cries for help! He will answer you when he hears your voice! (TPT)

At the sound of a crying child, all heads are turned and prepare for action. When a cry of distress is heard from a ship lost at sea or the flight deck of an airliner, support is mobilized immediately.

Crisis calls for action. Injury and calamity cannot be deferred. It's time for action ~ now.

If that's the way of the world, how much greater is God's response when we cry out for help? God will move heaven and earth to help His children.

Isaiah 30:19 reminds us that God is near and He hears our every heart cry. "How compassionate he will be when he hears your cries for help! He will answer you when he hears your voice!"

Does that truth touch your heart this morning? It touches mine.

God loves you so much He doesn't want you to suffer needlessly. The suffering He really wants you to avoid is the lie from the enemy of our soul whispers, "You are alone. God doesn't care about you." That is a lie. The truth is what we read here… as soon as God hears your cry for help, He will answer you. He will walk by your side through it all.

On the journey to Bill's healing, often the Lord heard our cry for help. And He always answered. Sometimes it was His peace. Other times it was a physical manifestation as in a healing miracle or the appearance of something we needed. Every single day we knew that God was near and He loved us.

The Glory Road is often filled with a lot of noise. It can wear you out rather than build you up. I often retreat to a quiet place ~ physically or in my spirit, and ask the Lord for help in that moment. He always answers.

Lord, thank you for the gift of a new day. You hear the cries of our heart and Your compassionate heart is moved to intervene on our behalf. We lean into the best You have for us today ~ whether that's through a valley or rejoicing on the mountaintop of victory. You are our refuge and strength, an ever-present help in time of trouble. We praise you, Lord, in Jesus' name, amen.

Thank you for your faithfulness.#Godisfaithful#TheGloryRoad

Day# 538 October 9

Anchor Verse: Colossians 1:3-4

Whenever we pray for you, we always begin by giving thanks to God the Father of our Lord Jesus Christ, for we have heard how much you trust the Lord, and how much you love his people. (TLB)

If we were together in a room, a large room, I would pose this question, "How many of you pray?" Likely most of you, if not all of you, would raise your hands or nod your heads.

Some people are dedicated prayer warriors who pray day and night, it's what God has called them to do. Others may have specific times they pray, and others may reach out to God only in desperate situations.

When you pray for others, do you thank God for them? Or are your prayers filled with a list of needs of what we want God to do?

As he writes to the church at Colossae, Paul says this, "Whenever we pray for you, we always begin by giving thanks to God the Father of our Lord Jesus Christ, for we have heard how much you trust the Lord, and how much you love his people." (Colossians 1:3-4)

On our journey to Bill's healing, prayer was as necessary as breathing. Our prayers were filled with thanksgiving as we watched God's hand move through His people. Your acts of love and bold prayers prayed on Bill's behalf are a testimony to your faith in God. God saw what you did for us, what you are still doing for me, and He will reward your obedience.

The Glory Road cuts through a time in history when prayer is more than just a habit or a ritual, it's as vital as our heart beating. Millions of prayers rise to heaven each day. We have all witnessed and been in prayer groups with a few or many. God's hand has moved because of our prayers. Others hear how much you trust the Lord and how much you love His people. Keep up the good work as you continue to be Jesus' hands and feet.

Lord, thank you for the gift of prayer. Bless your prayer warriors, heal them, fill them up with new hope and new joy. Exchange their weariness for strength. Extend the length of their days and crown them with Your love and mercy. Lord, all we have and all that we hope to be we give it all to You as an offering of praise. May we be a blessing everywhere our feet walk today. In Jesus' name we pray, amen.

Thank you for your love for me and others.#Godisfaithful#TheGloryRoad

Day#539 October 10

 Anchor Verse: Colossians 2:2
My goal is that they may be encouraged in heart and united in love... (NIV)

It's good to have goals. You have a target, something to prepare for, and dream about, and achieve.

One of my favorite quotes is by Napoleon Hill, "A goal is a dream with a deadline." Which of your dreams needs to have a deadline attached to it today?

In Colossians 2, Paul is writing to the believers there in Colossae but in verse one, Paul says he is not only contending for them but for those at Laodicea and for all he has not met personally.

Paul has a goal and it guides his actions and prayers. "My goal is that they may be encouraged in heart and united in love..." (Colossians 2:2)

The rest of the verse tells us the "why" behind it, "so that they may have the full riches of complete understanding, in order that they may know the mystery of God, namely, Christ."

For just a moment, ponder what it feels like when someone encourages you. They planted seeds of hope in your soul, when one of life's wildfires torched your plans and left it in ashes. When we are encouraged in heart, we are ready to take on life's battles again with confidence.

On our journey to Bill's healing, these two elements of Paul's goal, "encouraged in heart and united in love" were the fuel that sustained us on a challenging path. It was not only the bond Bill and I had together, but those God wove into the beautiful tapestry of our lives.

The Glory Road is like walking into the Promised Land. God is with me, the Holy Spirit directs my path, and Jesus is at my side to navigate the mountains and the valleys. My goals are similar ~ to encourage others, pray with them and over them, and share the love of Jesus so we are united in love.

Lord, we praise and thank you for the gift of time. We thank you that we are in the world for "such a time as this." We can be instruments of Your peace. Please bless those who are a blessing to others. In Jesus' name, amen.

Thank you for your faithfulness.#Godisfaithful#TheGloryRoad

Day#540 October 11

 Anchor Verse: Colossians 3:14
Above all, clothe yourselves with love, which binds us all together in perfect harmony. (TLB)

This morning as you got dressed and ready for the day did you put on love? The Amplified version says you are to "wrap yourselves in [unselfish] love."

Unity and perfect harmony occur when we are not thinking of ourselves alone, but of those around us~ "when one seeks the best for others." (AMP)

Paul is telling the believers, the church, to clothe themselves with these qualities "compassion, kindness, humility, gentleness and patience." In verse 14, Paul reminds them that even though all these are admirable qualities that ALL of it must be wrapped up in love that seeks that best for others.

On our journey to Bill's healing, our love took on new dimensions. God had called us off the beaten path years previously, but in this season, we chose to take our love to another level. God showed us what true love looks like when the Hallmark version of love is stripped away. God's love has no floor or ceiling. His love is unconditional and eternal.

The Glory Road gives me the opportunity to seek the best for others as I love with selfless love. That doesn't mean that I love myself less, but rather God's love in me overflows to others. My understanding of God's love for me increases every day. Because of God's love and goodness and grace and mercy and peace, I can be a light in the darkness of the world.

Lord, we praise and thank you for the gift of Your love through Jesus Christ your son. May we choose love over being right. May we choose harmony instead of discord. May we choose truth over the lie. May we choose faith instead of fear. Lord, help us where we are weak. We bow before You this morning, King of kings and Lord of lords. We will give You, all the praise and honor and glory in Jesus' name, amen.

Thank you for your faithfulness.#Godisfaithful#TheGloryRoad

Day#541 October 12

 Anchor Verse: Isaiah 40:25
"To whom will you compare me? Who is my equal?" asks the Holy One. (NLT)

Too often in our lives we compare ourselves to others. Often we feel like we fall short. Maybe come out on top in the comparison game, but usually it's the deficit we see.

In Isaiah 40, we read about the incredible feats of God and what He does. "He stretches out the heavens like a canopy." (verse 22) "He brings out the starry host one by one and calls forth each of them by name." (verse 26) His ways are beyond our understanding. His power and majesty without equal.

"To whom will you compare me? Who is my equal?" asks the Holy One." (Isaiah 40:25)

My soul responds this morning, "Lord, there is no one like you! For you are great, and your name is full of power." (Jeremiah 10:6)

When was the last time, you stopped running through the day and reflected on God's majesty, His grace, His mercy, or His peace?

Just a few verses later in verse 31 we find the key, "Those who WAIT on the Lord" … that is where is strength is found, our joy, our peace, and our power.

On our journey to Bill's healing, our lives came to halt, the lives we once knew. We entered into a new understanding, respect, honor, and the opportunity to see His glory because we stopped and stood in God's presence. Or more accurately fell to our knees as we recognized our need and His great presence. Lord, You have no equal.

The Glory Road is a place of revelation. Every day something new pops up. I learn more about myself and others, but infinitely more about God. He longs to be in relationship with you and me. There may be none other like Him, yet God stoops down from heaven to walk with us and talk with us daily.

Lord, You are not a small god we can fit in our pocket and take out when we need You. You are beyond understanding. You are greater than we can imagine. You are close as our very heartbeat and next breath. Thank you for Your love that passes all understanding. In Jesus' name, amen.

Thank you for your companionship.#Godisfaithful#TheGloryRoad

Day#542 October 13

 Anchor Verse: Isaiah 41:18
I will open up rivers for them on the high plateaus. I will give them fountains of water in the valleys. I will fill the desert with pools of water. Rivers fed by springs will flow across the parched ground. (NLT)

When you are thirsty, there is nothing that quenches your thirst like water. God created that thirst in us, not only to keep our bodies hydrated and healthy, but to thirst after Him.

Be thirsty for God? What? Maybe that's a new concept for you. But there is something inside of us that longs to be with God, our Creator. God is the river of life and our soul thirsts for Him.

When Jesus encounters the Samaritan woman at the well, He asks her for a drink of water. She is shocked a Jewish man would ask her, a Samaritan woman, for a drink. Jews and Samaritans didn't have anything to do with each other. Jesus speaks to her of "living water." (John 4:13-14)

We are reminded of God's ability to reverse situations and bring life where it seems death is winning. God always has the final word.

"I will open up rivers for them on the high plateaus. I will give them fountains of water in the valleys. I will fill the desert with pools of water. Rivers fed by springs will flow across the parched ground." (Isaiah 41:18)

On our journey to Bill's healing, we encountered desert places, places where no one else wanted to travel. God was always there. The river of life flowed into those places with fountains of water in the valleys, pools of water in the desert, and rivers fed by springs flowed across the parched ground.

The Glory Road is a place with so many different terrains. One minute, the highway, the next, a desert place or headed off into a briar patch to answer the call of someone in distress. God is with me directing my path and there is purpose to my journey.

Heavenly Father, You have created in us a thirst for You that only You can quench. We come and bring you our love and adoration this morning. We drink from the river of life as we tackle the challenges of this day knowing You are for us and not against us. We praise you in Jesus' name, amen.

Thank you for your persevering prayers.#Godisfaithful#TheGloryRoad

Day#543 October 14

 Anchor Verse: 1 Thessalonians 2:8
So we cared for you. Because we loved you so much, we were delighted to share with you not only the gospel of God but our lives as well. (NIV)

Taking care of others is a big responsibility and also a huge blessing.

At this time in our history, more people have become caregivers in one capacity or another than we can remember. Due to some external forces, families, friends, even strangers have come together in new ways.

1 Thessalonians 2:8, in the NIV version, starts out with a remnant from the previous verse as it talks about a nursing mother caring for her child… "so we cared for you." New moms not only give birth to their children, but provide life-giving sustenance. The baby is dependent on the mother for life. Paul and his team cared for those God had called them to love and minister to there in Thessalonica and elsewhere.

"So we cared for you. Because we loved you so much, we were delighted to share with you not only the gospel of God but our lives as well." (1 Thessalonians 2: 8)

On our journey to Bill's healing, our relationship gained new depth. We learned to care for each other in new ways. We were willing to give our lives for each other. All our love, all our strength, all our joy, everything we had we shared until God took Bill home. That is the level of commitment God is asking of us today. "Greater love has no one than this, than to lay down one's life for his friends." (John 15:13 NJKV)

The Glory Road is blazing a trail through new territory. The past is gone. We may have the memories, but what lies ahead of us is even greater than what is behind us. God needs us to give everything we have, leaving nothing on the table, so we can live lives that bring honor and glory to His name.

Lord, thank you for those who have left such an amazing selfless legacy of giving their all. It is not for their glory, fame, or riches, but for Your honor and glory. For those who are caregivers, we ask for an extra measure of strength. Open our eyes to see those in need around us and offer a cup of cold water in Jesus' name. In Jesus' name we pray, amen.

Thank you for your love.#Godisfaithful#TheGloryRoad

Day#544 October 15

 Anchor Verse: Isaiah 46:11
...What I have said, that I will bring about; what I have planned, that I will do. (NIV)

Plans... we all have plans ~ plans for today, plans for this week, this year, etc. How many of our plans actually come to pass? Many of them are left undone. Some are rescheduled by God and others fall to the ground.

Jeremiah 29:11 reminds us God's plans for us are good, to prosper us and not harm us, to give us hope and a future. We often "forget" the next verse, "Then you will call on me and come and pray to me, and I will listen to you." (Jeremiah 29:12) We can't achieve these "best" plans on our own.

"What I have said, that I will bring about; what I have planned, that I will do." (Isaiah 46:11)

Is this comforting? Maybe you are walking through deep waters right now and the water keeps rising higher. It's no longer around your ankles. The water has risen to your knees and it's heading for your waist.

Isaiah 43 promises that we will go "through" them, we will not be overcome by the waters, the rivers, or the fire... we are victorious in Jesus' name.

On our journey to Bill's healing, we became familiar with the roar of God, the Lion of the tribe of Judah. When God says it, He means it, and He has the power to make good on His promises. What a blessing to see God choreograph outcomes that otherwise would be impossible with man.

The Glory Road is a path of making new plans and walking new roads. There is great comfort to be found as you rest in the shadow of the Almighty. (Psalm 91) His ways are so much higher than my ways, and His thoughts than my thoughts.

Lord, thank you for the gift of this new day. You are the God who sees not only today but the future. Our times are in Your hands. The world may be in a season of unrest, but when we have faith in You we can sleep during the storm when You are at our side. Lord, we sing praises to Your name this morning. In Jesus' name we pray, amen.

Thank you for believing in miracles.#Godisfaithful#TheGloryRoad

Day#545 October 16

 Anchor Verse: Isaiah 49:25b
For I will fight those who fight you, and I will save your children. (NLT)

As we walk through this world, we will experience adversity and trouble. Life is not always easy. There are trials, temptations, and even battles.

The Prince of Peace reminds us there is nothing in our lives we will encounter that is bigger than our God. There are no depths of sorrow, dry desert places, swamps of despair and discouragement, or even mountains of victory that can match the splendor and majesty of our God.

It is a powerful concept to grasp that God is fighting for us. The world and our culture would have us believe we are walking this journey alone.

Throughout Isaiah 49, the Lord has been telling His people about how He will lead them to victory. In verse 23 it says, "Then you will know that I am the Lord; those who hope in me will not be disappointed."

Where have you placed your hope?

In verse 25, God makes this promise, "I will fight those who fight you, and I will save your children." Some translations use the word "contend" or "oppose" to describe His protection of us.

On our journey to Bill's healing, we witnessed God fighting for us. Countless times God's army of angels surrounded Bill. God moved supernaturally and through the hands of men to accomplish His purposes ~ life for Bill.

The Glory Road is a place where daily battles surround me. Some I hear from a distance and others are up close and personal. One thing I know, God is fighting for me. Some days it translates to sitting back and resting in Him and His ability to fight for me. Other days, God calls me to walk into the battle and through His strength, I am victorious. We must listen to the still, small voice of God to direct our path. We are victorious in Jesus' name.

Lord, You are our shield and defender. We are not defeated by the wiles and strategies of the enemy. We come humbly with hearts filled with gratitude. Our future is bright because of You. In Jesus' name we pray, amen.

Thank you for your faithfulness.#Godisfaithful#TheGloryRoad

Day#546 October 17

 Anchor Verse: Isaiah 52:1
Wake up, wake up, O Zion! Clothe yourself with strength. (NLT)

Do you have a wake-up routine in the morning? Do you wake up to an alarm at a specific time? Maybe hit the snooze button ~ once or twice?

Morning is more than just about the routine we have on the outside but rather what's happening inside of us. What's your attitude like? You might be slow to get started, even needing a cup of coffee to get your system going. Or you might jump out of bed fully awake and ready to go.

As believers, we have an "extra" layer, the armor of God. This is how we fight the battles we encounter throughout the day. Ephesians 6 outlines the pieces: belt of truth, breastplate of righteous, shoes of peace, helmet of salvation, shield of faith, and the sword of the Spirit (the Word of God).

In Isaiah 52:1, we read this message to Zion, but a message we can take to heart as well, "Wake up, wake up, O Zion! Clothe yourself with strength."

That is not the human strength we generate at the gym by working out, but rather the strength that comes from the Lord.

On our journey to Bill's healing, we learned that human strength can be quickly stripped away by an illness or injury. With God fighting for you, your strength is renewed as you wait on the Lord, and then you will soar again. We must wake up and not rely on our own strength but clothe ourselves with His strength. That's how we win the war.

The Glory Road gives me opportunities daily to clothe myself with strength. Not only when I begin my day, but throughout my day, as I stop to rest and reflect on the Lord, my strength is renewed. The Bible says, "The joy of the Lord is my strength." (Nehemiah 8:10)

Lord, today we come asking for Your help. At times we are weak, when we view the battles that surround us in the world. Lord, we turn to You this morning and ask to be clothed in Your strength for the battles we will face today. We choose faith over fear. We choose peace instead of chaos. We choose love instead of hate. We choose You, Lord, instead of the fleeting pleasures of the world. In Jesus' name we pray, amen.

Thank you for your persistent prayers.#Godisfaithful#TheGloryRoad

Day#547 October 18

 Anchor Verse: 2 Thessalonians 1:4

We point to you as an example of unwavering faith for all the churches of God. We boast about how you continue to demonstrate unflinching endurance through all the persecutions and painful trials you are experiencing. (TPT)

We all love to tell stories of victory, of people overcoming obstacles, stories with a happy ending. Through the generations, through our history as families as well as a nation, we remember people who with great determination kept pressing on and pushing through what seemed like insurmountable odds.

Your own family tree is filled with stories of those who went through hardship and never quit. That is why you are here today.

In 2 Thessalonians 1:4, in Paul's letter to the Thessalonian church, he begins by praising the church for their track record. "We point to you as an example of unwavering faith for all the churches of God. We boast about how you continue to demonstrate unflinching endurance through all the persecutions and painful trials you are experiencing."

As a nation, we are walking through a time of great challenges. Will we rise to the challenge like the Thessalonian church and face these times with unwavering faith and unflinching endurance?

On our journey to Bill's healing, we chose to have faith in God and put our hand in His hand, and trust Him to lead the way through our trials and challenges. Was it easy? No. Was God faithful? Yes, in every situation. We were given the opportunity to let His light shine through our lives.

The Glory Road passes through a world where there are persecutions and painful trials. This is the reality of our lives. When our eyes are turned toward heaven, we are blessed with courage, faith, and even joy through the trials.

Lord, we praise for the gift of this day. Your mercies are brand new. Whatever the challenges we face, we do not face them alone. Victories await us, we will cross the finish line by Your grace. We pray for those who are facing tests, trials, and temptations. May they be found faithful as they press on with unwavering faith. We love you in Jesus' name, amen.

Thank you for your persevering prayers.#Godisfaithful#TheGloryRoad

Day#548 October 19

 Anchor Verse: Isaiah 57:10
As I create the praise of his lips, Peace, peace, to him who is far away [both Jew and Gentile] and to him who is near!" says the Lord; "And I will heal him [making his lips blossom anew with thankful praise]." (AMP)

We are often impatient people. We want to see results and we want to see them now. That impatience often spills over to the people in our lives.

"Easy" looks different for everyone,

"As I create the praise of his lips, Peace, peace, to him who is far away [both Jew and Gentile] and to him who is near!" says the Lord; "And I will heal him [making his lips blossom anew with thankful praise]." (Isaiah 57:10)

Notice that God is speaking peace over all of them ~ those who are close and those who are far away. Those who know God intimately and those who are being drawn to the love of God, God is speaking peace over all of them. We should do the same. Love them with God the Father's love for them. It is God's love that draws us near to His heart.

Then comes the promise, "And I will heal him!" For those of us who need healing or have family or friends who need healing, we claim this promise today.

On our journey to Bill's healing, we were blessed in so many ways. God's peace was the undercurrent of our lives that kept us anchored to hope. We watched God heal Bill so many times. We gave thanks for our blessings.

The Glory Road traverses a land with overtones of chaos and confusion. But as we walk on the God's path, we will find peace. We each have our own unique journey. However, corporately as believers, we have the hope of Jesus Christ to keep us anchored in our faith so we can walk without stumbling or falling prey to the wiles and strategies of the enemy.

Lord, thank you for the gift of Your peace. We take a leap of faith into the hopes and dreams you have for us. Bind us together with cords that cannot be broken. Keep our hearts tender toward the wounded and broken. May Your love be the healing balm they need. In Jesus' name we pray, amen.

Thank you for your faithfulness.#Godisfaithful#TheGloryRoad

Day#549 October 20

 Anchor Verse: Isaiah 61:10a
I am overwhelmed with joy in the Lord my God! (NLT)

Overwhelmed with joy ~ when is the last time you felt that way?

We live in a world where joy can be a sacred, even scarce, commodity. The truth is, it doesn't have to be scarce.

"Why?" you ask. Because God is the source of all joy. The joy we find in the Lord is never extinguished. It is a fountain of life.

In the NIV translation, the word "joy" appears 242 times.

Isaiah 61:10a says, "I am overwhelmed with joy in the Lord my God!" It fills me with joy just to read those words.

To feel that joy sometimes we need to get away from the barrage of distractions of life and be in a quiet place. Joy is a precious oil whose fragrance infuses our days and our nights.

On our journey to Bill's healing, we found joy in the most unexpected places. Not only did God's joy fill us but we were blessed to share that joy with others. Not everyone can find joy in an ICU unit or a rehab hospital, but Bill did. It touched the lives of many people. I'm so grateful for my husband and the joy he brought to my life.

The Glory Road is a path where darkness and light collide, where joy and sorrow often are only a breath apart. As followers of Christ, our vessels of clay are filled with His resurrection power. Keeping our focus in the right place is crucial as we steward the gift of joy. Share your joy liberally. God will replenish what you give away.

Lord, we praise you for the gift of joy. It is a fruit of the Holy Spirit. Today may we choose joy to accompany us on our journey. Open our eyes to see, open our ears to hear, open our mind to understand Your will for us, O Lord, and then may we go out with joy singing, "The Lord has been so good to me." Thank you that the joy of the Lord is our strength, today and every day in Jesus' name we pray, amen.

Thank you for your persistent prayers.#Godisfaithful#TheGloryRoad

Day#550 October 21

Anchor Verse: Isaiah 62:10
Go through, Go through the gates! Prepare the way for the people; Build up, Build up the highway! Take out the stones, Lift up a banner for the peoples! (NKJV)

Progress takes effort. If we want a change in our lives, in our surroundings, we must do something about it. We can't just wish it away or put it on our to-do list. Preparation precedes progress.

You can't put the roof on a house before you have poured the foundation. Some things may be obvious, and others, we learn by experience what we should or shouldn't do.

I'm in the process of doing an "extreme" makeover in my office. It's been an interesting experience. It went from a thought to what do I want to change? It takes time, effort, energy, wise counsel, and lots of prayer.

In Isaiah 62:10, we see a project coming to life, "Go through, Go through the gates! Prepare the way for the people; Build up, Build up the highway! Take out the stones, Lift up a banner for the peoples!"

There is plan, specific steps, and an intended outcome.

What are the stones in your life that need to be removed so the highway is smoothed out as you travel God's path for you?

On our journey to Bill's healing, we were brought onto new paths. Often the preparation time was quick, but there were always stones that needed to be removed. Always the banner of God's love was raised high so we could focus on our destination daily ~ being at peace in His presence.

The Glory Road is not only a path for me but for others. Part of my mission is to smooth the highway, remove the boulders that would cause others to fall, and to lift high the banner of the Lord. In any race, if we keep our eyes on the prize, we will remain encouraged and win the race set before us.

Lord, we praise and thank you for the gift of this day. Please meet our every need so we can pass that blessing along to others. You have equipped us for the tasks we will face today. May we encourage those who we encounter this day with Your promises, Lord. Great are You, Lord, and greatly to be praised. We love you and praise you in Jesus' name, amen.

Thank you for your faithfulness.#Godisfaithful#TheGloryRoad

Day#551 October 22

 Anchor Verse: 1 Timothy 2:8
Therefore I want the men in every place to pray, lifting up holy hands, without anger and disputing or quarreling or doubt [in their mind]. (AMP)

Praying is more than just the words speak, the thoughts we think, the petitions and praise we lay on the altar, it's about the attitude of our hearts and minds.

Are we coming to God with clean hands and a pure heart or with a bad attitude asking God to do bad things to our perceived enemies?

Psalm 24:3-4 reveals more about who can come into the Lord's presence. "Who may climb the mountain of the Lord and enter where he lives? Who may stand before the Lord? Only those with pure hands and hearts, who do not practice dishonesty and lying."

Praying is as much about us as it is about those we are praying for and bringing their needs before the Lord.

In 1 Timothy 2:8, Paul is summoning people to pray. "Therefore I want the men in every place to pray, lifting up holy hands, without anger and disputing or quarreling or doubt [in their mind]."

To read Paul's specific words, "without anger and disputing or quarreling or doubt (in their mind), creates a picture in our minds of mayhem as people came together to pray in not a very holy posture.

On our journey to Bill's healing, prayer went before us, went with us, and followed us. Bill and I walked through some places where there were a lot of chaos, and even frustration and anger around us.

The Glory Road is a place of much prayer. If we could "see" in the supernatural realm, it would amaze us how many prayers ascend to heaven daily. Prayer is not a club we use as a weapon against our enemies or those who think differently than we do. It is a portal God has opened to come near Him and bring our requests, prayers, petitions, and praise.

Thank you, Lord, for Your love for us. Thank you for the gift of prayer. May we pray as Jesus prayed even with love for those who come against us. Lord, we thank you that in You we have victory in Jesus' name, amen.

Thank you for your love.#Godisfaithful#TheGloryRoad

Day#552 October 23

 Anchor Verse: Jeremiah 1:7
But the Lord said to me, "Do not say, 'I am [only] a young man,' Because everywhere I send you, you shall go, And whatever I command you, you shall speak. (AMP)

Excuses…they flow out of our mouth so easily. They are like a road block that prevents us from moving forward. In reality, they are like a paper tiger, empty and powerless.

In this first chapter of Jeremiah, we are introduced to Jeremiah, a young man, when the Lord comes to him and appoints him as a prophet to the nations. Commentators don't agree on what age Jeremiah was when he was called but it's in the range of 13-17 years old.

Verse 5 says, "Before I formed you in the womb I knew you, before you were born I set you apart; I appointed you as a prophet to the nations." (NIV) Jeremiah responds he doesn't know how to speak. I am too young.

"But the Lord said to me, "Do not say, 'I am [only] a young man,' Because everywhere I send you, you shall go, And whatever I command you, you shall speak." (Jeremiah 1:7)

When the Lord has a mission for you, your excuses will not hold any weight. God tells Jeremiah "everywhere" I send you, you shall go. And as the rest of the book of Jeremiah unfolds, that is exactly what Jeremiah did.

On our journey to Bill's healing, there were places we didn't feel qualified to walk the path ahead of us. Instead of too young, we might have entertained the thought we were too old or too sick. When God has a plan, He will move heaven and earth to accomplish it. He will move you.

The Glory Road has many new adventures ~ some of them familiar tasks and many are not. The enemy of my soul whispers I am not enough, but the God of angel armies quickly rushes in and reminds me, where He sends me, I will go, and I will be enough for the task. All I need His hand will provide.

Lord, we come today with heart's full of gratitude thanking you for what You have done in our lives. Thank you for the moments in our lives when we thought we weren't enough, and You showed us the opposite. Our obedience changes the world and breeds confidence in the faithfulness of God. We trust you to lead us on the path of victory that will encourage others and bring glory to Your name. We love you, in Jesus' name, amen.

Thank you for your faithfulness.#Godisfaithful#TheGloryRoad

Day#553 October 24

Anchor Verse: 1 Timothy 4:7b-8
*...discipline yourself for the purpose of godliness [keeping yourself spiritually fit].
For physical training is of some value, but godliness (spiritual training) is of value in
everything and in every way, since it holds promise for the present life and for the life to
come. (AMP)*

Our bodies are the temple of the Holy Spirit (1 Corinthians 6:19) and we are
to take good care of them.

Physical training is important but spiritual training has even greater value.
How much time do you spend with God as you read your Bible and pray? If
you put your physical training and spiritual training on a balance scale, which
way would the scale tip?

Paul is in his letter to young Timothy reminds him to train himself to be
godly. Yes, it takes training, just like building up the strength in our bodies;
we must do the same for our souls.

"...discipline yourself for the purpose of godliness [keeping yourself
spiritually fit]. For physical training is of some value, but godliness (spiritual
training) is of value in everything and in every way, since it holds promise for
the present life and for the life to come. (1 Timothy 4:7b-8)

On our journey to Bill's healing, we learned about discipline and training. As
Bill's healing progressed, physical therapy was needed to strengthen his body.
At the same time through prayer and time with God, Bill's spirit was
strengthened too. That's how we fight our battles and win.

The Glory Road requires self-discipline. Starting the day in the Lord's
presence and ending the day in His presence are the bookends that keep me
on track. Being a believer is not an easy task, but the eternal reward is worth
it. The payoff for godliness is not only for eternity but for this present life.

Lord, thank you for Your goodness and Your grace. We need Your help
daily as we pursue godliness in a world where many serve another master.
Thank you for calling us apart so we may enjoy the joy only to be found in
You. Strengthen the weary, Lord. We will give You all the praise and honor
and glory in Jesus' name we pray, amen.

Thank you for your persistent prayers.#Godisfaithful#TheGloryRoad

Day#554 October 25

 Anchor Verse: 1 Timothy 5:5
The widow who is really in need and left all alone puts her hope in God and continues night and day to pray and to ask God for help. (NIV)

God is faithful in every circumstance of our lives, the times of celebration and times of mourning. We don't often like to talk about the tough places ~ the places where tears are prevalent, and the enemy comes rushing in.

In 1 Timothy 5, Paul is sharing with his young friend Timothy, about various groups of people in the church and how to respond to their needs. One of those groups is the widows. In 1 Timothy 5:5 it says, "The widow who is really in need and left all alone puts her hope in God and continues night and day to pray and to ask God for help."

When little girls dream about getting married that picture doesn't include the time when their husband passes on to heaven. Having been a widow twice, I know the reality of walking this path as both a young widow and now an older widow. It's not easy. But God is so faithful. Just as it says in this verse, I put my hope in God and day and night He hears the prayers of my heart, often those prayers are for you and your needs.

On our journey to Bill's healing, life and death took on another dimension. We didn't stay focused on the end of the story but rather chose to live life daily savoring every moment. Bill was always concerned about me and making sure I would be okay. With God's help, Bill took care of me in his lifetime. And now God continues to take care of me.

The Glory Road is not without trials and speed bumps. There are many I encounter, both widows and widowers, who have known not only the magnitude of the loss but also the faithfulness of God. It's a blessing to walk next to those who need a helping hand, an encouraging word, and prayer as they navigate life alone.

Lord, thank you that You are always present. You are a husband to the widow, and a father to the fatherless. We are always on Your radar. I pray for those who have lost a husband or wife or they are facing that loss today. Lord, wrap them in Your arms of love. In Jesus' name we pray, amen.

Thank you for your persistent prayers.#Godisfaithful#TheGloryRoad

Day#555 October 26

 Anchor Verse: 1 Timothy 6:11
O Timothy, you are God's man. Run from all these evil things, and work instead at what is right and good, learning to trust him and love others and to be patient and gentle. (TLB)

How many of you have a mentor or are mentors to others?

Paul was Timothy's mentor, and really so much more. In the letters we read that Paul wrote to Timothy, we see Paul's heart for Timothy was to help him avoid trouble and live a godly life that pleased the Lord.

Since Timothy was younger, he had less experience and Paul wanted to point out the "potholes" before Timothy fell into them.

In 1 Timothy 6:11, Paul says, "O Timothy, you are God's man. Run from all these evil things, and work instead at what is right and good, learning to trust him and love others and to be patient and gentle."

Those are powerful words that hit my spirit this morning, "O Timothy, you are God's man." Do this for yourself ~ put your name in the blank. "O _____, you are God's man/woman."

On our journey to Bill's healing, we learned a lot about what to run toward and what to run away from as we fought for Bill's life. Often those decisions were made in a split second, not with days to ponder the right course. So grateful for the Holy Spirit who is our guide through life's challenges to help with choosing God's best for us.

The Glory Road is a place of God's glory. It's where His attributes shine brightly as I lay down my will and surrender all I have to Him, trusting Him to do what is best for me. All for Your glory, there is no greater joy. It's the only place I want to be. In Your presence, Lord, we experience the fullness of Your joy. You make known to me the path of life. (Psalm 16:11)

Lord, thank you for the gift of Jesus. We turn away from the trappings of this world which quickly vanish. Instead, we pursue You, and the fruit of the Spirit ~ love, joy, peace, patience, kindness, goodness, gentleness, faithfulness, and self-control. It's the path of victory in Jesus' name. Amen

Thank you for loving well.#Godisfaithful#TheGloryRoad

Day#556 October 27

 Anchor Verse: 2 Timothy 1:5
As I think of your strong faith that was passed down through your family line. It began with your grandmother Lois, who passed it on to your dear mother, Eunice. And it's clear that you too are following in the footsteps of their godly example. (TPT)

In 2 Timothy 1:5, Paul speaks to Timothy about his spiritual heritage. "…As I think of your strong faith that was passed down through your family line. It began with your grandmother Lois, who passed it on to your dear mother, Eunice. And it's clear that you too are following in the footsteps of their godly example."

There are many good memories stored in my heart of time spent with my grandma. Seeing her quiet faith walked out through acts of service and love impacted my life. She was a widow for many years, and endured much in her lifetime, but Grandma never grumbled or complained. The fruit of her life included love and joy, and her laughter was contagious.

Paul reminds us we are to "follow in the footsteps of their godly example." Someone recently shared a prophetic word about walking in Jesus' footsteps. When we place our feet where Jesus walked, we won't go astray.

On our journey to Bill's healing, we experienced the answers to our ancestor's prayers ~ prayers for life and healing, and a closer walk with God. Mixed with your prayers, we walked in victory and in the footsteps of Jesus. At the same time, our faith, our story, Bill's victory will add to the foundation of faith of those who come after us.

The Glory Road is a place of legacy-building. The seeds that are sown on this path will reap a harvest in years yet to come. So grateful for the gift of prayer, and an intimate relationship with God, God and God alone is the source of my strength and my song.

Lord, we praise and thank you for the gift of our godly heritage. Thank you for godly examples around us. May we be that godly example for others. We praise you and thank you in Jesus' name we pray, amen.

Thank you for your persistent prayers.#Godisfaithful#TheGloryRoad

Day#557 October 28

 Anchor Verse: 2 Timothy 2:9
...the Word of God can never be chained! (TPT)

There is power in the name of Jesus. "For the word of God is alive and powerful." (Hebrews 4:12)

We don't fully understand the power of God in our lives. The resurrection power that raised Jesus from the dead lives in us. Often we don't get it. We are stuck in our routines as the energy is sucked out of us by the world of chaos, conflict, and confusion in which we live and the enemy neutralizes us.

In 2 Timothy 2, Paul is reminding Timothy of the truth of Paul's message: Jesus Christ was raised from the dead, and Jesus is a descendent of David. Paul says this is his gospel, and in the first part of verse 9 it says, "For which I am suffering even to the point of being chained like a criminal."

And then comes the heart of the message, "But God's word is never chained." That is where we rejoice and sing praises to God.

Paul was willing to suffer for the sake of the gospel so others might know Jesus and have eternal life through Him. It was worth it all to Paul.

On our journey to Bill's healing, we saw God overcome what seemed impossible in the eyes of men and medicine. When God speaks a word, it happens. God rescued Bill when it appeared Bill was "chained" by an illness. But since God's word can never be chained, God's power broke Bill out of that bondage. Whom the Son sets free is free indeed.

The Glory Road is a place of revelation. As I watch God moving in my life and the lives of others, I sing praises to His name. When we see a brick wall, God sees an open door. When we hear harsh words and feel frustrated and even angry, God opens His loving arms to hold you. Where we see defeat in the flesh, God sees victory in the spirit. Lord, open our eyes to see.

Father, thank you for the gift of Jesus Christ. Lord, help us to understand Your word is never chained. Rescue the perishing. Give hope to those who are feeling hopeless. Quiet the storm and open our ears to hear the songs of deliverance You are singing over us. We praise you in Jesus' name, amen.

Thank you for your faithfulness.#Godisfaithful#TheGloryRoad

Day#558 October 29

 Anchor Verse: 2 Timothy 3:10-11
But you, Timothy, certainly know what I teach, and how I live, and what my purpose in life is. You know my faith, my patience, my love, and my endurance. You know how much persecution and suffering I have endured…but the Lord rescued me from all of it. (NLT)

In the marketplace, we have a resume listing our work experience, education, accomplishments, and sometimes our mission or purpose. It's like a score card that tallies up what we have done.

In 2 Timothy 3, Paul is addressing Timothy. Paul lists some details about his life and also his credentials.

"But you, Timothy, certainly know what I teach, and how I live, and what my purpose in life is. You know my faith, my patience, my love, and my endurance. You know how much persecution and suffering I have endured. You know all about how I was persecuted in Antioch, Iconium, and Lystra—but the Lord rescued me from all of it." (2 Timothy 3:10-11)

In Philippians 3:10 Paul says, "My determined purpose is that I may know Him…" From its creation in 1933, the Navigators ministry has upheld their mission, "To know Christ, make Him known, and help others do the same."

On our journey to Bill's healing, many things in life became crystal clear. God and His ways were always at the top of the list. Our purpose, our lives were to live for His glory and let our light shine wherever we walked. Praise the Lord for how God sustained Bill through the struggles and the suffering. Now Bill has been given the reward of eternal life, living in God's presence.

The Glory Road is a path of adventure. That became Bill's description of the unprecedented places God called us to walk. My determined purpose is to know God and to make Him known. What an honor and privilege to not only love Him and be loved by God, but to share our story, my story for God's glory. With every breath I take, every move I make, every word I write, that God would be honored and glorified.

Lord, we praise that You have a purpose for each one of us. You wrote a book about our lives. The pages are filled with the amazing things. May we love others with Your love. Open our eyes to see the joy You have set before us. Guide our steps this day in Jesus' name, amen.

Thank you for your faithful prayers.#Godisfaithful#TheGloryRoad

Day#559 October 30

 Anchor Verse: 2 Timothy 4:7
I have fought the good fight, I have finished the race, I have kept the faith. (NIV)

Life is like a race. It has a beginning, middle, and an end. There is a course for our lives that is designed by the Master of the universe, Lord God Almighty. He wrote a book about your life before you were born. (Psalm 139:16)

And yet, every day we get to choose what we will do, the direction we will take. Will I choose to follow God and do what is right or choose to wander off the path of life and make poor choices?

Paul experienced many hardships. When we read the list of what he endured, our tests and trials look really small. However, Paul didn't have his eyes set on the praises of men, but the praise of his heavenly Father.

In 2 Timothy 4:7, we hear Paul's words that are often spoken at the end of someone's life. It's like a memorial wreath, a golden crown placed on their head for a life well lived. "I have fought the good fight, I have finished the race, I have kept the faith."

On our journey to Bill's healing, Bill learned about persevering through adversity. In our years together, we walked through the refining fire more than once. But in the last stretch of Bill's life, he was taken to a new level of intimacy with his heavenly Father. Truly, I can say my husband fought the good fight, he finished the race, and kept the faith. I'm so proud of you, Bill. Well-done, good and faithful servant.

The Glory Road is a new leg of my journey, God's path for me. There are days the battle is fierce, as I fight my own battles, but also stand with you as you fight yours. My faith and trust are in my heavenly Father. He is unstoppable, unshakeable, and unmovable. Because of this strong foundation, I fight from a place of victory, not striving for victory.

Lord, thank you that we have victory through Jesus Christ, and His victory over death, hell, and the grave. May we come alongside those who need our help. Lift the arms of the weary and dry the tears of those who mourn. Lord Jesus, may we be Your hands and feet. In Jesus' name we pray, amen.

Thank you for your faithfulness.#Godisfaithful#TheGloryRoad

Day#560 October 31

 Anchor Verse: Jeremiah 23:23
Am I a God who is only close at hand?" says the Lord. "No, I am far away at the same time." (NLT)

Human beings are confined to being at one place at one time. It's true that with the advent of technology, we can be in one place physically and through our phones, Zoom, etc. we can also be present with people virtually.

The truth remains, we are where our feet are…and that's it.

Our heavenly Father, the Creator of the universe, Lord God Almighty is omnipresent ~ present everywhere at the same time. Truly that is beyond our understanding, our comprehension.

In Jeremiah 23:23 we read, "Am I a God who is only close at hand?" says the Lord. "No, I am far away at the same time." And in the next verse He goes on to say, "'Can anyone hide from me in a secret place? Am I not everywhere in all the heavens and earth?' says the Lord."

We can't hide from God. And if we love God, we don't want to hide from Him. We want to be in His presence all the time. Everything we desire is found in God's presence ~ unspeakable joy, unconditional love, forgiveness, amazing grace, and so much more.

On our journey to Bill's healing, God was with Bill at every hospital (5 of them) in two states, and when he came home. Bill was never outside of God's sight. Everything he needed, including comfort and confidence, was delivered from the heart of God.

The Glory Road is a path walked out in God's view. He has gone ahead of me, God is with me, and He has left a trail of His faithfulness behind me. I am safe in the hollow of His hands. Nothing I face is too hard for Him. I walk forward in confidence because He is with me.

Lord, we praise and thank you for the gift of life. You are nearby and also far away. You know our going out and our coming in. Lord, may we never run away from You but run into Your arms of love. We pray for those who are far from you today. Good Shepherd, go find them and bring them home to safety. In Jesus' name we pray, amen. Thank you for your persistent prayers.#Godisfaithful#TheGloryRoad

November 2021

Therefore my heart is glad, my tongue rejoices, my body will rest in hope.

~ Acts 2:26 ~

Day#561 November 1

 Anchor Verse: Jeremiah 20:13
Sing to God! All praise to God! He saves the weak from the grip of the wicked.
(MSG)

When God blesses you and turns what the enemy meant for evil to the good, do you praise the Lord? Do you sing praises to His name?

Remember the story of the 10 lepers who were crying out to Jesus to heal them? In Luke 17:14-16 it says, "When he saw them, he said, "Go, show yourselves to the priests." And as they went, they were cleansed. One of them, when he saw he was healed, came back, praising God in a loud voice. He threw himself at Jesus' feet and thanked him—and he was a Samaritan."

We live in a world where there is conflict and turmoil. Good and evil clash every day. But there is hope with God. One of the ways we continue to feed our souls with that hope is by singing praises to God and giving credit where it is due. We win our battles because God is fighting for us.

"Sing to God! All praise to God! He saves the weak from the grip of the wicked." (Jeremiah 20:13)

What battle are you fighting today that you need God's help?

On our journey to Bill's healing, there were battles and victories. They didn't come by our own strength but because of God's strength at work in us. I can remember sitting in a doctor's office receiving good news and giving thanks to the Lord. Bill's voice filled with thanksgiving still echoes in my ear.

The Glory Road is a place where the righteous and the wicked live side by side. The battle is intense but God is greater. So grateful our God loves us and fights for us. Singing praises to His name is how I fight my battles.

Lord, we praise and thank you for the gift of Your love. You are a fierce warrior. Jehovah Sabaoth is Your name ~ the Lord of Hosts, the God of Angel Armies. You are mighty in battle and mighty to save. We are so grateful that You fight for us. Be with those who are weak and weary who cannot fight for themselves. Carry them in Your arms of love. We love you, Lord, in Jesus' name, amen.

Thank you for your encouraging words.#Godisfaithful#TheGloryRoad

Day#562 November 2

 Anchor Verse: Jeremiah 29:14a
"I will be found by you," declares the Lord. (NIV)

Have you ever been lost? Not having a clue where you were? You took a wrong turn, missed the right exit, and now you're in a place you shouldn't be. It looks scary. It's unfamiliar and you need someone to rescue you.

Your GPS may be repeating those not helpful words, "Recalculating..." But God knows exactly where you are and He will get you back on track.

Jeremiah 29 is Jeremiah's letter to the exiles who were carried away by King Nebuchadnezzar from Jerusalem to Babylon. The Lord is encouraging them through the words of Jeremiah. It's a good news/bad news report.

The Lord says they will be there for 70 years which means some of them will never see their homeland again. Mixed with this bittersweet message is God's promise to prosper them even in the midst of their exile. "Seek the peace and prosperity of the city to which I have carried you into exile. Pray to the Lord for it, because if it prospers, you too will prosper." (Jeremiah 29:7)

In Jeremiah 29:11, we read about God's plans to prosper them and not harm them, to give them hope and a future. The people must call on God and pray and seek God with all their heart. Then in Jeremiah 29:14a, "'I will be found by you,' declares the Lord."

On our journey to Bill's healing, we ascended mountains and walked through deep valleys. Sometimes progress was slow ~ a snail's pace, but it was progress. God was always with us. His presence gave us peace and power. We could always find Him ~ anywhere.

The Glory Road is a place of pursuit ~ seeking God's best, seeking God's plan, always for His glory. There are times it seems like I am in a foreign land, a place so different than all the years with Bill at my side. But God's call is to pray for those around me, the place where my feet are planted, so the "city" will prosper and so will I. Always for my good, and for His glory.

Lord, we praise you that You always know where we are. We are never far from Your presence. You hear the cries of our heart as well as our verbal prayers. We are safe in the hollow of Your hand. You will be found when we seek You with all our heart. We will find You. In Jesus' name we pray, amen.

Thank you for your persevering prayers.#Godisfaithful#TheGloryRoad

Day#563 November 3

 Anchor Verse: Philemon 1:21
Confident of your obedience, I write to you, knowing that you will do even more than I ask. (NIV)

Confidence in another comes because of a proven track record. To use a baseball analogy, it means you have stepped up to the plate and knocked it out of the ballpark, not just once (a fluke) but consistently.

For example, as a parent, you will only leave your child in the care of someone you trust. That's the level of trust and integrity we should all walk in each day.

Paul has written this short letter to Philemon. Philemon hosted a church in his home and was a partner with Paul and Timothy in spreading the good news of Jesus. Paul is writing on behalf of Onesimus who was a runaway slave. In fact, Onesimus had run away from his master, Philemon. Onesimus is now a Christian, a fellow believer, just like Philemon himself. Paul is urging Philemon to forgive Onesimus. Paul is willing to pay his debt.

And in verse 21, Paul inserts this word of expectation, "Confident of your obedience, I write to you, knowing that you will do even more than I ask." It's like Paul saying, "I know you're a man of God, Philemon, and I'm confident you will do the right thing, and even more than I am asking."

On our journey to Bill's healing, we learned a lot about walking in obedience and doing more than what was asked. I saw Bill do this every day during his recovery and healing. But I also saw it in others, those who surrounded him that God brought into his life. We were so blessed.

The Glory Road is a path of obedience. It's an opportunity to listen to the voice of God, step out in faith, and do the "more" for others just like Jesus has done for me. It is such a blessing to have people in your life who you can count on to not only do what they are asked to do, but even more. As the saying goes, "like frosting on the cake." We are so grateful.

Lord, we praise and thank you for the gift of Your love. Thank you, Jesus, You were willing to step down from the glory of heaven to walk with us, and love us, and show us a better way to live ~ as we look out for the good of others and not just ourselves. May we be Jesus' hands and feet and walk in obedience to Your commands, Lord. In Jesus' name we pray, amen.

Thank you for your faithfulness.#Godisfaithful#TheGloryRoad

Day#564 November 4

 Anchor Verse: Jeremiah 32:19
You have all wisdom and do great and mighty miracles; for your eyes are open to all the ways of men, and you reward everyone according to his life and deeds. (TLB)

As we walk through our day, we don't fully comprehend the miracle it is that we can walk, talk, eat, sleep, and all the activities we do without a thought.

Until something goes wrong... and we have a pain, a struggle, an illness, a disease. Then through the revelation of the Great Physician, and human medical people, God reveals the intricacy of His ways, how we are wired.

How often do we take the time to acknowledge the majesty of God? Or the depths of His knowledge, His wisdom and understanding, and the compassion and love for those who are close to Him or far away?

"You have all wisdom and do great and mighty miracles; for your eyes are open to all the ways of men, and you reward everyone according to his life and deeds." (Jeremiah 32:19)

It's a call for us to go higher with Him. It's a call to confession and repentance, if we have walked away from the narrow way. It's an opportunity to praise Him because God sees it all. He also is a God of compassion, with a loving Father's heart who hears our cries for mercy and catches every tear.

On our journey to Bill's healing, God opened the door so we could see things we had never seen before, both on earth and in heaven. The depths of His love, His mighty miracles, His compassion, and yes, His all-seeing eyes ~ each part was such a gift.

The Glory Road is a place of deeper revelation. Every breath we take, every move we make is a testimony to God's faithfulness. When God is mending the broken pieces in your life, know that He is El Roi, the God who sees. He is Jehovah Jireh, the God who provides. He is Jehovah Shalom, our peace.

Lord, thank you for the gift of this day. You meet each of us individually, and yet, You know all things about all people. Our minds cannot comprehend the complexity of our God, yet our heart embraces the depth of Your love. Thank you for fighting for us. In Jesus' name we pray, amen.

Thank you for your persistent prayers. #Godisfaithful#TheGloryRoad

Day#565 November 5

 Anchor Verse: Jeremiah 35:14
But I have spoken to you again and again, and you refuse to obey me. (NLT)

From an early age, children are taught to listen to their parents and obey them. It's for the child's good and for their safety.

Every family derives a "system" designed for a good outcome and it includes listening and obedience. Some have the "1-2-3" warning system and what follows are consequences if the child doesn't comply.

We see this walked out in daily living, but it is also true in our spiritual lives. The Bible contains God's instructions to live a holy life, a life that can be filled with God's blessings if we obey. There are consequences if we disobey.

Throughout the Old Testament, we read about the children of Israel and the many times they chose to disobey God's commands.

Jeremiah has been given the task of relaying messages from God to His people and the consequences of their disobedience. It wasn't always an easy message to deliver, but Jeremiah was faithful, even with the prospect of his own personal harm. "Don't kill the messenger" comes to mind.

We hear God's voice of frustration, as He speaks the truth about their actions. "But I have spoken to you again and again, and you refuse to obey me." (Jeremiah 35:14) In verse 17, God continues to say, "I spoke to them, but they did not listen; I called to them, but they did not answer."

On our journey to Bill's healing, our ears were tuned to hear the voice of God. Obedience always brings life. When the world is calling you to walk one direction, the still small voice of God will always guide you.

The Glory Road is like a motion picture with people's lives and choices on stage to the right and to the left. I hear the call of the Lord to walk the straight and narrow path. When I listen to His voice and choose obedience, His peace is my portion and His love knows no bounds.

Lord, we praise and thank you for Your mercy. Your path is the path to life and glory. You set before us an open door; may we walk through it. Rescue those walking in sin's dark night. Lord, You are great and greatly to be praised. In Jesus' name, amen.

Thank you for your faithfulness.#Godisfaithful#TheGloryRoad

Day#566 November 6

 Anchor Verse: Hebrews 3:13
Speak to [Encourage] each other about these things every day while there is still time so that none of you will become hardened against God, being blinded by the glamor of sin. (TLB)

Besides what we do in the natural for ourselves and our families, there are thoughts and actions God is calling us to do.

In the Old Testament, the priests made daily sacrifices/offerings on behalf of the people. In the New Testament, in Matthew 6:11, as part of the Lord's Prayer, Jesus said, "Give us this day our daily bread." In Luke 9:23, Jesus reminded his followers they were to take up their cross daily and follow Him.

We are called to encourage each other daily. "Speak to each other about these things every day while there is still time so that none of you will become hardened against God, being blinded by the glamor of sin."

Encouraging each other to stay on the path to life is like giving water to one who is thirsty or food to someone who is hungry ~ even starving. Just like Jesus did, whatever we have been given, we are encouraged to share.

On our journey to Bill's healing, we learned more about the power of encouragement. An encouraging word can pierce the darkness and lift heavy burdens. Bill had many opportunities to not only be encouraged by others but to speak an encouraging word. You might think that is impossible when you are going through your own challenges to speak life into someone else, but I watched Bill do it every day.

The Glory Road is an intersection where light and darkness collide daily. There is hope and hopelessness. Those who have a vision for tomorrow and those who can't see past today walk the streets of our cities. There is joy and sorrow, mourning and dancing. First, last, and always there is Jesus and His love for us. His unconditional love allows us to encourage others daily.

Lord, thank you for the gift of each new day. Your mercies are new every morning and great is Your faithfulness. Our eyes are on You. We remember Your indescribable love and joy. We pray for those going through deep valleys and ask You to carry them and their burdens. May they know the fullness of Your joy, in Jesus' name, amen.

Thank you for your encouraging words.#Godisfaithful#TheGloryRoad

Day#567 November 7

 Anchor Verse: Hebrews 4:15
He [Jesus] understands humanity, for as a man, our magnificent King-Priest was tempted in every way just as we are, and conquered sin. (TPT)

When we don't know how to do a particular task or a new skill, we ask someone who does. My paternal grandfather was very good at this especially during the Depression years when jobs were scarce. When presented with a work opportunity, he jumped in and learned quickly from the person working next to him.

In Matthew 4, we read the story of Jesus being tempted in the wilderness by the devil. Jesus fasted for 40 days and 40 nights. During the time, three times the devil came to Jesus with an "offer" and each time Jesus refused to "take the bait" by quoting from the Word of God ~ the Bible.

Jesus tempted like we are, but He said "no" to sin and conquered it. His victory over sin through trials and temptations can be our victory.

In Hebrews 4, Paul reminds the church of how Jesus helps us daily as we walk through the battles in our lives. "He understands humanity, for as a man, our magnificent King-Priest was tempted in every way just as we are, and conquered sin." (Hebrews 4:15)

On our journey to Bill's healing, Jesus was our ever-faithful companion. The Bible reminded us of God's promises and God would be our ever-present help in time of trouble. And He was, and still is. Thank you, Lord, for the victory we have in Jesus and in His victory over death, hell, and the grave.

The Glory Road is a place lived in the presence of God. Jesus is my constant companion. When I put my hand in His hand, I know He will lead the way, even when I can't see the path ahead. He is so faithful, and gentle and kind. Jesus, thank you for showing me how to walk in victory every day.

Lord, we praise and thank you for the gift of Your son, Jesus Christ. Because of Jesus' obedience, we know ALL things are possible with You. We don't need to suffer needlessly or throw up our hands in frustration, but we can rest in Your arms of love and walk out our victory. We surrender ourselves anew to You today. We love you and praise you, in Jesus' name, amen.

Thank you for your persistent prayers.#Godisfaithful#TheGloryRoad

Day#568 November 8

 Anchor Verse: Hebrews 5:11

I have a lot more to say about this, but it is hard to get it across to you since you've picked up this bad habit of not listening. (MSG)

The apostle Paul traveled around the region teaching and preaching. However, there were many times he was unable to travel and instead wrote letters of instruction, which later became books in the Bible.

For those of you who are teachers, thank you for your service, perseverance, and yes, long-suffering, as you attempt to teach lessons even though they are not always well received.

In Hebrews 5, Paul is teaching them about Jesus, but in verse 11 Paul says, "I have a lot more to say about this, but it is hard to get it across to you since you've picked up this bad habit of not listening." (Hebrews 5:11) Ouch!

The Amplified version says it a little more descriptively, "Concerning this we have much to say, and it is hard to explain, since you have become dull and sluggish in [your spiritual] hearing and disinclined to listen." The believers Paul is addressing have become dull and sluggish in their spiritual hearing.

Could the same be said of us? Lord, open our ears to hear and our hearts to receive Your message of hope and joy.

On our journey to Bill's healing, Bill's hearing became even more acute. My husband had great hearing before this illness (just like my mom) but during the trials, his ability to hear, both in the natural and spiritual realm increased. His ears were tuned to God's voice. God's voice brought him hope and life.

The Glory Road calls for greater understanding of God and His truths. I cannot be complacent or "settle" for milk, but I must crave solid food ~ the truth found in the Word of God. We must continue to mature in Christ if we are going to succeed in our Christian walk.

Lord, thank you for the gift of Your love. You have done great things. Open our ears to hear, may our hearts not grow dull, our feet not grow weary on the path of right living. Thank you for the Holy Spirit who is our comforter, and for Jesus who lived on earth and knows our every test, trial, and temptation. We are victorious in Jesus' name. Amen.

Thank you for your faithfulness.#Godisfaithful#TheGloryRoad

Day#569 November 9

 Anchor Verse: Hebrews 6:15
Then Abraham waited patiently, and he received what God had promised. (NLT)

Let's face it, patience has a bad reputation.

Often the way we get patience isn't through a magic pill or a God download, but rather we go through a life situation that cultivates the fruit of patience.

When God has promised your descendants will be more numerous than the sands on the seashore or the stars in the sky, and you don't even have one child, that's a tough spot. Some may have doubted God's word, but Abraham at 100 years old still believed God could do what He promised.

What promise has God given you that hasn't been fulfilled yet?

"Then Abraham waited patiently, and he received what God had promised." (Hebrews 6:19)

Patience is a gift from the heart of God. It's also a posture, a choice we make about how we will face adversity, illness, unfilled promises, even the death of one we love.

On our journey to Bill's healing, we learned about patience. Bill and God had discussions about Bill not being a patient man. Through the years of Bill's illness and healing, God gave him the gift of patience…through the things he suffered. Bill was grateful to receive that gift. Thank you, Lord, for Your kindness and gentleness. You are a good, good Father.

The Glory Road is also a path of patience. God promised my healing from the moment I was diagnosed with breast cancer. I have stood on that promise, and continue to stand there. God has given me a great perspective about this journey. It's not just about my healing; God wants to do a greater work, just like He did in Bill's life. There are many who need to see God at work in me as I walk out this path of healing, not only physically, but the grief wound from Bill's death. I know He can do it.

Thank you, Lord, for Your faithfulness. You don't make promises You will not keep. God, You do not lie. Thank you for Your promises and words of truth spoken to us and over us. We walk in the light of Your love. We praise you, Lord. In Jesus' name we pray, amen.

Thank you for your patient endurance.#Godisfaithful#TheGloryRoad

Day#570 November 10

 Anchor Verse: Hebrews 7:1
This Melchizedek was king of Salem and priest of God Most High. He met Abraham returning from the defeat of the kings and blessed him. (NIV)

Sometimes a scripture verse reaches right off the page and grabs your attention. Do you know what I mean?

We likely have read the passage many times, but in that moment, the Lord highlights it for us, for a purpose. He has a message just for you.

In Hebrews 7, we read about Melchizedek the priest and as the chapter goes on, about how Jesus is like Melchizedek.

"This Melchizedek was king of Salem and priest of God Most High. He met Abraham returning from the defeat of the kings and blessed him."

The person who greets Abraham is Melchizedek, who was not only a priest of God Most High but also the king of Salem. Salem means peace. He was the King of Peace. And Melchizedek means "king of righteousness."

This man representing peace and righteousness comes to Abraham and blesses him as the victorious hero returns home. It's quite a contrast. But what a powerful illustration that no matter how we look or where we have come from, whether victory or defeat, Jesus will meet us and bless us.

On our journey to Bill's healing, we often met Jesus in unusual places. Whether fresh off the battlefield from a health challenge or at home learning to walk better and enjoy life again, Bill was always in the presence of Jesus whose desire was to bless him. Thank you, Jesus.

The Glory Road is a place of battles and blessings. Jesus who sacrificed His life for us, the greatest sacrifice of all, is our High Priest and King of kings and Lord of lords. Because Jesus was victorious, so are we every day.

Lord, we praise and thank you for the gift of this day. We thank you for always being with us. You never leave us or forsake us. Not only do we thank you for our blessings, but we bless you, Lord Jesus, and kneel before you this morning, as King of kings and Lord of lords. You are great and greatly to be praised. In Jesus' name we pray, amen.

Thank you for your persistent prayers.#Godisfaithful#TheGloryRoad

Day#571 November 11

 Anchor Verse: Jeremiah 50:4
Then the people of Israel and Judah shall join together, weeping and seeking the Lord their God. (TLB)

History has often shown when we go through hard times as individuals, families, even nations, in those moments, we are drawn together. King Solomon, the wisest man who ever lived, speaks about this in Ecclesiastes. "Two are better than one, because they have a good return for their labor: If either of them falls down, one can help the other up." (Ecclesiastes 4:9-10).

It reminds me of how this nation rallied together after the events of 9/11, not only in neighborhoods, but at sporting events in cities across the nation. There was no east and west, we were one nation under God in that moment. Barriers were torn down and "God Bless America" echoed from sea to sea.

"Then the people of Israel and Judah shall join together, weeping and seeking the Lord their God. They shall ask the way to Zion and start back home again. "Come," they will say, "let us be united to the Lord with an eternal pledge that will never be broken again." (Jeremiah 50: 4-5)

They recognized their sin and shortcomings and ran back to the Lord confessing their mistakes (sins) so they can be united with the Lord once again. Like the parable of the Prodigal Son in Luke 15:11-32.

On our journey to Bill's healing, we experienced the power of unity, not only with others but with the Lord. When you are walking with Him, there is no greater joy, even in the tough places. God always had His arms extended to welcome us, no matter our geographical location.

The Glory Road is like a collage with so many different facets. There are pockets of unity and discord. Places where people agree and disagree. It's a study in contrasts, but over and above it all, is God's banner of love. God has open arms to receive all who would enter in to His rest. We just have to turn our backs on the old ways of the world and embrace His grace.

Lord, we praise and thank you for the gift of Your unconditional love. We are so grateful Your love never changes; it only gets stronger. We are so blessed daily by the gifts that come from Your hand and Your heart. May we walk in unity with each other. We are overcomers in Jesus' name. Amen.

Thank you for your persevering prayers.#Godisfaithful#TheGloryRoad

Day#572 November 12

 Anchor Verse: Jeremiah 51:46a
Do not lose heart or be afraid when rumors are heard in the land. (NIV)

If all the words that you heard or read in a day were put in a pile, you would be surprised. In fact, the pile might be way bigger than you are.

But not everything we hear is the truth. In fact, much of it is rumor, gossip, presumption or even lies.

"Do not lose heart or be afraid when rumors are heard in the land." (Jeremiah 51:46a)

Rumors may not be true but they sure can spread like wildfire. Rumors normally don't bring warm fuzzies, they often breed fear.

"For God has not given us a spirit of fear, but of power and of love and of a sound mind." (2 Timothy 1:7 (NKJV)

Where do we find truth to combat rumors and lies? In the Word of God, the Bible.

God's promises are true. They have held up for generations and will for all eternity. Heaven and earth will pass away, but my words will never pass away. (Luke 21:33 NIV)

On our journey to Bill's healing, we were faced with many places where we had to hold on to the truth God spoke to us. There were thoughts, opinions, even rumors, about what might happen next, but God's plans were the only ones that prevailed. Bill and I stood on the truth, the solid rock of Jesus, and we were not moved. God always held us in His arms of love.

The Glory Road is thick with words. Some days we must hold up our shield of faith just so we aren't buried by them. We need wisdom and discernment to know what to take into our spirits and what needs to be kept out of our hearts and minds, and our ears too. Keep rumors and half-truths from coming out of our own mouth, be a guard to our lips, O Lord.

Lord, we praise and thank you that You are truth. There is no greater authority than You. There is no greater love than Your love. May we walk in truth today, and not listen to the rumors around us. In Jesus' name, amen.

Thank you for your love and kindness.#Godisfaithful#TheGloryRoad

Day#573 November 13

 Anchor Verse: Isaiah 11:3a
His delight will be obedience to the Lord. (TLB)

The Bible is God's instruction manual for living the Christian life and so much more. God has given us a guide, about how we can live this life well so there is joy on the journey.

Unfortunately, we don't always choose the path to obedience right away. There may be some wandering before we realize there is no greater joy than obeying and walking with Jesus.

Isaiah 11 is painting a picture of Jesus, the Messiah who was yet to come. It is a description of God's promise that would bring hope to His people.

"His delight will be obedience to the Lord." (Isaiah 11:3)

Is our delight to obey the Lord?

In the previous verse, we read of the seven spirits that equip Jesus for the task ahead. The Passion translation used very descriptive words. "The Spirit of Yahweh will rest upon him, the Spirit of Extraordinary Wisdom, the Spirit of Perfect Understanding the Spirit of Wise Strategy, the Spirit of Mighty Power, the Spirit of Revelation, and the Spirit of the Fear of Yahweh."

On our journey to Bill's healing, our delight, our joy was in walking in obedience to the Lord. God's ways are often higher, better than our first "human" thought. There are times we have to stand up and stand with the Lord, rather than the favor of men. The Lord equips us just as He did Jesus to face trials, tests, and temptations so we may walk in victory with Him.

The Glory Road is a place where daily I must choose to obey the Lord rather than my own wishes or those of others. Listening to His still small voice is my guiding light. Asking for extraordinary wisdom, perfect understanding, wise strategy, mighty power, revelation and the fear (respect and adoration) of the Lord, allows me to walk this walk honorably.

Lord, thank you for the gift of Jesus. You have called us by name and we belong to You. Nothing will separate us from the love of Christ. Today we choose You, Lord. Thank you for helping us to walk this walk by grace and with the power of the risen Lord, in Jesus' name, amen.

Thank you for your faithful prayers.#Godisfaithful#TheGloryRoad

Day#574 November 14

 Anchor Verse: Hebrews 10:35
So do not throw away this confident trust in the Lord. Remember the great reward it brings you! (NLT)

Trust is fragile. It is not easily earned but it can quickly be destroyed. Human relationships can fall short at times but God is always trustworthy.

Abraham is a great example of trusting God. God told Abraham to go to a land He would show him. And Abraham left everything behind and walked out in faith, and God rewarded his faithfulness.

How much are we supposed to trust God? With our whole heart and not lean on our own understanding, He wants all of us ~ heart, mind, soul, and body. (Proverbs 3:5-6)

The answer we seek is a long time coming. We may be growing weary and wonder if our prodigal child will come home or our spouse will return to the love we once shared. God is faithful in the waiting.

"So do not throw away this confident trust in the Lord. Remember the great reward it brings you!" (Hebrews 10:35) Hold on to hope, hold on to God's hand as you walk through the calm and the storm. God is faithful, what He starts He always completes. (Philippians 1:6)

On our journey to Bill's healing, we learned a lot about trusting God, even until Bill drew his final breath. The path wasn't always easy, but God was always faithful. We couldn't have walked this path without Him. Because we chose to trust God ~ confidently, He never let us down. Thank you, Lord.

The Glory Road is a path where God and I daily walk together, trusting each other. God can always be trusted, with every detail of my life. He has tested me to see how much I can be trusted. As our trustworthiness muscle is developed, God can entrust us with greater tasks. Great is the joy of hearing God say, "Well done, good and faithful servant."

Lord, we surrender ourselves anew to You today. We trust You even when our eyes can't see the outcome. What is ahead of us is far greater than what lies behind us. We trust you with all we have ~ our time, our talents, our people, and our possessions. All of them are a gift from Your hand. We entrust them to Your loving care today. In Jesus' name we pray, amen.

Thank you for believing in miracles.#Godisfaithful#TheGloryRoad

Day#575 November 15

 Anchor Verse: Hebrews 11:13a
All these people were still living by faith when they died. (NIV)

Living by faith… it's something God asks us to do every day. Faith isn't something we take out of our pocket on special occasions or only in desperate situations. It is a lifestyle. It is a choice. It is glorious.

Hebrews 11 is filled with examples of several people who walked by faith. This is not an exhaustive list, but the people who were highlighted as the text of the Bible was "downloaded" from heaven.

Often called the "Hall of Faith" we are reminded of what faith in action looks like.

Each of us has moments in our lives when we must walk by faith, because we can't see the way ahead of us. We must trust God in the darkness of the trial. We know He is always in the light. He is our source of hope even on our darkest night.

On our journey to Bill's healing, we learned so much more about walking by faith even when the way ahead was unseen. Often what looked like it was the road, the path changed… because God had a better plan. There were moments where your neck would almost get whiplash because the prayers of God's people moved the hand of God so quickly. God's ways are so much higher than our ways and His thoughts than our thoughts.

The Glory Road is a place where daily I walk by faith. God is faithful because that is His testimony. Nothing is too hard for Him and so nothing is too hard for me. I will choose faith until I draw my final breath on earth and enter heaven's glory when He says the book about my life has been written, and lived out. (Many years from now.)

Lord, we praise and thank you for the gift of faith. For the examples of those who lived by faith and for those were still living by faith when they died as we read in Hebrews 11. Our faith is not mustered up by our own strength but through His grace and power. Lord, we stand in awe of You this morning. In Jesus' name, amen.

Thank you for your persevering prayers.#Godisfaithful#TheGloryRoad

Day#576 November 16

 Anchor Verse: Ezekiel 3:10
And he said to me, "Son of man, listen carefully and take to heart all the words I speak to you. (NIV)

Listening is a lost art to many today. Our lives are filled with so much noise, and many distractions. We are barraged by videos, news reports, people speaking ~ family, co-workers, bosses, pastors, etc.

No one on earth has greater wisdom than heaven's wisdom. Nothing is more powerful than the truth of God. No one has a greater interest in your life, your health, your future than your heavenly Father.

In Ezekiel 3, God is speaking to Ezekiel to give him a prophetic word to speak to the people of Israel. God tells Ezekiel the people have not been listening to God and so he should not expect they will listen to him either.

In verse 10, I hear a tenderness in God's voice as He speaks to Ezekiel, "And he said to me, "Son of man, listen carefully and take to heart all the words I speak to you." In the next verses it says, "Go now to your people in exile and speak to them…. Whether they listen or fail to listen."

When God has an assignment for us, our responsibility is to complete the task, speak the message, walk in obedience. The outcome is not in our hands.

On our journey to Bill's healing, Bill often heard the voice of God directing his path and encouraging him. There were also occasions when God gave him a message to share with others, which he did. Obedience brings life. God will equip you for the assignments He has for you. Be strong and courageous do not be afraid, just do what God says to do.

The Glory Road is filled with opportunities to be God's hands and feet. It is also a place to speak His word ~ words of life, words of hope, words of love to those who are walking through a barren land. Listen and obey ~ it's that simple. The task may not be easy. The message we are called to deliver may not be popular, but what we do know is that God is faithful.

Lord, thank you for the gift of Your love, Your life. Thank you for reaching out to us even when we have wandered away from You. Lord, be honored and glorified in our lives. In Jesus' name we pray, amen.

Thank you for your words of life.#Godisfaithful#TheGloryRoad

Day#577 November 17

 Anchor Verse: Hebrews 12:3
Just consider and meditate on Him who endured from sinners such bitter hostility against Himself [consider it all in comparison with your trials], so that you will not grow weary and lose heart. (AMP)

It's easy to sell ourselves short when we start comparing what we have to others. There will always be someone in the world who has "more" than what you have of something. When we do that, we miss the blessings God has placed in our hands. We miss the joy of the adventures God has planned.

Hebrews 12 is a powerful chapter that starts out with the great cloud of witnesses cheering us on in the race we are called to run.

"Just consider and meditate on Him who endured from sinners such bitter hostility against Himself [consider it all in comparison with your trials], so that you will not grow weary and lose heart." (Hebrews 12:3)

Jesus is our example of how to go through great adversity, even "bitter hostility" from others, and not give up. When we compare our lives to what Jesus went through, our trials, no matter how difficult, look small.

On our journey to Bill's healing, we experienced an avalanche of health challenges. Places we had never walked before, and never with the speed and intensity with which those challenges kept coming. Through it all, our eyes were on the Lord, even if they were clouded by tears. We chose not to fear but put our trust in the only one who could help us overcome the challenges.

The Glory Road intersects new territory each day. Jesus offers to walk with me through the unknown places, new horizons, and even down memory lane. He often speaks those words softly and gently, "Don't grow weary and lose heart, for I have overcome the world." Then I take another step of victory and declare His promises are true. I am an overcomer in Jesus' name.

Lord, thank you for the gift of Jesus and His victory over death, hell, and the grave. We stand on Your promises this morning and declare that You are great and greatly to be praised. We shift our burdens to Your shoulders today, Jesus, since they are too heavy for us to carry alone. Thank you that Your love sustains us in Jesus' mighty name, amen.

Thank you for your persistent prayers.#Godisfaithful#TheGloryRoad

Day#578 November 18

 Anchor Verse: Hebrews 3:3
Remember those in prison, as if you were there yourself. Remember also those being mistreated, as if you felt their pain in your own bodies. (NLT)

Often we live our lives in our own little bubble unaware of the lives of those around us. In the pandemic season, this perception, this reality has been compounded as we all have had to be isolated at times.

In Hebrews 3, we are invited into a spot that might feel uncomfortable to some of you, maybe to all of us at times.

"Remember those in prison, as if you were there yourself. Remember also those being mistreated, as if you felt their pain in your own bodies."

Here two people groups are identified: those in prison and those being mistreated. Personally, your daily life may not include either one of these groups, or you try and avoid walking in either camp.

But this is who Jesus loved, those who were different because of their experience. Those who were hurting, Jesus felt their pain, and He calls us to do the same.

On our journey to Bill's healing, Bill and I stepped off the main road where most of you travel. For a time, we became a part of a group we often do not notice, and truthfully, forget to some degree. Those who are in prison, mistreated, homeless, sick, who are different from us in some way, by society are given the tag "those people." It breaks my heart every time I hear it spoken. It breaks Jesus' heart too.

The Glory Road is a road where I encounter the beautiful bouquet of God's children. Many don't look the same as me and we have very different life experiences. But each one of them needs Jesus, they need to know His love, mercy, grace, and peace. And through His light in me, I can point them to the Savior, to the lighthouse, to Jesus, the hope of the world.

Lord, today we thank you for the gift of Your love. No one is excluded in Your kingdom. You are the Good Shepherd who goes looking for the lost sheep. May our eyes be peeled to do the same. And when we find them, we bind up their wounds and we love them with the love of Jesus. There is no greater love. In Jesus' name we pray, amen.

Thank you for your love for others.#Godisfaithful#TheGloryRoad

Day#579 November 19

 Anchor Verse: James 1:16
Don't be deceived, my dear brothers and sisters. (NIV)

We live in a world where truth is valued more highly by some than others. There are those who walk in darkness rather than the light who are willing to deceive others for personal gain without feeling remorse. It's not pretty.

But lest we condemn them without a trial, we, too, are guilty of deception, because sometimes we deceive ourselves. How do we do that? By believing something that isn't true.

James says, "Don't be deceived, my dear brothers and sisters." (James 1L16)

The enemy will use others to be instruments of his dirty work, but in every situation, you and I have a choice. In Galatians 6:7 it says, "Do not be deceived: God cannot be mocked. A man reaps what he sows." For those not familiar with reaping and sowing, it's a term related to planting seed and the harvest that comes from it.

It's the same way in our own lives, if you "plant seeds" through your good actions, good deeds, then good things will come out of it, for yourself and others. On the other hand, if you are lying and cheating, etc. nothing good will come out of that but more darkness.

On our journey to Bill's healing, God called us to walk in the truth He spoke over Bill. Listening to God's voice we filtered out the negative and choose to walk in the light, where God's blessings flowed over us, not in the darkness. We walked in some pretty "dark" places, but God's love sustained us.

The Glory Road is filled with people with different experiences, different motives. It is through God's wisdom and His grace I make good decisions. Not everyone has my best interests in mind, it's about what's best for them, and for some, the cost to others is irrelevant. By His grace, I will not be deceived by the actions of others, or my own mental gymnastics.

Lord, You are the firm foundation on which we stand. Your words are truth and they are unshakable. We ask for Your wisdom to guide us and protect us from words of deception spoken by others. Our hope comes in the name of the Lord, Maker of heaven and earth. In Jesus' mighty name we pray, amen.

Thank you for your faithful prayers.#Godisfaithful#TheGloryRoad

Day#580 November 20

 Anchor Verse: James 2:26b
...Faith without works [of obedience] is also dead. (AMP)

Faith is more than just believing that God is who God says He is. Faith is also walked out in our lives. What does that mean?

In James 2, James talks us through the debate about faith and works, and what some people were saying about which was better. James comes to this conclusion when he compares faith to a human body. Once there is no breath, no life in a person, they are dead. So too when it comes to faith, "faith without works [of obedience] is also dead. (James 2:26b)

What is the "fruit" of your faith that is seen by others? Our actions ~ the way we love others and care for them is so important. Jesus, as He walked this earth, loved others and showed it in so many ways. Jesus would listen to people, ask about their need, and meet it the best He knew how ~ sometimes physically, mentally, emotionally, or spiritually.

On our journey to Bill's healing, we were blessed by many who had faith and also kind deeds that went along with their faith. Sometimes those deeds included praying as well as meeting our tangible needs. Bill and I had the opportunity to do the same for others. Give what the Lord has given you without counting the cost and God will reward you.

The Glory Road intersects the lives of many people ~ some who live only for themselves, their world is small. Others have big hearts and see a need and rush in to fill it. Jesus gave us an example to walk in His steps. They are big shoes to fill. We freely give what we have received from Him.

Lord, we praise you and thank you that You alone are worthy of our praise. Thank you for giving us faith that is activated by our actions. It is not merely words or just thoughts, but we have the opportunity to be Jesus' hands and feet. Open our eyes to see what You see and be moved to do what we can do. We love you and praise you in Jesus' name, amen.

Thank you for loving others well.#Godisfaithful#TheGloryRoad

Day#581 November 21

 Anchor Verse: James 3:2a
We all stumble in many ways. (NIV)

The message from James this morning is short and powerful. "We all stumble in many ways." (James 3:2a) In other words, we're not perfect. You're not perfect. I'm not perfect. Only Jesus is perfect.

James 3 talks a lot about taming our tongue and what a challenge it can be. He compares our tongue to a bit in a horse's mouth or the rudder on a ship. Just like a small spark can set a whole forest on fire, our tongue is also a fire.

The fact we all stumble isn't license to keep on stumbling. It's an opportunity to try and do better. If we know we have a propensity to mess up, especially when we speak, then we need to ask for help. The first place to seek help is from our heavenly Father, and then from those around us.

Let's focus on those moments when our words fitly spoken were like apples of gold in settings of silver. (Proverbs 25:11) Recall times when words spoken in love, with patience, encouraging words, words that were life-giving actually changed the course of a person's life. We don't always know the effect of the "good" words we speak, but quickly we see the results of words spoken in anger or frustration.

On our journey to Bill's healing, we learned about the power of words, not only the ones we spoke, but those spoken to us and about us. Words can be like a razor cut, a paper cut, they are sharp and cut quickly. Negative words can be like weeds which quickly take over the garden of our mind.

The Glory Road is a place where I am very aware of words ~ especially those I choose to take into my spirit. God said, "Let those words pass over you, don't take them into your spirit." This was very sage advice I still follow today. You and I both need to be mindful of our words before they pass our lips. Will this build others up or tear them down? Choose good seed, good words, bring life to those around you.

Lord, thank you for the gift of communication. Forgive us for words we have spoken that have wounded others. Thank you for Your words that have brought life. Purify our hearts and our minds so all we do and say would bring honor and glory to Your name. In Jesus' name we pray, amen.

Thank you for your encouraging words.#Godisfaithful#TheGloryRoad

Day#582 November 22

 Anchor Verse: James 4:1
What is the cause of your conflicts and quarrels with each other? Doesn't the battle begin inside of you as you fight to have your own way and fulfill your own desires? (TPT)

The book of James talks about some very practical things, hard things. In chapter 4, James talked about matters of the heart and submitting ourselves to God.

"What is the cause of your conflicts and quarrels with each other? Doesn't the battle begin inside of you as you fight to have your own way and fulfill your own desires?" (James 4:1)

The conflicts and quarrels in us and around us, come from the battle within.

In my mind's eye, I see two bears attacking each other, and growling, with those paws and long nails accentuating their point. This is a picture of our spirit as we are battling each other.

Thanksgiving is right around the corner and in some gatherings, there will be those who are diverse in their beliefs and lifestyles. How will they interact that day? Will they extend an olive branch representing peace or words that ignite a wildfire of trouble? What will you do?

On our journey to Bill's healing, we encountered those who were different and believed differently. There were those who were angry at the world, angry at God ~ just angry. When life is filled with unexpected hiccups, we try and wade through the muck and mire, and sometimes this mudslinging extends to others. We tried to be a fire hydrant filled with the love of God that could extinguish those fiery flames.

The Glory Road has many sights and sounds, some near, some far away. The noise of conflict and quarrels has an edge to it, it touches your soul. We must examine our own hearts and ask hard questions, "Am I seeking to have my desires fulfilled or God's way, and offering others the love of Jesus?"

Lord, we thank you for showing us the better way. We can find peace in You, Lord. May we lay down our burdens and our battles at Your feet and walk away with Your peace and Your power, because we have been in Your presence. May we be peacemakers, in Jesus' name we pray, amen.

Thank you for loving others so well.#Godisfaithful#TheGloryRoad

Day#583 November 23

 Anchor Verse: James 5:17
Elijah was a man with human frailties, just like all of us, but he prayed and received supernatural answers. (TPT)

When you read the Bible and the stories of men and women who did extraordinary things, do you see them as superheroes? Bigger than life people who have nothing in common with you and me?

The truth is each one of them had the same start as we did. Some of them came into a challenged world, just like you may have done.

"Elijah was a man with human frailties, just like all of us, but he prayed and received supernatural answers." (James 5:17)

Elijah was just like you and me ~ a man with human frailties. The Amplified Version says, "A man with a nature like ours [with the same physical, mental, and spiritual limitations and shortcomings]." BUT… he prayed and received supernatural answers.

Elijah prayed and it didn't rain for three and a half years. God stopped the rain in answer to his prayers and the rain began again when Elijah asked.

On our journey to Bill's healing, as ordinary people, we saw God move in extraordinary ways. Bill and I could both testify of God's miraculous ways, the signs and wonders that were manifested in our lives, in Bill's body. We prayed believing God could move…and He did.

The Glory Road explores land I have never seen before. It is a place where daily I have the opportunity to partner with heaven. Some of you have known me since my childhood and can testify that I am an ordinary person. I have scars from childhood skinned knees to prove it. But when you choose to put your faith in God, the same God who created the universe, the same Jesus who healed, delivered, and set people free, and the Holy Spirit who comforts and guides us, you will see the extraordinary happen.

Lord, thank you that You love us with an everlasting love. Our times are in Your hands. You hear and answer our prayers. Thank you for opportunities to bring our friends, families, and even strangers to the throne room of grace where they will find help in the hour of their need. In Jesus' name, amen.

Thank you for believing in miracles.#Godisfaithful#TheGloryRoad

Day#584 November 24

 Anchor Verse: 1 Peter 1:22b
...love one another from the heart [always unselfishly seeking the best for one another]. (AMP)

Love is something we talk about a lot. Millions of dollars annually are spent in the name of love. But love is best expressed not by gifts purchased at a store, but love from the depths of our heart.

In 1 Peter 1:22, Peter starts off by saying sincere love for each other starts off by obeying the truth of God. And out of that obedience and love, we can love one another. "Love one another from the heart [always unselfishly seeking the best for one another]."

Always seeking the best for one another ~ it's such a fun way to live and quite the adventure.

On our journey to Bill's healing, God's love was magnified in our lives. When God's love fills your heart, you want to love each other more, always seeking the best for one another. Sincere love takes on another dimension when your loved one is going through the valley of illness.

The Hallmark style of love quickly is escorted out the door, and the Garden of Gethsemane love of Jesus, willing to sacrifice all you have for the one you love, takes its place. Faith, hope, and love remain but truly the greatest of these is love.

The Glory Road is crowded with people who need to be loved. There are those who have never known Jesus' love, that unconditional, sacrificial love. Those who have loved and have lost the one they love. We have the opportunity to be Jesus' hands and feet, but also His arms of love to hold those who need to feel strong arms that remind them they are not alone.

Lord, thank you that Your love is greater than life. Your love is unconditional and eternal. It never fades, it never falters, and it never fails. Today we pray for those who are hurting, wounded, lost, and feeling rejected. Show them Your love through us today. May we always unselfishly seek the best for others ~ our family, friends, and even strangers. Help us to love them all. We love you, Lord, in Jesus' name we pray, amen.

Thank you for your love.#Godisfaithful#TheGloryRoad

Day#585 November 25

 Anchor Verse: 1 Peter 2:9b
He called you out of darkness to experience his marvelous light, and now he claims you as his very own. He did this so that you would broadcast his glorious wonders throughout the world. (TPT)

Today is Thanksgiving Day 2021 in the United States. Traditionally, it is a day set aside to count our blessings and gather with family and friends to celebrate, usually with a large meal. Whatever your tradition, new or old, it's an opportunity to turn away from what's wrong and celebrate what's right.

In 1 Peter 2:9, Peter reminds us of our amazing heritage and God's gift to us. "He called you out of darkness to experience his marvelous light, and now he claims you as his very own. He did this so that you would broadcast his glorious wonders throughout the world."

Good news isn't meant to be kept to ourselves but we are to spread that news to others. We are called out of darkness into the light of God, His wonderful love, the light of life. It's brighter than any lighthouse on a dark, stormy night at sea.

Peter not only tells us God saved us and claims us as His own, but now we have been commissioned to share the good news. Where? Throughout the world… yes, share His glorious wonders to people both near and far.

On our journey to Bill's healing, we were blessed with the opportunity to share the miracles God did in Bill's life across the world. When God moves in your life, when what was wrong is made right, it's a joy to tell the story. Thanks to technology, both prayer requests and praise reports were broadcast, locally and across the world.

The Glory Road is a path that touches the world. My physical feet may be in the United States, but my footprints can be found on foreign soil. I'm so grateful for the international friendships God has blessed with as I move forward in this new season. Truly we are one family of God, and what a blessing to share what the Lord has done with each other.

Lord, thank you for the gift of being part of the family of God. We pray for those who are in need this morning, show us how to be Your hands and feet. We sing praises to Your name this morning as our hearts are filled with joy and thanksgiving. In Jesus' mighty name we pray, amen.

Thank you for your kindness.#Godisfaithful#TheGloryRoad

Day#586 November 26

 Anchor Verse: 1 Peter 3:9
Don't repay evil for evil. Don't retaliate with insults when people insult you. Instead, pay them back with a blessing. That is what God has called you to do, and he will grant you his blessing. (NLT)

Words quickly slip through our lips, a text message is sent, a quick response to a social media post, all of it happening within a breath.

Sometimes it's as if our brain becomes disengaged, and the result is a disaster. People are hurt, relationships are shattered, and our words have wounded someone we love. But it doesn't have to be that way. Peter proposed a different response.

As you read these words in 1 Peter 3:9, it may surprise you, or your response may be, "No way. I couldn't do that." Maybe in your own flesh it may seem impossible, but that's God specialty, doing the impossible.

"Don't repay evil for evil. Don't retaliate with insults when people insult you. Instead, pay them back with a blessing. That is what God has called you to do, and he will grant you his blessing." (1 Peter 3:9)

On our journey to Bill's healing, we had many opportunities to do what seemed contrary to a "normal" human response. When we respond this way, people take notice. Why are you different? It's a great opportunity to let the light and love of Jesus shine through you. You should try it.

The Glory Road walked out in an environment where there is still much hostility, division, and disagreement often feels like a war zone. But it's in those places where the peace of God shines most brightly. Love is stronger than hate, and blessing overrides curses. Offering a hand up rather than pushing someone down. This is the way Jesus lived.

Lord, we praise and thank you that Your heart for us is filled with blessings. We need Your help as we convert our reflex of speaking without thinking to responding with Your words of love and blessings. Put a guard on our lips. May our words build up instead of destroying others. Let us love as Jesus loved. In Jesus' mighty name we pray, amen.

Thank you for your kind words.#Godisfaithful#TheGloryRoad

Day#587 November 27

 Anchor Verse: 1 Peter 4:7b
Therefore, be sound-minded and self-controlled for the purpose of prayer [staying balanced and focused on the things of God so that your communication will be clear, reasonable, specific and pleasing to Him.] (AMP)

Self-control is always a popular topic. As 2021 marches forward, and December will soon be here, we often look ahead to determine what we want to do differently in the new year.

In 1 Peter 4, Peter is talking about how we should live for God and what that means according to our actions. You may have heard the expression a tree is known by its fruit. The same is true for us, especially as believers in Christ.

There is a purpose, an end result for being self-controlled. "Therefore, be sound-minded and self-controlled for the purpose of prayer [staying balanced and focused on the things of God so that your communication will be clear, reasonable, specific and pleasing to Him.]" (1 Peter 4:7)

Self-control is for the purpose of prayer. The Amplified version gives us a more detailed picture which includes that we will stay balanced and focused on the things of God. When we do that, our prayers are more powerful and pinpointed, so God can partner with us in seeing miracles happen..

On our journey to Bill's healing, Bill learned about discipline and self-control. Our thoughts, actions, and attitude shape our daily lives. When we surrender to the Lord and ask Him to take control of our lives, the outcome is much better.

The Glory Road leads through a place of opposites, self-control and no control. Our world is a study in contrasts but God's kingdom is one of order. Praise the Lord. When we keep our eyes focused on Jesus and walk in His steps, there is abundant joy and great grace for daily living.

Lord, we praise and thank you for Your help. We can't do life well without You, but with Your help ALL things are possible. We believe in miracles. Thank you for the opportunity to partner with heaven on behalf of friends, family, and strangers. In the name of Jesus we pray, amen.

Thank you for your persistent prayers.#Godisfaithful#TheGloryRoad

Day#588 November 28

 Anchor Verse: 1 Peter 5:2
Feed the flock of God; care for it willingly, not grudgingly; not for what you will get out of it but because you are eager to serve the Lord. (TLB)

We are all called upon to be a shepherd to a flock at some time in our lives.

Peter is upfront in his teaching. "Feed the flock of God; care for it willingly, not grudgingly; not for what you will get out of it but because you are eager to serve the Lord." (1 Peter 5:2)

There are two strong points. We are to care for others willingly not grudgingly, and not for our gain but because we are eager to serve the Lord.

Anybody squirming in your chair? The two points that Peter speaks about are patterns we see in the world's structure. Those that are in leadership positions but doing it because they have to and trying to figure out how it benefits them. Is it the same in our churches? I pray it is not.

Jesus showed us how to walk in this world serving others for the joy of serving and being the hands and feet of God, and His voice too. We have the honor and privilege of serving others and seeing them flourish and grow.

On our journey to Bill's healing, as much as Bill was cared for by others, he also fed the flock of God. Because of Bill's choices to put his hand in God's hand, so many of us were blessed in the process and the blessings continue.

The Glory Road offers me an opportunity to feed God's flock. Not only from the lessons I learned walking alongside Bill on his journey to healing, but now on my own healing journey. It is an honor and privilege to care for others and to serve without counting the cost, and expecting nothing in return. God always rewards those who diligently seek Him (Hebrews 11:6). It's not about the reward; it's about the joy of serving.

Lord, we praise and thank you for the opportunity to walk with You and work with You. I pray for those who are weary in their leadership and caregiving responsibilities today. Infuse them with new hope, new love, new joy. Thank you for the blessing of serving others that You would be honored and glorified in Jesus' name, amen.

Thank you for your love and care.#Godisfaithful#TheGloryRoad

Day#589 November 29

 Anchor Verse: 2 Peter 1:16
For we have not been telling you fairy tales when we explained to you the power of our Lord Jesus Christ and his coming again. My own eyes have seen his splendor and his glory. (TLB)

In a world where there is much that is counterfeit, copycat, or a wannabee, Peter, the author of this chapter, shares with us what it real.

Peter is the same man who was one of Jesus' disciples. The one who Jesus called to get out of the boat and walk to Him on the water, Peter who denied Jesus three times on the night of His betrayal, but also the one who Jesus restored after His resurrection.

"For we have not been telling you fairy tales when we explained to you the power of our Lord Jesus Christ and his coming again. My own eyes have seen his splendor and his glory." (2 Peter 1:16)

Peter saw Jesus for "real" in the flesh. With his own eyes, Peter saw Jesus. Peter knew Jesus' voice. He saw Jesus heal people, teach the disciples, laugh with them, rejoice with them, but also saw Jesus' anguish, not only as He went to the cross but as He felt the betrayal of others.

On our journey to Bill's healing, we saw the difference between those who had stories to tell and those who had walked the path themselves. There is something so powerful about describing what you have seen with your own eyes. Bill was also honored to have dreams and visions the last couple years of his life, as God revealed great things to him. What a joy to be God's child.

The Glory Road is a place of further revelation. I have walked the path of healing alongside many others but now it's personal. The battle and the victory are in my own body, and great is God's faithfulness on this journey. The revelation of God is not a fairy tale. The blood of the Lamb and our testimonies help us defeat the enemy of our souls. (Revelation 12:11)

Lord, You are real. You are not a character in a fairy tale. May we walk in the truth and let the truth set us free. As we stand on Your promises, may others be drawn to the light of the love of Jesus in us. We pray for those who are lost in the darkness, or wandered away from the light, bring them home, Good Shepherd. We love you and praise you in Jesus' name, amen.

Thank you for your prayers.#Godisfaithful#TheGloryRoad

Day#590 November 30

 Anchor Verse: Ezekiel 38:23
In this way, I will show my greatness and holiness, and I will make myself known to all the nations of the world. Then they will know that I am the Lord. (NLT)

As we enter this Advent season, in anticipation of the celebration of Jesus' birth, we have an opportunity to slow down for a moment, and revel in the miracle of Jesus' coming, and God's gift to us in the person of Jesus Christ.

God is not only a personal God but the God of all the nations.

"In this way, I will show my greatness and holiness, and I will make myself known to all the nations of the world. Then they will know that I am the Lord." (Ezekiel 38:23)

In Ezekiel 38, there's a lot going on ~ a lot of mayhem, mischief, and destruction. Out of that mess emerges God's holiness and glory. There will come a time where every knee will bow and every tongue confess that Jesus Christ is Lord to the glory of God the Father. (Philippians 2:10-11)

On our journey to Bill's healing, God spoke in a still small voice to encourage Bill daily on his journey to healing. Then there were days when the Lion of the tribe of Judah roared, "Enough!" and the Red Sea parted, and the miracle of healing was manifested in Bill's body. God used Bill's life as a beautiful example of what happens when a man surrenders to the Lord, and allows God's glory to be seen in him.

The Glory Road is filled with opportunities both big and small to be Jesus' hands and feet. In the serving, in the surrender, in the submission to His will and not mine, there is a beacon of light sent out into the darkness and people are drawn to Jesus. May our lives reflect His love, His glory, His beauty every day. He is alone is worthy of our praise.

Lord, we praise and thank you for the gift of Jesus. Heavenly Father, when You speak, Your voice can be heard around the world, and in another moment, only in the depths of my heart. Thank you for Your presence with us. We love you, Lord, in Jesus' name we pray, amen.

Thank you for being a vessel of honor.#Godisfaithful#TheGloryRoad

December 2021

Let us hold unswervingly to the hope we profess for he who promised is faithful.

~ Hebrews 10:23 ~

Day#591 December 1

 Anchor Verse: 2 Peter 3:9
The Lord does not delay [as though He were unable to act] and is not slow about His promise, as some count slowness, but is [extraordinarily] patient toward you, not wishing for any to perish but for all to come to repentance. (AMP)

Delays… waiting… unexpected disturbances and distractions… we don't like them. Our very nature… the one placed in us at creation as we were made in the image of God, is to have our lives in order.

If you look at your surroundings, the piles of things in your office or home, you may not think that is true. But your spirit was designed to walk with God, your heart to beat with the heart of God.

God operates on a different time schedule than we do. "A day is like a thousand years, and a thousand years like a day."

Sometimes we don't get that whole concept of time, because we are driven by alarms and alerts, and calendars, and smartphones, and so much more, trying to remind us what we should be doing.

"The Lord does not delay [as though He were unable to act] and is not slow about His promise, as some count slowness, but is [extraordinarily] patient toward you, not wishing for any to perish but for all to come to repentance." (2 Peter 3:9)

On our journey to Bill's healing, there were places of delay, waiting, and being patient. Bill said he wasn't a patient man, but God changed him. Bill learned to wait on the Lord and His perfect timing.

The Glory Road is like living on a superhighway and other times like a dirt road in the country. Quickly the day may speed by or the cadence is slower and each step is measured. God is the one who directs the tempo of my life, what is accomplished quickly and what is left undone. Lord, set my pace that I might accomplish Your will for Your glory.

Lord, we praise and thank you for the gift of Your rhythm. You have called us by name and we belong to You. Lord, thank you for Your patience. Your perfect timing in our lives. For those walking in the darkness, may they walk into the light of Your love. We love you, Lord. In Jesus' name, amen.

Thank you for your faithfulness. #Godisfaithful#TheGloryRoad

Day#592 December 2

 Anchor Verse: 1 John 1:4
We are writing these things so that you may fully share our joy. (NLT)

For a moment, use your imagination to consider what it would have been like to walk with Jesus. Not only to walk with Him as His disciples did, but to hear His voice and see the love in His eyes as Jesus spoke with others and touched and healed them.

In 1 John1:2, John, Jesus's disciple who wrote this book of the Bible says, "The life appeared; we have seen it and testify to it, and we proclaim to you the eternal life, which was with the Father and has appeared to us." John is describing Jesus. From this first-hand account, this eyewitness testimony, John invites us to share in that moment.

"We are writing these things so that you may fully share our joy." (1 John 1:4)

To "fully" share in the joy ~ not just a little bit, but be immersed in the joy that comes from knowing Jesus and walking with Him. We can have that honor and privilege today as we say "yes" to Jesus.

On our journey to Bill's healing, we experienced the joy that comes through walking with the Prince of Peace through hard places. It did not always change our circumstances, but it definitely changed our perspective.

Psalm 16:11 says, "You will show me the path of life; In Your presence is fullness of joy; At Your right hand are pleasures forevermore." (NKJV)

The Glory Road is a path of further revelation of who God is moment by moment. Unspeakable joy can only be found in the presence of God. Who wants to leave His presence where we experience life in ways we cannot imagine? Thank you, Lord, for the gift of Your joy, the gift of Jesus.

Lord, we praise and thank you for this Advent season. As we receive the fullness of Your joy, we can share it with others. There is nothing that is too hard for You, absolutely nothing. We lean in today to hear Your voice as we seek Your wisdom. God, may You be honored and glorified in our lives today. In Jesus' name we pray, amen.

Thank you for sharing your joy.#Godisfaithful#TheGloryRoad

Day#593 December 3

 Anchor Verse: 1 John 2:10-11
It's the person who loves brother and sister who dwells in God's light and doesn't block the light from others. But whoever hates is still in the dark, stumbles around in the dark, doesn't know which end is up, blinded by the darkness. (MSG)

Darkness and light – every day we see this contrast in nature. The darkness dissolves when light breaks forth in the pre-dawn hours.

As believers in Jesus, we have chosen to walk away from the darkness into the light of God's love. In 1 John 2, John talks about love and hatred among fellow believers. Shouldn't we love each other? Yes, we should.

In 1 John 2:6, John says, "Whoever claims to live in him must live as Jesus did." We have Jesus' example, the Holy Spirit to guide us, and a heavenly Father who is ever vigilant to fight for us.

"It's the person who loves brother and sister who dwells in God's light and doesn't block the light from others. But whoever hates is still in the dark, stumbles around in the dark, doesn't know which end is up, blinded by the darkness." (1 John 2:10-11MSG)

You may have lost power due to a natural storm. When there is no light, the darkness is so dark that it's disorienting. Greater still is the darkness of the soul. When hatred clouds our vision, it puts up a wall so we can no longer see the light of God's love. It is the darkest place on earth.

On our journey to Bill's healing, we fought battles in both the darkness and the light. Choosing to love others and speak words of life in the difficult places with difficult people is something that can only be done with God's love in your heart. With God all things are possible.

The Glory Road is a place of choices. Choosing to love others, when the world speaks hate to us. In the body of Christ, we are called to love as Jesus loves. Daily, I must choose the path I walk. The path of love and truth follows the light, while the path that follows the enemy is lined with grumbling, lies, and darkness.

Lord, we praise and thank you for the gift of Your love. Jesus' love paid the price for my sins. God's love restored my relationships and gave me life. May we be givers of life in our words and actions. In Jesus' name we pray, amen.

Thank you for your persevering prayers.#Godisfaithful#TheGloryRoad

Day#594 December 4

 Anchor Verse: 1 John 3:17
If anyone sees a fellow believer in need and has the means to help him, yet shows no pity and closes his heart against him, how is it even possible that God's love lives in him? (TPT)

Living as Jesus lived; loving as Jesus loved ~ this is our daily call to action.

Sound like too great of a challenge? It might be if we had to do it on our own, but we don't have to walk this path alone. God promised to NEVER leave us or forsake us. (Hebrews 13:5)

Throughout the Bible, we are taught that our faith, saying we are Christians, needs to extend beyond our words, our actions need to reflect it.

In Matthew 25, Jesus shared the parable about the sheep and the goats. "Then the righteous will answer him, 'Lord, when did we see you hungry and feed you, or thirsty and give you something to drink? When did we see you a stranger and invite you in or needing clothes and clothe you? When did we see you sick or in prison and go to visit you?' "The King will reply, 'Truly I tell you, whatever you did for one of the least of these brothers and sisters of mine, you did for me.'" (Matthew 25:37-40)

1 John 3:17 says, "If anyone sees a fellow believer in need and has the means to help him, yet shows no pity and closes his heart against him, how is it even possible that God's love lives in him?"

On our journey to Bill's healing, we had both the opportunity to give and to receive. It may not be financial resources or possessions God is calling you to share, but it could be the gift of your time, your talent, or your prayers.

The Glory Road is filled with so many opportunities to share with others. Daily, hourly, minute by minute, we can share the gift of hope, words of life and encouragement, prayers for strength, and sometimes beyond that, giving of our possessions. There isn't a one-size-fits-all pattern, God deals with each of us individually.

Lord, we praise and thank you for the gift of today. Thank you for the opportunity to be a blessing to others. It's not about what we own or where we live, but how we use the gifts you have given us for Your honor and glory. Let people see Your love in us, O Lord. In Jesus' name we pray, amen.

Thank you for being a blessing.#Godisfaithful#TheGloryRoad

Day#595 December 5

 Anchor Verse: Daniel 1:5
They were to be trained for three years, and after that they were to enter the king's service. (NIV)

When we think about difficult things happening in our lives, we reason that we can make it through almost anything for a short time. This was not the case for these young men. "They were to be trained for three years, and after that they were to enter the king's service." (Daniel 1:5)

King Nebuchadnezzar had a lifetime change in mind for them. First, there would be three years of training. Three years is a long time in a place you don't know, with people who do not follow your God, your religious practices, or even what you eat. The king has in mind they will serve him for as long as he is on the throne – a new assignment for a lifetime.

God has a different plan, and these young men who had been trained by their parents and religious leaders, stood up for what they believed. Daniel in verse 8 asked the chief official to not eat the royal food and defile (pollute, dishonor) himself in this way, but instead to just give them vegetables to eat and water to drink. It was agreed this would happen for 10 days. And at the end of it, these young men were healthier than all the others.

What a great illustration and reminder that as believers we are called to be set apart and follow God even in a foreign land. It's not so much about the actual food in this case, but what God is calling us to do and how to conduct our lives to keep ourselves holy and righteous before Him.

On our journey to Bill's healing, we entered a foreign land. It wasn't about the physical location but God set us apart to follow Him, and do what He said to do. We were preserved and protected everywhere we went as we honored the Lord in thought, word, and deed.

The Glory Road crosses lands and people that are different than me and my past experience. God calls me to remain holy and put Him first in my life. He is my shield and defender in a foreign land, in places I do not know.

Lord, we praise and thank you that wherever we go, You are there. May we set our hearts and minds on following You. May we walk in love and invite others to join us there. Thank you for Your hand of protection over Your children. You are great and greatly to be praised. In Jesus' name, amen.

Thank you for your love and prayers.#Godisfaithful#TheGloryRoad

Day#596 December 6

 Anchor Verse: Daniel 4:2
I want you all to know about the miraculous signs and wonders the Most High God has performed for me. (NLT)

Good news is too good to keep to yourself. And when that good news is a miraculous sign and wonder from God, the enthusiasm and passion to share it is multiplied.

Not only here in the Old Testament do we see this to be true but also in the New Testament when Jesus performed miracles and people were healed, and the 5000 were fed with five loaves and two fish.

King Nebuchadnezzar, the king of Babylon, was a powerful king. But his power and success took hold of his life in a bad way. The king makes a huge gold image and everyone is supposed to fall down and worship the image when they heard the music play. The three young men from Israel, Shadrach, Meshach, and Abednego refused to do so, because they only worshiped God. They are thrown into the fiery furnace for defying the king.

King Nebuchadnezzar praises God who sent His angel and rescued these young men and decreed that no one should speak against the God of Shadrach, Meshach, and Abednego.

In Daniel 4:2, Nebuchadnezzar says, "I want you all to know about the miraculous signs and wonders the Most High God has performed for me."

On our journey to Bill's healing, we encountered miraculous signs and wonders God did in Bill's life. We knew the source of the miracles; others were surprised about what happened because it defied explanation. They even called Bill, the "Miracle Man." Bill and I sang praises to God's name.

The Glory Road is filled with the signs and wonders of God in my life and the lives of others. Even those who do not call themselves Christians are amazed at what God has done in us.

Lord, we praise and thank you for Your blessings in our lives. You are a God who heals, delivers, and sets people free. We pray for those who are in need of a miracle. Do what only You can do, Lord, and we will give You all the praise and honor and glory in Jesus' mighty name, amen.

Thank you for believing in miracles.#Godisfaithful#TheGloryRoad

Day#597 December 7

 Anchor Verse: 2 John 12
I have much more to say to you, but I don't want to do it with paper and ink. For I hope to visit you soon and talk with you face to face. Then our joy will be complete. (NLT)

Many thoughts and ideas race through our minds in a day, and for some, through the night.

Some things work well to share on paper, or through an email or text message. There are some blessings and conversations that need to happen face to face.

John, as he writes this letter and brings it to a close, expresses this exact sentiment. "I have much more to say to you, but I don't want to do it with paper and ink. For I hope to visit you soon and talk with you face to face. Then our joy will be complete." (2 John 12)

As we have traveled through a season when a virus has drastically changed our interactions with each other, we no longer take for granted in-person interactions.

On our journey to Bill's healing, there were stretches of the road where written communication was the best we could offer. In those special moments, the God-ordained and arranged, "look what the Lord has done" moments, our joy was multiplied, our joy was complete.

The Glory Road is a place of strategic interactions, ordained by the hand of God. Many times my path intersects those God has personally sent so I can show them the love of Jesus. We are called to not only be His hands and feet but also His voice, that speaks with love and compassion.

Lord, thank you for the gift of Your love. You have a plan and purpose for our lives. Thank you that what You do, God, You do well. Thank you for every face-to-face encounter we have with each other – friend, loved one, or stranger. May our words be full of hope and Your love this day. We are blessed to be a blessing in Jesus' mighty name, amen.

Thank you for your encouraging words.#Godisfaithful#TheGloryRoad

Day#598 December 8

 Anchor Verse: Daniel 10:12
Then he said, "Don't be frightened, Daniel, for your request has been heard in heaven and was answered the very first day you began to fast before the Lord and pray for understanding; that very day I was sent here to meet you." (TLB)

We are a results-driven people. We like our answers, our food, our wants, needs, and desires fulfilled… NOW! That sounded a little bit like a two-year-old's temper tantrum. Forgive us, Lord.

In Daniel 10, Daniel receives a vision from the Lord and all his strength is gone. He had fallen into a deep sleep. In verse 10, a messenger from heaven arrives and tells Daniel to stand and receive this word from the Lord.

"Then he said, "Don't be frightened, Daniel, for your request has been heard in heaven and was answered the very first day you began to fast before the Lord and pray for understanding; that very day I was sent here to meet you."

This angelic messenger had been detained for 21 days, but the archangel Michael had come to help him (Gabriel) defeat this spiritual enemy.

We can find encouragement in this verse. Your request has been heard in heaven and was "answered" the very first day you began to fast and pray for understanding. A messenger from heaven was sent that very day to deliver the message, the answer you were waiting for.

On our journey to Bill's healing, our prayers and your prayers rose to heaven, day and night, on Bill's behalf. What a great assurance to know that God had a plan, a healing, a purpose for Bill's earthly journey. It was not only ultimately for Bill's good, as it drew him closer to God, but also to bring God glory. Delay is not denial. God's answers are worth waiting for today.

The Glory Road is filled with the prayers of the saints. If we could see into the spiritual realm, we would see prayers and their answers passing back and forth between earth and heaven, and heaven and earth. We might catch a glimpse of the skirmish that is causing the delay. We know God's promises are true, and so we wait in expectation, filled with hope, for their completion.

Lord, thank you for the gift of Your love, mercy, grace, and peace. You hear the cries of our hearts even when we haven't received the answer we seek. Thank you for trusting us in the waiting as our faith grows stronger. We will hold on to Your hand and never let go. In Jesus' name, amen.

Thank you for your faithfulness.#Godisfaithful#TheGloryRoad

Day#599 December 9

 Anchor Verse: Jude 22
Keep being compassionate to those who still have doubts. (TPT)

This small book of the Bible, Jude, starts off in verse 2 with this statement. "Mercy, peace and love be yours in abundance." (NIV)

Those words roll easily off our tongues, but each word is powerful and pregnant with meaning. Mercy. Peace. Love. Take a moment and savor the flavor of them, like a tasty morsel, food for our souls.

God's love is the greatest act of mercy when He sent Jesus to die for us. As sinners, we can't stand before a holy God, but Jesus took our punishment and now our relationship with our heavenly Father has been restored.

We now have the opportunity to share that mercy, grace, and compassion with others. In verse 22, Jude reminds us of our commission, "Keep being compassionate to those who still have doubts."

What a great opportunity to come alongside those who are struggling, who are wavering in their faith, and lift them up, just as Jesus does for us. May we not forget we came from the dark night of chaos. Even now as we stand in the light of His glorious presence that brings life to our souls, may we extend our hands, our hearts, and bring others out of the cold through our prayers.

On our journey to Bill's healing, we were blessed with many opportunities to extend compassion, mercy, grace, and yes, love, to those who still had doubts. Even those who were walking the path with us didn't always see what the Lord was showing us. We held them up in our prayers and asked the Lord to give them eyes to see His goodness, grace, and love.

The Glory Road travels through a time when God's mercy and forgiveness are needed daily. We are called to broker that hope and extend our hands, and listen to those who are lost in a world of doubt. Let us offer an open hand of grace rather than a closed heart that seeks to be right.

Father, thank you for Your new mercies, not only in our lives, but so we can plant them in the lives of others. Every word is a seed planted in the heart and mind of another. Help us love as Jesus loved, and speak words of kindness and compassion. May their doubts be extinguished in the river of Your love. We love you, Lord, in Jesus' name amen.

Thank you for your heart of compassion.#Godisfaithful#TheGloryRoad

Day#600 December 10

 Anchor Verse: Hosea 2:15a
I will return her vineyards to her and transform the Valley of Trouble into a gateway of hope. (NLT)

When your life has been chosen to have God's prophetic word lived out through you, it's an interesting road.

God told Hosea to marry a promiscuous woman and have children with her. God even picked out their names, which were a message to the people of Israel. Hosea did not have an easy life, yet he chose to follow God.

Your life may not be easy either but when you are walking in obedience, He will make even the rough places smooth, and the crooked places straight.

"I will return her vineyards to her and transform the Valley of Trouble into a gateway of hope." (Hosea 2:15)

Let's dwell in that gateway of hope for a moment as the Lord takes us out of the Valley of Trouble. God is reminding us that this is not our final destination. Even if we have made poor choices, we can let them go, and run to the Lord and be filled with hope for the bright future that lies ahead of us.

On our journey to Bill's healing, we walked through the Valley of Trouble many times. For a while, it seemed like we were doing laps, and it was a track that had no end. God knew where He would open a gateway of hope that led to miracles and victory. With our eyes focused on the Lord, we listened for His words of instruction and His very heartbeat that drew us forward in hope away from the depths of darkness.

The Glory Road is filled with people in chaos and confusion. Alongside them are others filled with peace, hope, and joy. Which camp do you fall into the morning? As followers of Jesus Christ, our hope comes in the name of the Lord. We will walk out of this Valley of Trouble onto the path of light.

Lord, we thank you for the gift of Your love. You are the light of the world. Thank you for helping us even while we still may be in the Valley of Trouble. You will make a way out of it. It might not be today, but You have a plan and a purpose even in the hard places. We trust you. In Jesus' name, amen.

Thank you for your persistent prayers. My next MRI is Tuesday, Dec. 14#Godisfaithful#TheGloryRoad

Day#601 December 11

 Anchor Verse: Revelation 2:7
Whoever has ears, let them hear… (NIV)

"Are your ears awake?" That's what the Message translation of Revelation 2:7 says. It's really a great question. Because sometimes our ears aren't awake, they're asleep. We are deaf to the cries of those around us, and most of all deaf to the Spirit of the Lord speaking to us.

Hearing and listening are two powerful gifts that we can give ourselves and others. My dear husband used to say that he learned so much more by listening than when he was talking.

How long has it been since you had a listening day? Maybe it's been too long.

God's Word, the Bible, is filled with great truth, amazing promises, and stories of those who chose the best path and those who did not. All of this holds great lessons for us to learn. The added bonus is to listen to the Holy Spirit, our guide, and those who have walked with God for a long distance who have learned the wisdom of His ways. Listening will glean great results.

On our journey to Bill's healing, we learned the value of the art of listening. Most of all what God said, the best source of wisdom and knowledge. Bill learned so much as he listened to his heavenly Father, and I learned so much by listening to Bill. What a blessing to hear your husband breathe and listen to words of wisdom that come from God's heart. I am a blessed woman.

The Glory Road offers many opportunities to be still in God's presence and to listen, and obey. It is in the quietness of my heart and often my surroundings that I hear the heartbeat of God. I hear His still small voice giving me instructions and calling me forward. When I listen, I can hear the cry of the lonely heart of others and those asking for help who often go unheard in the noise of life. Lord, teach me to listen.

Lord, You speak to us and long for us to hear Your instructions. Thank you for the opportunity to not only be Your hands and feet, and voice, but also Your ears, to hear the silent cries of others, and how we can meet their needs. May today be a "listening day." In Jesus' name we pray, amen.

Thank you for the gift of listening.#Godisfaithful#TheGloryRoad

Day#602 December 12

 Anchor Verse: Hosea 11:8
My heart is torn within me, and my compassion overflows. (NLT)

Lord God Almighty, Maker of heaven and earth created emotions when He created us. Our heavenly Father walks with us through the winding roads of our lives and every emotion too.

In the Old Testament, we read many passages that describe God's emotions, from great love to great frustration and anger at the children of Israel. We are so grateful that God is a God of mercy as well as justice.

In Hosea 11 in the midst of the details of destruction, we read these words, "My heart is torn within me, and my compassion overflows." (Hosea 11:8)

Thank God for His compassionate heart. It overflows with love. It is moved by our circumstances. And ultimately, His compassion overflows like a river.

Do you and I have that same trait as our heavenly Father? Is our heart torn at times and ultimately does our compassion overflow?

On our journey to Bill's healing, we walked through some harsh terrain, but we were not alone. Many others were also having difficult experiences. Bill and I had the opportunity to come alongside of them, experience their brokenness, and speak life and hope, and Jesus' love to them.

The Glory Road is filled with lots of emotion in this Advent season. Not just in those around me, but in my own heart and life. My mind is taken back to the birth of Jesus in a world that was troubled, people who were weary, much like today. God had a great gift in mind, Jesus, the hope of the world was about to enter their darkness. Jesus is still our best gift today.

Lord, we are so grateful Your heart overflows with compassion. We pray for those who are weary, who feel alone and their hope level is low. Fill them up with new joy. As we praise and worship you, King of kings and Lord of lords, a fountain of new life will erupt in us. In Jesus' name, amen.

Thank you for your persistent prayers.#Godisfaithful#TheGloryRoad

Day#603 December 13

 Anchor Verse: Hosea 14:9
Who is wise? Let them realize these things. Who is discerning? Let them understand. The ways of the Lord are right; the righteous walk in them, but the rebellious stumble in them. (NIV)

How many of you have ever taken the wrong exit? Turned left instead of right? Or stumbled over something in the dark, and ended up with a hurting body part?

We all have experienced the wrong way. The right path is the one where the Lord abides. It's where we walk and talk with Jesus, and we are given wisdom and understanding for every situation we face.

"Who is wise? Let them realize these things. Who is discerning? Let them understand. The ways of the Lord are right; the righteous walk in them, but the rebellious stumble in them." (Hosea 14:9)

Would you consider yourself righteous or rebellious?

Wisdom and understanding come from the heart of God. King Solomon knew that and that's why he asked the Lord for wisdom above all else. God not only gave him wisdom and understanding, He also rewarded Solomon with so much more.

On our journey to Bill's healing, we were given the opportunity to choose God's way or the way of the world. God's path still has hills and valleys but when you are walking with the Lord, He makes your paths straight. To quote my husband, "You will do the things you think you cannot do." Amen.

The Glory Road is a crowded highway at times, and then in some places, there are few people around me. The path of God's best is often narrow and less traveled. The Good Shepherd knows the way and His feet are sure-footed, and He will lead me safely to our destination. Thank you, Jesus.

Lord, we praise for the gift of Your goodness and grace. Your peace is multiplied even in the midst of difficult situations. Please go before us and also be our rearguard. You alone are worthy of our praise. Lord, we pray you would open the eyes of the rebellious to see You. In Jesus' name, amen.

Thank you for your faithfulness. Prayers appreciated for this devotional project and my MRI tomorrow.#Godisfaithful#TheGloryRoad

Day#604 December 14

 Anchor Verse: Revelation 5:11
Then I looked and heard the voice of many angels, numbering thousands upon thousands, and ten thousand times ten thousand. They encircled the throne and the living creatures and the elders. (NIV)

Voices singing ~ it changes the atmosphere…it brings heaven to earth.

The last book of the Bible, the book of Revelation can be difficult to wrap your head around. I remember as a teenager studying Revelation in our youth group, and honestly, a lot of what we talked about scared me.

What a scene we see depicted in this passage this morning.

"Then I looked and heard the voice of many angels, numbering thousands upon thousands, and ten thousand times ten thousand. They encircled the throne and the living creatures and the elders." (Revelation 5:11)

Even doing the math, we can't comprehend the number of angels surrounding the throne. Can you imagine how beautiful their songs of praise must sound? Thank you, Lord, for giving us just a small taste of heaven

On our journey to Bill's healing, Bill was blessed with many encounters with the Lord, through both dreams and visions. I was also blessed as Bill shared some of those encounters. There were other nights that the conversation was to stay between Bill and God. Some revelations are meant to be pondered in our own hearts rather than shared with many. God will give you direction about what to share and what to hold close to your heart.

The Glory Road is a place where angels walk with me. The presence of heaven touches earth. There are times when I see God's hand at work and hear His voice. Every day I am invited to praise the Lord for what He is doing in my own life. He alone is worthy of my praise.

Lord, we praise and thank you for the gift of Your love for us. The steadfast love of the Lord never ceases. We rest on Your faithfulness. May Your name be lifted high. We love you and praise you in Jesus' name amen.

Thank you for your powerful prayers. MRI today (12.14.22) for me.#Godisfaithful#TheGloryRoad

Day#605 December 15

 Anchor Verse: Amos 3:4
Will a lion roar in the forest, when he has no prey? Will a young lion cry out of his den, if he has caught nothing? (NKJV)

There are so many unanswered questions in our lives. We don't have all the answers but we know the one who does ~ God, and God alone.

I have heard others say, "When I get to heaven, I have a list of questions to ask God." It's a great plan, but I don't think our lists will go with us. When we enter heaven's glory, our questions will disappear as we stand in awe and wonder.

In our humanity, there are mysteries we try and solve. Paths we seek to places we desire to go. We try and make sense of things that are a stretch to our imagination. We won't even try and figure out those the age-old question about why bad things happen to good people.

"Will a lion roar in the forest, when he has no prey? Will a young lion cry out of his den, if he has caught nothing?" (Amos 3:4)

Is the answer the most important part of our journey? Or are there some things best left as a mystery?

Our times are in His hands (Psalm 31:15) and that's where we need to rest.

On our journey to Bill's healing, we encountered some crossroads that caught us off-guard. There were places we didn't have the answers, but we knew God did. So, we ran to Him. We laid our concerns at His feet and asked for wisdom to continue. I saw Bill do this often. It was a beautiful picture of a man completely surrendered to God.

The Glory Road is a place filled with questions and mysteries. Many times, I don't know the answer. I cry out to the Lord for wisdom and understanding and trust Him to make a way where there doesn't seem to be a way. He is unshakable, unstoppable, and unmovable.

Lord, we praise and thank you that You are the answer to our every question. You are the light in the darkness. You are the bright and morning star. We love you and praise you this morning for who You are. You are enough. We love you, Lord. In Jesus' name, amen.

Thank you for your love and support. MRI went well. God was there. I don't meet with the doctor until January 2022.#Godisfaithful#TheGloryRoad.

Day#606 December 16

 Anchor Verse: Revelation 7:17
For the Lamb at the center of the throne will be their shepherd; 'he will lead them to springs of living water.' 'And God will wipe away every tear from their eyes.'"
(NIV)

Are you a "picture" person or a "word" person? Are you more visual, you need a picture of something, have that object in your hands rather than words on a page or a description of an item?

In Revelation 7:9 it says, "After this I looked, and there before me was a great multitude that no one could count, from every nation, tribe, people and language, standing before the throne and before the Lamb. They were wearing white robes and were holding palm branches in their hands."

Then John has a discussion with one of the elders about who these people. They have come out of the great tribulation. "Never again will they hunger; never again will they thirst. The sun will not beat down on them,' nor any scorching heat." They are delivered from all their human wants and needs.

"For the Lamb at the center of the throne will be their shepherd; 'he will lead them to springs of living water. And God will wipe away every tear from their eyes.' (Revelation 7:17)

No more tears. No more sorrow. Everything they need the Lamb, their shepherd, will provide.

On our journey to Bill's healing, often our needs were great, beyond what we could do for ourselves. So many gifts came from God's heart and hands through others, and often through His own words of encouragement.

The Glory Road has been a place of tears, many of them. Some tears were born out of the loss of my husband, and my mom, but they are mixed with tears of gratitude and joy for how God has moved on my behalf. God will wipe away every tear from my eyes. None of us will lack anything.

Lord, You are an ever-present help in time of trouble just as You are the first to rejoice in our victories. We are so blessed to be called the children of God. May our lives reflect Your light and Your love. In Jesus' name, amen.

Thank you for your persevering prayers. Pray that the way is clear for me to go home for Christmas to be with my family. Nothing is too hard for God.#Godisfaithful#TheGloryRoad

Day#607 December 17

 Anchor Verse: Revelation 8:1
When the Lamb broke the seventh seal on the scroll, there was silence throughout heaven for about half an hour. (NLT)

Silence ~ it can make some people uncomfortable. Our world is filled with a lot of noise. Sounds of daily living in a modern world.

In Revelation 8:1, we read about the Lamb breaking open the seventh seal on the scroll. The Bible says, "There was silence throughout heaven for about half an hour."

Silence in heaven where normally the air, the atmosphere is filled with praises and people worshipping the King of kings and the Lord of lords.

The air is saturated with awe and wonder of what would happen next. They "held their breath" for a moment in anticipation of God's next move.

On our journey to Bill's healing, there were moments of silence. Yes, there are those moments in hospital rooms, in doctor's offices when the news you have been told takes your breath away. There is also the silence of blessing when you are with someone you love. I remember the car rides Bill and I would take when he would ask that there be no conversation so he could take in his surroundings, and absorb life. Silence can also be beautiful.

The Glory Road has its own pockets of silence. My home is often too quiet without the sound of Bill's voice and his laughter. But in the silence, I sense my heavenly Father's presence beckoning me to come closer to Him. He wraps me in His arms of love and reminds me that everything will be alright. Silence is my friend in the pre-dawn hours as I hear the voice of the Lord through scripture reminding me that He is very near.

Lord, we praise and thank you for the gift of silence. We thank you that silence often precedes a big event, a breakthrough, a lesson, a blessing. We pray for those who are struggling with the silence in their lives. We ask for Your presence to fill that hole and that they would be complete in You. Lord, may we walk according to the unforced rhythm of Your grace.

Thank you for your encouraging words. Travel plans (2021) have changed due to icy conditions. Moving on to Plan B.#Godisfaithful#TheGloryRoad

Day#608 December 18

 Anchor Verse: Obadiah 1:3a
The pride and arrogance of your heart have deceived you. (AMP)

Obadiah was a prophet, not always an easy job to speak to God's people and deliver God's message.

The Edomites were coming against the people of Judah and God had a message for them. If they didn't stop, bad things were about to happen. He calls them out and doesn't mince any words.

"The pride and arrogance of your heart have deceived you." (Obadiah 1:3)

Since they lived high on a mountain, they could look down on everything below. However, it was more than just their elevation, it was their attitude. They considered themselves better than the people who lived in the valley below. Their pride and arrogance were their undoing.

Is there any pride or arrogance in our hearts that is deceiving us?

If the answer is yes, then we need to run to God in prayer and admit we have a wrong attitude, (and maybe actions too), and ask for His forgiveness. Then we change direction, and we don't do that anymore. Give us a clean heart and clean hands, O Lord.

On our journey to Bill's healing, we learned a lot about the power of position. The best way to live is to come alongside someone, and give them a hand up. In our years working with people who were going through hard times, we learned they are just like us with hopes and dreams. Never call others "those people" because we are all the same – God's children.

The Glory Road has mountains and valleys, and people reside in different places at different elevations. A mountain and valley are only about geography, what really matters is the position of our hearts. Christmas is a great opportunity to reach out to others and share what we can. May we not hoard our time, talent, and resources but rather with open hands be Jesus' hands and feet to those who need to know someone cares.

Thank you, Lord, for the gifts that come from Your hands. May our hearts not be filled with pride and arrogance. May we give You all the praise, honor, and glory due Your name. We love you, Lord, in Jesus' name we pray, amen.

Thank you for loving well.#Godisfaithful#TheGloryRoad

Day#609 December 19

 Anchor Verse: Jonah 3:8
People and animals alike must wear garments of mourning, and everyone must pray earnestly to God. They must turn from their evil ways and stop all their violence. (NLT)

God is a God of love but He's also a God of justice. He will only tolerate evil for so long before He takes action.

The book of Jonah tells the story of a man, a stubborn man, who God wanted to use to save the people of Nineveh. It was a very large city. It took three days to walk across it. God loved them, but could no longer tolerate the evil that He saw there.

God asks Jonah to go. Jonah says no and runs the other direction. Many of you know the story of Jonah and the whale. Yes, God goes to extraordinary means even to save those who are running away from Him.

Here in Jonah 3, Jonah completes his assignment and the people hear his warning and in Jonah 3:5, it says, "The Ninevites believed God." In fact, a fast was proclaimed, and all of them from the greatest to the least put on sackcloth, clothes of mourning, praying God would have mercy.

On our journey to Bill's healing, there was much chaos in the land. We were on the front edge of the pandemic, and much turmoil and confusion were everywhere. Bill and I ran to the Lord, prayed, and stayed in His presence where we found His peace and the fullness of His joy.

The Glory Road is filled with reports of evil prospering, and violence abounding. It is only when people turn away from evil toward good that love will fill the land. The change begins in each one of us. Our heart must seek the Lord while He may be found, call on Him while He is near. (Isaiah 55:6) His heart is filled with love and mercy, but we must choose to receive it.

Lord, we praise and thank you for the gift of Your love and mercy. Father, we know that we are a sinful people. We choose wrong over right. We choose the easy way, instead of Your way. May the words of our mouth and the meditation of our heart be acceptable in Your sight, O Lord, our Strength and our Redeemer. In Jesus' name we pray, amen.

Thank you for your faithfulness in prayer.#Godisfaithful#TheGloryRoad

Day#610 December 20

 Anchor Verse: Acts 12:5
So Peter was kept in prison, but fervent and persistent prayer for him was being made to God by the church. (AMP)

There is a price to pay when we follow Jesus. This is not something new, but it has been happening for generations.

In the book of Acts, we read of the early church and how King Herod began arresting and persecuting those who belonged to the church. In Acts 12:3, we read about King Herod arresting Peter, which met with the approval of the Jews. His plan was to put Peter on public trial after the Passover.

But Peter wasn't alone, even in prison.

"So Peter was kept in prison, but fervent and persistent prayer for him was being made to God by the church." (Acts 12:5)

There was intense intercession by the church when one of their own was in trouble. Today, it may not be that a church member is in prison, but facing a life-threatening illness, financial concerns, broken relationships, etc. The answer is for the church, a group of believers to surround you and pray.

On our journey to Bill's healing, many came around us in prayer, especially our church family, as well as all of you. There were prayers that ascended to heaven, day and night, from those who had never met Bill in person. Hearing his story, others were moved to ask God for the miracle that Bill needed.

The Glory Road is a place of prayer. It is a place of miracles, not only in my life but the lives of others. What a blessing to come together as believers and believe that God can do what we can't ~ immeasurably more than ALL we can ask or think (Ephesians 3:20). Even as I press in for my healing miracle, I stand with those who need their own miracle. I know that God's arm is not too short (Isaiah 59:1) to do what the hands of man cannot do.

Thank you, heavenly Father that You are the God of miracles. At Your word, people are healed. You delight to partner with us in prayer, as we ask and believe for what we cannot see. We pray for those who need Your healing touch today. Comfort those who mourn that they may be comforted. We rest on Your promises. In Jesus' name we pray, amen.

Thank you for believing in miracles.#Godisfaithful#TheGloryRoad

Day#611 December 21

 Anchor Verse: Micah 4:4b
… no one will make them afraid, for the Lord Almighty has spoken. (NIV)

In the Bible, there are many types of stories. There are historical accounts, genealogies, poetry, parables, songs (psalms), prophecy, and so much more.

Micah 4 speaks of a time when there will be no more war. "Nation will not take up sword against nation, nor will they train for war anymore. Everyone will sit under their own vine and under their own fig tree." (Micah 4:3-4a) It speaks of a time of peace and prosperity.

Our focus is on the latter part of verse 4, "No one will make them afraid, for the Lord Almighty has spoken."

For a moment, just ponder what it will be like when no one or nothing will make you afraid. No longer will a virus or the armies of a nation, or your neighborhood, or a bully, or financial concerns, or a wayward child, or abusive partner make you afraid. The peace of the Lord will reign in the hearts of those who know Him and have chosen to walk with Him.

On our journey to Bill's healing, we encountered many different seasons in our lives, not only seasons in nature, but of Bill's health. There were some scary moments, I won't deny that, but we always found comfort in the words the Lord spoke to us. We leaned into His truth and rested on His word.

The Glory Road is walked through terrain that is spotted with conflict and peace. Navigating the storms of life can be a daily battle. Choosing where to focus and who to listen to and who to ignore, we must rely on the wisdom of God, and walk according to His word.

Lord, we praise and thank you for the gift of Your tender care. You fight for us and nothing can separate us from Your love. We choose You today. We choose to walk with You and live for You. We pray for those who are struggling that they might find comfort in Your arms of love. Thank you for the gift of Your son, Jesus. In Jesus' name we pray, amen.

Thank you for your persistent prayers.#Godisfaithful#TheGloryRoad

Day#612 December 22

 Anchor Verse: Micah 7:15
As in the days when you came out from the land of Egypt, I shall show you marvelous and miraculous things. (AMP)

Comparing your life, your circumstances, your gifts to others, often we come up short, or we are filled with pride. Too often it's easy to fall into the trap that we are not good enough or good stuff happens for others but not me.

Maybe you think signs, wonders, and miracles were only for those who lived in Old Testament times or when Jesus walked the earth, not today. The truth is… God still does miraculous things today.

In Micah 7:15, we read, "As in the days when you came out from the land of Egypt, I shall show you marvelous and miraculous things."

When the Israelites left Egypt, God changed the heart of Pharaoh who was determined to keep the people of Israel in captivity. He had a good thing going with all those people working for him, but God knew there was a day they would be set free. God used ten plagues to accomplish His purposes.

On our journey to Bill's healing, we saw God's hand miraculously. Even now I can remember times, it looked like the end of the road for Bill, heart, lungs, other things were failing, but God said, "It's not time. There is still work for Bill to do." And Bill miraculously lived. With joy, I will continue to tell others what the Lord has done for us for the rest of my life.

The Glory Road on the surface often looks like a place of chaos. It might even resemble Egypt. But the truth is, it's a perfect place for us to see God's miraculous ways. As I pray for others, day and night, we see the hand of God move and do mighty miracles. I don't always understand His ways, but I trust Him to do what is best for us.

Lord, we praise and thank you for Your love for us. Thank you for Your hedge of protection around us and how You save us in ways we don't even know or understand. You are the God of miracles, not only in the past but for today and all our tomorrows. May we walk in obedience to Your commands, and may we rejoice in the wonders of Your love. We love you and praise you in Jesus' name we pray, amen.

Thank you for believing in miracles.#Godisfaithful#TheGloryRoad

Day#613 December 23

 Anchor Verse: Nahum 1:3
The Lord is slow to get angry, but his power is great, and he never lets the guilty go unpunished. He displays his power in the whirlwind and the storm. The billowing clouds are the dust beneath his feet. (NLT)

As we walk through our lives and face trials, tests, we become acquainted with God who will fight for us. God's love has no boundaries; He is the Good Shepherd in Psalm 23 who will pursue the lost sheep.

In Nahum 1, we read of the power of God. "The Lord is slow to get angry, but his power is great, and he never lets the guilty go unpunished. He displays his power in the whirlwind and the storm. The billowing clouds are the dust beneath his feet." (Nahum 1:3)

When we think about storms that destroy things in their path, we think they are bad, or even evil. But the nature of a storm is to clear a path before it and to rain buckets of water from heaven.

God who knows me and loves me is all-powerful. There is nothing that can stop Him. His heart is moved by injustice yet filled with great compassion. If heaven and earth need to be moved to accomplish His purposes for me and you, He not only can do that, but He will.

On our journey to Bill's healing, we went through many storms. But we quickly were made aware that God was there in the storm with us. Just like He was with Daniel in the lions' den and Shadrach, Meshach and Abednego in the fiery furnace, God is with us in the deepest valleys of trouble and the highest mountains of victory. Look for Him the next time you're in a storm.

The Glory Road is guarded by a powerful God. Daily, He fights for me. He will contend against those who contend against me. When I heard the crack of lightning or the roar of thunder, mountains of snow, dust storms, or the beauty of a sunny day with a light breeze, I know He is there. Every breath I take is at His command and He watches over me as I sleep. His justice keeps evil in check, and when I hear His roar, I know that He has had enough.

Lord, we thank you for the gift of life. You are all-powerful. Your steadfast love never ceases, Your mercies never come to an end. Lord, we pray for those in a storm. Your power is tempered by Your grace and Your love. We are so grateful for the peace we find in You. In Jesus' name we pray, amen.

Thank you for your faithfulness.#Godisfaithful#TheGloryRoad

Day#614 December 24

 Anchor Verse: Habakkuk 2:3

But these things I plan won't happen right away. Slowly, steadily, surely, the time approaches when the vision will be fulfilled. If it seems slow, do not despair, for these things will surely come to pass. Just be patient! They will not be overdue a single day! (TLB)

It's Christmas Eve. Our children are anxious to see the gifts waiting for them under the tree. Many anticipate Christmas with great excitement, so much sleep will be elusive tonight.

As adults, we know that there is an even greater miracle in the making. It's about the celebration of Jesus' birth, the newborn King, who came to earth to bring hope to the world, the greatest gift ever.

It's not just about the presents under the tree or the wrappings of the celebration, it's about the presence of Jesus, our greatest gift.

Habakkuk 2:3 reminds us God has a plan, He has a vision, and it always comes to pass at the appointed time. "But these things I plan won't happen right away. Slowly, steadily, surely, the time approaches when the vision will be fulfilled. If it seems slow, do not despair, for these things will surely come to pass. Just be patient! They will not be overdue a single day!"

There are many things in our lives that we would like to tidy up, and get through, or find the solution, but there's something about the process that is part of God's plan too. It's not just about the destination.

On our journey, God made it abundantly clear that all things are made beautiful in His time. Two years ago (12.24.19), Bill was released from the hospital after having three stents put in his heart to improve the blood flow. Miraculous how God made that possible. Thank God for His perfect timing.

The Glory Road is a place of promises not yet fulfilled as I wait in expectation. but there are so many lessons, so many blessings on the journey. God said the things He had planned for us wouldn't happen right away, but we patiently await the fulfillment of His promises in our lives.

Lord, thank you for the gift of Your love. Your timing is always perfect even when ours is not. We ask for Your hand of protection over us. Thank you for the gift of Jesus, the best gift of all. In Jesus' name we pray. Amen.

Thank you for the gift of being you.#Godisfaithful#TheGloryRoad

Day#615 December 25

 Anchor Verse: Luke 2:20
Then the shepherds went back again to their fields and flocks, praising God for the visit of the angels, and because they had seen the child, just as the angel had told them. (TLB)

It's Christmas Day. We celebrate Jesus, the greatest gift of all, the hope of the world who came as a little baby. Thank you, Lord.

The birth of Jesus extraordinary, not only did He leave His home in glory to take on human flesh, born in a stable because there was no room for Him in the inn, but shepherds were the first to greet Him.

Shepherds were tending their flocks that night, a quiet night, listening for their sheep but also ready to address any threat.

An angel of the Lord appears and brings good tidings of great joy that shall be for ALL the people (Luke 2:10).

"Then the shepherds went back again to their fields and flocks, praising God for the visit of the angels, and because they had seen the child, just as the angel had told them." (Luke 2:20)

They went back to work, back to the sheep, but as they went they told everyone what they had seen. They returned "glorifying and praising God" (NIV) about all they had seen and heard.

On our journey to Bill's healing, the good news of Christmas, the hope of the world, Jesus, was Bill's hope every day. It was because of Jesus and His strength Bill could fight the health issues he faced.

The Glory Road has many opportunities to share what God has done for me. With Jesus by my side, I can face any obstacle, and offer His encouragement and words of life to others. Rejoice with me today and glorify and praise God for the gift of Jesus, the gift of life, and His love.

Lord, we thank you for Jesus, born as a baby but now victorious in heaven. I pray for those who are going through deep waters. Lord Jesus, be a friend that is closer than a brother. May our hearts be filled with joy because of Jesus' love in us. Jesus is the greatest gift of all. In Jesus' name, amen.

Thank you for your love. Merry Christmas!#Godisfaithful#TheGloryRoad

Day#616 December 26

 Anchor Verse: Haggai 2:19b
But from this day onward I will bless you. (NLT)

When God makes a promise, He keeps it. He does not take His commitments lightly. He is the Promise Keeper.

What we find amazing about God's promises is God knows the outcome before even one step is choreographed, one step taken on this new stretch of highway. He knows the end from the beginning (Isaiah 46:10) and that should bring us great comfort. This is not a haphazard out of control life we are living. Our times are in His hands (Psalm 31:15).

There is a greater description as to what that looks like in the earlier part of Haggai 2:19a, "I am giving you a promise now while the seed is still in the barn. You have not yet harvested your grain, and your grapevines, fig trees, pomegranates, and olive trees have not yet produced their crops."

Lean in and listen, this is His promise spoken over you, "But from this day onward I will bless you." (Haggai 2:19b)

On our journey to Bill's healing, God was there too, at the beginning and the end. Every step of the way, God's will, God's best for us was being rolled out. I know God delighted in the miracles that surprised us, but didn't surprise Him. He is a good, good Father.

The Glory Road is a place of God's blessings. I believe God spoke words of blessing over me the morning Bill died in April 2020. That continues to be His promise and His pleasure. As 2021 comes to a close and a new year is ahead of us, there too His promises will be kept and His blessings will be multiplied. Praise the Lord for His faithfulness.

Lord, we praise and thank you for the gift of a new day. Thank you, Lord, that Your promises are true and they are from everlasting to everlasting. The whole earth is filled with Your glory from the moment the sun rises until it sets. We look forward to Your blessings as we walk in obedience to Your commands. We love you and praise you. In Jesus' name, we pray, amen.

Thank you for your faithfulness.#Godisfaithful#TheGloryRoad

Day#617 December 27

 Anchor Verse: Zechariah 2:5
For I, declares the Lord, will be a wall of fire around her [protecting her from enemies], and I will be the glory in her midst. (AMP)

In the last books of the Old Testament, there are many prophetic images and messages. This passage in Zechariah 2:5 portrays a very powerful image.

"For I, declares the Lord, will be a wall of fire around her [protecting her from enemies], and I will be the glory in her midst."

He is speaking of the city of Jerusalem in this verse and how the Lord will protect this holy city and be the glory within her.

Today, as believers, God lives in us, we belong to Him. As He dwells in us, He is a wall of fire around us protecting us from our enemies and His glory resides in us, around us, and shines out of us. It's a glorious promise.

When Moses had been in the presence of the Lord, his face was so radiant he had to cover it with a veil as he went back to his people. That's the power of God's presence and glory in us. (Exodus 34:35)

On our journey to Bill's healing, we saw these characteristics of God in Bill's life. He was a wall of fire around Bill. And the glory of the Lord was seen in Bill, reflected in his countenance and also how Bill lived his life during his healing journey. What a privilege to be God's vessel of honor.

The Glory Road is walked out in a land of darkness where the light of the Lord shines brightly. Gratitude is too small of a word to describe how full my heart is as God fights for me. We must choose to walk with God and let His glory be reflected in us, and not muddied up by our misdeeds.

Thank you, Lord, for the gift of Your presence. Thank you, Lord, for the gift of joy and the pleasure of living life with You by our side. Your love never ceases and because of Your great love, You will fight for us. You always win. Lord, I pray for those in the darkness today, lead them to the light of Your love. May Your church radiate Your glory, in Jesus' name, we pray, amen.

Thank you for your faithful prayers.#Godisfaithful#TheGloryRoad

Day#618 December 28

 Anchor Verse: Zechariah 8:13
Just as you, Judah and Israel, have been a curse among the nations, so I will save you, and you will be a blessing. Do not be afraid, but let your hands be strong. (NIV)

One of the amazing blessings about following Jesus is that He can redeem your past and put you on the "right" path. Your past does not define your future. You will no longer be a "curse" but a "blessing."

This are the words of Zechariah to Judah and Israel but as we stand on the threshold of a new year, they can be God's promise us too. We don't need to be afraid, but our hands (and hearts) can be strong.

There are so many choices that we make daily that determine the course of our lives. And in the process, we are role models, examples to others. Whether with our families, our friends, strangers, people we meet in the grocery store or even online, we impact everyone we meet.

Some of you may believe that your life doesn't matter. (That's a lie.) Every day our thoughts, our words, and our actions shape not only our own lives but the lives of others. That is the measure of influence the Lord has placed in your hands. (Something we can reflect on as we enter 2022.)

On our journey to Bill's healing, we were blessed to be a blessing. Wherever Bill went, others were impacted by his life, by his actions, and most of all, his attitude. Bill chose to be an overcomer, victorious rather than a victim. Thank you, Lord, for my husband's legacy.

The Glory Road offers me the same opportunities to influence the world and to do good, not harm. You may not realize, or recognize, the seeds you are planting daily, but know that you are planting them. What do you want the harvest of your life to look like? My prayer is that my legacy will be one of blessing. Thank you, Lord, for making that possible for each one of us.

Lord, we praise you for the opportunities to bless others. Thank you that You never leave us alone but You are always close by to carry us through the storms of life. Even in our most difficult challenges, You can shine brightly through us. May we be a vessel of honor for God, today and every day. We love you and praise you, Lord. In Jesus' name we pray, amen.

Thank you for being a blessing to me.#Godisfaithful#TheGloryRoad

Day#619 December 29

 Anchor Verse: Zechariah 10:6
I will strengthen Judah and save the tribes of Joseph. I will restore them because I have compassion on them. (NIV)

God has many facets to His character. Honestly, way more than we can even comprehend. But that's what makes God, God. His ways are higher than our ways and His thoughts than our thoughts.

He has great power but also great compassion. Jesus is the Lamb of God (John 1:29) but also the Lion of the tribe of Judah. (Revelation 5:5)

In our humanity, we may not be able to reconcile how that all works, but that's where we take a leap of faith and believe.

Zechariah 10:6 tells us how God will strengthen and save His people. Why? "I will restore them because I have compassion on them." (Zechariah 10:6)

"I know their pain and will make them good as new. They'll get a fresh start, as if nothing had ever happened. And why? Because I am their very own God, I'll do what needs to be done for them."

On our journey to Bill's healing, God was so good to us. His heavenly Father knew Bill's pain. God restored Bill so many times, both physically and spiritually. The old was gone and the new had come. Just like He said, "I'll do what needs to be done for them." He is a good, good Father.

The Glory Road is walked hand in hand with Jesus, He who knows me so well, my comings and goings. My heavenly Father is the God of angel armies who protects me and makes a way for me. He knows my pain and sorrow, but then fills me with great joy. He does what needs to be done for me. I'm so grateful for God's love in every season of my life.

Lord, thank you for the gift of life. Thank you for the gift of Your love, mercy, and grace. You restore us when our lives are in chaos. You bring blessings when the world gives us sorrow. God's love never fails and Your mercies are new every morning. Great is Your faithfulness, O Lord. We love you and praise you in Jesus' name, amen.

Thank you for your faithful prayers.#Godisfaithful#TheGloryRoad

Day#620 December 30

 Anchor Verse: Revelation 21:23
And the city has no need of sun or moon to light it, for the glory of God and of the Lamb illuminate it. (TLB)

God's first act of creation in Genesis 1:3 was to bring light out of the darkness. "Let there be light."

In the book of Revelation, chapter 21:23, we are told of the new city, the city of God that will one day come. Reading and understanding the many details can stretch us a little. One thing that stands out is this, "And the city has no need of sun or moon to light it, for the glory of God and of the Lamb illuminate it."

The glory of God and the Lamb (Jesus Christ) will light the whole city. There will be no more night, no more darkness. We will rejoice and live in His presence with fullness of joy – forever.

On our journey to Bill's healing, our blessings were multiplied in the presence of God. Bill's encounters with the Lord gave him a whole new perspective about life, both here on earth and for eternity. Just like Moses was radiant after his encounter with God, Bill's countenance changed too. You and I, as believers, will experience that same blessing for all eternity.

The Glory Road is a place of further revelation about who God is. It is a path that leads to the fullness of joy in His presence. When that day comes for all of us, "He will wipe every tear from their eyes. There will be no more death or mourning or crying or pain, for the old order of things has passed away." (Revelation 21:4) Until then, we love, we live, we walk as Jesus did, we are called to be His hands and feet.

Lord, we thank you for the future plans You have for us. We don't have to wait until we get to heaven, You are here for us today. You are as close as our next breath. Thank you for loving us so well. We pray for those who are mourning today, whose hearts are heavy, fill them with Your love and new joy. We love you and praise you in Jesus' name, amen.

Thank you for loving others so well.#Godisfaithful#TheGloryRoad

Day#621 December 31

 Anchor Verse: Malachi 3:7
Now return to me, and I will return to you," says the Lord of Heaven's Armies.
(NLT)

Here we stand on the last day of 2021, with many days, many thoughts, many actions behind us. And before us lies the uncharted land of 2022.

What lies before us may be unknown territory but one thing we know is that God is with us, God is for us, and that will never change.

In Malachi 3:6 it says, "I the Lord do not change." That brings us great comfort. In a world where things are always in a state of flux, God is unchangeable, unshakable, and unstoppable.

There are many things we have no control over, but we do get to choose where we stand and how we stand. May the Lord find us faithful.

There is hope that comes in the name of the Lord. God's promises are always true, they never fade, they never fail. "Now return to me, and I will return to you," says the Lord of Heaven's Armies." (Malachi 3:7)

Where do you stand today? Have you stood strong with the Lord, or have you walked away?

On our journey to Bill's healing, God was always there. Sometimes He was quiet and was vigilant in the silence as He wove together the beautiful tapestry of our lives. Other times, He moved in a way for the entire world to see. We never doubted God's love. His arms were always open wide for us.

The Glory Road has been filled with so many emotions, circumstances, and events since Bill walked from earth into heaven. Even though Bill is not by my side in the flesh, what I learned from him continues to shape my life. God's love tenderly guides me. His hope lifts me up when the chaos of the world comes to my doorstep. His faithfulness continues to be a shining light for this generation and generations yet to come.

Lord, we thank you for Your faithfulness. On this last day of 2021, we turn our eyes toward heaven and ask that You would turn Your ear toward us. We confess we have not always lived or loved as we should. Restore us, O Lord, that we might shine brightly for others. In Jesus' name, amen.

Thank you for 365 days of faithful prayers.#Godisfaithful#TheGloryRoad

Author's Note

Go back to the place of the miracle.

These are the words God spoke to me the night God took Bill home to heaven in the early morning hours of April 19, 2020.

If you have ever experienced a miracle in your own life, you understand that your perspective is forever changed. Life is never quite the same because you have seen God do the impossible.

As I read through every day of this devotional, once again I was brought back to some life-changing moments. Even my final goodbyes to my husband, since his celebration of life service and cemetery service were delayed for over a year due to Covid.

And yet, I have hope. I have joy. I have peace. Because I have seen the hand of God move and I believe He has more miracles in store for all of us.

"God's Hope on the Glory Road" is a reminder we can have hope on the darkest nights and in the deepest valleys. Christ in you, is the hope of Glory. (Colossians 1:27)

If your own flame of hope is growing dim, I'd like to pass a cup of hope to you, put another log on the fire in your heart. God is faithful. All you have to do is ask and He will come running to you with arms wide open.

The next book in this devotional series will be released in December 2023. Every day as I write my daily devotion to post on Facebook, God gives me further revelation about who He is and who I am called to be. May the wisdom of heaven be yours and the joy of the Lord be your strength.

If you want to get a fresh word from the Lord, look for my daily devotion on my Facebook page: Barb Hollace.

If your life has been touched by our journey, please share your story with me at barbara@barbarahollace.com.

Check out my website for future book releases: www.barbarahollace.com.

Other Books

Barbara Hollace, Contributing Author

- *Light for the Writer's Soul:* 100 Devotions by Global Christian Writers: Armour Publishers
- *Love, Animals and Miracles:* New World Library
- *Gonzaga Book of Prayer:* Gonzaga University
- *A Miracle under the Christmas Tree:* Harlequin
- *And Then What Happened:* CreateSpace
- *Love is a Verb Devotional:* Bethany House
- *A Book of Miracles:* New World Library
- *Faith, Hope and Healing:* John Wiley and Sons
- *SpokeWrite: Journal of Art and Writing (3 issues):* Gray Dog Press
- *A Cup of Comfort for Military Families:* Adams Media
- *Mistletoe Madness:* Blooming Tree Press
- *God's Words for the Young:* Choat &Lederman
- *The Art of Brave Living:* Diane Cunningham
- *Divine Interventions:* Heartwarming Stories of Answered Prayer: Guideposts
- *Yes, God!:*Releasing in 2023

About the Author

Barbara Hollace is a Christian woman who loves the Lord. God has called her to be a prayer warrior and a writer. Her greatest joy is to pray for others and see God's miracles happen. Through both her and her husband's health challenges, Barbara learned prayer can move mountains in our lives.

Her love of writing blossomed from an early age when she started creating her own greeting cards for family and friends. In 1985, Barbara self-published her first poetry book, "From Dust to Dust." Barbara has been published in 24 books [as author or contributing author] and numerous newspaper articles, with other books in progress. She has written 15 novels and is pursuing publication options.

Professionally, she is an author, editor, writing coach, and speaker. Owner of Hollace Writing Services, Barbara's goal is to "identify the good and magnify it!" This includes helping a person get the story in their heart on the page, editing the story, and pursuing publication options. She recently opened her own publishing company, Hollace House Publishing, and continues to expand its reach.

Barbara has a Bachelor's degree in Business Administration from Western Washington University and a Juris Doctor degree from Gonzaga University School of Law. She was also recently certified as a Prayer-Powered Mastermind Facilitator. Barbara is the Communications Director at Spokane Dream Center church in Spokane Valley, Washington.

For more information about Barbara and her business, go to www.barbarahollace.com.

Made in United States
Troutdale, OR
11/19/2023

14721754R00236